The Realignment of Pennsylvania Politics Since 1960

The Realignment of Pennsylvania Politics Since 1960

Two-Party Competition in a Battleground State

RENÉE M. LAMIS

With a Foreword by James L. Sundquist

THE PENNSYLVANIA STATE UNIVERSITY PRESS
UNIVERSITY PARK, PENNSYLVANIA

Library of Congress Cataloging-in-Publication Data

Lamis, Renee M.
    The realignment of Pennsylvania politics since 1960 : two-party competition in a
battleground state/Renee M. Lamis.
        p.   cm.
    Includes bibliographical references and index.
Summary: "Explores electoral changes in Pennsylvania since 1960, finding that the recent
'culture-wars realignment' has significantly altered the old New Deal party system, especially
since the early 1990s. Contains illustrations plotting political alignment of Pennsylvania
counties"—Provided by publisher.

    ISBN 978-0-271-03420-1 (pbk : alk. paper)
    1. Elections—Pennsylvania—History—20th century.
    2. Elections—Pennsylvania—History—21st century.
    3. Pennsylvania—Politics and government—1951– .
    I. Title.

JK3690.L36 2009
320.9748—dc22   2008047573

It is the policy of The Pennsylvania State University Press to use acid-free paper. Publications
on uncoated stock satisfy the minimum requirements of American National Standard for
Information Sciences—Permanence of Paper for Printed Library Material, ANSI Z39.48–1992.

To *Alec*, *Peter*, and *Alexander*, the three loves of my life

Your love, support, and patience were my constant motivation and inspiration.

Contents

Figures

Tables

Foreword

Anyone who was an observer of, or participant in, the politics of Pennsylvania a half-century ago, in the late 1950s (both of which I happened to be), learned at the outset this certitude: the state's political geography was a fixture, reliable and predictable. Some of its sixty-seven counties were Republican, always had been—since the time of the New Deal and Franklin Roosevelt, that is—and always would be, and others were just as solidly Democratic. Very few of the counties were genuinely "swing" territory, that might go either way, and they were small ones. So, the question in each election was simply which one of the major parties would compile the bigger margin in "its" segment of the state's political map—what these days would be called the "red" and the "blue" counties respectively.

The Democratic bastions were the city of Philadelphia (which had only recently been converted from historically entrenched Republican control), the blue-collar, steel-making, and coal-producing counties that made up the Pittsburgh metropolitan area, and the anthracite region of Lackawanna and Luzerne counties. The rest of the state belonged to the Republicans, but in terms of population the bedrock of their strength was the crescent of upscale suburban counties surrounding Philadelphia—Bucks, Montgomery, Delaware, and Chester. This red–blue division of the commonwealth would be carried forward from election to election with only the slightest changes. And while in statewide contests the parties might be sometimes closely matched and competitive, the state's "normal" tilt was in the Republican direction.

If one turned attention, at that time, from state to national political geography, one also seemed to see stability. Like Pennsylvania, the North as a whole was one broad Republican belt, except for its major cities, which appeared as isolated Democratic islands. And the South would still be referred to as the Solid South because of the overwhelming dominance of the Democratic party.

Even at that time, however, had appeared the first signs of erosion of the South's solidity, and in the next few decades that region produced the clearest and most dramatic example in modern times of what political scientists and historians have termed "realignment"—that is, the transfer of allegiance by large segments of the voting population from one political party to another. From its status as the virtually one-party base of the Democratic party, it has transformed itself into the most reliable bulwark of Republican strength in the nation. Where once Republican candidates for president did not even bother to campaign south of the Mason-Dixon line, it is now the Democratic candidates who choose not to waste much time there.

But if everybody recognizes, and accepts, that a realignment in the South has clearly taken place, has the rest of the country been stable, or has it realigned as well? That is the question that Renée Lamis set out to answer with respect to just one state—Pennsylvania—and her technique has been to subject that state's changing political configuration to what is surely the most intense, microscopic scrutiny ever given to any state's electoral landscape over a comparable period of time.

Her findings and conclusions are a resounding yes. What could scarcely have been imagined half a century ago has occurred, transforming the political map of Pennsylvania. Those Philadelphia suburban counties that then seemed so impregnable for Democrats have undergone (like the South) a role reversal, shifting heavily to the once-hopelessly outnumbered Democratic party. And the once-solid Democratic area centered on Pittsburgh has seen a flow in the opposite direction, toward the GOP. Because the movement in the more populous eastern counties has outweighed that in the west, the state that had been historically Republican ever since the Civil War and still gave that party a distinct edge after World War II is now considered normally Democratic—a blue state.

The author analyzes in exhaustive detail the where, the when, and the why of this realignment. For the where and when, she applies what is surely every pertinent statistical technique known to political science to interpret the data provided by election returns and party registration figures, county by county. For the why, she draws upon public opinion polls and the wisdom of the journalists who cover electoral campaigns and the strategists who manage them, as well as her own commonsense observations of political happenings during the period that she covers. Her conclusion is that the transformation in Pennsylvania politics is the result of the "culture wars"—a cluster of interrelated social issues that arose in the 1960s (abortion, school prayer, civil rights and racial integration, the anti-Vietnam protests and youthful rebellion in general, the liberalization of sexual behavior, and so on) and continued in the subsequent decades of what she calls the "aftershocks" of the 1960s turmoil.

In demonstrating by her statistics and her logic that a realignment has indeed taken place in Pennsylvania, Dr. Lamis presents a compelling validation of the whole concept of realignment as, in the words of the subtitle of Theodore Rosenof's 2002 book on the topic, "The Theory That Changed the Way We Think about American Politics."[1] Her data refute those critics who have argued that we live in a period not of realignment but of "dealignment," in which political allegiances are so unstable and volatile that patterns firm enough to be considered alignments and therefore subject to realignment cannot be discerned. She demonstrates that the pattern in place at the beginning of the 1960s, when her study begins, had been a stable one, and the configuration that replaced it four decades later was likewise well established and, from all the evidence, durable. The long transition from the one firm pattern to the other showed volatility between successive elections, of course, but when the

---

1. Theodore Rosenof, *Realignment: The Theory That Changed the Way We Think About American Politics* (Lanham, MD: Rowman & Littlefield, 2002).

short-term ups and downs are smoothed out, the underlying trend lines prove to be straight and steady. In the numbers that make up her rich mass of data, there is little to suggest that dealignment has been the dominant characteristic of the period; they are, rather, consistent and mutually reinforcing in support of what David R. Mayhew terms the "realignment perspective," embodied in writings that he dubs the "realignment genre."[2]

In this highly original, groundbreaking contribution to the genre, Dr. Lamis chooses to examine the realignment phenomenon in depth rather than breadth. She focuses her searchlight on a limited geographical area—one state—and covers a limited time period, just under half a century. We finish the book feeling that we truly understand what happened in that time and place. When her approach has been replicated for other states (graduate students in search of dissertation topics, please take note), the basis will exist for generalizing more confidently about the processes of realignment, the causes and the circumstances, and how much realigning may have been going on at any given time—such as the present.

But even in the absence of counterpart studies of similar depth and intensity, this study of a single commonwealth adds a rich lode of data to be mined by the scholars who are currently contributing to the realignment genre. Those data are sure to influence every study in the field, and one contribution in particular is bound to have a profound impact on the theoretical structure that underpins the empirical literature concerning realignments.

That is the decoupling of two phenomena that have been seen from the beginning, by many scholars, as inextricably related—"party realignment" and "critical elections." It is difficult to say which of these was noted first and then associated with the other, but that does not matter; when the realignment genre was born (Rosenof's history attributes the fatherhood to Samuel Lubell's 1952 book, *The Future of American Politics*,[3] but political scientists are more likely to credit a 1955 journal article[4] by one of their own, V. O. Key Jr., a piece invariably referred to as "seminal"), the two were immediately linked. Some elections, it was seen, appeared to create new, durable patterns of political party allegiance while others did not. The former were termed "critical"; the latter were seen as simply sustaining, or reinforcing, existing patterns. The creation of the new configuration during, or by, a critical election was, of course, called "realignment." The two phenomena were seen as so interdependent and inseparable that the terminology sometimes was even merged; scholars wrote of "critical realignments." And critical elections were viewed as so crucial in American history that Walter Dean Burnham entitled his influential 1970 book *Critical Elections and the Mainsprings of American Politics*.[5]

---

2. David R. Mayhew, *Electoral Realignments: A Critique of an American Genre* (New Haven: Yale University Press, 2002).

3. Samuel Lubell, *The Future of American Politics* (New York: Harper & Brothers, 1952).

4. V. O. Key Jr., "A Theory of Critical Elections," *Journal of Politics* 17 (February 1955), 3–18.

5. Walter Dean Burnham, *Critical Elections and the Mainsprings of American Politics* (New York: W. W. Norton, 1970).

Now comes Dr. Lamis to tell us, through a powerful array of statistics, that, in the words of the musical, "It ain't necessarily so." The realignment in Pennsylvania, whose course she traces, occurred over a span of several decades, with no single election standing out as "critical." Yet it undeniably occurred. The answer, obviously, is that realignments and critical elections are not interdependent after all.

This should have been clear all along, as scholars developed the realignment genre, but when critical elections did occur they were so spectacular and attention-grabbing that they bedazzled the writers and obscured the obvious. Yet those who relied on critical elections to explain realignments often had difficulty deciding which were the elections that earned the label. Did the last great political transformation that everyone agrees happened—the one brought about at the time of the Great Depression, the New Deal, and Franklin Roosevelt—have its critical election in 1932, when FDR won his first term, or in 1936, with his reelection, or even in 1928, when Al Smith's candidacy had its profound impact on both urban and rural voting patterns? There is evidence in electoral results to support any of these dates; in other words, the realignment occurred at different times in different places, and it is futile to try to identify any election as "critical" for the nation as a whole. So the term "realigning eras" began to appear in the realignment genre as a substitute for "critical elections." But even these eras can be long drawn out. In some places, the transfiguration that occurred so suddenly and sharply elsewhere in the 1930s did not take shape until after World War II, notably in the 1950s, and to some extent may still be going on, hidden in the redrawing of the political map brought on by other, newer realigning forces.

Since Dr. Lamis's work fits so squarely within the realignment genre—and makes such a contribution to it—it becomes obligatory, in any praise of it, to acknowledge that the whole idea of realignment, and the entire body of literature devoted to it, has recently come under attack by reputable scholars. Just a year before Rosenof published his short volume explicating the centrality of realignment theory in the study of American electoral politics (2003), David Mayhew had produced a treatise, of almost equal length, debunking the entire concept and pleading for its abandonment. He denounced realignment theory, and all its terminology, as "too slippery, too binary, too apocalyptic."[6]

Mayhew is certainly accurate enough in applying the label "slippery." The notion of realignment, and the word itself, have been used so freely and so variously by journalists, statesmen, and scholars that they have never attained clarity and stability of meaning. After every election, learned commentators debate in the press and on television the question of whether a realignment has taken place, and each has his or her own unstated and implied definition of the term. But the answer is not to discard the concept and its vocabulary. That would get us nowhere. A phenomenon is out there—the kind of significant and durable shift in patterns of attachment of voters to their political parties that this book describes and analyzes in such exquisite detail—that demands to be measured, dissected, and explained,

6. Mayhew, *Electoral Realignments*, 165.

and for that to happen it must first be given a label. For decades now, the term "realignment" has been used, by political scientists, historians, and journalists alike, and if that label were to be abandoned, a substitute would have to be adopted or coined—and, to critics such as Mayhew, it would no doubt be just as slippery and troublesome.

To achieve some greater degree of clarity, writers have adopted adjectival modifiers: major or minor, national or regional or local, secular or critical. But these distinctions beg many of the questions. Where, for instance, is the dividing line between major and minor? Can a series of minor realignments achieve a cumulative magnitude that qualifies the end result as major? How much local and regional realigning, if it occurs at different times in different places but apparently from the same causes, has to occur before we call it national? Should changes in electoral patterns that arise not from shifts in party allegiance among established voters but simply from the addition of new voters, such as immigrants and their descendants, or the mobility of partisans across jurisdictional lines, be considered realignment at all? And, if not, how can those changes be excluded from the registration and election figures by which realignments are measured?

In the search for clearer definition, one must begin by recognizing that shifts in the allegiance of voters to political parties are not the actions of a national electorate, or a state electorate, or even a county, ward, or precinct citizenry. Any realignment is the product of a myriad of separate decisions, by individual voters. We tend to say, for instance, that Texas, or South Carolina, has shifted from being a Democratic to a Republican state. But it was not the state that acted, nor the state's collective citizenry, but just a fraction of the state's individual voters—enough to recolor the state from blue to red on electoral maps, but nevertheless a fraction.

And the causes that lead individuals to change allegiance, to reidentify themselves politically (or new voters to adopt identities different from their parents, in generational change) are likewise infinitely varied. In studying political realignments of the past, scholars have searched through documents of the period—political platforms, campaign speeches, newspaper editorials, diaries and memoirs, and so on—to find what the issues were that moved individual voters, enabling them to speculate about the causation of electoral change. Since the mid-twentieth century, students have had available an increasingly sophisticated body of information that bears directly on the question of why citizens change political allegiance: public opinion polls. Dr. Lamis expertly mines these data to reach her conclusion that the realignment she narrates was the product of the "culture wars" that broke out in the 1960s and have been a crucial determinant of political behavior ever since.

So, as individual citizens find themselves changing political allegiance (or their successors in the next generation do so), some degree of realignment is always going on. When the question is asked, after each presidential election, "Was that a realigning election?" the answer has always to be "somewhat," not "yes" or "no." The latter, as Mayhew complains, would indeed make the concept "too binary." Of course, if a very high proportion of the individual realignment decisions happen to be made in a single election (or, more accurately, recorded then after having been made at any time since the last balloting), that election will inevitably be called "critical" and the realignment "major." But, at other times, a lower proportion of realignment decisions does not mean that none occurred at all. That is the either/ or fallacy when what is being considered is properly measured only as a matter of degree.

Thus, when Mayhew asserts that "No certifiable electoral realignment has occurred since 1932,"[7] he is entrapped in that fallacy; his interpretation, in his own phrase, is "too binary." Moreover, his conclusion implies that to be certifiable, a realignment must be national in scope. No one, surely, could deny that the South as a region has dramatically and drastically realigned since 1932—specifically, since the 1950s. If such a transformation is not to be called a "certifiable electoral realignment," then another term must be found, for a historical phenomenon of that magnitude cannot simply be ignored. And now Dr. Lamis has shown, again beyond any reasonable doubt, that realignment has occurred in one Northern state, Pennsylvania. It remains for other studies of electoral change in the North, for which this study provides an ideal model, to determine whether those changes are, like those in the South, regionwide.

To quote Mayhew yet again, in refuting his premise of "no realignment since 1932," this study demolishes his conclusion that follows, that "the realignment genre . . . has ceased to be relevant."[8] Indeed, this book is a compelling reaffirmation of its relevance, as well as a major contribution to its theoretical and empirical bases. Those who have believed all along in the utility of the realignment perspective in analyzing political history and electoral current events will find their faith confirmed in this work, and it is difficult to see how any open-minded skeptic of the genre could read this treatise in its entirety without having his or her doubts satisfied and confidence restored.

James L. Sundquist

---

7. Ibid., 35.
8. Ibid., 35.

Preface

As an Erie, Pennsylvania, native and life-long resident of the Keystone State, I have been intrigued by the politics of my home state. While in graduate school in political science at Case Western Reserve University, I became acquainted with the rich literature on American electoral and party system change, which illuminated for me the complex electoral paths the country has followed since the upheavals of the Civil War era.

This extensive reading also taught me that for the most recent period—since the early 1960s—there was considerable interpretive confusion over what has happened in the nation's electoral politics. Have we had another realignment along the lines of the New Deal "earthquake" of the 1930s? If so, how did it play out across the country?

I also puzzled over what I had been observing firsthand in Pennsylvania politics. For example, I knew that registered Democrats had outnumbered registered Republicans by half a million voters for several decades. However, I also knew that many Republicans had been elected to major statewide offices in recent decades, including my own congressman, Republican Tom Ridge of Erie, who was elected governor twice in the 1990s.

These statewide Republican successes, which included near total dominance of both U.S. Senate seats, occurred despite the fact that Pennsylvania voted for the Democratic party's nominee for president in all four elections since 1992. What explained these disparate outcomes?

With these questions uppermost in my mind, in the summer of 2003, I began the study that resulted in this book. I set out to find the answers to the above questions and many more by thoroughly studying Pennsylvania's electoral experience.

I realized that I could not answer completely the Pennsylvania questions without understanding, at least in a tentative fashion, the broader topic of recent national electoral change.

Further, it was clear to me that full comprehension of national developments in the post-1960 period would require extensive study of many states, something I was not undertaking. Rather, it was my hope at the outset that I could clarify the national picture in the process of fully comprehending what had happened in the Keystone State. While the reader will be the ultimate judge, I believe, as I state in the concluding chapter, that I accomplished the task.

The landmark 2006 election occurred several months after I completed my manuscript and submitted it to Pennsylvania State University Press. After it was accepted for publication in early 2007, I had the opportunity to expand the study to include the memorable results of that election.

I decided to confine my discussion of the 2006 election to the book's final chapter, although for the convenience of the reader, I updated several figures and tables in earlier chapters to include the 2006 results. Placing my analysis of the 2006 election at the end allowed me to treat the latest election as something of a test of the ideas elucidated in the previous six chapters. Fortunately, Pennsylvania's voters in 2006 produced results that exhibited amazing continuity with the trends I had previously identified. In addition, because publication of this book was slated for January 2009, my publisher kindly allowed me to write a postscript covering the exciting and historic 2008 presidential election.

In the preparation of this book, I received assistance from many people, and I would like to thank them now, beginning with three people who saved me precious hours time and again.

First is Dr. Harold E. Cox, founder and director of the Election Statistics Project at Wilkes University in Wilkes-Barre, Pennsylvania. Thanks to his tireless efforts to see that two centuries of Pennsylvania county-level election returns are freely available, I was able to assemble quickly in digital form the data I needed to hit the ground running. The electoral data archive established by Dr. Cox, an emeritus professor of history at Wilkes University, is a gem. I can't thank him enough for providing this terrific service to the public as well as for his personal feedback and encouragement given to me during several long phone conversations.

Next, I want to thank Allison Deibert, the former voter registration coordinator in the Bureau of Commissions, Elections, and Legislation in the Pennsylvania Department of State in Harrisburg, who kindly, cheerfully, and quickly responded to my many requests for registration data and aided me in getting the story straight as to exactly how the reporting of those who do not affiliate with the Republican or Democratic party is handled in Pennsylvania. Allison, who was recently promoted to the Pennsylvania Gaming Control Board, was a pleasure to work with!

The third lifesaver of this trio is David L. Thomas, "research technician lead" at the Inter-University Consortium for Political and Social Research (ICPSR) at the University of Michigan in Ann Arbor. I can't recall how many times I e-mailed or called David for help in setting up a survey on my computer or in finding out specific information that wasn't available in the codebooks. David always got back to me in a timely and congenial manner. His advice and help with the surveys was invaluable, saving me from hours of futility; I know this for sure because in the beginning, before I came in contact with David, there were a lot of hours of futility. I don't know what I would have done without his enthusiastic direction and guidance. His cheerful nature made having to e-mail him over and over and over again quite a bit easier.

If it had not been for this trio's knowledge, data, expertise, and willingness to help, my work would have been much more difficult and my project would have taken much longer. The time they all gave and the long-distance smiles and interest with which they gave their time were truly heartwarming!

My debt to James L. Sundquist is enormous. First, I gained invaluable guidance from studying his insightful work on electoral change, as the reader will observe in the pages that follow. Next, he did me the honor of reading and commenting extensively on my manuscript in advance of it being accepted for publication. Further, he generously agreed to write the foreword to my book and, in the process, place my research in a context that only a scholar of his caliber could do. Finally, on a personal note, I had the pleasure to spend a delightful afternoon with him and his wife Gerry at their home in Arlington, Virginia, in August 2007, during which he regaled us with many amusing tales drawn from his personal recollection of Pennsylvania politicians.

Another prominent scholar, A. James Reichley, kindly read my study and offered keen insights based on his personal involvement in Pennsylvania politics as well as his own research and writing on American politics. I am grateful for the time he spent advising me, including sharing several hilarious stories about the politicians he knew.

I profited greatly from the advice of Robert Speel and Terry Madonna, who reviewed the manuscript for Pennsylvania State University Press. Their careful scrutiny of the manuscript was evident in the many useful comments they provided. In addition, Professor Speel's path-breaking book on electoral change in the North laid the foundation for my Pennsylvania study.

Joe Lenski of Edison Media Research, the company that conducted the 2004 and 2006 exit polls for the five major television networks and the Associated Press, provided me with an invaluable map that specifies the division of Pennsylvania's counties into the five analytical regions built into the exit-poll samples. This map of the "Geocode" was extremely helpful for the survey analysis presented in the second half of chapter 6.

Next, I want to thank two women at Case Western Reserve University's Kelvin Smith Library who made my life much easier. Karen Thornton, the subject specialist for government documents, repeatedly came to my aid when I was having difficulty locating needed census data. Elsie Finley, social and behavioral sciences liaison, helped by locating and quickly acquiring numerous publications and books relevant to my study.

I would like to express my appreciation to Dr. Vince McHale of Case Western Reserve University's Political Science Department, a Wilkes-Barre native, who offered sensible guidance and served as my informal factor-analysis coach. Dr. David Hammack of Case's History Department brought the perspective only a historian could add to such a work of political science, and I am thankful to have had his counsel.

In addition, I wish to thank my Master's of Public Administration (MPA) students at Gannon University in Erie, where I served as director of the MPA program from 1998 to 2007. Their constant encouragement (and their understanding) kept me going. Specifically, I would like to recognize the following students who took my course on Pennsylvania Politics in the Fall of 2006 and served as "guinea pigs" for my study, reading and commenting on various chapters. They are Jorge Alvear, Daniela Baban, Bob Currie, Adam Mook, Daniel Moore, Matty Njie, Ben Oduho, Andrew Spencer, and Gemma Thomas. I am also grateful to my dear friend and Gannon colleague, Dr. Mary Anne Rivera, whose support was a true blessing!

The following people also helped me in various respects along the way, which I much appreciate: Carol Perry, Anita Miller, Sharon Krahe, John Elliott, Ann Badach, Erin Heslin Slattengren, John Johnston, and Bob Sparks.

I would also like to thank all of those at Pennsylvania State University Press who had a hand in bringing this book into print. It has been a pleasure to work with Sandy Thatcher, the director of the Press, who handled the manuscript expertly throughout and who also had the terrific idea to ask Jim Sundquist to write the book's foreword. Special thanks to Jennifer Norton, design and production manager, with whom I exchanged several e-mails and phone calls during the early phases leading up to production, and to Kathryn Yahner, editorial assistant, and Cherene Holland, managing editor, for their assistance. My thanks to Carol Lallier, the book's copyeditor, and to Nick Maier and Carolyn Albee of diacriTech, who were skillful at shepherding the manuscript through the production process.

Last but not least, I would like to thank my family. Without their patience, love, and help, I may never have finished this undertaking.

First, to my parents, Tom and Ena DeGeorge, who have always supported my educational aspirations and were exemplary parents. They worked hard and sacrificed much so that they could provide me and my brother and sister with fine educations, and as a result, instilled in us a hard work ethic. And, they are probably as exhausted as I am for having watched their grandchildren countless hours while I worked on this book.

Next, to Alec Lamis, my husband and best friend, who served as my mentor, informal advisor, and in-house sounding board for this project, while operating a quasi-efficient "Daddy Daycare" center. His constant love and devotion and support were the glue that got me through. In addition, his book, *The Two-Party South*, which analyzed electoral change in his native region, inspired me to research the politics of my home state of Pennsylvania.

And, finally, to my two little guys, Peter, who turned seven on April 5, 2008, and Alexander, who turned five six days later on April 11. They heard a lot of, "Mommy can't play right now. Mommy has to work. You go out with Daddy." And "Mommy will be done soon—just a little while longer." In the face of all of that, they were real troupers, taking quality time with Mommy when they could get it and learning how to entertain themselves (which unfortunately often meant jumping off of radiators and couches). Well guys, I'm happy to report, "Mommy's all done. Let's play!"

Renée M. Lamis
Erie, Pennsylvania

The Realignment of Pennsylvania Politics Since 1960

1

Electoral Realignments and Pennsylvania from the Civil War, Through the New Deal, and into the Early Twenty-First Century

I n this book, I seek to understand Pennsylvania electoral and party system change since 1960 and to place the Keystone State's experience within the broader context of national electoral change. In the process, my goal is to illuminate both the complex nature of the electoral politics of this large and diverse Northeastern state as well as to contribute to our knowledge of how and why the national party system was transformed over these years.

There has been considerable analysis and speculation concerning whether the United States has undergone an electoral realignment since the establishment of the New Deal party system in the 1930s and its penetration during the 1940s and 1950s throughout the North in a series of "aftershocks" of the initial New Deal "earthquake," to borrow the terms of James L. Sundquist, a major scholar of American electoral change.[1] My study contributes to the ongoing debate by examining the topic within the confines of Pennsylvania. Such a case study cannot answer all the questions that realignment scholars have raised and are currently debating. But, it does add to our knowledge by bringing into the equation a solid understanding of the recent electoral experience of this important yet little-studied state.[2]

Robert W. Speel, in *Changing Patterns of Voting in the Northern United States: Electoral Realignment, 1952–1996*, a leading study in the field, strongly argues for the

---

1. James L. Sundquist, *Dynamics of the Party System: Alignment and Realignment of Political Parties in the United States*, rev. ed. (Washington, DC: Brookings Institution, 1983), 193–268.

2. On the value of case studies, see John Gerring, "What Is a Case Study and What Is It Good For?" *American Political Science Review* 98 (May 2004), 341–54.

importance of and need for more state-level studies.[3] In fact, he contends that part of the reason there is so much disagreement over the direction of the American electoral and party system in recent decades lies in the failure to appreciate regional and state differences. Concentrating on "broad national socioeconomic groups in surveys often reveals important political changes, such as the gender gap and racial attitudes," Speel writes, but, he argues further, such approaches "can actually miss much of the diversity of the states and their electoral patterns. . . . By focusing almost exclusively on national survey data to analyze modern realignment, some political scientists have completely missed either the existence or the best explanation of realignments in many of the states."[4]

After decrying the lack of state-level studies in the modern period, Speel presents case studies of Vermont and Rhode Island and examines in less detail changes in other parts of the country "west of New England," as he puts it. He writes practically nothing about Pennsylvania.

Throughout his book, Speel demonstrates an appreciation for the nuances and diversity found in our national party system in addition to expressing his strong position in favor of more studies of individual states. My book is an effort to fill part of the gap to which Speel points.

Pennsylvania is a fascinating state to examine because its partisan transformation has been dramatic and full of contradictions. Between 1860 and 1932, Pennsylvania supported every Republican presidential nominee, and the GOP dominated state politics as well. Then, the New Deal realignment of the 1930s ushered in an era of two-party competition. By the 1990s, Pennsylvania had become an important component of a new national Democratic coalition that gradually emerged after yet another major disruption in the party system began in the 1960s. In fact, the Democratic national nominee has carried the Keystone State in each of the presidential elections from 1992 to 2004, although the Democratic standard-bearer could win only two of these last four nationwide elections.

How this shift in the national position of the Keystone State occurred requires untangling two major periods of electoral change: the New Deal realignment as well as the changes that resulted from the disruption of the national party system starting in the mid-1960s, a transformation that I call the "culture-wars realignment." I examine these remarkable developments in the rest of this first chapter and in chapter 2.

Then, in chapters 3 and 4, I shift attention to the major electoral contests in Pennsylvania below the presidential level, that is, to elections for governor and U.S. senator. This focus takes us deeper into the Keystone State's electoral politics and requires becoming acquainted with the various politicians who sought and won the top public offices from 1962 to 2004. As is shown in an important party-strength figure introduced shortly, Pennsylvania Republicans were highly competitive in

---

3. Robert W. Speel, *Changing Patterns of Voting in the Northern United States: Electoral Realignment, 1952–1996* (University Park: Pennsylvania State University Press, 1998), 9–15.

4. Ibid., 13.

these elections for governor and U.S. senator from 1962 to 2004. This state-level GOP strength held firm even as the performance of the national Republican party exhibited, as mentioned previously, considerable weakness in Pennsylvania in the last four presidential elections. Why did Pennsylvania Republicans do so well in a period of impressive Democratic presidential strength in the Keystone State? This puzzling result is fully explored in chapters 3 and 4.

In chapter 5, I analyze a wealth of electoral and party registration data to highlight changes in the state's partisan patterns that have occurred from 1960 to 2004, including the use of an extensive county-level analysis that captures the most recent direction of change in each of the state's sixty-seven counties. In chapter 6, I mine a treasure trove of Pennsylvania public opinion surveys and election-day exit polls to illuminate further the recent changes that have occurred in the state's electorate. In chapter 7, I analyze fully the 2006 election in Pennsylvania, which witnessed a remarkable surge in Democratic party strength. My chief goal in this chapter is to understand this election within the context of ongoing electoral change in the Keystone State, concluding with cautious speculation concerning future prospects for Pennsylvania two-party politics. The book then closes with a postscript analyzing the 2008 election.

I turn now to national realignment theory for aid in understanding what has happened in Pennsylvania.

National Realignments and Pennsylvania from the Civil War Through the New Deal

V. O. Key Jr. is credited by political scientists with starting the field of realignment studies in his path-breaking 1955 article, "A Theory of Critical Elections."[5] Studying New England presidential voting patterns from 1916 to 1952, Key found

> the existence of a category of elections in which voters are, at least from impressionistic evidence, unusually deeply concerned, in which the extent of electoral involvement is relatively quite high, and in which the decisive results of the voting reveal a sharp altera-tion of the pre-existing cleavage within the electorate. Moreover, and perhaps this is the truly differentiating characteristic of this sort of election, the realignment made manifest in the voting in such elec-tions seems to persist for several succeeding elections.[6]

Working nearly a decade and a half after Key's pioneering study, Sundquist produced a comprehensive theory of realignment in his much-praised *Dynamics of the Party System: Alignment and Realignment of Political Parties in the United States.* Accepting the existence of electoral realignments, Sundquist sought to lay out exactly

---

5. V. O. Key Jr., "A Theory of Critical Elections," *Journal of Politics* 17 (February 1955), 3–18.
6. Ibid., 4.

how they occur and why. Drawing on the work of E. E. Schattschneider, Sundquist defined electoral realignments as "those redistributions of party support . . . that reflect a change in the structure of the party conflict and hence the establishment of a new line of partisan cleavage . . . within the electorate."[7] After a realignment has occurred, he wrote, "The parties quarreled over a different set of issues. . . . The line of cleavage between the parties cut across the electorate in a new direction; the party system shifted on its axis."[8]

At the core of the process Sundquist described is the rise of a powerful new issue (or cluster of issues) that cuts across the existing line of cleavage in the party system. If the political parties take opposing polar positions over the new issue or cluster of issues, a realignment results, and there is significant change in the nature of the party system. Not all "crosscutting" issues that arise lead to realignment.[9] However, it is essential that the two parties go to opposite poles on the new crosscutting issue; if they both embrace it, as more or less occurred during the Progressive era at the beginning of the twentieth century, no realignment results.

Further, Sundquist emphasized—and I agree with him completely—that realignments are national phenomena. After recognizing this essential fact, however, we then must look at specific states to understand the impact of the national changes on individual states and to seek to understand the variations in state patterns that result.[10] In the process, there is a basic reality that must be kept in mind: We have fifty separate state party systems that are connected to an overarching national party system. Thus, to fully comprehend electoral change in the United States, we must understand electoral change in individual states.[11]

During the period of his study, roughly from the 1830s through the early 1980s, Sundquist found three major realignments: the Civil War–era realignment, the Populist-era realignment, and the New Deal–era realignment. Of course, these were watershed periods in American political history, and the changes that occurred during these eras affected considerably more than electoral politics. Still, there is much to learn from a closer examination of Sundquist's interpretation, one that

---

7. Sundquist, *Dynamics of the Party System*, 14. The first edition of Sundquist's classic appeared in 1973.

8. Ibid., 13.

9. Ibid., 1–49, 298–321.

10. As Sundquist wrote in his chapter 3, "The Realignment Process: A Preliminary Statement:" "National parties in this country are not unified bodies, but federations of state parties, each of which responds to national and local forces in its own way. . . . So the course and extent of a realignment are determined by the course and extent of the myriad semi-independent state and local realignments that may be set in motion by a common circumstance or single series of events" (ibid., 49). And, earlier in his book in discussing the "geographic scope" of realignments, he asserted: "The assumption that critical elections, or realignments, occur across the whole nation at the same time can severely distort reality" (10).

11. This is a position with which Speel would doubtless agree.

is invaluable for understanding not only national electoral change but also the Pennsylvania experience.

The crosscutting issue that precipitated the Civil War–era realignment was the question of slavery, or, more precisely in the beginning, what to do about the extension of slavery into new states to be formed in the western territories. Needless to say, the slavery question was not the central issue that divided the Whig party and the Democratic party during the years before the realignment; they did political battle over a host of other issues that defined their separate identities and their followers. The Civil War–era realignment witnessed the demise of the Whig party in the early 1850s, the birth of the Republican party in the mid-1850s, the fighting of a bloody Civil War, and then Reconstruction. When it was over, a new period of partisan conflict between a transformed Democratic party and the victorious Republican party of Abraham Lincoln was ushered in.[12]

The second realignment had its origins during the 1870s and 1880s in the grievances of the nation's farmers against both political parties—the Republicans and the Democrats—and the farmers' fury over the lack of acceptable response from the two established parties. They carried forward their cluster of crosscutting issues—inflation of the currency to ease their debt burden, regulation of discriminatory railroad rates, a progressive income tax, and so on—by creating the People's party in 1891. When the Democratic party in 1896 nominated William Jennings Bryan of Nebraska, a skilled orator with strong appeal to farmers, the Populists made common cause with the Democrats in the critical election of that year. Bryan's defeat by the Republican William McKinley, caused in no small measure by the failure of the Democratic–Populist forces to make inroads among the industrial workers in the eastern states, ushered in an era of Republican dominance that persisted to the end of the 1920s and the onset of the Great Depression.[13]

An exception to national Republican ascendancy was found in the one-party Democratic South that formed throughout the former states of the Confederacy by the dawn of the twentieth century. The purpose of Democratic unity in Dixie was to preserve racial segregation there and to keep that region's African American population in a second-class status. The rationale for the one-party South would break down in the 1960s when the nation resolved the civil rights impasse and would lead to the partisan transformation of the region, a story that becomes relevant later in my study when considering post-1960 national electoral change.[14]

12. Sundquist, *Dynamics of the Party System*, 50–105.

13. Ibid., 106–69.

14. Alexander P. Lamis, *The Two-Party South*, 2nd expanded ed. (New York: Oxford University Press, 1990), 3–19. The classic treatment of the politics of the one-party Democratic South is found in V. O. Key Jr., *Southern Politics in State and Nation* (New York: Alfred A. Knopf, 1949).

In all of these nineteenth-century and early twentieth-century changes, Pennsylvania was in the thick of the action, as professors Philip S. Klein and Ari Hoogenboom recount in their book *A History of Pennsylvania*, the best relatively recent history of the commonwealth.[15] This early "action" in the Keystone State was dominated by the Republican party, which, as mentioned previously, received the commonwealth's electoral votes in every one of the nineteen presidential elections from 1860 to 1932 (of course, the post–Civil War Democratic party won only five of those presidential elections). In fact, Pennsylvania's James Buchanan in 1856 was the last Democrat to carry the state until Franklin D. Roosevelt in 1936 began the first of his three straight victories in Pennsylvania and the second of four straight in the nation.

"Republican domination of Pennsylvania [between 1860 and the early 1930s]," Klein and Hoogenboom wrote, "owed much to the exploitation of Civil War hatreds, to support from businessmen, farmers, and immigrants, and above all to superb political leadership and organization."[16] That leadership was supplied over the years by three remarkable Pennsylvania Republicans: Simon Cameron, Matthew Quay, and Boies Penrose. "The Cameron-Quay-Penrose [Republican] organization was so successful and long-lived," Klein and Hoogenboom wrote, "that more than any other organization it deserved the title 'machine,' which expressed the mingled hatred, despair, and admiration of its enemies."[17]

A useful way to visualize Pennsylvania's partisan path during these decades of Republican domination and later is to employ a measure of party strength and plot it over time. This is done for the Democratic party in Figure 1.1, using a measure devised by Paul T. David, a University of Virginia political scientist.[18] To get his measure of party strength, David averaged the vote in each biennial election year for three major offices: governor, U.S. senator, and U.S. representative with each counting a third (all the U.S. House elections are averaged to get their one-third contribution).[19] The resulting index, which is plotted in Figure 1.1 as a solid line, provides a reasonable gauge of a political party's strength, because a party that is unable to do well in these three categories is clearly not doing well. Incidentally, the dotted line in the figure is the quadrennial Democratic vote for president in the state, a valuable percentage to use for comparison with David's party strength index.

Figure 1.1 highlights the devastating impact of the Populist-era realignment on the post–Civil War Pennsylvania Democratic party. After being mildly

---

15. Philip S. Klein and Ari Hoogenboom, *A History of Pennsylvania*, 2nd ed. (University Park: Pennsylvania State University Press, 1980).

16. Ibid., 360.

17. Ibid.

18. Paul T. David, *Party Strength in the United States, 1872–1970* (Charlottesville: University Press of Virginia, 1972). Professor David updated his party strength figures for 1972 to 1976 in three *Journal of Politics* research notes. The updated figures through 2006 were calculated by Andrew M. Lucker for Alexander P. Lamis, who made them available to me.

19. Interpolation is used when there is no gubernatorial or U.S. Senate election in any particular year.

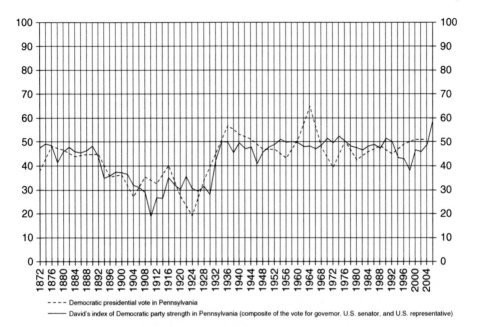

Fig. 1.1. Democratic Party Strength in Pennsylvania, 1872–2006

competitive with the Republican party until the early 1890s, the state's Democrats descend below the 40 percent line and remain there until the New Deal era, even dipping below the 30 percent line during several election cycles. When compared to the states of the North as a whole, Pennsylvania exhibited somewhat more Republican strength than found in the region through the 1920s, even though the GOP dominated the North as it did Pennsylvania.[20] Figure 1.2, which charts David's index of Democratic party strength for the North,[21] allows for this comparison with the Pennsylvania pattern in Figure 1.1.

20. In their chapter entitled "The Evolution of a One-Party State," Klein and Hoogenboom explain how and why the Republican party came to dominate Pennsylvania politics in a narrative that stressed the financial and leadership advantages of the Grand Old Party as well as the many difficulties encountered by the Democrats. On the latter, for example, they wrote: "Laborers became distinctly cool to Democrats in the 1890s. Laborers were convinced not only that Democratic tinkering with the protective tariff had caused the Panic of 1893 and their distress but also that the Democratic party was hostile to their aspirations. [Erie industrialist William L.] Scott, an enemy of organized labor, had led Pennsylvania Democrats, and two years before [Democratic President Grover] Cleveland broke the 1894 Pullman Strike with Federal troops, [Democratic Governor Robert E.] Pattison had broken the Homestead Strike with state militia." *History of Pennsylvania*, 371–73.

21. Population is taken into account when constructing the regional figures by using the number of members in the U.S. House allocated to each state. The South consists of the eleven former Confederate states along with Kentucky and Oklahoma. Thus, the North is made up of the other thirty-seven states.

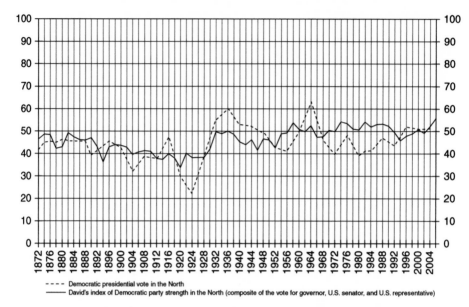

Fig. 1.2. Democratic Party Strength in the North, 1872–2006

A dramatic upturn in Democratic fortunes in Pennsylvania and through-out the North occurred in the 1930s as a result of the emergency of the Great Depression and the favorable popular response given to the New Deal initiatives of President Roosevelt, who led the Democratic party out of the political wilderness to become the country's new majority party during the New Deal realignment, an epoch-shattering phenomenon. Figures 1.1 and 1.2 show the trend. The crosscutting issue involved in this transformation, to return to Sundquist's realignment frame-work, was the proper role of the federal government in the social and economic life of the nation. At the head of an activist national government, Roosevelt pioneered, through his New Deal program, in a host of areas from Social Security to labor law reform that were embraced by Americans of limited financial means.

As Sundquist put it: "[T]he party system that emerged from the revolution of the 1930s reflected a pronounced class cleavage [that it did not have before]. Businessmen and professional men were preponderantly Republican and the working class predominantly Democratic."[22] Commenting further concerning the class-based rationale of the new party system, Sundquist wrote: "[I]t was the lower economic classes who most actively sought to expand the scope of government, seeking to use its powers for the relief of economic hardship and the reform of the economic system in their interests."[23] The Republican party, holding to traditional notions of a limited role for the federal government, "remained," in Sundquist's phrase, "immobile at the conservative pole."[24]

22. Sundquist, *Dynamics of the Party System*, 217.

23. Ibid.

24. Ibid., 213.

Perhaps nowhere in the nation did the New Deal realignment have a bigger impact than in Pennsylvania. As the historians Klein and Hoogenboom put it, "The Depression changed the Democratic party [in Pennsylvania] from a laughingstock to a vital organization."[25] They added:

> The Depression, and particularly Roosevelt's New Deal efforts to combat it, won laborers, immigrants, and blacks to the Democratic party. In the 1920s Democratic strength had been conspicuous in some agricultural areas and in a few mining counties, but the outstanding industrialized sections were solidly Republican.[26]

While Klein and Hoogenboom are correct in pointing to the importance of Roosevelt and the New Deal for transforming the Democratic party in Pennsylvania, they overlook the significance of the 1928 presidential election for setting in motion part of the change. This is understandable because on the surface the 1928 results seemed a continuation of the dismal Pennsylvania performance of the Democratic party in previous decades. Herbert Hoover, the victorious Republican nominee in 1928, carried the state with 65.2 percent to 33.9 percent for Governor Alfred E. Smith of New York, the Democratic standard-bearer, a result similar to the GOP presidential victory percentages in 1920 and 1924. But, as Samuel Lubell wrote in his "Forgotten Warrior" section of the important "Revolt of the City" chapter in his classic *The Future of American Politics*, "Before the Roosevelt Revolution there was an Al Smith Revolution."[27] Smith, the first Catholic nominee of the Democratic party, a "wet" on Prohibition, and a Northeastern urban sophisticate, shattered GOP strength in northern urban areas. According to Lubell, the four-term New York governor in 1928 swung 122 northern counties out of the 1924 Republican column, and of those, 77 were predominantly Catholic.[28] Lubell wrote further:

> Before Smith the Democrats were little more of an urban party than were the Republicans. In Pennsylvania, for example, the three counties the Democrats won in 1920 and 1924 were largely rural and native born. These counties swung for Hoover in 1928. In their place, the Democrats captured three mining and industrial counties—Elk,

25. Klein and Hoogenboom, *History of Pennsylvania*, 455. They note here that "from 1893 to 1931 Democrats lost ninety-five out of ninety-six statewide elections." For more on Pennsylvania and the New Deal realignment, see Walter Dean Burnham, *Critical Elections and the Mainsprings of American Politics* (New York: W. W. Norton, 1970), 54–59.

26. Klein and Hoogenboom, *History of Pennsylvania*, 455.

27. Samuel Lubell, *The Future of American Politics* (New York: Harper & Brothers, 1951), 35. In his influential article, "A Theory of Critical Elections," Key places emphasis on the "critical" nature of the 1928 election, at least for New England, writing: "In New England, at least, the Roosevelt revolution of 1932 was in large measure an Al Smith revolution of 1928" (4). Incidentally, in his article Key makes reference to Lubell's "Forgotten Warrior" section.

28. Lubell, *The Future of American Politics*, 35.

Luzerne and Lackawanna—which had not gone Democratic since at least 1896.[29]

"What Smith really embodied," Lubell explained, "was the revolt of the underdog, urban immigrant against the top dog of 'old American' stock," pointing out that the "new" wave of immigrants after 1885 came from predominantly Catholic countries in Europe, while earlier immigrant groups—the Irish were an exception—came from predominantly Protestant Europe.[30] Further, as Sundquist notes, there was an anti-Smith reaction in smaller cities and rural areas in the Northeast as well as elsewhere in the country where Democrats had strength prior to 1928.[31] Both Sundquist and Lubell make clear that Smith, whose campaign was tied up in issues of religion and Prohibition and whose chief backers included prominent American millionaires, did not press class conflict. For these reasons, Sundquist concludes, "The minor realignment of 1928 in the cities can therefore be considered an episode in American politics distinct from the realignment of the 1930s."[32] Lubell reaches a similar conclusion by pointing out that the urban population of native American stock "had still to be roused," but, he added, they would be in the next decade.[33] The remainder of his "Revolt of the City" chapter details this "rousing."[34] In my analysis of presidential election patterns in chapter 2, I demonstrate the significance of the 1928 election for the abrupt shift in Pennsylvania county-level electoral patterns that took place in the late 1920s and in the 1930s, a remarkable departure of considerable durability and importance.

In the 1934 elections, Pennsylvania Democrats elected their first governor of the twentieth century, George H. Earle, and their first U.S. senator since the 1870s, Joseph F. Guffey. The Democrats understood why they had won. Governor-elect Earle put it bluntly: "I literally rode into office on the coat-tails of President Roosevelt, and I have no hesitation in saying so."[35] Proposing a Little New Deal for Pennsylvania, Earle declared in his inaugural address, "My fundamental conviction is that life must be made secure for those millions who, by accident of birth, are left at the mercy of economic forces."[36] The governor's Little New Deal program achieved notable success after the 1936 election resulted in heavy Democratic majorities in the legislature.[37] But, as Klein and Hoogenboom observed, "the

---

29. Ibid., 40.

30. Ibid., 39.

31. Sundquist, *Dynamics of the Party System*, 193. For more on this topic, see "The 'Al Smith Revolution' in the East," in Sundquist's "Minor Realignments of the 1920s" chapter in ibid, 191–97.

32. Ibid., 197.

33. Lubell, *Future of American Politics*, 41.

34. See ibid., 41–57, especially the table on page 50.

35. Klein and Hoogenboom, *History of Pennsylvania*, 457.

36. Ibid.

37. See Richard C. Keller, *Pennsylvania's Little New Deal* (New York: Garland, 1982).

brief Little New Deal interlude" ended with the election in 1938 of the first of four straight Republican governors.[38]

Throughout the North, state and local Democrats struggled in the late 1930s and throughout World War II to build on their surge in strength as a result of the popularity of Roosevelt and the New Deal. Sundquist argues that it wasn't until after World War II that sustained Democratic support was achieved in the region as a whole in a process he called delayed "aftershocks" of the New Deal "earthquake," using terms I mentioned at the beginning of this chapter. In an insightful chapter entitled "Aftershocks of the New Deal Earthquake—in the North," Sundquist describes how it required several decades for the changes started by Roosevelt at the national level to penetrate and transform politics in various northern states.[39] Figures 1.1 and 1.2 show that Democratic strength in Pennsylvania and the North dropped back in the late 1930s even though Roosevelt's majorities remained strong. What accounted for this delay, according to Sundquist, was "the unattractive character of the state and local Democratic parties."[40] What was needed was the ascendancy in the various states of a new generation of "programmatic liberals." These programmatic liberals were, to quote Sundquist further, "as issue oriented as the old leaders were patronage oriented. They had been attracted into politics by the excitement of the New Deal . . . and while they were ambitious, it was not for the pecuniary rewards of politics. They were intellectual and argumentative, devoted followers of the Roosevelt New Deal, as liberal as their elders were conservative."[41]

In considering the aftershocks process specifically in Pennsylvania, Sundquist concluded, in one of only four short, northern-state case studies he used in *Dynamics of the Party System*, that the penetration of the New Deal realignment in Pennsylvania was unique, illustrating several diverse patterns.[42] He wrote that in some parts of Pennsylvania there was a drastic, single-stage realignment, while other parts of the state experienced a two-stage aftershocks process and still others realized no net shift at all.[43] To explain these differences in Pennsylvania, Sundquist wrote:

> [N]ew party identifications were formed by voters in the 1930s and were immediately reflected in all aspects of political behavior, including registration, wherever the Democrats were able to win locally; where they did not, the expression [of the new Democratic strength] (except in presidential voting) was delayed. Eventually,

38. Klein and Hoogenboom, *History of Pennsylvania*, 465.

39. Sundquist, *Dynamics of the Party System*, 240–268 (chapter 11).

40. Ibid., 262.

41. Ibid., 263.

42. Ibid., 252.

43. Ibid., 252–56. Sundquist titled this section "Pennsylvania: Patronage Republicans Switch Parties."

however, identification with the party at the presidential level proved controlling. Once the Democrats broke through at the local level, the party's hidden strength was finally reflected in the registration figures and in sustained local Democratic victories.[44]

David's index in Figure 1.1 confirms that sustained Democratic victories in Pennsylvania took hold in the late 1940s and in the 1950s following the classic aftershocks pattern suggested by Sundquist. In fact, Sundquist marks the 1949 off-year elections in Philadelphia as the Democratic breakthrough point. In that year, Philadelphia Democrats, to quote Sundquist's account,

> elected Richardson Dilworth as city treasurer and Joseph S. Clark as city controller—the first local Democratic victories in decades. Dilworth and Clark, like their counter-parts in the upper Midwest, were aggressive New Dealers, determined to use a revived Democratic party as a vehicle for a liberal program, but they were also urban political reformers, campaigning against corruption and a patronage-oriented political system.[45]

Dilworth and Clark each went on to be elected mayor of Philadelphia in succession. Clark won a U.S. Senate seat in 1956 and served two terms. Dilworth sought the governorship unsuccessfully in 1950 and 1962. They epitomized the programmatic liberals who were at the forefront of transforming the Democratic party at the state level in the North during this delayed aftershocks phase. Incidentally, Sundquist's notion of delayed realignment aftershocks is an important insight that I apply in later discussion to help explain the transformation that occurred in Pennsylvania and the nation after the main events of the "culture-wars realignment" had occurred. Like the New Deal realignment aftershocks, the culture-wars aftershocks were felt in Pennsylvania and the nation for well over a decade after this latest realignment had occurred, a point discussed at greater length later in the chapter.

The Democratic party's ability to compete with the once dominant Pennsylvania Republican party received a big boost in 1954 with the election of George M. Leader as the first Democratic governor since Governor Earle's Depression-era victory twenty years earlier. This was followed by the election of another Democratic governor, David L. Lawrence, in 1958, and continued Democratic successes in Philadelphia in 1955 and 1959.

Thus, by the time the 1960s arrived, Pennsylvania had been transformed by the New Deal realignment into a competitive two-party state. Two political scientists, G. Terry Madonna and Robert J. Bresler, in a brief, eight-page survey of the state's party history and organization, echo this point: "In the 1950s Pennsylvania emerged

---

44. Ibid., 256.
45. Ibid., 255.

as a genuinely competitive two-party state."[46] In fact, by the time of the balloting for president in November 1960, Democratic party voter registration in Pennsylvania narrowly passed Republican registration for the first time in the twentieth century. Democratic registration continued to outstrip the GOP's totals by several hundred thousand voters from then to the present with the exception of a few years in the late 1960s and early 1970s.[47]

As Pennsylvania entered the 1960s, the driving force behind its partisan politics was still the ongoing penetration of the New Deal realignment and the amazing transformation it had wrought on the Keystone State's politics. Starting in the mid-1960s, another cluster of crosscutting issues would enter the national party system and launch yet another transformation. But the new culture-wars realignment did not have the force to supplant the underlying cleavages brought to the state during the New Deal realignment and its aftershocks. Thus, the older New Deal cleavages persisted as the bedrock of the state's politics. Sundquist impressively captured this process of the intermingling of successive eras of change in his concluding section to chapter 1 of *Dynamics of the Party System*, which is entitled "The Infinite Complexity of Political Alignments." He wrote:

> Successive realignments can best be understood as new patterns drawn on transparent overlays. Each overlay defines a new line of party cleavage within the electorate (or redelineates an old line) and so distributes some elements of the voting population on either side of that line in new arrangements. But beneath the latest overlay can be discerned all the lines of cleavage of the past, some more distinct than others by virtue of their recency or the strength of the color in which they were originally drawn.[48]

The New Deal realignment in Pennsylvania was drawn in a very bright color indeed. Its persistence amid the new changes that started to arrive in the middle to late 1960s is an important part of the story to come.

National Electoral Change Since 1960:
The Culture-Wars Realignment and
Its Implications for Pennsylvania

The American political party system in the early years of the twenty-first century is very different than it was in 1960 even though elements from the previous era

46. G. Terry Madonna and Robert J. Bresler, "Pennsylvania," in Andrew M. Appleton and Daniel S. Ward, eds., *State Party Profiles: A 50-State Guide to Development, Organization, and Resources* (Washington, DC: CQ Press, 1997), 273.

47. Pennsylvania party registration figures since 1926 are presented in Table 5.5 in chapter 5.

48. Sundquist, *Dynamics of the Party System*, 17.

persist. How and why did the changes occur, and what explains the persistence of certain older features? Finally, what are the implications of these national changes for Pennsylvania politics?

For guidance in this inquiry, I rely again on Sundquist, the theorist who, in my view, has offered the most comprehensive and accurate explanation of overall U.S. electoral change. As sketched previously, Sundquist's realignment theory requires a new issue or cluster of issues to arise and cut across the existing line of party cleavage. Although many scenarios can occur based on how the crosscutting issue is handled by the existing political parties, no significant change will occur, in Sundquist's view, without such a new crosscutting force.

The Democratic and Republican parties coming out of the New Deal realignment of the 1930s and its aftershocks were mainly differentiated by their positions on the proper role of the federal government in the economic life of the nation, as already mentioned. The Democrats favored an activist government pushing a host of programs designed to deal with the material needs of citizens, while Republicans placed more emphasis on the private sector as the key engine of economic prosperity. In the GOP view, as the economy grew and expanded in an economic environment with little governmental intervention, citizens would prosper and be in a position to take care of their own needs.

The key to understanding the post-1960 era is the recognition that, starting in the mid-1960s, a series of new issues rose to prominence that were different from the issues that defined the New Deal party system. The process followed the classic Sundquist-described pattern involving a cluster of new issues cutting across the existing line of cleavage between the two parties. These new issues were cultural ones that divided the electorate in ways quite different from the economic and role of government issues of the New Deal realignment. They were the hot-button social and cultural issues of the day—race relations and other related racial concerns such as affirmative action and school busing; abortion; prayer in the schools; gay rights; gun control; the death penalty; "activist" judges "legislating" rights not clearly written in constitutional texts; and so on. There was also a foreign and defense policy dimension to this partisan transformation that flowed from the domestic battles over the Vietnam war. Although President Lyndon Johnson, a Democrat, prosecuted the war, the major opposition arose within the "peace wing" of the Democratic party. That faction in the years that followed became stigmatized—to its electoral detriment—as "weak on defense" and somehow not quite up to the struggles of the Cold War.

As mentioned in the introduction to this chapter, I call this latest transformation of the party system the culture-wars realignment. Its effects fueled partisan changes over several decades and continued to play out after 1992 as the aftershocks from this latest partisan earthquake worked their way into our decentralized party system. The end result is a striking post-realignment party configuration that took hold toward the end of the 1990s and persisted through the 2004 election, showing high correlations in partisan electoral patterns during the early elections of the twenty-first century. National and Pennsylvania data substantiating this end result of the culture-wars realignment are presented in the next chapter.

When these emotional issues swept into our national life starting in the mid-1960s, along with the divisiveness stemming from the Vietnam war, they played out first and most prominently at the national level in presidential elections. Republican presidential candidates were the main beneficiaries, and the GOP nominees won five of the six presidential elections from 1968 to 1988, starting with Richard Nixon's comeback victory eight years after his narrow defeat by John F. Kennedy in 1960, an election fought under very different circumstances and over very different issues compared to those Nixon confronted in his winning 1968 campaign.

The capstone election of this realignment was the fifth Republican win, the 1988 triumph of George H. W. Bush over Michael Dukakis, the Democratic governor of Massachusetts. This election, which I discuss further below, exhibited virtually all of the crosscutting issues of the culture-wars realignment, making it the showcase election of this latest national transformation of the party system. In the next presidential election, the 1992 Democratic nominee, Arkansas governor Bill Clinton, went to great lengths to distance himself from what he viewed as the losing Democratic stances of the culture-wars realignment, which spanned most of his life in politics. Thus, by defining himself as a "New Democrat," different from his losing predecessors, namely George McGovern, Walter Mondale, and Dukakis, Clinton conceded the success of the pro-Republican realignment that had occurred during the years after 1964. In essence, Clinton did what "me too" Republican politicians like Governor Thomas E. Dewey of New York did in order to survive the onslaught of the New Deal revolution in the 1940s, which was to embrace popular New Deal policies. "It is not the function of a political party to die fighting for obsolete slogans," Dewey said at the time.[49] Although the 1992 election had more than its share of features specific to that year, such as Ross Perot's powerful articulation and denunciation of the burgeoning national debt, Clinton stood out by his effort to place distance between himself and the orthodox liberal positions held by a majority of the politicians in his party. Here's how the historian James T. Patterson described Clinton's positioning:

> Democrats, [Clinton] said, would never win unless they avoided overidentification with interest groups such as labor unions. Though they must protect entitlements such as Social Security and Medicare, they had to cast aside their "old tax-and-spend policies." Again and again, Clinton insisted that his party must stand for "opportunity," "responsibility," and "community." Like Jimmy Carter [the lone Democrat to win a presidential election between Lyndon Johnson in 1964 and Clinton in 1992], he said he was a born-again man of faith. During the campaign, he stood behind the death penalty. [Patterson relates later that Clinton left the campaign trail and returned to Arkansas "to approve the execution of a mentally retarded black

49. Ibid., 335.

prisoner."[50]] He promised to reform welfare, primarily by limiting the length of time that recipients might receive cash assistance.[51]

By becoming a "me too" Democrat on more than a few of the divisive social and cultural issues that had arisen between the mid-1960s and the 1992 election, Clinton ratified the transformation that had occurred. In a sense, Clinton's Democratic campaign in 1992 brought a measure of closure to the latest realignment because, by doing what he did, Clinton ratified and legitimated the culture-wars transformation just as Dukakis in his hapless 1988 role highlighted all the negative effects for Democrats that the culture-wars realignment had wrought up to then. But, as is shown below, the culture-wars realignment did not mean that the Democratic party was doomed to minority status. It did mean that the national Democrats' majority status, a legacy of the New Deal era, was at an end. The new party system, as mentioned above, exhibited a fairly even balance between the two major parties, a reality that was reflected in the "perfect tie" presidential election of 2000.[52]

The end result of this recent realignment was to graft onto the party system a new set of issues dividing the parties and, in the process, reorder the fundamental nature of American two-party politics. For example, the divisions witnessed in the 2000 and 2004 presidential elections (apart from those directly attributable to the terrorist attacks of September 11, 2001, and the Iraq war) owed much to the culture-wars realignment, starting with the reordering of the partisan lineup of the states and extending to shifts in various voting blocs as revealed by national survey data, all of which is shown in chapter 2. In fact, I argue later in this chapter that the forces unleashed during the culture-wars realignment have been responsible for driving cultural liberals to the Democratic party and cultural conservatives to the Republican party, resulting in the very recent and stable state-by-state outcomes presented in chapter 2. I view these post-1992 trends as aftershocks of the culture-wars realignment.

Now that I have introduced the end point of the culture-wars realignment and its aftermath, I go back to fill in the details of the latest realignment from its beginnings in the mid-1960s through the "ratifying" election of 1988 and into the current post–culture-wars realignment period we entered in the 1990s and are still in today.

After President Kennedy's assassination in November 1963, President Johnson pushed to passage in Congress many of Kennedy's major initiatives, which themselves flowed from liberal Democratic policy debates in the late 1940s

---

50. James T. Patterson, *Grand Expectations: The United States, 1945–1974* (New York: Oxford University Press, 1996), 252.

51. James T. Patterson, *Restless Giant: The United States from Watergate to* Bush v. Gore (New York: Oxford University Press, 2005), 248–49.

52. In fact, two political scientists used the phrase as the title of their book: James W. Ceaser and Andrew E. Busch, *The Perfect Tie: The True Story of the 2000 Presidential Election* (Lanham, MD: Rowman & Littlefield), 2001.

and 1950s. This liberal agenda included the Civil Rights Act of 1964, Medicare and Medicaid in 1965, significant federal aid to education, and urban development programs. Johnson, who hoped to pick up where President Franklin Roosevelt left off, added an ambitious agenda of his own aimed at creating a Great Society, including the elimination of poverty in America.[53] This burst of governmental activism helped fuel a "rights revolution" that took off in the middle to late 1960s. As Patterson explained in *Grand Expectations: The United States, 1945–1974*, an excellent treatment of the country's political history during that era:

> Rising living standards [expanded] expectations, particularly among the huge and self-assertive cohorts of young people—the baby boom generation—who had grown up in the abundance of the postwar world. By the late 1960s these expectations also affected Americans of less favored socio-economic backgrounds. Blacks, having achieved legal protections under the civil rights legislation of 1964 and 1965 [the latter being the Voting Rights Act of that year], were quick to demand social and economic equality. Poor people, including welfare recipients, insisted on their "rights" to better benefits. Ethnic groups, notably Mexican- and Native-Americans, grew increasingly self-conscious and, like blacks, turned to direct action to achieve their goals. Women, too, raised the banner of equal rights. In 1966 expectant leaders formed the National Organization for Women.
>
> Most of these groups turned eagerly to government, especially Washington, for redress of their grievances. Like liberals, whom many protestors came to disdain, they hoped that they could influence the system and expand the Great Society. Their expectations, however, had grown grand indeed, and they were impatient. Increasingly, they sought not only benefits but also guarantees and entitlements. The rise of rights-consciousness, having flourished in the early and mid-1960s, became central to the culture by 1970.[54]

In the midst of this liberal rights revolution and burgeoning federal involvement in the lives of citizens, there developed a backlash against this unprecedented governmental activism that went far beyond the basic New Deal initiatives centered on Social Security, minimum wage laws, labor law reform, and the basic policing of certain key economic institutions by agencies like the Securities and Exchange Commission. Patterson also succinctly captures the nature of the "backlash" in his chapter "Rights, Polarization, and Backlash, 1966–1967." He wrote:

53. Patterson, in *Grand Expectations*, recounts this burst of domestic activism in his chapter 18, "Lyndon Johnson and American Liberalism," 524–61, and in chapter 19, "A Great Society and Rights-Consciousness," 562–92.

54. Ibid., 637–38.

The escalating demands for rights after 1965, and especially the [race riots and other protests in the later part of the 1960s], did more than bewilder people. They also aroused significant backlash, the most vivid of the many reactions that arose amid the polarization of the era. It long outlasted the 1960s. . . .

Many of these angry whites could hardly be called "conservative" in a traditional sense. They included millions of struggling, often class-conscious people who raged with almost equal fervor at what they perceived as the special privileges of corporate elites, Establishment priests and ministers, wealthy medical practitioners, liberal school boards, permissive bureaucrats and judges, and "experts" in general. They displayed a mounting unease with much that was "modern," including the teaching of Darwinian theories in the schools, and with much that "know-it-all" social engineers told them to believe. They were disturbed by feminists, sexual liberation, radicals, and . . . demonstrators [against the Vietnam war], and they were outraged by the "idolatrous" and "criminal-coddling" Warren Court. Many perceived a conspiracy that was masterminded by an eastern Establishment. Threatened by the insouciance of the younger generation, they especially resented the contempt that they received from more secular Americans. By 1966 they were beginning to take part in politics as never before. . . . [Ronald] Reagan was but the best-known of the anti-liberal office-holders who actively politicized their concerns and benefited from what became identified in the 1970s as a new and powerful Religious Right.[55]

Coupled with the backlash against the rights revolution was the bitter division in the country over the Vietnam war. Antiwar protestors became identified with yet another development that spawned backlash, those associated with the "hippie" counterculture. "Their unconventional ways, moreover, made them easy targets for ridicule by conservative politicians," according to Patterson, who added: "Governor Reagan [of California] delivered perhaps the most famous one-liner [about them]. A hippie, he said, is someone who 'dresses like Tarzan, has hair like Jane, and smells like Cheetah.' "[56]

Corroborating Patterson's interpretation is the analysis of Thomas Byrne Edsall and Mary D. Edsall in their well-regarded book *Chain Reaction: The Impact of Race, Rights, and Taxes on American Politics.* They wrote:

As the civil rights movement became national, as it became clearly associated with the Democratic party, and as it began to impinge on local neighborhoods and schools, it served to crack the Democratic loyalties of key white voters. Crucial numbers of voters—in the white, urban and suburban neighborhoods of the North, and across

55. Ibid., 668–69.
56. Ibid., 670.

the South—were, in addition, deeply angered and distressed by aspects of the expanding rights revolution. It has been among the white working and lower-middle classes that many of the social changes stemming from the introduction of new rights—civil rights for minorities, reproductive and workplace rights for women, constitutional protections for the criminally accused, immigration opportunities for those from developing countries, free-speech rights to pornographers, and the surfacing of highly visible homosexual communities—have been most deeply resisted. Resentment of the civil rights movement among key white voters was reinforced and enlarged by cultural and economic conflicts resulting from the rights revolution.[57]

As was discussed earlier, these new crosscutting issues were cultural. The historian Patterson, who continued his chronicle of these issues in his 2005 sequel to *Grand Expectations*, entitled *Restless Giant: The United States from Watergate to Bush v. Gore*, wrote the following in a chapter devoted to Jimmy Carter, Ronald Reagan, and the rise of the New Right: "Many conservatives in the 1970s did not focus their fire on foreign policies, big government, or taxes. Instead, they targeted social and cultural evils—as they perceived them—such as abortion, 'women's lib,' gay rights, and pornography."[58] Patterson added that the 1973 Supreme Court *Roe v. Wade* decision legalizing abortion in many circumstances "aroused special outrage among conservative Catholics, who swelled the membership of a National Right to Life Committee—and in short order, the voting power of Republican political candidates."[59] Some of these conservative activists called abortion "child murder" and the "slaughter of the innocent."[60]

Long before Patterson and the Edsalls wrote their similar interpretations of the rise of these divisive crosscutting issues in American politics, Samuel Lubell and Kevin Phillips captured the essence of what was happening in books published at the start of the new era. Both placed early emphasis on race. In *The Hidden Crisis in American Politics*, Lubell wrote in 1970 that the "New Deal coalition has not collapsed in one heap, but broke down at one enormously important point, that of racial conflict."[61] In his 1969 book, *The Emerging Republican Majority*, Phillips asserted:

> The principal force which broke up the Democratic (New Deal) coalition is the Negro socioeconomic revolution and liberal Democratic ideological inability to cope with it. Democratic "Great Society" programs aligned that party with many Negro demands, but the

57. Thomas Byrne Edsall and Mary D. Edsall, *Chain Reaction: The Impact of Race, Rights, and Taxes on American Politics* (New York: W. W. Norton, 1991), 5.

58. Patterson, *Restless Giant*, 133.

59. Ibid.

60. Ibid., 136.

61. Samuel Lubell, *The Hidden Crisis in American Politics* (New York: W. W. Norton, 1970), 29.

party was unable to defuse the racial tension sundering the nation. The South, the West and the Catholic sidewalks of New York were the focal points of conservative opposition to the welfare liberalism of the federal government; however, the general opposition which deposed the Democratic Party came in large part from prospering Democrats who objected to Washington dissipating their tax dollars on programs which did them no good. The Democratic Party fell victim to the ideological impetus of a liberalism which had carried it beyond programs taxing the few for the benefit of the many (the New Deal) to programs taxing the many on behalf of the few (the Great Society).[62]

Prominent in the minds of Lubell and Phillips was the then recently concluded presidential election of 1968, which featured the third-party "white backlash" candidacy of George Wallace, the segregationist former Democratic governor of Alabama, and the more subtle "southern strategy" and "law-and-order" campaign approach of Richard Nixon. As Patterson wrote in a *Grand Expectations* chapter devoted just to 1968 and entitled "The Most Turbulent Year":

Wallace was indeed a frightening force in 1968. . . . As in [his past campaigns], Wallace commanded enthusiastic support among southern segregationists. Most far-right organizations, including the KKK, Citizens' Councils, and the John Birch Society, openly aided his operations. . . .

The appeal of Wallace in 1968, however, transcended regional lines, important though those were. It rested also on his evocation of backlash in many working-class areas of the North. Wallace was an energetic, aggressive, caustic, sneering, often snarling campaigner. Eschewing openly racist oratory, he called for "law and order" in the streets and denounced welfare mothers who he said were "breeding children as a cash crop." He gleefully assailed hippies, leftists, and radical feminists, some of whom picketed the Miss America pageant in Atlantic City just after the Democratic convention [in Chicago], dumped what they called objects of female "enslavement"—girdles, bras, high-heeled shoes, false lashes, and hair curlers—into a "freedom trash can," and earned the label forever after of "bra-burners." Wallace took special pleasure in attacking anti-war demonstrators, often with thinly veiled references to violent retribution that excited many of his followers. "If any demonstrator ever lays down in front of my car," he proclaimed, "it'll be the *last* car he'll ever lay down in front of." . . .

62. Kevin P. Phillips, *The Emerging Republican Majority* (New Rochelle, NY: Arlington House, 1969), 37.

Wallace seemed most passionate in attacking know-it-all federal bureaucrats and self-styled experts who tried to tell honest working-class folk what to do. "Liberals, intellectuals, and long-hairs," he cried, "have run the country for too long." His audiences cheered when he denounced "over-educated, ivory-tower folks with pointed heads looking down their noses at us." These were "intellectual morons" who "didn't know how to park a bicycle straight." He added, "When I get to Washington I'll throw all these phonies and their briefcases into the Potomac."[63]

The title of a 1995 biography of Wallace, *The Politics of Rage: George Wallace, the Origins of the New Conservatism, and the Transformation of American Politics,*[64] aptly sums up this fiery politician's role. In the 1968 election, Wallace won 13.5 percent of the vote nationwide. In the thirteen southern states, he received 32.5 percent compared to 7.9 percent in the North.[65] (In Pennsylvania, Wallace won 8.0 percent.) I analyze the Wallace vote further in chapter 2.

As Patterson put it, "On domestic matters Nixon echoed Wallace, but in a more genteel fashion, by catering to the contemporary backlash. (Humphrey mocked Nixon as a 'perfumed, deodorized' version of Wallace.) This meant celebrating 'law and order,' denouncing Great Society programs, rapping liberal decisions of the Supreme Court, and deriding hippies and protestors."[66] This distinguished historian concluded that the turbulent year of 1968 was "a pivotal year in the postwar history of the United States. The social and cultural antagonisms that rent the country, having sharpened appreciably since 1965, widened so significantly [as a result of the traumatic events of 1968] that they could not thereafter be resolved."[67]

With Wallace not running as a third-party candidate in 1972 and with President Nixon facing George McGovern, the liberal U.S. senator from South Dakota, a Democratic presidential nominee who could easily be identified with the social permissiveness fueling the backlash so widely prevalent at the time, the Republican President triumphed with 60.7 percent of the vote to McGovern's 37.5 percent. Nixon's forced resignation in August 1974 as a result of the Watergate scandal temporarily halted the Republican surge of the early 1970s, as did the 1976 election of Democrat Jimmy Carter, the former Georgia governor.

However, partly as the result of Carter's poor performance in the White House and partly as a result of economic and foreign policy woes that may have been beyond his control, the 1980 Republican presidential nominee, Ronald Reagan, who

---

63. Patterson, *Grand Expectations*, 698–99.

64. Dan T. Carter, *The Politics of Rage: George Wallace, The Origins of the New Conservatism, and the Transformation of American Politics* (New York: Simon & Schuster, 1995).

65. As is the case for the party-strength figures, the South is defined as the eleven states that left the Union during the Civil War plus Kentucky and Oklahoma.

66. Patterson, *Grand Expectations*, 701.

67. Ibid., 709.

had cut his political teeth on the conservative side of the divisive cultural issues of the mid-1960s, triumphed in the national election of that year. As Patterson aptly expressed it:

> By 1980, however, several previously unconnected groups—white blue-collar workers, southern white foes of civil rights, Republicans who opposed big government, and socially conservative Catholics and evangelical Protestants—were converging to crusade for a range of causes and to fight on behalf of candidates who would promote them. This conservative coalition, adeptly exploited by Reagan, dramatically altered the landscape of politics in the United States.
>
> Many of the new conservatives, so-called Reagan Democrats, were white working-class people in the North who still supported a range of liberal bread-and-butter economic programs. But like white Democrats in the Sunbelt who had earlier been turning to the GOP, these blue-collar Americans resented the "reverse discrimination," as they saw it, of social policies, such as busing and affirmative action. They raged at the growth of crime, which they blamed on violent and lawless blacks. Some of these white Americans, having backed the presidential candidacies of Richard Nixon or Alabama governor George Wallace in the 1960s and the 1970s, seethed at the derisive and supercilious "elitism," as they perceived it, of well-educated, upper-middle-class intellectuals and prominent figures in the media and Hollywood. Defending their ways of life, they were gathering together to fight against what they damned as the culturally permissive legacies of the 1960s.[68]

Two other writers, John B. Judis and Ruy Teixeira, offer an insightful analysis and description of this realignment:

> Two main factors propelled the Republicans into a majority. White opposition to civil rights continued to be a major factor in Democratic defections to the Republican Party. The cluster of issues that Wallace had evoked had, if anything, expanded, for now they included busing and affirmative action. As politicians were quick to understand, evoking any part of this cluster called up the whole and created a ready-made constituency among angry downscale whites who would otherwise have been expected to vote Democratic. By the time Ronald Reagan ran for president in 1980, it wasn't necessary any longer for politicians to make explicit racial appeals. He could use traditional code words such as state's rights, as Reagan did in his opening September campaign speech in Philadelphia, Mississippi, or could champion one of the issues at the margins of the racial

---

68. Patterson, *Restless Giant*, 131.

cluster such as "law and order," "welfare cheating," or even capital punishment.[69]

Judis and Teixeira later added:

> Reagan and the Republicans were also able to draw on some vot-
> ers' discomfort with the counterculture of the sixties, including
> feminism, gay rights, abortion, decriminalization of drugs, and
> sexual freedom. As early as 1966, Reagan, running for governor of
> California, had successfully singled out the "filthy speech move-
> ment" (a successor to the "free speech movement") in winning
> blue-collar votes. In 1972, Nixon had campaigned against "acid,
> amnesty, and abortion," a slogan he borrowed from McGovern's
> Democratic critic Senator Henry Jackson. These appeals exploited
> the generation gap between parents and children, but also the gap
> between the blue-collar and middle-class taxpayers who funded
> universities and the long-haired upper-middle-class students who
> attended them.[70]

A second issue driving the triumph of Reagan Republicanism, according to Judis and Teixeira, was economic, namely "stagflation" in the late 1970s and the doubts it raised about the wisdom of Democratic party economic policies at a time when a Democrat, President Carter, occupied the White House and there were Democratic majorities in Congress. But, economics was also tied to these other grievances. As the authors put it:

> The stagflation fed resentments about race—about high taxes for
> welfare (which was assumed to go primarily to minorities) and
> about affirmative action. But it also sowed doubts about Democrats'
> ability to manage the economy and made Republican and business
> explanations of stagflation—blaming it on government regulation,
> high taxes, and spending—more plausible. In 1978, the white back-
> lash and doubts about Democratic economic policies had helped
> fuel a nationwide tax revolt. In 1980, these factors led to a massive
> exodus of white working-class voters from the Democratic ticket.
> These voters had once been the heart of the New Deal coalition, but
> in the 1980 and 1984 elections, Reagan averaged 61 percent support
> among them.[71]

Sundquist also came down on the side of a post–New Deal realignment in an article written not long after Reagan's landslide reelection victory over Walter

69. John B. Judis and Ruy Teixeira, *The Emerging Democratic Majority* (New York: Scribner, 2002), 21–22.
70. Ibid., 24.
71. Ibid., 22.

Mondale, entitled "The 1984 Election: How Much Realignment?": "What, then, is the degree of realignment in 1984? [M]uch less than in 1936, but more than at any other time in the half century since then. The Reagan Revolution does not match the Roosevelt Revolution in its impact on the party system, but it has brought about the greatest transformation in five decades—and the realigning forces are still at work."[72] In the 1983 revised edition of *Dynamics of the Party System*, Sundquist had examined in a comprehensive fashion the new crosscutting issues that entered the party system in the mid-1960s in two insightful final chapters entitled "Years of Disruption: Crosscutting Issues Nationwide" and "The Reagan Revolution—and After."[73] Sundquist completed that second and last edition of his classic work shortly after the 1982 election, which saw a surprising twenty-six-seat Democratic gain in the U.S. House just two years after Reagan was overwhelmingly elected president. It also was a time of economic recession and a period when Reagan's public approval rating dropped from 49 percent in January 1982 to 41 percent in December of that year and continued downward, hitting 35 percent at the end of January 1983. By October 1983, Reagan's approval rating had risen to 49 percent, going steadily up thereafter until it reached 58 percent shortly before he won an overwhelming reelection victory in November 1984.[74] Catching the "Reagan Revolution" at low tide may have led Sundquist to hedge his early-1980s conclusions about the permanence of these disruptive crosscutting issues that he, Patterson, Judis and Teixeira, and many others had noted.[75] But by 1985, in the article "The 1984 Election," he came down strongly on the side of realignment.[76]

The 1988 presidential election between Vice President Bush and Michael Dukakis, the liberal governor of Massachusetts, was a culminating event of the culture-wars realignment. On display were all the negative factors that had worked

72. James L. Sundquist, "The 1984 Election: How Much Realignment?" *The Brookings Review* (Winter 1985), 9.

73. Sundquist, *Dynamics of the Party System*, 376–449.

74. Lyn Ragsdale, *Vital Statistics on the Presidency* (Washington, DC: CQ Press, 1998), 210–12.

75. In his concluding 1983 chapter, Sundquist suggested that continuity in the form of a "revitalization of the New Deal party system" was a distinct possibility. However, Sundquist added the following: "To say the New Deal party system can be revitalized is not, however, to say that the Democrats will necessarily recover and maintain their old advantage. The Republicans will gain if the Reagan administration turns out, despite the setbacks of its first two years, to be markedly successful." Sundquist, *Dynamics of the Party System*, 447–48.

76. These four books provide part of the context for the cultural cleavages involved in the realignment: John Kenneth White, *The Values Divide: American Politics and Culture in Transition* (New York: Chatham House, 2003); David C. Leege, Kenneth D. Wald, Brian S. Krueger, and Paul D. Mueller, *The Politics of Cultural Differences: Social Change and Voter Mobilization Strategies in the Post–New Deal Period* (Princeton, NJ: Princeton University Press, 2002); Geoffrey Layman, *The Great Divide: Religious and Cultural Conflict in American Party Politics* (New York: Columbia University Press, 2001); and James Davison Hunter, *Culture Wars: The Struggle to Define America* (New York: Basic Books, 1991).

against Democratic nominees since 1968. Patterson relates two prominent episodes from the campaign that illustrate the point:

> Bush . . . seized on the fact that Dukakis in an earlier term as governor in 1977 had vetoed a law requiring teachers to lead students in reciting the Pledge of Allegiance. Dukakis's advisers had told him, correctly, that the measure, which would have subjected non-complying teachers to criminal charges, was unconstitutional. Bush was unmoved, labeling Dukakis a "card-carrying member of the American Civil Liberties Union." . . .
>
> Republicans zeroed in with special zeal on what they called the "revolving door prison policy" of Dukakis's governorship. This was a program—instituted by a Republican predecessor—which enabled prisoners to take brief furloughs. Most states, including California during Reagan's tenure as governor, had comparable programs, as did the federal prison system, though only Massachusetts made it available to lifers. One of these Massachusetts prisoners was Willie Horton, a convicted first-degree murderer, who on a weekend furlough had repeatedly beaten and stabbed a man and assaulted and raped his fiancée. Dukakis, defending the program, did not discontinue it until April 1988. Some of Bush's state party committees and independent groups circulated pictures of Horton, an ominous-looking black man, and produced TV ads that showed streams of prisoners going in and out of prison via a turnstile. Though Bush's national committee disavowed material that identified and pictured the prisoner, there was no doubting that the Bush team knew and approved of the ads.[77]

The Republicans also portrayed Dukakis, who lacked extensive foreign and defense policy experience, as "weak on defense" by attempting to tie him—with some success—to policy positions held by the "peace wing" of his party.[78]

Bush, never close to the socially and culturally conservative wing of the Republican party, embraced their causes in the 1988 campaign, opposing abortion except in rare circumstances, favoring voluntary prayer in the public schools, opposing gun control, and demonizing the "L" word, liberal.[79] "Among the aides who helped him get in touch with socially conservative religious people," Patterson wrote, "was his eldest son,

---

77. Patterson, *Restless Giant*, 221–23.

78. Patterson added: "Republicans made fun of an ad, intended by Democratic strategists to show that Dukakis would be a strong commander-in-chief, which showed him grinning foolishly, clad in a jumpsuit and an outsized, Snoopy-style helmet while riding a tank. Bush quipped, 'He thinks a naval exercise is something you find in Jane Fonda's exercise books' " (ibid., 221).

79. Patterson suggested the term "demonizing" in his account of the 1988 election, which I relied upon here (ibid., 222).

George W. Bush. Young George had kicked a serious drinking habit two years earlier and had found God. 'It was goodbye Jack Daniels, hello Jesus,' he said."[80]

For his part, as the journalist Jules Witcover wrote, Dukakis "proved to be a willing accomplice by turning the other cheek to all the accusations against him, naively believing the truth would be apparent to voters."[81] There were, of course, other reasons Bush won in 1988, starting with the strength of the economy, the popularity of President Reagan, and a feeling among many voters that the Republicans deserved "credit for having lifted the spirits of Americans during the previous eight years."[82] Still, the easy manner in which a Democratic nominee could be stigmatized to his electoral detriment by association with culturally liberal positions remained a key feature of the 1988 election. As related earlier, Bill Clinton, reacting to what had happened to Dukakis and other liberal Democratic presidential nominees, distanced himself as much as he could from many of those previously "losing" positions in his successful 1992 campaign. Later in the 1990s, as we shall see, being on the liberal side of the cultural divide did not necessarily mean being in the minority forever. In any event, the cleavages of this realignment restructured the American party system. Here's how Patterson sketched the new division in a *Restless Giant* chapter devoted to the "culture wars" in the 1990s: "Cultural conservatism developed increasing appeal to people—notably white working-class Americans—in the South and in the Plains and Rocky Mountain states, while liberal ideas continued to appeal to well-educated academic and professional people on the east and west coasts and in the metropolitan centers of the East and Midwest."[83]

I turn briefly now to two other important lines of interpretation concerning recent electoral and party system change, neither of which I view as incompatible with my embrace of the Sundquist realignment framework even though they are sometimes portrayed that way.[84] The two alternative schools of thought consist of "dealignment" proponents and scholars who favor a long-term or evolutionary explanation of electoral change and who, in the process, reject the realignment framework.

80. Ibid., 222.

81. Jules Witcover, *Party of the People: A History of the Democrats* (New York: Random House, 2003), 639.

82. Patterson, *Restless Giant*, 223.

83. Ibid., 264. The exact title of his chapter is " 'Culture Wars' and 'Decline' in the 1990s," pp. 254–91.

84. David R. Mayhew in *Electoral Realignments: A Critique of an American Genre* (New Haven: Yale University Press, 2002) offers a devastating attack on those who subscribe to a cyclical view of realignment, particularly Walter Dean Burnham. But, in his short book, Mayhew fails to make a convincing case against Sundquist's detailed and sophisticated insights into electoral change. The "realignment" concept that Mayhew attacks in his long essay is unrecognizable to careful readers of *Dynamics of the Party System*. While I do agree with Mayhew's criticisms of cyclical notions of realignment, I disagree that realignment theory should be thrown out as I amply demonstrate by my reliance in this book on the valuable insights of Sundquist and other realignment scholars.

A scholar of the history of American electoral studies, Theodore Rosenof, in his fine book *Realignment: The Theory That Changed the Way We Think about American Politics*, offers a helpful summary of the dealignment approach. He wrote:

> The most pervasively held alternative concept to come out of the period of upheaval and revision was that of dealignment. This view held that the decline of party identification and the growth of political independence had created an electorate without moorings; instead of a politics of continuity characterized by party loyalties and group traditions, politics was now geared more to the short run, to individual candidates and campaigns. In such a context of flux and instability, the very notion of realignment appeared outlandish to many: How could there be a realignment without an enduring alignment from which to realign?[85]

Most prominently associated with this school of thought was Paul Allen Beck,[86] but many other scholars regularly turned to dealignment as they attempted to assess recent electoral politics. For example, William H. Flanigan and Nancy H. Zingale, at the end of the "Partisanship" chapter of their widely praised overview of the field of electoral studies, *Political Behavior of the American Electorate*, ask in the heading to a two-paragraph section: "Has There Been a Realignment?" They answer:

> Some analysts have argued that the movement of white southerners into the Republican Party and the movement of blacks and some northern whites toward the Democratic Party constitutes a realignment and should be regarded as the start of a new party system. Disagreement arises about when this realignment occurred. Some date it from the 1960s, with the start of Republican dominance in presidential voting. Others view it as a "Reagan realignment" of the 1980s.
>
> There is no question that there has been a lot of voter movement and electoral volatility since the 1960s. It is also true that much of this movement has been a sorting-out process whereby some voters are finding their natural home in a political party that shares their views on issues that concern them most. It is equally true, however, that over this same time period, a sizable number of voters have found neither political party a congenial place to be and have demonstrated this by becoming independent, or not adopting a party identification in the first place, or supporting an independent

85. Theodore Rosenof, *Realignment: The Theory That Changed the Way We Think About American Politics* (Lanham, MD: Rowman & Littlefield, 2003), 129.

86. Paul Allen Beck, "Partisan Dealignment in the Postwar South," *American Political Science Review* 71 (June 1977). See also Jerome M. Clubb, William H. Flanigan, and Nancy H. Zingale, *Partisan Realignment: Voters, Parties, and Government in American History* (Beverly Hills, CA: Sage, 1980), 119–54.

> candidate such as Perot. . . . In these circumstances, we find it more
> useful to consider the current situation as a continuation of a period
> of *dealignment*.[87]

Their approach typifies those who employ dealignment.[88]

The attraction of dealignment is simple: No one can deny that there are signs of a lessening of party attachment in the nation and in Pennsylvania. For example, party registration data introduced in chapter 3 strikingly show the rapid recent increase in those Pennsylvania voters who did not affiliate with either major party when they registered to vote. The percentage opting for the "other" category in 1970 was 2.1 percent; in 2005, it had increased to 11.6 percent, a gigantic increase. Further, there has been considerable "volatility" in the Pennsylvania electorate since 1960, as manifested in the widespread "ticket-splitting" that is detailed in chapters 3 and 4 of this book. Recognizing the reality of the rise of independents and ticket-splitting, it is hard to discount dealignment as a factor. Yet, there may be rational reasons voters are splitting their tickets, as I discuss later. And while that phenomenon may lead to more volatility in the electorate, it does not preclude the presence of realignment. It may simply mean that somewhat fewer voters are engaged enough with the parties to participate in a realignment. In my view, and in the view of many others cited previously, we have gone through a post–New Deal realignment despite the growth of independents and ticket-splitters.

Others have argued in favor of a long-term or evolutionary explanation of electoral change, rejecting the realignment framework in the process. In Rosenof's history of realignment, he concluded that the "lack of cataclysmic transformation along New Deal lines underlay the continued [reliance of some scholars] on more gradual versions of electoral change."[89] Changes going back to the 1960s could be explained, argued adherents of the gradualist school, "by incremental, continuous movement, rather than by quick, dramatic upheaval."[90] Everett Carll Ladd was a leading scholar who rejected the realignment framework in favor of the "laborious and prosaic" task of "charting the many shifts that have occurred in the party system . . . and seeking their diverse sources and implications." He preferred this process, he wrote, to the alternative view that "the realignment perspective

---

87. William H. Flanigan and Nancy H. Zingale, *Political Behavior of the American Electorate*, 10th ed. (Washington, DC: CQ Press, 2002), 73.

88. Another example is found in the following statement by Paul R. Abramson, John H. Aldrich, and David W. Rohde at the end of their concluding chapter in a recent volume of their excellent series of books on each presidential election since 1980: "For the moment, *dealignment* seems to be an accurate term to describe the American party system. The old party system is in disarray, but nothing has replaced it." Paul R. Abramson, John H. Aldrich, and David W. Rohde, *Change and Continuity in the 2000 and 2002 Elections* (Washington, DC: CQ Press, 2003), 295.

89. Rosenof, *Realignment*, 144.

90. Ibid.

requires," namely, "to ask why the partisan 'Big Change' has not occurred—and when it will."[91] Thus, he asserted, realignment theory "continues to tease us with the promise that an enormously complex reality will submit to a very simple and highly parsimonious theoretic organization."[92]

In my view, gradualists like Ladd are too hasty in tossing out the realignment framework, which has proven quite useful in understanding past American electoral and party system change. Further, a premier realignment theorist, Sundquist, recognizes that change ("redistributions of party support") is always taking place and "can be of any magnitude."[93] Further, Sundquist answers Ladd's concern about the unending wait for the "big event" in a valuable section of his first chapter of *Dynamics of the Party System* that discusses gradations in the size of realignments, dismissing a notion like Ladd's as an "all-or-nothing-fallacy." One must reject the idea, Sundquist warns, that only "a redistribution of party support on a scale beyond some undefined boundary constitutes a realignment while anything less does not."[94]

Probably more important in regard to meeting the gradualists' argument is Sundquist's invaluable analysis and description of the aftershocks process that can flow from a realignment earthquake. In his chapter devoted to aftershocks, Sundquist is actually describing gradual change that flows from a previous disruption. What Sundquist so richly offers are impressive explanations as to how

91. Everett Carll Ladd, "Like Waiting for Godot: The Uselessness of 'Realignment' for Understanding Change in Contemporary American Politics," in Byron E. Shafer, ed., *The End of Realignment? Interpreting American Electoral Eras* (Madison: University of Wisconsin Press, 1991), 34. He likens the process to a central theme in Samuel Beckett's play *Waiting for Godot*, in which two main characters wait for something that never comes (ibid., 24–25).

92. Ibid., 34. Edward G. Carmines and James A. Stimson also offer another gradualist explanation under the rubric of "issue evolution." Rosenof explains Carmines and Stimson's approach as follows: "At times issues become so powerful and enduring, [Carmines and Stimson] held, combining 'great salience and longevity' with electoral shifts, as 'to define the party system.'" For them, the struggle over race in the mid-1960s was such an issue. Rosenof, *Realignment*, 144–45. Carmines and Stimson wrote: "The American party system, in sum, was fundamentally transformed during the mid-1960s. The progressive racial tradition in the Republican party gave way to racial conservatism, and the Democratic party firmly embraced racial liberalism." The time of issue intensity that Carmines and Stimson point to sets in motion "a gradual reorientation of the electorate along different issue lines and [accounts] for the break in politics dating to that time." Edward G. Carmines and James A. Stimson, *Race and the Transformation of American Politics* (Princeton, NJ: Princeton University Press, 1989), 58.

93. Sundquist, *Dynamics of the Party System*, 7. He argues that "gradations in size [of change] can be indicated by adjectives or prefixes. Major realignments can be distinguished from minor [ones]" (ibid., 8).

94. Ibid. Incidentally, when discussing gradual change, many scholars regularly cite the influence of V. O. Key's "other" major electoral-change article, "Secular Realignment and the Party System," in which Key discusses long-term change, using a less-than-common definition of the term "secular." V. O. Key Jr., "Secular Realignment and the Party System," *Journal of Politics* 21 (May 1959), 198–210.

and why these disruptions—no matter their magnitude—occur. On the other hand, the gradualists rarely offer a causal explanation to account for the change. Further, Sundquist couples his causal propositions with a conception of how change flows into our "uniquely decentralized" party system, to borrow Sundquist's phrase. Thus, when Sundquist introduced his chapter on the important aftershocks process in the North, he wrote: "Most of what has appeared as party realignment in the decades since the 1930s—including much of what is happening at the present time—has to be understood as simply a later phase of the realignment of the 1930s, a phase during which the new alignment settled into place."[95] Some could look at those later changes and call them "gradual," but Sundquist's conception links them to a previous realignment and, in doing so, gives a political cause for the "gradual" change. I prefer to look at the process the way Sundquist does—that is, as aftershocks where appropriate—because identifying causal factors is more valuable than merely pointing out change without offering an explanation of why the change is occurring.

Thus, I disagree with those arguing for a dealignment or a gradualist approach. Instead, I am in complete agreement with the important three-sentence conclusion Rosenof reached in the final paragraph of his 224-page history of realignment theory:

> Still, the kernel of realignment theory as set forth by [V. O.] Key—the focus on durable change in electoral patterns—did fit the new era. Realignment theory thus retains qualities essential to the retrospective analysis of American politics. This in turn assures realignment theory a continuing role in the future of American electoral study.[96]

Therefore, I find realignment theory, as expounded by Sundquist, to be highly useful for explaining what has happened nationally in the post-1960 era in American electoral politics. However, it is a framework that offers only a general understanding of the "big picture." State case studies such as mine are needed to fill in the details and capture variations across the country.

Before turning to an in-depth look at post-1960 presidential electoral change in the nation and Pennsylvania in chapter 2, I explore the ideas of the authors of two books that I find especially useful for understanding the most recent trends in Pennsylvania and other parts of the nation, those of Judis and Teixeira in *The Emerging Democratic Majority* and those of Speel in *Changing Patterns of Voting in the Northern States*.

Judis and Teixeira offer an insightful analysis that helps explain why the Democratic party attracted certain types of voters during the "aftershocks" phase of the culture-wars realignment both in Pennsylvania and elsewhere in the country. The other author, Speel, offers a sensible explanation for how major statewide Pennsylvania Republican candidates, as well as Republicans similarly

95. Ibid., 240.
96. Rosenof, *Realignment*, 167.

situated in other states, were able to sidestep a voter shift away from the national Republican party in their areas and continue to win elections. To fully appreciate the value that the insights of Judis and Teixeira and Speel have for Pennsylvania requires greater familiarity with the details of what happened in the Keystone State, which comes in the next three chapters. Thus, their ideas are employed in subsequent chapters as those details are covered. It is appropriate at this point, however, to introduce their ideas in the chapter containing other theoretical frameworks useful for my study.

As the data analysis in the next three chapters strikingly documents, voters in the populous suburban counties surrounding Philadelphia (Montgomery, Chester, Bucks, and Delaware) have been trending away from their once dominant Republican voting patterns in the last decade or so. To understand how Judis and Teixeira account for this shift requires a brief presentation of their main argument.

Judis and Teixeira describe the transformation of American cities and suburbs during the last decades of the twentieth century as follows:

> [A] new geographical formation has emerged—the postindustrial metropolitan area. It combines city and suburb in a seamless web of work and home. As manufacturing has moved to the suburbs and even the country, cities like Boston and Chicago have become headquarters for the production of ideas. Both city and suburb have become filled with the shops, stores, and institutions of postindustrial capitalism, from café-bookstores to health clubs to computer learning centers. Many are the site of major universities, which since the sixties have been the crucible of the new postindustrial work and values. . . .
>
> These new postindustrial metropolises . . . are peopled by the new professionals who live according to the ethics of postindustrial society. Their socially liberal values and concerns with the quality of life permeate the population, including the white working class. The result is widespread and growing support for the Democrats' progressive centrism. In the past, cities like Chicago, Philadelphia, and San Francisco were Democratic, while the surrounding suburbs were Republican. Now the entire metropolitan area in many of these locations has become strongly Democratic.[97]

The authors label these postindustrial metropolises "ideopolises," or cities and suburbs where the production of ideas and services has replaced the production of things. Judis and Teixeira foresee an "emerging Democratic majority" propelled by voters in these ideopolises. Support for Republicans, they argue, is strongest

---

97. Judis and Teixeira, *Emerging Democratic Majority*, 8–9.

in communities that have lagged behind in the transition from manufacturing to a postindustrial economy. They explain that the most integrated ideopolises are those where "the work and culture of the ideopolis pervades the entire metropolitan area."[98] They contend:

> The Democrats' vote in these integrated ideopolises included, of course, professionals, women, and minorities, but it also included relatively strong support from the white working class—the very group that had begun to abandon the Democrats during the sixties and that formed the backbone of the Reagan majority. In the most advanced ideopolises, the white working class seems to embrace the same values as professionals, and in some of them, white working-class men vote remarkably similarly to their female counterparts. As a result, Republican appeals to race (or resentment against immigrants), guns, and abortion have largely fallen on deaf ears, and these voters have not only rejected Republican social conservatism, but also reverted to their prior preference for Democratic economics.[99]

As mentioned earlier, data in subsequent chapters point to the Judis and Teixeira analysis as a valuable explanation for the recent behavior of voters in the important suburban counties surrounding Philadelphia. In fact, as we shall see, these populous suburban Philadelphia voters have been casting ballots for winning statewide Democrats since a special U.S. Senate election in 1991. In an October 1996 *Baltimore Sun* article, a nationally syndicated political columnist, Jack Germond, focused on this movement of moderate Republicans whose distaste for the social conservatism of the national Republican party caused them to vote for Democrats, split their tickets, and in some cases, even switch parties. In his column, Germond introduces a Republican Chester County commissioner, Karen Martynick, whose 15-year-old son was confronted by a rival Republican candidate at a polling place on the day of the primary. Martynick recalled the altercation: "They told him, your mother's a baby-killer. She has blood on her hands." Germond reports further:

> This is not the kind of politics that Martynick, 44, bargained for when she began a long career as a Republican activist. . . .
> But it is the kind of politics being played out in the Republican Party these days in the comfortable suburbs of Philadelphia. And it is the kind of politics, Martynick says, that will cost Bob Dole [the 1996 Republican presidential nominee] heavily in support from political moderates Nov. 5.

98. Ibid., 73.
99. Ibid., 74.

"I think suburban Republicans are scared off by some of the rhetoric of the far right in the Republican Party, especially women," Martynick says. "I think this is difficult for the Republican Party. I don't think it's anti-Dole—nobody dislikes Dole. But it's a general fear of what the Republican Party stands for.

"It's not just [Newt] Gingrich. It's the total picture that includes Ralph Reed, Pat Robertson, Pat Buchanan. Dole comes with all that on his shoulders."[100]

In order to better understand why these movements are taking place, Judis and Teixeira studied NES surveys and census data, finding several interesting changes among professionals, women (especially those who are working, single, and highly educated), and minorities. Throughout the 1950s, those employed in professional occupations, as defined by the census separate from managers, had aligned themselves with the Republican party in opposition to "big government" initiatives. According to Judis and Teixeira:

> No group used to be as dependably Republican as highly skilled professionals, a group that includes architects, engineers, scientists, computer analysts, lawyers, physicians, registered nurses, teachers, social workers, therapists, designers, interior decorators, graphic artists, and actors. This group dutifully backed Eisenhower in 1952 and 1956, Nixon in 1960, 1968, and 1972, Ford in 1976, and Reagan in 1980 and 1984. But their anti-Democratic proclivities began to soften as early as 1972, and by 1988, they were supporting Democrats for president and have continued to do so. In the fifties, their choices didn't matter that much: they made up only about 7 percent of the workforce. But by 2000, they made up 15.4 percent. Moreover, they have the highest turnout rate of any occupational group. As a result, they compose about 21 percent of the voting electorate nationally and are likely near one-quarter in many Northeastern and Far Western states.[101]

In 1972, their support for Nixon waned because many of them identified with the civil rights, feminist, antiwar, consumer, and environmental movements of the 1960s, but they continued to vote Republican because of their skepticism regarding the economic policies of the Democrats. The failure of President George H. W. Bush's fiscal policies in 1991–1992 and the redefining of the Democratic party under Bill Clinton from one of "tax-and-spend liberals" to one in favor of deficit

---

100. Jack W. Germond, "GOP Turns Off Moderates in Pa. Suburbs; Social Divisions Hurt Dole, Observers Say," *Baltimore Sun*, October 2, 1996.

101. Judis and Teixeira, *Emerging Democratic Majority*, 39.

reduction and fiscal restraint led many professionals to crossover to support the Democrats, Judis and Teixeira assert.[102]

Women were another group that trended Republican throughout the 1950s. Many women during that time were nonworking wives and mothers whose place was in the home. According to Judis and Teixeira, these women comprised nearly two-thirds of female voters and were much more likely to vote Republican than were working men and women. In the 1960s, the women's movement, coupled with the accelerated rate in which women were entering the workforce, contributed to changing the manner in which women thought about politics. Then, in the 1970s and 1980s, political events would push women toward the Democratic party, namely, the controversies over equal rights for women, the position of conservative Republicans that women belonged in the home, and, perhaps most importantly, the parties' differing stances on abortion. Specifically, many working women were turned off by the Republican party's prolife position and saw it as a direct affront to their personal freedoms.[103]

And, in terms of minorities, African Americans have voted solidly Democratic since President Kennedy introduced the Civil Rights Bill in 1963 and President Johnson pushed it through Congress in 1964. Hispanics and Asians are trending that way as well.

Finally, I turn to an explanation of the voting behavior of the white working class, as described by Judis and Teixeira:

> The most important reason why many of these voters returned to the Democrats in the early nineties was the recession that occurred during the Bush administration. The recession wiped out not only jobs, but white working-class confidence that Republicans could manage the economy better than Democrats. Clinton also successfully countered the image of the Democrats as the "black party" by his advocacy of welfare reform and the death penalty. . . . Clinton's success in 1992 and 1996 was particularly notable among unionized white working-class voters—a group that would be most susceptible to the Democrats' economic argument. Reagan had won these voters in 1980 and 1984, and Bush had barely lost them 52–48 percent in 1988, but Clinton won them by an average of 23 percent in 1992 and in 1996.
>
> [Al] Gore's problems with white working-class voters were due partly to . . . the boom of the late 1990s; in such flush times, working-class voters thought less about the economy and more about the issues on which they preferred Republicans, such as gun control, abortion, or affirmative action. Gore did particularly poorly among white working-class voters in rural areas and in the

102. Ibid., 47–49.
103. Ibid., 51–54.

South—the two groups most susceptible to Republican appeals on these issues.[104]

In sum, Judis and Teixeira argue that a new Democratic majority is emerging[105] as a result of (1) the failure of Republicans to effectively manage the economy, (2) the extremism of the Religious Right, and (3) the evolving postindustrial economy in the ideopolises. As *The Emerging Democratic Majority* authors put it:

> A look at the voting patterns for president and Congress during the 1990s clearly indicates that while the conservative Republican majority was crumbling, a new Democratic majority was germinating. It would include white working- and middle-class Democrats . . . who have returned to the Democrats in the nineties because they (or their progeny) believe the Democrats are more responsive to their economic situations. They are responding primarily to the Democratic Party's Jacksonian and New Deal past—its commitment to economic security for the average American.
>
> But it would also include three groups of voters who clearly appeared in George McGovern's loss to Richard Nixon: minority voters, including blacks, Hispanics, and Asian-Americans; women voters, especially single, working, and highly educated women; and professionals. While the ranks of white working-class voters will not grow over the next decade, the numbers of professionals, working, single, highly educated women, and minorities will swell. They are products of a new postindustrial capitalism, rooted in diversity and social equality, and emphasizing the production of ideas and services rather than goods. And while some of these voters are drawn to the Democratic Party by its New Deal past, many others resonate strongly to the new causes that the Democrats adopted during the sixties.[106]

104. Ibid., 64–65.
105. Judis and Teixeira see the 1990s as the start of the "disintegration of the conservative Republican majority" that resulted from "the triumph of Reagan Republicanism," to quote the title of their sections on each development. (Their section entitled "The Triumph of Reagan Republicanism" is on pages 21 to 27 of *The Emerging Democratic Majority*, and their section entitled "The Disintegration of the Conservative Republican Majority" is on pages 27 to 32.) The authors view the latter process as caused primarily by the overreaching of the GOP social conservatives and the backlash those extreme positions produced in the country's ideopolises. Of course, the central theme in their book, captured in its title, *The Emerging Democratic Majority*, is that another realignment is going to occur in the latter part of the first decade of the 2000s centered on the themes that play well in the ideopolis. This realignment, they say, will make the Democratic party the country's majority party once again. They make their prediction for the future in the final section of their first chapter, "An Emerging Democratic Majority?" on pages 32 to 35.
106. Ibid., 34–35.

I agree with the basic Judis and Teixeira thesis. As the concluding sentence of the last quoted passage makes clear, this new surge of Democratic voting strength in the ideopolises (or even elsewhere) is tied directly to a positive assessment of the socially liberal positions the Democratic party became associated with during the culture-wars realignment and to a negative assessment of the socially conservative positions of the Republican party. I view this same phenomenon in a way that runs parallel to how Judis and Teixeira see the situation.

My position is that these recent Democratic gains are aftershocks of the culture-wars realignment playing out after the main event of the realignment has occurred, exactly as the New Deal earthquake set in motion aftershocks that were instrumental in restructuring the party system in the states decades after the New Deal realignment occurred, in a process so effectively analyzed by Sundquist. For example, as the data in my chapters to come also show, the counties surrounding Pittsburgh/Allegheny County exhibited a movement away from the Democratic party and toward the Republican party. The voters in these counties are more culturally and socially conservative than those in the Philadelphia suburbs, as polling data introduced later show. In my view, the aftershocks of the culture-wars realignment are benefiting the Republican party in the counties surrounding Pittsburgh/Allegheny County just as they have hurt the Republican party in the suburban counties close to Philadelphia.[107]

Finally, I return to the political scientist I mentioned at the beginning of the chapter who is a strong advocate of individual state case studies—Robert Speel. Besides being an advocate for the type of study I do in this book, Speel offers a valuable insight into recent American electoral change that I find extraordinarily helpful in understanding Pennsylvania patterns. As stated early in this chapter, a key question I examine concerning recent Keystone State elections is, Why did Pennsylvania Republicans do so well in a period of impressive national Democratic strength in the state?

Speel argues that such a result, which clearly entails considerable ticket-splitting, may very well be a reasonable response by voters to the choices they are faced with at both ballot levels, that is, the vote for president and the vote for major statewide offices, namely, governor and U.S. senator. He writes: "Rarely considered is the possibility that voters may actually have strategic reasons for choosing a Republican for one office and a Democrat for another office, reasons other than either a preference for divided party government or differing expectations of institutions."[108] Then, Speel presents his concept of "federalized realignment," which he says allows for the possibility that voters are splitting their ballots between the major parties in a rational way. He writes:

107. From Judis and Teixeira's perspective, one could argue that the Pittsburgh area has yet to reach the status of an ideopolis, a defensible position. Both ways of looking at the situation reach a similar conclusion because the core idea uniting the Judis/Teixeira view and the aftershocks perspective is the same.

108. Speel, *Changing Patterns of Voting in the Northern United States*, 14.

> If the national Republican party stresses lots of defense spending and prayer in the schools, while the state Republican party [opposes] cuts in government spending and environmental regulation, any voter could easily and rationally vote against a Republican presidential candidate and for a Republican gubernatorial candidate. And in addition, if the national Democratic party opposes school prayer and favors cuts in defense spending, while the state Democratic party takes the opposite stands, any voter could rationally vote for different parties at different office levels.[109]

He explains further:

> For this reason, national Democratic support for socially liberal policies has lost the party many supporters in the South and among certain ethnic groups. Meanwhile, national Republican conservative policies have gained support among these groups. What has been less noticed is that such conservative policy stands may have lost the Republicans support in some of the party's historically stronger areas outside the South.[110]

Finally, he drives home the point:

> If voters in an area consistently vote for candidates that express a similar set of values and views, and do not support those with opposite values and views, it seems highly inaccurate to label these voters as ideologically adrift in a sea of candidate personalities and transient issues. And if parties at the state level relatively consistently nominate candidates with similar values and views, even if these differ from the values and views of the national party's candidates, and if voters of the state respond by generally favoring one party for state elections, even if the same group of voters favor a different party in presidential elections, it seems highly inaccurate to label such a pattern only with the somewhat negatively tainted term of "dealignment" without also acknowledging some of the consistency and rationality of the state's voter behavior. Instead the voters could be more accurately labeled as undergoing a federalized realignment.[111]

After thoroughly presenting the details of what occurred in major Pennsylvania elections, that is, at the end of the second of my two narrative chapters, I apply Speel's appealing "federalized realignment" notion in analyzing what happened.

---

109. Ibid.
110. Ibid., 8.
111. Ibid., 15.

I do have a small terminological disagreement with Speel. Since he really isn't using realignment in the classic sense that realignment scholars like Sundquist use the term, I prefer to think of Speel's "federalized realignment" insight as an explanation of a federalized accommodation or adjustment to a national realignment. The value of his insight, however, is not reduced by this minor difference of opinion over phrasing.

With the central questions presented, the theoretical terrain explored, and the outline of my book delineated, I turn next, in chapter 2, to presidential electoral change in the nation and in Pennsylvania since 1960.

2

Presidential Electoral Change in the Nation and in Pennsylvania Since 1960

This chapter examines presidential electoral change in the nation and in Pennsylvania. Viewing the nation first provides me the opportunity to elucidate the broader context in which the Keystone State's voters were behaving as they made their presidential choices from 1960 to 2004. I do this in the first section of this chapter before turning directly to Pennsylvania voters in the chapter's second and last section.

The Nation

Using realignment theory in chapter 1, I presented my understanding of how the national party system changed since 1960, that is, how the culture-wars realignment disrupted the party system established after the New Deal realignment. In this section, I examine the national changes brought by these partisan shifts in greater detail.

Figure 2.1 shows the state-by-state victory pattern of John F. Kennedy in the 1960 election, the starting point for my study. His winning electoral-college pattern differs substantially from the state-by-state Democratic presidential configuration found in the 2000 and 2004 elections, as a comparison of 1960 with the last two elections shows.

The five-election composite trend map in Figure 2.2 classifies the states according to how many times the Democratic or Republican nominee carried each state in the five elections from 1988 to 2004. The states that were won by Al Gore in 2000 and John Kerry in 2004 are easy to spot in the Figure 2.2 composite map. The Gore–Kerry states are either in dark gray (five Democratic wins) or medium gray (four Democratic wins, one Republican win) with just three exceptions: Gore carried New Mexico (in light gray); Kerry did not carry the medium gray state of Iowa, but he did carry the light gray state of New

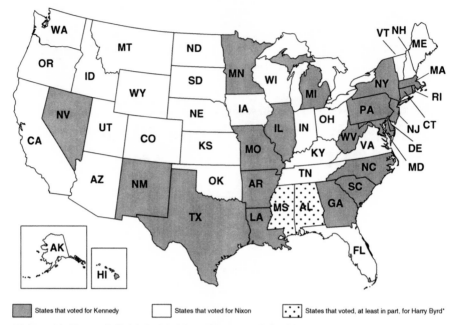

Fig. 2.1. Map of the Vote for President by State, 1960

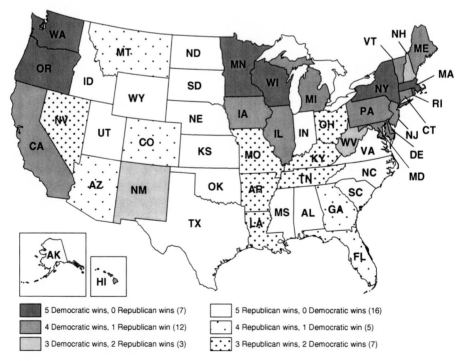

Fig. 2.2. Map of the Vote for President by State, 1988–2004

Hampshire.[1] (Neither Gore nor Kerry carried the only other light gray state—West Virginia.)

The most striking change between 1960 and 2000–2004 is the dramatic transformation of the American South. Kennedy was the last of the post-1960 nonsouthern Democratic nominees (Humphrey, McGovern, Mondale, Dukakis, and Kerry) to win in the South with the lone exception of Hubert Humphrey, who carried just one state, Texas, in 1968. Even Gore, a Tennessean, carried no state in his native region, not even his home state. Only Johnson, Carter, and Clinton, all southerners, won states in the South, with Carter doing the best in 1976, winning ten of the eleven former states of the Confederacy.

This dramatic political transformation of the South since 1960 is a familiar story to all students of American politics. With the passage of the Civil Rights Act in 1964 and the Voting Rights Act in 1965, the rationale for the old solidly Democratic South—that is, white unity in the Democratic party to preserve racial segregation—evaporated, and the South began to develop a permanent two-party system. The pattern is starkly illustrated in Figure 2.3, which charts Democratic party strength in the same manner employed in chapter 1 in similar figures for Pennsylvania (Figure 1. 1) and for the North (Figure 1.2). Actually, southern white unity in the Democratic party at the presidential level took its first drop after President Harry Truman undertook several civil rights initiatives in 1947 and 1948, leading to the Dixiecrat third-party revolt in the 1948 election. In Figure 2.3, this presidential decline is shown by the path of the dotted line. Note that Democratic party strength in the South—that is, the measure of the composite vote for governor, U.S. senator, and U.S. representative but not including the presidential vote—does not plunge until the first years of the 1960s.

Of course, the breakup of southern white unity in the Democratic party, the main purpose of which was to keep African Americans in a second-class status, was directly linked to the race issue. However, as a two-party system developed in the South over the next four decades, its newly emerging two-party politics became suffused with the entire cluster of crosscutting issues associated with the culture-wars realignment, not just the race issue.[2] Ronald Reagan, for example, was wildly popular among many white southerners from the time he entered politics in the

---

1. In the book's maps, I use shades of gray to identify Democratic voting strength and white and patterns of dots for Republican strength. As a result of the use of red and blue by the major television networks in their widely watched election programming, it has become common to refer to states regularly carried by Republican presidential candidates as "red" states and those by the Democrats as "blue" states. Two political scientists even adopted the color scheme as the title of their book on the 2004 presidential election: James W. Ceaser and Andrew E. Busch, *Red Over Blue: The 2004 Elections and American Politics* (Lanham, MD: Rowman & Littlefield, 2005).

2. For the partisan development of the South over these four decades, see Alexander P. Lamis's introductory and concluding chapters in his edited book, *Southern Politics in the 1990s* (Baton Rouge: Louisiana State University Press, 1999), 1–49, 377–406, as well as his *The Two-Party South*, 2nd expanded ed. (New York: Oxford University Press, 1990). See also Earl Black and Merle Black, *The Rise of Southern Republicans* (Cambridge, MA: Harvard University Press, 2002).

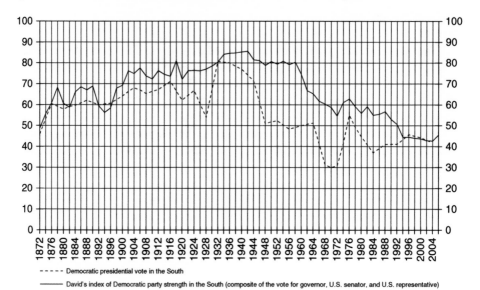

Fig. 2.3. Democratic Party Strength in the South, 1872–2006

mid-1960s. The region voted heavily for him in 1980 and 1984, and, in fact, the South became a Republican party bastion in presidential elections except for Carter's first election; in his failed reelection bid in 1980, Carter carried only his home state of Georgia.[3] To visualize these changes quickly via national maps, contrast the southern portion of the 1960 map in Figure 2.1 with Dixie's performance in the five presidential elections from 1968 to 1984, which is depicted in a composite map of these elections in Figure 2.4.

Apart from its value in showing the southern patterns, Figure 2.4, the twin of Figure 2.2, captures the state-by-state patterns for the main presidential elections involved in the culture-wars realignment. As related in chapter 1, this partisan transformation was highly favorable to the Republican party, which had not enjoyed such national strength since the 1920s, that is, until right before the New Deal realignment made the Democratic party the country's majority party. In the map in Figure 2.4, the fifty states are covered in white (five Republican wins), light dots (four Republican wins, one Democratic win), and heavy dots (three Republican wins, two Democratic wins). Only Minnesota, the home state of Walter Mondale, Carter's vice presidential running mate in 1976 and 1980 and himself the Democratic nominee in 1984, managed to make it to medium gray (four Democratic wins, one Republican win). Just three states—Maryland, Rhode Island, and West Virginia—fell in the category of three Democratic wins and two Republican wins (light gray). No state had five Democratic wins (dark gray).

3. See Black and Black, *The Vital South: How Presidents Are Elected* (Cambridge, MA: Harvard University Press, 1992).

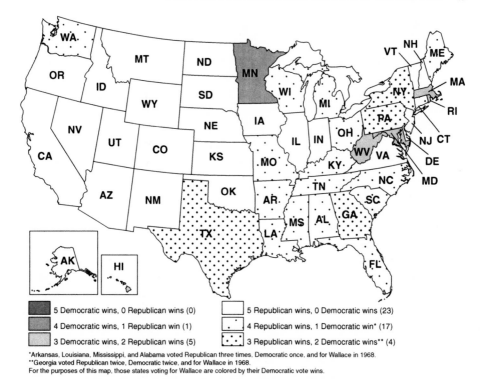

5 Democratic wins, 0 Republican wins (0)
4 Democratic wins, 1 Republican win (1)
3 Democratic wins, 2 Republican wins (5)

5 Republican wins, 0 Democratic wins (23)
4 Republican wins, 1 Democratic win* (17)
3 Republican wins, 2 Democratic wins** (4)

*Arkansas, Louisiana, Mississippi, and Alabama voted Republican three times, Democratic once, and for Wallace in 1968.
**Georgia voted Republican twice, Democratic twice, and for Wallace in 1968.
For the purposes of this map, those states voting for Wallace are colored by their Democratic vote wins.

Fig. 2.4. Map of the Vote for President by State, 1968–1984

This all changes in the next five elections, 1988 to 2004, the last four of them occurring during the period I view as being dominated by the aftershocks of the culture-wars realignment. Note in Figure 2.2 that the Pacific Coast states have moved into the national Democratic camp, including the country's most populous state, California, which voted Democratic in the last four elections. Even Dukakis carried Washington and Oregon, making it five for five for the Democrats there. Further, note Democratic strength throughout the Northeast, including Maine, Vermont, and to a lesser extent New Hampshire, three New England states that had voted against their fellow New Englander, Kennedy, in 1960. In the Midwest, significant recent Democratic gains have occurred in Illinois, Wisconsin, Michigan, Minnesota, and Iowa over the last five elections. The new Democratic presidential coalition that formed in the aftermath of the culture-wars realignment consisted, in essence, of the more culturally liberal states, not a surprising development given the nature of the cleavages that had sundered the national political party system from the mid-1960s into the early 1990s.

Another way to depict these varied patterns in the North is to look more closely at the party-strength figures for the northern states. I do this by first looking at the three regions of the North—Northeast, Midwest, and West—and then examining in a cursory way the patterns in three northeastern states, the latter providing comparative data for placing the Pennsylvania pattern in a broader context. Figures 2.5, 2.6, and 2.7 depict the three northern regions. The illustration for the Northeast (Figure 2.5) strikingly shows the recent overall strength of the Democratic party in this region at the presidential level and at the state level. The trend lines in the Midwest (Figure 2.6) capture the battleground nature of this region both in presidential elections and in state-level party strength. The graph for the West (Figure 2.7) is somewhat less useful because of the sharp divergence in recent years between the voting patterns of the Pacific Coast states and the less populous but more numerous Rocky Mountain states, not to mention the big differences between Hawaii and Alaska. Still, the western pattern contributes to completing the national picture when coupled with the figure for the South (Figure 2.3).

Clearly, in order to study in detail these regions and their states, one would want to examine individual state party-strength figures, which I do briefly here for just three states in Pennsylvania's region, the Northeast. Among the twelve northeastern states, there is a fair amount of variation in the state patterns, as depicted in their individual party-strength figures. Look, for example, at Democratic party strength in New Jersey (Figure 2.8), Connecticut (Figure 2.9), and New York (Figure 2.10). To understand the twists and turns in the respective Democratic-strength lines (the solid line in the figures) of these three northeastern states would require the type of detailed analysis I do in this book only for Pennsylvania; the same is true, of course, for the other states of the region. As I argued in chapter 1, full comprehension of electoral change in the United States requires attention to these variations for all of the states.

Recognizing that the ideal of full comprehension is not within the scope of a lone, state-focused analyst, how can the overall national patterns be further understood in order to have a basis for understanding the Pennsylvania changes

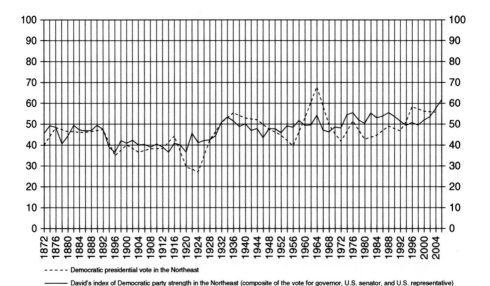

- - - - - Democratic presidential vote in the Northeast

——— David's index of Democratic party strength in the Northeast (composite of the vote for governor, U.S. senator, and U.S. representative)

Fig. 2.5. Democratic Party Strength in the Northeast, 1872–2006

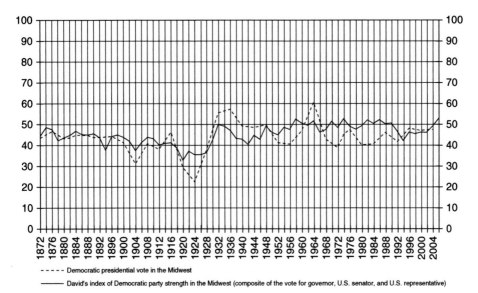

Fig. 2.6. Democratic Party Strength in the Midwest, 1872–2006

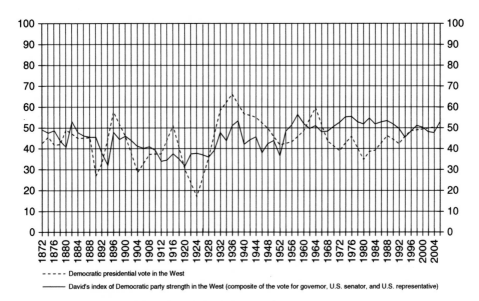

Fig. 2.7. Democratic Party Strength in the West, 1872–2006

within the national context? I have made a beginning with the composite national electoral maps introduced earlier. Now I turn to a useful and easily understood statistical technique, simple correlation, for further guidance. In fact, this tool is so valuable that I employ it throughout the book to examine patterns among Pennsylvania's sixty-seven counties. However, I use it at this point to study patterns among the fifty states.

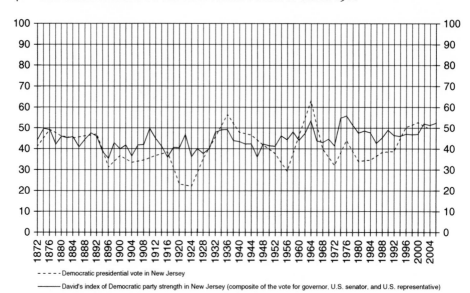

Fig. 2.8. Democratic Party Strength in New Jersey, 1872–2006

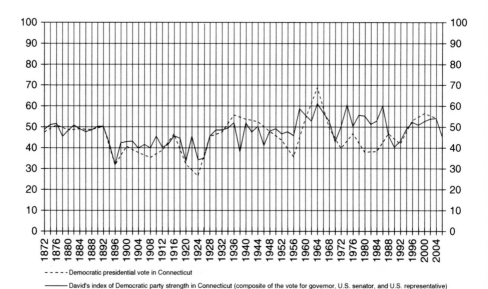

Fig. 2.9. Democratic Party Strength in Connecticut, 1872–2006

Here's how the correlation technique works. Imagine we had in front of us two columns of percentages indicating the Democratic vote for president in the 1960 and the 2004 elections in each of the fifty states listed in alphabetical order. If we spent ten minutes or so studying and comparing the vote for Kennedy in 1960 and Kerry in 2004 in each state, we could draw reasonable conclusions from the percentages as to how the two Democrats differed or were the same in various states

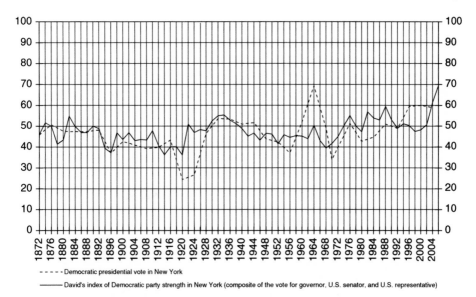

- - - - - Democratic presidential vote in New York

——— David's index of Democratic party strength in New York (composite of the vote for governor, U.S. senator, and U.S. representative)

Fig. 2.10. Democratic Party Strength in New York, 1872–2006

in those two elections. The correlation technique does the same thing, but it does it instantly and far more precisely, allowing one to examine many elections together over time to determine patterns of continuity or disruption. The technique consists of a mathematical formula that yields a coefficient that varies from 1.0 to –1.0, which provides an invaluable measure of the relationship of the two columns of presidential vote percentages.[4]

If Kennedy and Kerry had received roughly the same proportion of their support in the same states in 1960 and 2004, then the correlation coefficient produced by the mathematical comparison of those two columns of percentages would have been close to 1.0. In other words, these two Democratic candidates would be demonstrating that the partisan cleavage—at least as measured by state percentages[5]—has been undisturbed in any major way between these two elections.

4. Concerning this statistical technique, V. O. Key Jr., the twentieth century's premier political scientist specializing in American politics, wrote: "The process of correlation constitutes one of the most valuable tools for the analysis of political data." Key, *A Primer of Statistics for Political Scientists* (New York: Thomas Y. Crowell, 1954), 124. In fact, Key's "Simple Correlation" chapter in his *Primer* (pp. 105–29) constitutes a lucid, invaluable, and even witty explanation of the technique. For more recently written explanations of simple correlation, see Janet Buttolph Johnson and Richard A. Joslyn, *Political Science Methods*, 2nd ed. (Washington, DC: CQ Press, 1991), 293–338; and W. Phillips Shively, *The Craft of Political Research*, 6th ed. (Upper Saddle River, NJ: Pearson/Prentice Hall, 2005), 110–30.

5. As with all measures, there are limitations. Thus, just because an electoral unit—a state or a county—does not change its percentages for candidates of the same party very much over two elections, this doesn't mean that no change has occurred within the unit. We must always keep in mind that we are working with aggregate numbers within electoral units. Thus, with

Incidentally, a coefficient of exactly 1.0 is considered a perfect positive correlation, which rarely happens in electoral correlations; coefficients as high as 0.96 or 0.97 do occur, however, as we shall see.

If the Kennedy and Kerry patterns had been completely opposite to one another (that is, in states where one candidate was strong, the other was weak, and vice versa), then the correlation coefficient would approach –1.0. Such a strongly negative correlation among fellow partisans between elections almost never happens. Even a fairly low negative correlation (for example, in the –0.30 range) would indicate that a major disruption in the normal partisan patterns had occurred.

Finally, if the Kennedy and Kerry state-by-state percentages showed neither a positive nor a negative relationship, but exhibited merely a random pattern, then the correlation coefficient would be zero or close to it. As with a negative correlation, a finding of a random relationship between two fellow partisans would indicate that big changes had occurred in the party system, or at least that something unusual was going on in the pair of elections being correlated.[6]

In sum, the correlation technique[7] is a useful tool for determining if a political party's electoral pattern of support is remaining consistent from election to election or is deviating significantly. The best way to do this is to correlate pairs of elections over many years and to present the correlation coefficients in a matrix, as I do in Table 2.1 for all the Democratic presidential nominees from 1960 to 2004. Overall, this matrix reveals considerable discontinuity over the forty-four-year period, which is not surprising in light of the breakup of the solidly Democratic South and the events of the culture-wars realignment and its aftershocks as the more culturally liberal states moved toward the Democratic party in presidential elections and the more culturally conservative states became the mainstay of the Republican party in national elections. In fact, the Kennedy–Kerry correlation

this type of correlation analysis, we don't know what shifts may be occurring among individuals within a unit even if the unit's total candidate percentages have remained fairly constant. Therefore, in electoral research, it is vital to rely on multiple sources of information and to employ various analytical techniques.

6. For other examples of the use of state-by-state correlations to study electoral change, see Jerome M. Clubb, William H. Flanigan, and Nancy H. Zingale, *Partisan Realignment: Voters, Parties, and Government in American History* (Beverly Hills, CA: Sage, 1980), especially chapter 2, "Identifying Realignments: Correlation Analysis," 47–76; and Gerald Pomper, "Classification of Presidential Elections," *Journal of Politics* 29 (August 1967), 535–66.

7. Incidentally, after explaining how the correlation technique works, Professor Key offered his readers this charming advice about how to the present the findings: "A question of practical tactics in correlational analysis is how to present the findings. To most audiences to which one directs his findings, the coefficient of . . . correlation is a symbol devoid of content. Often the entire conclusion can be translated into English and the statistical analysis discarded. . . . By the exercise of a modicum of ingenuity, the most hardened audience of skeptics about statistics may be seduced into following the findings of a correlation analysis. In the process it is often just as well to avoid employing the term correlation" (*Primer of Statistics for Political Scientists*, 125–26).

Table 2.1 Correlations of the Democratic Vote for President in the United States, 1960–2004

	1960	1964	1968	1972	1976	1980	1984	1988	1992	1996	2000	2004
1960	1.00											
1964	0.20	1.00										
1968	0.32	0.83	1.00									
1972	0.34	0.69	0.86	1.00								
1976	0.58	−0.07	−0.02	0.08	1.00							
1980	0.49	−0.08	0.04	0.07	0.88	1.00						
1984	0.48	0.34	0.55	0.65	0.61	0.71	1.00					
1988	0.32	0.52	0.71	0.77	0.36	0.43	0.87	1.00				
1992	0.49	0.24	0.32	0.41	0.72	0.77	0.83	0.66	1.00			
1996	0.51	0.42	0.59	0.60	0.55	0.60	0.82	0.71	0.88	1.00		
2000	0.48	0.40	0.56	0.58	0.47	0.55	0.79	0.67	0.82	0.95	1.00	
2004	0.42	0.50	0.67	0.69	0.33	0.42	0.77	0.69	0.75	0.91	0.95	1.00

coefficient is a weak 0.42. The matrix also reveals that the disruptions of the period from 1960 to 1980 give way to a new pattern of consistency in the state-by-state partisan patterns that starts to take shape in 1984. Walter Mondale's losing Democratic pattern in that election correlates more strongly with the Democratic candidates to follow than with those who came before him. Thus, in retrospect, it appears that the Mondale election and that of the Democratic loser, Michael Dukakis, four years later, paved the way for a new Democratic correlation consistency that took hold in the 1990s. Or, one could just as appropriately view the situation from a Republican perspective and say the smashing reelection triumph of Ronald Reagan in 1984 and the ratification of that victory in the easy victory of Reagan's vice president, George H. W. Bush, in 1988, ushered in a new Republican pattern. In fact, the correlations among Clinton in 1996, Gore in 2000, and Kerry in 2004 are very high, indeed, hitting 0.95 for Gore–Kerry. In my view, the matrix in Table 2.1 confirms that the disruptions of the culture-wars realignment yielded in the 1990s to a more stable party system as the aftershocks of this latest national realignment played themselves out in the fifty states and reshaped the party system in conformity with the new partisan rationale that emerged during the culture wars.

Let's look more closely at several key elections depicted in the matrix by using an illustrative analytical tool—the scatter diagram, usually referred to by the briefer term scattergram—that allows a visual depiction of the pattern of any correlation of two elections. (Later in this chapter and throughout the book, I employ scattergrams extensively to examine Pennsylvania county-by-county correlation patterns in pairs of interesting elections, but the technique is used here first for states.) A scattergram like the one in Figure 2.11 is produced by plotting on a graph the position of each state (or county) using the percentages attained by both candidates in the two elections being analyzed. Incidentally, the black diagonal line found in each scattergram is known as the "best-fit" line because it defines the only possible straight line that could fit the scattergram's unique spread of dots (actually, in my figures, the "dots" are small diamonds representing the position of each state or county) when vertical lines are drawn either upward or downward from the dots.[8] Figure 2.11 presents the scattergram of the Kennedy–Kerry correlation of 0.42, which allows for a more precise depiction of the shifts among the fifty states over the forty-four-year period.

States located to the right of the 50-percent broken line running down the center of the figure and below the 50-percent broken line running across the figure were Kennedy states that went for the Republican nominee in 2004, President George W. Bush. They are mostly southern states, but Nevada, West Virginia, and Missouri are also there. Those to the left of the vertical centerline but below the horizontal 50-percent line did not go for the Democrat either time, although the scattergram shows a variety of percentage shifts among these states. For example, Kennedy had respectable losing percentages in Utah, Wyoming, and Idaho, which wasn't the case for Kerry.

8. Ibid., 114.

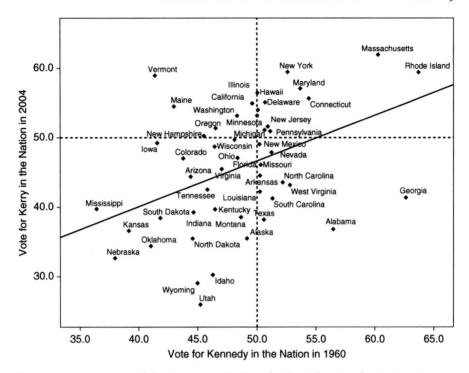

Fig. 2.11. Scattergram of the Democratic Vote for President in the Nation in 1960 and 2004

Above the horizontal 50-percent line are the old Democratic states (that is, those to the right of the vertical 50-percent line in the upper right-hand quadrant) and the new Democratic states (that is, those to the left of the vertical line or the upper left-hand quadrant). In the "new" category are California, Oregon, Washington, Maine, and Vermont. Note that Vermont exhibited an amazing pro-Democratic turnaround, one comparable to Georgia's dramatic movement in a pro-Republican direction. As just illustrated, scattergrams are especially useful for identifying such "far outliers" like Vermont and Georgia in the Kennedy–Kerry correlation. Examining units in a scattergram that exhibit such extreme behavior can unearth important novel developments, as we shall see in upcoming analyses of Pennsylvania counties in recent elections. As Phillips Shively pointed out, users of the correlation/scattergram technique "far too rarely go on to the creative and exploratory labor of examining the [far outliers]. . . . Usually, the spread of dots around the [best-fit line] is treated as an act of God, or a measure of the basic uncertainty of human affairs. On the contrary, it is a trove in which new variables lie waiting to be discovered."[9]

In the "old" Democratic category, New York grew more Democratic by about 6 percentage points between 1960 and 2004. Massachusetts and Rhode Island

9. Shively, *Craft of Political Research*, 121.

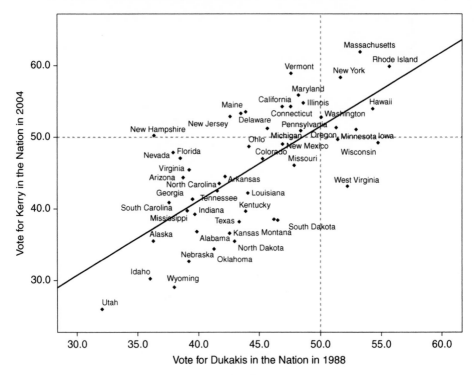

Fig. 2.12. Scattergram of the Democratic Vote for President in the Nation in 1988
and 2004

remained strongly Democratic; Maryland and Connecticut retained a solid
Democratic edge. Pennsylvania is clustered with Minnesota and Michigan, all with
very similar Democratic percentages around 51 in both the 1960 and 2004 elections. Keep in mind that even if a state doesn't change in its overall percentage,
there very well could be significant change going on within the state. In fact, as
we shall see with the county-by-county analysis of the Pennsylvania trends, that
is exactly what happened in the Keystone State (and probably in Michigan and
Minnesota, too).

Because the Dukakis–Bush election was instrumental in shepherding in a new
national Democratic (and Republican) pattern, I present a scattergram of the correlation of Dukakis in 1988 and Kerry in 2004 (coefficient of 0.69) in Figure 2.12 in
order to capture these most recent shifts among the states. As with Figure 2.11, the
new and old Democratic states are portrayed above the horizontal 50-percent line.
Of the Republican states below the 50-percent line in Figure 2.12, note that West
Virginia and Iowa and, to a lesser extent, Wisconsin,[10] are states that have declined

10. Kerry did carry Wisconsin in 2004, but his winning percentage of 49.7 (to Bush's 49.3) was
down from Dukakis's 51.4. For West Virginia, the fall-off was 9 percentage points from
Dukakis's 52.2 percent to Kerry's 43.2 percent. For Iowa, the drop-off was 5.5 percentage points
from Dukakis's 54.7 percent to Kerry's 49.2 percent.

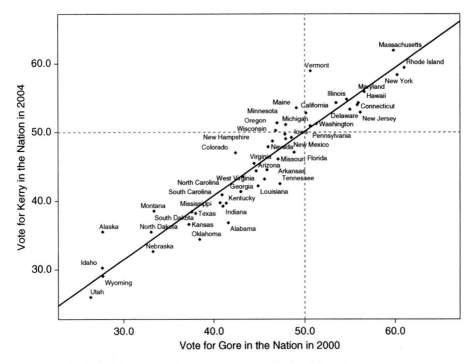

Fig. 2.13. Scattergram of the Democratic Vote for President in the Nation in 2000
and 2004

in the percentage of their Democratic presidential vote since being carried in 1988
by the losing Democratic national nominee that year, Dukakis. Note how far many
of the "new" Democratic states in the Kerry camp had come in the sixteen years
since Dukakis's defeat. For example, New Jersey gave Dukakis only 42.6 percent of
its vote compared to 52.9 percent for Kerry.

To visualize the new partisan pattern as it emerged in the early twenty-
first century, scrutinize Figure 2.13, a scattergram of the highly correlated
Gore–Kerry state-by-state lineup in 2000 and 2004 (coefficient of 0.95, as mentioned previously). Depending on whether you start at the top or the bottom
of the best-fit line that defines the correlation pattern, this illustration presents
an array of the American states from most Democratic or most Republican
and in the process shows in rough form how the voters in the fifty American
states sorted themselves out in the latest two elections of the post–culture-wars
realignment era.[11]

11. In an effort to better understand the relationship among the culture-wars realignment elections, I conducted a factor analysis of the Democratic vote in the fifty states in each presidential election from 1960 to 2004. Factor analysis is a method of data reduction that takes
large amounts of data and breaks them down into a few factors, or components, to determine
where the relationships exist. It grouped the 1960 to 2004 presidential elections into two
components that explained 80.8 percent of the variance. In the first component, there was

With this national overview of post-1960 presidential electoral change completed, I now turn to an analysis of presidential elections in Pennsylvania.

Pennsylvania

Concentrating primarily on Pennsylvania's presidential vote from 1960 to 2004, this section examines the Keystone State's voting behavior in presidential elections during these forty-four years and thus offers a comparison with the national patterns covered in the chapter's first section. However, unlike the analysis for the nation, for Pennsylvania, I begin with the late nineteenth century in order to provide a broader perspective on the Keystone State's partisan path and to emphasize and substantiate points made in chapter 1 concerning Pennsylvania developments throughout the twentieth century.

As related in chapter 1, Pennsylvania was wedded to the Republican party from the election of Abraham Lincoln in 1860 through the early 1930s. Thus, the county-by-county Pennsylvania map in Figure 2.14, depicting the number of times the Republicans or the Democrats carried each of Pennsylvania's sixty-seven counties in five selected presidential elections from 1896 to 1920, illustrates this overwhelming Republican dominance as well as pinpointing where Republican and, to a considerably lesser extent, Democratic strength was. (The shades of gray, white, and dotted patterns introduced in Figure 2.4 are used here as well and in similar illustrations that follow.) Note that the state's two main population centers, Philadelphia and Pittsburgh (the latter a part of Allegheny County), are white—five Republican wins, no Democratic wins. That situation changes dramatically after the New Deal "earthquake" strikes in the 1930s, and, by 2004, Philadelphia is by far the most Democratic county in Pennsylvania with Allegheny County a distant second.[12]

---

a considerable amount of state-by-state electoral turmoil from 1960 to 1980, as evidenced by the low component scores and the breakout of a second factor to help explain the elections of 1964, 1968, and 1972, and to a lesser extent, 1988 and 2004. Then, in 1984, just as was demonstrated in the correlation matrix in Table 2.1, a stronger relationship developed among the Democratic candidates. These patterns are consistent with those illustrated in the scattergrams in Figures 2.11, 2.12, and 2.13. In chapter 5, I profitably and more extensively employ factor analysis to better understand recent Pennsylvania patterns. At that point in the book, I fully explain the factor-analysis technique in the process of presenting the Keystone State's county-by-county findings.

12. In 1896 in Philadelphia, William Jennings Bryan, the Democratic presidential nominee, received 25.9 percent of the vote to Republican William McKinley's 72.1 percent; in Allegheny County, the percentages in 1896 were 27.6 for Bryan, 70.9 for McKinley. In 2004 in Philadelphia, John Kerry received 80.4 percent of the vote to Republican President George W. Bush's 19.3 percent; in Allegheny County the percentages in 2004 were 57.2 for Kerry, 42.1 for Bush.

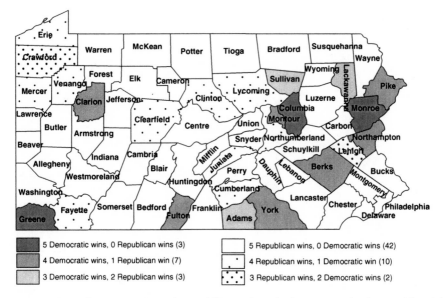

Fig. 2.14. Map of Democratic and Republican Victories by County in the Presidential Elections of 1896, 1900, 1908, 1916, and 1920

Before delving more deeply into the shifting Pennsylvania county-by-county patterns, it is essential to take a short geographic and demographic tour of the state in order to prepare for the extensive scrutiny of the state's political patterns that follows in this chapter and throughout the book. Providing assistance in this tour are two Pennsylvania maps—Figures 2.15 and 2.16—that supplement the rather Spartan basic state map—like the one in Figure 2.14—that I use throughout the book to identify county-level patterns. The map in Figure 2.15 contains the names of the state's sixty-seven county seats, which in most cases identifies a significant city or town in each county. Figure 2.16, taken from the fine Pennsylvania chapter in Neal R. Peirce's *The Megastates of America*,[13] is an illustrated map that shows important geographical features of the state. Both maps are useful aids for understanding Pennsylvania political geography.

A fundamental fact about Pennsylvania's population is illustrated in Table 2.2, namely, that 52.2 percent of the state's 12.3 million people live within the Philadelphia and Pittsburgh metropolitan areas, as recorded in the 2000 census. A whopping 31.4 percent (3,849,647 people) are found in the five main Philadelphia area counties— Philadelphia city/county[14] and Montgomery, Bucks, Delaware, and Chester counties. Incidentally, the percentage of the state's population from these five counties has

13. Neal R. Peirce, *The Megastates of America: People, Politics, and Power in the Ten Great States* (New York: W. W. Norton, 1972), 229.

14. Philadelphia, the state's largest city by far, functions administratively within the state like a county.

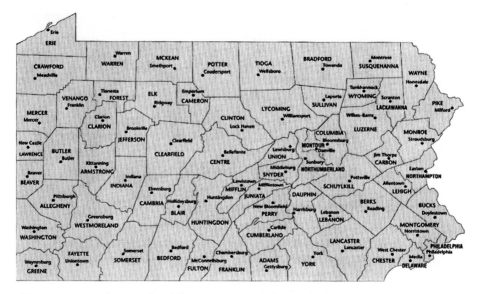

Fig. 2.15. Map of Pennsylvania's Counties and County Seats

Source: E. Willard Miller, ed., *A Geography of Pennsylvania* (University Park: Pennsylvania State University Press, 1995). Miller's map of Pennsylvania's counties is located at the beginning of the book to the left of the title page; there is no page number.

Fig. 2.16. Map Portraying Pennsylvania's Various Geographic Features

Source: Neal R. Peirce, *The Megastates of America: People, Politics, and Power in the Ten Great States* (New York: W. W. Norton & Company, 1972), 229. Permission to use this map was attained from W. W. Norton & Company.

Table 2.2 Population of Philadelphia and Pittsburgh Metro Areas in 2000

Philadelphia Metropolitan Area		
	2000	Percentage of State Population
Philadelphia	1,517,550	12.4%
Montgomery	750,097	6.1%
Bucks	597,635	4.8%
Delaware	550,864	4.5%
Chester	433,501	3.5%
Total of 4 Surrounding Counties	2,332,097	18.9%
Total Philadelphia Metro Area	3,849,647	31.3%
Pittsburgh Metropolitan Area		
	2000	Percentage of State Population
Allegheny	1,281,666	10.4%
Westmoreland	369,993	3.0%
Washington	202,897	1.7%
Beaver	181,412	1.5%
Butler	174,083	1.4%
Fayette	148,644	1.2%
Lawrence	94,643	0.8%
Armstrong	72,392	0.6%
Greene	40,672	0.3%
Total Pittsburgh Metro Area	2,566,402	20.9%
Total Philadelphia and Pittsburgh Metro Area	6,416,049	52.2%
Total Pennsylvania Population	**12,281,054**	

remained roughly consistent for over two centuries,[15] although the rapid, post–World War II suburbanization of the outlying Philadelphia counties has redistributed the proportion significantly within the five-county metropolitan area. In the 2000 census, Montgomery, Bucks, Delaware, and Chester held 18.9 percent of the state's population compared to approximately 6 percent in 1900. Philadelphia made up 12.4 percent of the state's population in 2000, down from about 20 percent in 1900.[16]

The state's other large population center is the Pittsburgh metropolitan area, consisting of Allegheny County[17] and its surrounding counties of Beaver, Lawrence, Butler, Armstrong, Westmoreland, Fayette, Greene, and Washington. It contained 2,566,402 people in 2000, or 20.9 percent of the state's total, as shown in Table 2.2.

To continue this quick overview of the state's population distribution, glance at Table 2.3, which presents all of the state's counties in descending order of population. The bottom thirty-seven counties fall in the category of less than 100,000 people, ranging from Lawrence, northwest of Pittsburgh and included in the Pittsburgh metro area, with 94,643, to three counties with less than 10,000 people spanning the north-central portion of the state from west to east—Forest (4,946), Cameron (5,974), and Sullivan (6,556).

Of the top ten counties in Table 2.3, seven fall in the core Philadelphia and Pittsburgh metropolitan areas. The other three are Lancaster (470,658) and York (381,751), two rapidly growing southeastern counties west of Philadelphia, and Berks (373,638), which has its county seat at Reading and is part of the far outer Philadelphia orbit of counties. In addition to three additional Pittsburgh-area counties, Washington, Beaver, and Butler, the next ten largest counties include the old anthracite coal mining centers of Luzerne (319,250), county seat of Wilkes-Barre, and Lackawanna (213,295), county seat of Scranton and the home of two important post-1960 governors, William W. Scranton, a Republican, and Robert P. Casey, a Democrat. Luzerne and Lackawanna are in northeastern Pennsylvania. South of them and north of Philadelphia are two other counties in this population classification—Lehigh (312,090), county seat of Allentown, and Northampton (267,066), county seat of Easton and containing the city of Bethlehem. Rounding out this category are the counties of Erie (280,843), in the far northwest and the state's only outlet on Lake Erie; Dauphin (251,798), where the state capital of Harrisburg is located; and Cumberland (213,674), county seat of Carlisle, in the south-central part of the state.

The next ten counties range from Cambria (152,598) in the west-central part of the state, where the main city is Johnstown, to Lycoming (120,044), county

15. In 1810, these counties made up 28 percent of the state's population, according to Paul D. Simkins, "Growth and Characteristics of Pennsylvania's Population," in E. Willard Miller, ed., *A Geography of Pennsylvania* (University Park: Pennsylvania State University Press, 1995), 90.

16. Ibid.

17. Allegheny County includes much more than the city of Pittsburgh; for example, Pittsburgh's population in 2000 was 334,563, which was only 26.1 percent of the population of Allegheny County (1,281,666).

Table 2.3 Pennsylvania Population by County, 2000

1	Philadelphia	1,517,550	34	Crawford	90,366
2	Allegheny	1,281,666	35	Indiana	89,605
3	Montgomery	750,097	36	Clearfield	83,382
4	Bucks	597,635	37	Somerset	80,023
5	Delaware	550,864	38	Armstrong	72,392
6	Lancaster	470,658	39	Columbia	64,151
7	Chester	433,501	40	Bradford	62,761
8	York	381,751	41	Carbon	58,802
9	Berks	373,638	42	Venango	57,565
10	Westmoreland	369,993	43	Bedford	49,984
11	Luzerne	319,250	44	Wayne	47,722
12	Lehigh	312,090	45	Mifflin	46,486
13	Erie	280,843	46	Pike	46,302
14	Northampton	267,066	47	McKean	45,936
15	Dauphin	251,798	48	Jefferson	45,932
16	Cumberland	213,674	49	Huntingdon	45,586
17	Lackawanna	213,295	50	Warren	43,863
18	Washington	202,897	51	Perry	43,602
19	Beaver	181,412	52	Susquehanna	42,238
20	Butler	174,083	53	Clarion	41,765
21	Cambria	152,598	54	Union	41,624
22	Schuylkill	150,336	55	Tioga	41,373
23	Fayette	148,644	56	Greene	40,672
24	Monroe	138,687	57	Clinton	37,914
25	Centre	135,758	58	Snyder	37,546
26	Franklin	129,313	59	Elk	35,112
27	Blair	129,144	60	Wyoming	28,080
28	Lebanon	120,327	61	Juniata	22,821
29	Mercer	120,293	62	Montour	18,236
30	Lycoming	120,044	63	Potter	18,080
31	Lawrence	94,643	64	Fulton	14,261
32	Northumberland	94,556	65	Sullivan	6,556
33	Adams	91,292	66	Cameron	5,974
			67	Forest	4,946

Total Population: 12,281,054

seat of Williamsport, located on the West Branch of the Susquehanna River in the north-central part of the state. Also included in this category of counties are Schuylkill (150,336), county seat of Pottsville and northwest of Philadelphia; Fayette (148,644), county seat of Uniontown, south of Pittsburgh; Monroe (138,687), in the Pocono Mountains in the northeastern part of the state bordering the Delaware River and New Jersey; Centre (135,758), home of the main campus of Pennsylvania State University at State College; Franklin (129,313), county seat of Chambersburg, in the south-center of the state bordering Maryland; Blair (129,144), in the west-center with its main city of Altoona; Lebanon (120,327), just east of Harrisburg; and Mercer (120,293), located two counties south of Erie bordering Ohio.

Running through the center and much of the northern part of the state are the Allegheny and Appalachian Mountains, which encompass most of the remaining thirty-seven rural, small-town counties, that is, those with populations below 100,000. I return in chapter 5 to the state's demography when I use U.S. census data from 1960 to 2000 in an effort to further understand the recent behavior of the Pennsylvania electorate.

With this quick portrait of Pennsylvania in front of us, let's continue to examine the composite election maps for additional insight into the state's presidential electoral patterns. As was the case for Figure 2.14, in the following four composite maps, I display the shifting county-level patterns of partisan strength in Pennsylvania since 1928 by calculating the number of times the Democratic and Republican presidential nominees have carried each county over the last twenty presidential elections, taking the elections in groups of five.

Figure 2.17, the composite map of the five elections from 1928 to 1944, shows the effect of the New Deal realignment. Philadelphia turns light gray (three

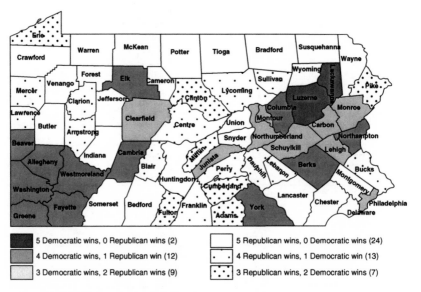

Fig. 2.17. Map of Democratic and Republican Victories by County in the Presidential Elections, 1928–1944

Democratic wins, two Republican wins), Luzerne and Lackawanna turn dark gray (five Democratic wins, no Republican wins), and the counties surrounding the Pittsburgh area turn to medium gray (four Democratic wins, one Republican win). Note that the four counties surrounding Philadelphia are heavily Republican in this map. Note also that the northern tier of the state is unchanged, remaining white (five Republican wins, no Democratic wins).

The composite map of the vote for president from 1948 to 1964, Figure 2.18, shows that several of the Pittsburgh-area counties and Philadelphia have now turned dark gray during this twenty-year period in which the aftershocks of the New Deal realignment continued to remake electoral patterns in the state. Remember, it was not until November 1960 that Democratic voter registration surpassed GOP registration for the first time in the twentieth century. Incidentally, if it had not been for the landslide election of President Lyndon B. Johnson in 1964, all of the lightly dotted counties would be white. As it is, only four Republican counties—Wayne, Union, Snyder, and Lebanon—bucked the Johnson landslide, becoming the four most Republican counties in the state during the 1948 to 1964 period.

The next series of five elections, those of 1968 to 1984, shown in Figure 2.19, reflect the strong Republican presidential victories nationwide and in Pennsylvania during the culture-wars realignment, especially the landslide elections of 1972, 1980, and 1984. Note that Philadelphia's heavily populous, suburban counties—Chester, Montgomery, Delaware, and Bucks—remain solidly in the Republican column during this twenty-year period, voting for the Republican nominee in all five elections. Also, four counties adjacent to as well as south of Allegheny County weaken slightly in their Democratic support, moving from dark gray to medium gray, compared to their performance in the previous five elections.

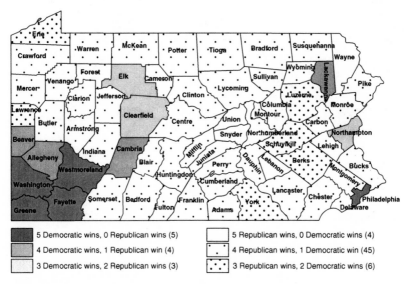

5 Democratic wins, 0 Republican wins (5)   5 Republican wins, 0 Democratic wins (4)

4 Democratic wins, 1 Republican win (4)   4 Republican wins, 1 Democratic win (45)

3 Democratic wins, 2 Republican wins (3)   3 Republican wins, 2 Democratic wins (6)

Fig. 2.18. Map of Democratic and Republican Victories by County in the Presidential Elections, 1948–1964

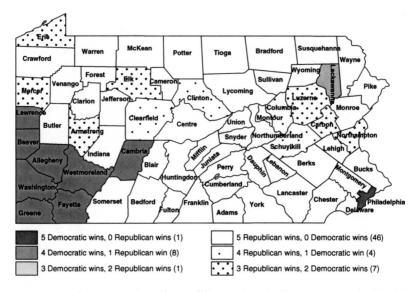

Fig. 2.19.   Map of Democratic and Republican Victories by County in the Presidential
Elections, 1968–1984

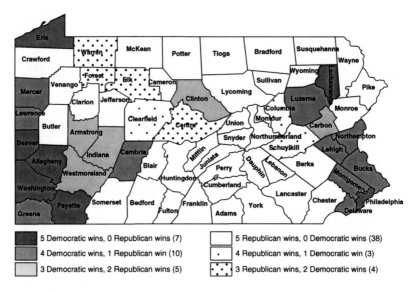

Fig. 2.20.   Map of Democratic and Republican Victories by County in the Presidential
Elections, 1988–2004

In the final series, from 1988 to 2004, Figure 2.20 depicts a striking new development in the Philadelphia area. Montgomery, Bucks, Delaware, and Lehigh counties
move from white (five Republican wins, no Democratic wins) to medium gray
(voting four out of five times for the Democratic presidential nominee). This is a
remarkable turnaround, and I devote considerable attention to this development
throughout this book, linking the changes to the aftershocks of the culture-wars
realignment. Also, Allegheny returns to five straight Democratic wins, or dark gray,
along with Beaver, Washington, and Fayette counties, but Westmoreland, the largest
Pittsburgh-area suburban county (population of 369,993 in 2000), moves to light
gray, recording only three of five Democratic wins during the latest period. These
interesting and complex changes in the Pittsburgh metro area also receive considerable attention below.

Further, Erie turns dark gray (five Democratic wins) from heavy dots (two
Democratic wins), and Luzerne and Mercer change from heavy dots to medium
gray. This composite map also vividly depicts the Republican "T" that commentators on the state's politics regularly refer to, that is, the strong GOP strength in the
rural, small-town counties in the northern and central part of the state that seem
to form a large T shape on a map of the state.[18]

With the completion of this introductory overview via composite maps of over
a century of presidential electoral change in Pennsylvania, I now examine in more
detail the Keystone State's presidential election patterns using county-level correlations as well as scattergrams of several key elections. Also, I present two revealing
state maps pinpointing county-level partisan strength in the "bookend" elections
of the 1960 to 2004 period.

In the manner of the national state-by-state analysis done in Table 2.1, Table 2.4
presents a correlation matrix of the county-by-county patterns for all of the
Democratic presidential nominees from 1896 to 1956, and Table 2.5 does the same
thing for the elections from 1960 to 2004. The first correlation matrix confirms
the major disruption of Pennsylvania electoral patterns that occurred during the
New Deal realignment period. Starting with the "Al Smith Revolution" in 1928 and
continuing through Franklin Roosevelt's 1932 and 1936 elections, past county-level
patterns break down. A renewed consistent pattern begins again with a high correlation between the 1936 and 1940 Democratic county-level patterns in Pennsylvania
(correlation coefficient of 0.97).

As Table 2.5 shows, these strong correlations continue into the 1960s and
1970s.[19] Table 2.5 also demonstrates that presidential patterns in the state from

18. See John J. Kennedy, *The Contemporary Pennsylvania Legislature* (Lanham, MD: University
    Press of America, 1999), 8–11. "The Pennsylvania 'T'" is the title of this three-page section in
    Kennedy's first chapter, "Overview of the Keystone State."

19. A factor analysis of the Democratic vote for president in Pennsylvania from 1896 to 2004
    groups these elections into three components that explain 90.1 percent of the variance. For
    the elections between 1896 and 1924, which were grouped together in the second compo-
    nent, there is a high degree of stability. Then, starting in 1928, major disruptions occur,
    producing the first component, which groups the elections from 1928 to 2004. It was in the

Table 2.4 Correlations of the Democratic Vote for President in Pennsylvania, 1896–1956

	1896	1900	1904	1908	1912	1916	1920	1924	1928	1932	1936	1940	1944	1948	1952	1956
1896	1	0.94	0.85	0.90	0.85	0.90	0.80	0.72	0.32	0.68	0.37	0.34	0.29	0.38	0.22	0.22
1900		1	0.94	0.98	0.94	0.93	0.87	0.80	0.31	0.66	0.37	0.36	0.29	0.33	0.17	0.17
1904			1	0.96	0.96	0.89	0.86	0.85	0.24	0.63	0.34	0.34	0.25	0.28	0.14	0.14
1908				1	0.96	0.94	0.90	0.83	0.34	0.69	0.43	0.42	0.35	0.38	0.23	0.23
1912					1	0.92	0.89	0.88	0.20	0.61	0.31	0.32	0.22	0.26	0.12	0.13
1916						1	0.90	0.85	0.23	0.68	0.42	0.41	0.32	0.37	0.22	0.22
1920							1	0.89	0.24	0.69	0.49	0.52	0.40	0.42	0.30	0.32
1924								1	0.06	0.56	0.25	0.28	0.15	0.21	0.06	0.11
1928									1	0.68	0.57	0.56	0.65	0.64	0.62	0.59
1932										1	0.74	0.72	0.69	0.74	0.66	0.66
1936											1	0.97	0.94	0.92	0.89	0.85
1940												1	0.96	0.91	0.90	0.87
1944													1	0.95	0.96	0.91
1948														1	0.95	0.92
1952															1	0.97
1956																1

Table 2.5 Correlations of the Democratic Vote for President in Pennsylvania, 1960–2004

	1960	1964	1968	1972	1976	1980	1984	1988	1992	1996	2000	2004
1960	1											
1964	0.87	1										
1968	0.93	0.96	1									
1972	0.90	0.90	0.93	1								
1976	0.90	0.93	0.94	0.92	1							
1980	0.86	0.86	0.90	0.88	0.93	1						
1984	0.86	0.84	0.91	0.89	0.90	0.95	1					
1988	0.85	0.84	0.91	0.89	0.90	0.95	0.99	1				
1992	0.85	0.81	0.89	0.90	0.88	0.90	0.96	0.96	1			
1996	0.84	0.79	0.86	0.89	0.84	0.81	0.87	0.86	0.95	1		
2000	0.82	0.73	0.83	0.85	0.78	0.70	0.80	0.78	0.89	0.97	1	
2004	0.75	0.66	0.76	0.80	0.69	0.61	0.71	0.70	0.83	0.92	0.98	1

1960 to 2004 were not disrupted in the dramatic fashion that occurred during the New Deal realignment. Instead, there was a weakening of the Democratic pattern in the middle years of the table, 1980 to 1992. Then, starting with President Bill Clinton's reelection in 1996, a very strong set of correlations appears again among the Democratic county-by-county presidential election patterns from 1996 to 2004.

In three Pennsylvania scattergrams, I look more closely at the Kennedy–Kerry (1960/2004) correlation (coefficient of 0.75), the Kennedy–Dukakis (1960/1988) correlation (coefficient of 0.85), and the Dukakis–Kerry (1988/2004) correlation (coefficient of 0.70) in order to highlight the areas of significant presidential change in the Keystone State, which I link to the effects of the national culture-wars realignment in the state.

The fact that Pennsylvania patterns were not disrupted in a stronger fashion is the result of at least two factors. First, this realignment was not as powerful as the New Deal realignment. Second, a national realignment does not exhibit uniform levels of change in every American state. Some states are affected more, some less. Some are affected earlier and for a longer time period; others later and for a shorter period. And there are other possible combinations. A good way to begin to glean these diverse comparative effects is to note the degree of partisan change demonstrated by the various states between 1960 and 2004, which was shown in the national scattergram in Figure 2.11. Many states shifted much more radically than Pennsylvania. After all, Pennsylvania maintained its Democratic tilt in both elections, as did Michigan and Minnesota, as mentioned earlier. As shown in the state-by-state scattergram in Figure 2.11, the Keystone State kept its distance from major state switchers, such as Georgia, Alabama, and South Carolina, which became much more Republican, and Vermont, Oregon, and Washington, which became more Democratic. States showing more radical shifts, such as these six, were more likely to manifest great disruption in their county-level correlation patterns than was found in the Keystone State.

To substantiate this notion, I calculated county-level Democratic presidential election correlations for two of these states, South Carolina and Oregon, and for Michigan, which tracked closely with Pennsylvania in the national scattergram. As can be seen in Table 2.6, South Carolina's county patterns were dramatically disrupted, starting in 1968 and continuing into the 1980s. The restructuring appeared to end in 1984, and a new consistent partisan pattern settled in. The Oregon correlations, displayed in Table 2.7, exhibited considerable turmoil throughout the

---

1936 election when the new configuration, which was being fueled by the substantive New Deal policy initiatives, took hold. This pattern persisted and grew even stronger into the 1960s and 1970s until 1980, when a weakening of the pattern began to appear, culminating in a third factor breaking out in 1992. This third factor is instrumental in helping to explain the county-level presidential patterns that coalesced after 1992. In chapter 5, I rely heavily on several factor analyses of the Pennsylvania vote over many elections, including the presidential elections from 1896 to 2004. Supporting calculations for these factor analyses appear in Appendix C.

Table 2.6 Correlations of the Democratic Vote for President in South Carolina, 1960–2004

	1960	1964	1968	1972	1976	1980	1984	1988	1992	1996	2000	2004
1960	1											
1964	0.82	1										
1968	-0.30	-0.27	1									
1972	-0.20	-0.14	0.93	1								
1976	0.54	0.47	0.38	0.52	1							
1980	0.36	0.32	0.52	0.65	0.91	1						
1984	-0.06	-0.09	0.81	0.88	0.67	0.84	1					
1988	0.03	0.00	0.78	0.86	0.71	0.86	0.97	1				
1992	-0.03	-0.03	0.77	0.84	0.67	0.84	0.96	0.98	1			
1996	0.00	0.01	0.75	0.83	0.68	0.84	0.94	0.97	0.98	1		
2000	-0.12	-0.07	0.80	0.85	0.60	0.76	0.92	0.93	0.96	0.98	1	
2004	-0.22	-0.17	0.81	0.85	0.50	0.69	0.90	0.91	0.94	0.94	0.98	1

Table 2.7 Correlations of the Democratic Vote for President in Oregon, 1960–2004

	1960	1964	1968	1972	1976	1980	1984	1988	1992	1996	2000	2004
1960	1											
1964	0.63	1										
1968	0.57	0.88	1									
1972	0.38	0.76	0.91	1								
1976	0.64	0.74	0.77	0.75	1							
1980	0.21	0.68	0.85	0.89	0.66	1						
1984	0.29	0.69	0.83	0.94	0.65	0.91	1					
1988	0.29	0.71	0.86	0.93	0.62	0.91	0.97	1				
1992	0.07	0.51	0.72	0.85	0.43	0.86	0.91	0.94	1			
1996	0.01	0.57	0.73	0.78	0.37	0.87	0.83	0.90	0.93	1		
2000	-0.07	0.44	0.66	0.78	0.34	0.82	0.82	0.87	0.94	0.94	1	
2004	-0.07	0.43	0.64	0.77	0.32	0.79	0.82	0.86	0.94	0.92	0.98	1

Table 2.8 Correlations of the Democratic Vote for President in Michigan, 1960–2004

	1960	1964	1968	1972	1976	1980	1984	1988	1992	1996	2000	2004
1960	1											0.60
1964	0.88	1										0.61
1968	0.95	0.92	1									0.62
1972	0.79	0.82	0.86	1								0.73
1976	0.77	0.81	0.80	0.76	1							0.60
1980	0.78	0.81	0.86	0.86	0.90	1						0.73
1984	0.81	0.78	0.87	0.87	0.86	0.93	1					0.75
1988	0.76	0.77	0.81	0.86	0.84	0.90	0.95	1				0.80
1992	0.70	0.74	0.78	0.83	0.83	0.91	0.94	0.94	1			0.83
1996	0.62	0.68	0.67	0.77	0.76	0.83	0.80	0.86	0.91	1		0.92
2000	0.53	0.58	0.55	0.66	0.58	0.69	0.65	0.72	0.77	0.92	1	0.92
2004	0.60	0.61	0.62	0.73	0.60	0.73	0.75	0.80	0.83	0.92	0.95	1

late 1960s and 1970s, stabilizing by the mid-1980s. The Michigan pattern, shown in Table 2.8, resembles the Pennsylvania pattern, except that the deviation from continuity starts four years earlier—in 1972—in this large, industrial, Midwestern state. Like Pennsylvania, a cohesive partisan configuration reemerges in the 1996 election and continues through 2004.

These three comparative state examples reinforce the reality that national realignments work their way through our complex, decentralized party system in varying ways. If I were to calculate similar correlations for the other forty-six states, my hunch is that I would find several distinct state patterns emerging during the years of the culture-wars realignment. Of course, even with this glimpse at South Carolina, Oregon, and Michigan, we know nothing about the political dynamics peculiar to each of these states nor anything about electoral competition below the presidential level there. As I argued in chapter 1 and as I assert again in the conclusion to this book, understanding electoral patterns throughout the fifty states is imperative if we are to have a full understanding of national electoral change.

Now that the overall 1960 to 2004 presidential patterns have been presented, it seems appropriate to specify exactly how the vote went in Pennsylvania in each of these last twelve presidential elections. Table 2.9 gives the raw numbers and percentages. Starting with John Kennedy's victory over Richard Nixon in the state in 1960 (51.1 percent to 48.8 percent), Pennsylvania became an important component in the national Democratic presidential coalition through to the end of the century and continuing in the 2004 presidential election. In fact, of the twelve elections in this period, the Democratic presidential nominee carried Pennsylvania eight times, three more times than the Democratic party was able to win the nation. The three Democrats who carried Pennsylvania but lost the national election were Hubert Humphrey in 1968 with 47.6 percent to Nixon's 44.0 percent (George Wallace received 8.0 percent); Al Gore in 2000 with 50.6 percent to George W. Bush's 46.4 percent; and John Kerry in 2004 with 51.0 percent to President Bush's 48.5 percent.[20]

Pennsylvania was also vital to Jimmy Carter's narrow 1976 victory over President Gerald R. Ford; the Georgia Democrat carried the state with 50.4 percent to Ford's 47.7 percent. In fact, in the post-1960 period, the national Republican nominees have carried Pennsylvania only in elections in which they have won nationwide by substantial margins:[21] Richard Nixon in 1972, Ronald Reagan in 1980 and 1984, and George H. W. Bush in 1988. Incidentally, the Bush victory in Pennsylvania in 1988 over Democrat Michael Dukakis was the only close contest in Pennsylvania of

20. This was quite a turnaround for Pennsylvania. In the 1948 election, when President Harry Truman defeated the Republican nominee, Thomas E. Dewey, nationally, Pennsylvania gave its electoral votes to the Republican with 50.9 percent of the vote to Truman's 46.9 percent.

21. This was also the case for Dwight Eisenhower's two Pennsylvania victories: in 1952 with 52.7 percent to 46.9 percent for the Democratic nominee, Adlai Stevenson, and in 1956, when President Eisenhower carried the state a second time with 56.5 percent to Stevenson's 43.3 percent.

Table 2.9 Pennsylvania Vote for President, 1960–2004

Year	Democratic Candidate	Republican Candidate	Dem Vote	Rep Vote	Other Vote	Total Vote	Plurality		% Dem	% Rep
2004	John F. Kerry	George W. Bush	2,938,095	2,793,847	33,822	5,765,764	144,248	D	51.0	48.5
2000	Al Gore	George W. Bush	2,485,967	2,281,127	146,025	4,913,119	204,840	D	50.6	46.4
1996	Bill Clinton	Robert Dole	2,215,819	1,801,169	489,130	4,506,118	414,650	D	49.2	40.0
1992	Bill Clinton	George H. W. Bush	2,239,164	1,791,841	928,805	4,959,810	447,323	D	45.1	36.1
1988	Michael Dukakis	George H. W. Bush	2,194,944	2,300,087	41,220	4,536,251	105,143	R	48.4	50.7
1984	Walter Mondale	Ronald Reagan	2,228,131	2,584,323	32,449	4,844,903	356,192	R	46.0	53.3
1980	Jimmy Carter	Ronald Reagan	1,937,540	2,261,872	362,089	4,561,501	324,332	R	42.5	49.6
1976	Jimmy Carter	Gerald Ford	2,328,677	2,205,604	86,506	4,620,787	123,073	D	50.4	47.7
1972	George McGovern	Richard Nixon	1,796,951	2,714,521	80,634	4,592,106	917,570	R	39.1	59.1
1968	Hubert Humphrey	Richard Nixon	2,259,405	2,090,017	398,506	4,747,928	169,388	D	47.6	44.0
1964	Lyndon Johnson	Barry Goldwater	3,130,954	1,673,657	18,079	4,822,690	1,457,297	D	64.9	34.7
1960	John F. Kennedy	Richard Nixon	2,556,282	2,439,956	10,303	5,006,541	116,326	D	51.1	48.7

Note:

In 2000, 103,392 of the votes within the other vote column were cast for Ralph Nader of the Green party.

In 1996, 430,984 of the votes within the other vote column went to independent Ross Perot.

In 1992, 902,677 of the votes within the other vote column were cast for Reform party candidate Ross Perot.

In 1980, 292,921 of the votes within the other vote column were cast for independent John Anderson.

In 1968, 378,582 of the votes within the other vote column were cast for George Wallace.

Source: Rhodes Cook, Alice V. McGillivray, and Richard M. Scammon, *America Votes: Election Returns by State, 2005–2006,* vol. 27 (Washington, DC: CQ Press, 2007).

these lone four GOP wins out of the twelve 1960 to 2004 elections. Bush received 50.7 percent to Dukakis's 48.4 percent in Pennsylvania, while the Republican won nationwide with 53.4 percent to Dukakis's 45.6 percent. Bill Clinton easily defeated President Bush in the state in 1992 with 45.1 percent to the incumbent president's 36.1 percent; Ross Perot received 18.2 percent. And Clinton again carried the state in 1996 with 49.2 percent to 40.0 percent for Bob Dole, the Republican nominee; Perot's percentage dropped to 9.6. The line chart in Figure 2.21 traces the Pennsylvania Democratic presidential vote along with the national Democratic vote from 1960 to 2004. Also note that Figure 2.21 traces the substantial difference between the presidential vote in the North and in the South, a point that becomes more significant as I analyze national and Pennsylvania survey data in chapter 6.

A useful way to gain insight into the changing county-level presidential voting patterns in Pennsylvania is to examine more closely the two "bookend" elections of the main period under study in this book—1960 and 2004. This is done first with a pair of maps and then with a scattergram of the Kennedy–Kerry correlation of 0.75. Then, four additional scattergrams are examined for what they reveal about the evolving changes.

The county-level maps for the 1960 and 2004 elections, shown in Figures 2.22 and 2.23, classify Pennsylvania counties into four categories. If the county was carried by the Democratic nominee, then the county is shaded dark gray. The other three categories denote the strength of the GOP margin of victory. The

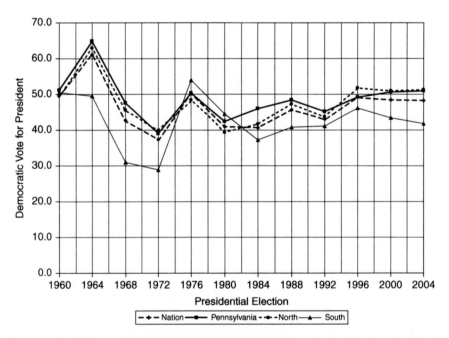

Fig. 2.21. Line Chart of the Democratic Vote for President in the Nation, the North, the South, and Pennsylvania, 1960–2004

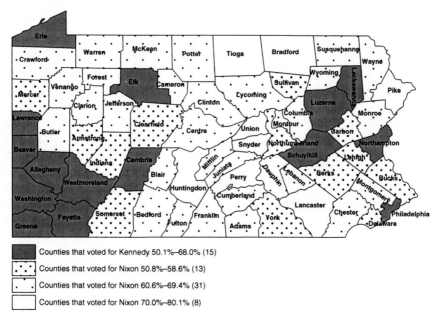

Counties that voted for Kennedy 50.1%–68.0% (15)

Counties that voted for Nixon 50.8%–58.6% (13)

Counties that voted for Nixon 60.6%–69.4% (31)

Counties that voted for Nixon 70.0%–80.1% (8)

Fig. 2.22. Map of the Vote for President in 1960 with Four Levels of County Support

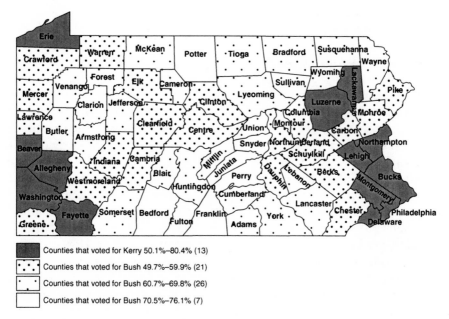

Counties that voted for Kerry 50.1%–80.4% (13)

Counties that voted for Bush 49.7%–59.9% (21)

Counties that voted for Bush 60.7%–69.8% (26)

Counties that voted for Bush 70.5%–76.1% (7)

Fig. 2.23. Map of the Vote for President in 2004 with Four Levels of County Support

weakest Republican counties are denoted with heavy dots (percentages in the 50s), stronger counties contain a lighter dot pattern (percentages in the 60s), and those counties with a GOP margin of victory over 70 percent are white. The 1960 map in Figure 2.22 offers a rough picture of the basic Pennsylvania partisan land-scape at the start of the main period under study. Democratic strength then was located in Philadelphia (but not its surrounding suburbs), in Allegheny County and six of the eight surrounding counties that make up the Pittsburgh metro-politan area, in the old coal mining counties of Lackawanna and Luzerne, plus a few others, including Erie, a heavily Catholic manufacturing center in the far northwest. Republican strength ran throughout the famous T—the rural, small-town counties that stretch through the state's northern tier and down the center, ending in the heavily populated suburban counties surrounding Philadelphia and including the populous counties of York and Lancaster, west of the Philadelphia suburbs.

By 2004, as the map in Figure 2.23 shows, the state's partisan landscape had been altered considerably. The most striking change is found in the populous suburban Philadelphia counties of Montgomery, Delaware, and Bucks, plus nearby Lehigh; Kerry carried them all. Even Chester gave Kerry a healthy 47.5 percent of its vote compared to only 36.2 percent for Kennedy forty-four years earlier. Further, a very different picture is visible in the Pittsburgh metro area, which in 2004 was no longer the solid Democratic bastion it had been in 1960. Three counties in the Pittsburgh area, led by Westmoreland, the populous suburban county directly east of Allegheny County, voted Republican, and the winning 2004 Democratic percentages were down in all of the other Pittsburgh-area counties compared to Kennedy's vote with the exception of Allegheny. Also, several south-central Republican counties, namely Bedford, Fulton, Franklin, Juniata, and York, were even more Republican in 2004 than in 1960.

Although the maps are visually useful, a scattergram of the correlation of these two bookend elections, shown in Figure 2.24, provides greater precision in mark-ing Pennsylvania's changing voting patterns. This is because the county positions on the graph represent the actual percentages each candidate received in the vari-ous counties; with the two maps of the 1960 and 2004 elections, the counties are grouped into just four categories. Thus, the scattergram is able to nicely pinpoint the extent of the weakening of Democratic voting strength in the counties sur-rounding Allegheny/Pittsburgh. For example, Washington County, which Kerry narrowly won with 50.1 percent to Bush's 49.6 percent, had given Kennedy nearly 58.2 percent of its votes in 1960. The scattergram shows a similar weakening of Democratic support in Fayette and Greene counties. Likewise, the scattergram brings more precision in following the opposite trend in the Philadelphia suburban counties, which gave Kerry much larger percentages than Kennedy. For example, Montgomery county, something of a far outlier, went from a Kennedy vote of 39.2 percent to a Kerry vote of 55.6 percent, and Delaware county, which had given Kennedy 47.8 percent, gave Kerry 57.1 percent of its votes.

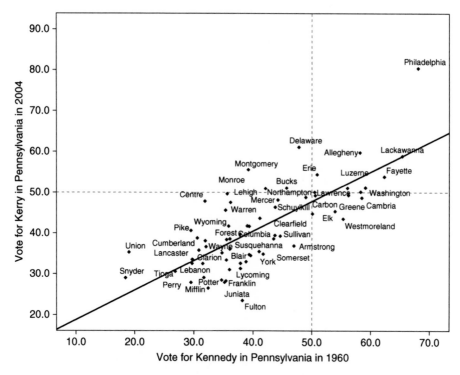

Fig. 2.24. Scattergram of the Democratic Vote for President in Pennsylvania in 1960 and 2004

By looking at the two scattergrams that "split" the Kennedy and Kerry elections at 1988, we see that the bulk of the big changes in the Philadelphia and Pittsburgh areas did not occur until after 1988. Figure 2.25, which depicts the scattergram of the Kennedy–Dukakis correlation (coefficient of 0.85), locates most of the Pittsburgh-area counties, even Westmoreland, in the top right quadrant of the graph that contains the counties that voted Democratic both in 1960 and in 1988. Similarly, the Philadelphia suburban counties, which stand out so vividly in their 1960 to 2004 movement in the two bookend maps, are safely found in the quadrant at the bottom left where counties that voted Republican in both elections are located. By contrast, the scattergram of the Dukakis–Kerry correlation (coefficient of 0.70) in Figure 2.26 captures fully the divergent movements in the Pittsburgh and Philadelphia areas that we witnessed in the Kennedy–Kerry scattergram in Figure 2.24. As I wrote in chapter 1 and earlier in this chapter for the national scene, I link these changes directly to the aftershocks of the culture-wars realignment. In essence, the more culturally liberal Philadelphia suburban counties have moved toward the national Democrats, and the more culturally conservative Pittsburgh-area counties have become more Republican, not unlike the paths of various states depicted in the first section of this chapter devoted to national trends. In chapters 5 and 6, I offer further evidence to help explain the voter shifts taking place in these

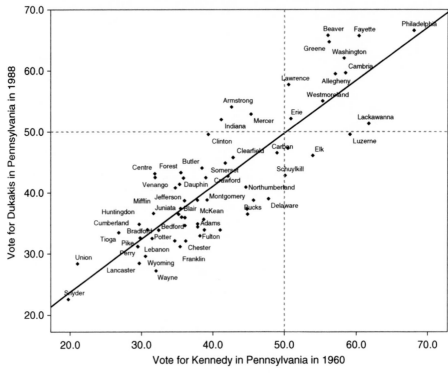

Fig. 2.25. Scattergram of the Democratic Vote for President in Pennsylvania in 1960 and 1988

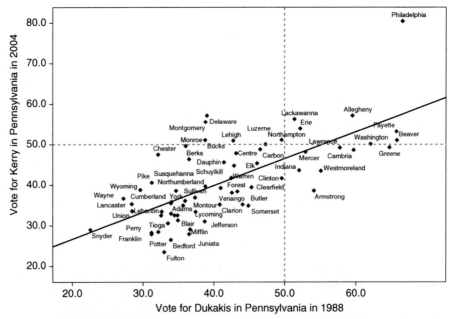

Fig. 2.26. Scattergram of the Democratic Vote for President in Pennsylvania in 1988 and 2004

counties, information that supports and expands the interpretation I have already stated. Also, in chapters 3 and 4, I examine related shifts in the context of gubernatorial and U.S. Senate elections in Pennsylvania.

The scattergram in Figure 2.27 illustrates the stable county-by-county Pennsylvania partisan pattern witnessed in the last two presidential elections (and in the previous 1996 election as well) by portraying the nearly perfect positive correlation found between Gore in 2000 and Kerry in 2004 (coefficient of 0.98!). Whether one runs down from the top of the best-fit line, starting with Democratic stronghold of Philadelphia, or up from the bottom at Fulton, Snyder, and Perry counties, three counties that are nearly as Republican as Philadelphia is Democratic, the ordering of the counties reveals the basic presidential two-party pattern that formed in the Keystone State in the early twenty-first century.

A final scattergram captures the breathtaking changes that occurred in Pennsylvania presidential patterns over the 108-year period from 1896 to 2004. Figure 2.28 depicts the correlation of William Jennings Bryan, the 1896 Democratic presidential nominee, with Senator Kerry in 2004, which yields a coefficient of –0.06 and reveals a

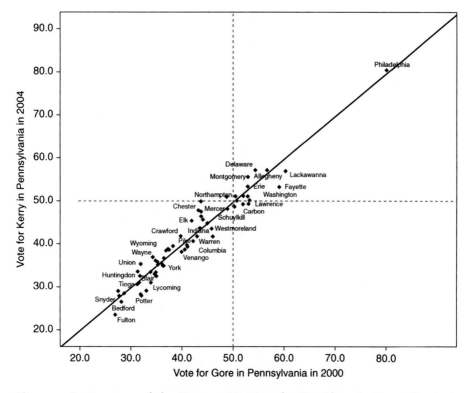

Fig. 2.27. Scattergram of the Democratic Vote for President in Pennsylvania in 2000 and 2004

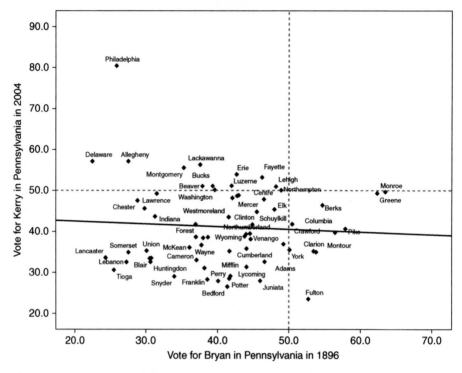

Fig. 2.28. Scattergram of the Democratic Vote for President in Pennsylvania in 1896 and 2004

random, slightly negative relationship between the two Democratic standard-bearers separated by over a century of partisan change.[22]

I return to an analysis of Keystone State presidential election patterns in greater detail in chapters 5 and 6 as well as to the patterns for the other major state-wide elections in Pennsylvania, that is, those for governor and U.S. senator. In those two chapters, I employ additional aggregate data and a wealth of Pennsylvania and national survey data. Attention now shifts in chapters 3 and 4 to a detailed election-by-election consideration of the major statewide elections in the state from 1962 to 2004. Competition for these two major statewide positions is at the core of electoral politics in any state, and that certainly was the case in Pennsylvania from 1962 to 2004, as the next two chapters demonstrate.

22. See Appendix A for a full array of Pennsylvania county-level correlation data for both the Democratic and Republican parties in the presidential elections from 1896 to 2004. The Bryan–Kerry correlation of –0.06 is found here.

3

Electoral Competition in Pennsylvania from 1962 to 1990: An Examination of Gubernatorial and U.S. Senate Elections

There is no substitute for knowing what happened in key individual elections when one is trying to understand electoral change. Thus far, I have tried to place Pennsylvania's partisan path in perspective by drawing on the electoral realignment literature and by examining presidential elections in Pennsylvania and the nation using composite maps of election outcomes, correlation analysis, and scattergrams. These sources of information and methods of analysis have yielded promising results for understanding Pennsylvania electoral change.

In the next two chapters, I explore the details of the important post-1960 statewide elections—those for governor and U.S. senator—using historical and journalistic accounts along with the various analytical tools introduced and employed in the first two chapters. This investigation immerses us in a sea of details involving ambitious politicians fiercely battling for political power in election after election. No one can come away from this account without an appreciation for the vigorous nature in which Republican and Democratic candidates for these two high offices in Pennsylvania conducted their struggles for ascendancy.

The percentages of the two-party vote, displayed in Table 3.1 for governor and Table 3.2 for U.S. senator, illustrate strikingly how closely contested these elections were. With only a few exceptions, namely the relatively easy reelection contests of the most recent governors and a couple of reelection contests of long-serving U.S. senators, most of these twelve gubernatorial and seventeen senatorial elections were close fights indeed. Further, as we shall see, important battles were also waged at critical moments among fellow partisans for their own party's nomination in hard-fought, contested primaries that yield valuable insights into the divisions in each party.

Table 3.1 Pennsylvania Vote for Governor, 1962–2006

Year	Democratic Candidate	Dem Vote	Republican Candidate	Rep Vote	Other Vote	Total Vote	Plurality		% Dem	% Rep
2006	Ed Rendell	2,470,517	Lynn Swann	1,622,135	3,425	4,096,077	848,382	D	60.3	39.6
2002	Ed Rendell	1,913,235	Mike Fisher	1,589,408	80,536	3,583,179	323,827	D	53.4	44.4
1998	Ivan Itkin	938,745	Tom Ridge	1,736,844	349,563	3,025,152	798,099	R	31.0	57.4
1994	Mark Singel	1,430,099	Tom Ridge	1,627,976	527,451	3,585,526	197,877	R	39.9	45.4
1990	Robert P. Casey	2,065,244	Barbara Hafer	987,516		3,052,760	1,077,728	D	67.7	32.3
1986	Robert P. Casey	1,717,484	William Scranton III	1,638,268	32,523	3,388,275	79,216	D	50.7	48.4
1982	Allan Ertel	1,772,353	Richard Thornburgh	1,872,784	38,848	3,683,985	100,431	R	48.1	50.8
1978	Pete Flaherty	1,737,888	Richard Thornburgh	1,966,042	38,039	3,741,969	228,154	R	46.4	52.5
1974	Milton Shapp	1,878,252	Andrew "Drew" Lewis	1,578,917	34,065	3,491,234	299,335	D	53.8	45.2
1970	Milton Shapp	2,043,029	Raymond Broderick	1,542,854	114,177	3,700,060	500,175	D	55.2	41.7
1966	Milton Shapp	1,868,719	Raymond P. Shafer	2,110,349	71,600	4,050,668	241,630	R	46.1	52.1
1962	Richardson Dilworth	1,938,627	William Scranton	2,424,918	14,497	4,378,042	486,291	R	44.3	55.4

Note: In 1998, 315,761 of the votes within the other vote column were cast for Constitutional Party candidate Peg Luksik. In 1994, 460,269 of the votes within the other vote column were cast for Constitutional Party candidate Peg Luksik.

Source: Rhodes Cook, Alice V. McGillivray, and Richard M. Scammon, *America Votes: Election Returns by State, 2005–2006*, vol. 27 (Washington, DC: CQ Press, 2007).

Table 3.2 Pennsylvania Vote for Senator, 1962–2006

Year	Democratic Candidate	Republican Candidate	Dem Vote	Rep Vote	Other Vote	Total Vote	Plurality		% Dem	% Rep
2006	Bob Casey	Rick Santorum	2,392,984	1,684,778	3,281	4,081,043	708,206	D	58.6	41.3
2004	Jim Hoeffel	Arlen Specter	2,334,126	2,925,080	299,319	5,558,525	590,954	R	42.0	52.6
2000	Ron Klink	Rick Santorum	2,154,908	2,481,962	98,634	4,735,504	327,054	R	45.5	52.4
1998	Bill Lloyd	Arlen Specter	1,028,839	1,814,180	114,753	2,957,772	785,341	R	34.8	61.3
1994	Harris Wofford	Rick Santorum	1,648,481	1,735,691	129,189	3,513,361	87,210	R	46.9	49.4
1992	Lynn Yeakel	Arlen Specter	2,224,966	2,358,125	219,319	4,802,410	133,159	R	46.3	49.1
1991	Harris Wofford	Richard Thornburgh	1,860,760	1,521,986		3,382,746	338,774	D	55.0	45.0
1988	Joseph Vignola	John Heinz	1,416,764	2,901,715	48,119	4,366,598	1,484,951	R	32.4	66.5
1986	Bob Edgar	Arlen Specter	1,448,219	1,906,537	23,470	3,378,226	458,318	R	42.9	56.4
1982	Cyril Wecht	John Heinz	1,412,965	2,136,418	54,725	3,604,108	723,453	R	39.2	59.3
1980	Pete Flaherty	Arlen Specter	2,122,391	2,230,404	65,247	4,418,042	108,013	R	48.0	50.5
1976	William Green	John Heinz	2,126,977	2,381,891	37,485	4,546,353	254,914	R	46.8	52.4
1974	Pete Flaherty	Richard Schweiker	1,596,121	1,843,317	38,374	3,477,812	247,196	R	45.9	53.0
1970	William Sesler	Hugh Scott	1,653,774	1,874,106	116,425	3,644,305	220,332	R	45.4	51.4
1968	Joseph Clark	Richard Schweiker	2,117,662	2,399,762	106,794	4,624,218	282,100	R	45.8	51.9
1964	Genevieve Blatt	Hugh Scott	2,359,223	2,429,858	14,754	4,803,835	70,635	R	49.1	50.6
1962	Joseph Clark	James Van Zandt	2,238,383	2,134,649	10,443	4,383,475	103,734	D	51.1	48.7

Note: In 2004, 220,056 of the votes in the other vote column were cast for Constitutional candidate James Clymer. The remainder went to Libertarian Betsy Summers.

In 1998, 68,377 of the votes in the other vote column were cast for Constitutional candidate Dean Snyder. The others went to Libertarian Jack Iannantuono.

In 1994, 69,825 of the other votes were cast for Patriot Diane Blough with 59,115 cast for Libertarian Donald Ernsberger.

In 1992, the 219,319 other votes were cast for Libertarian John F. Perry.

Source: Rhodes Cook, Alice V. McGillivray, and Richard M. Scammon, *America Votes: Election Returns by State, 2005–2006*, vol. 27 (Washington, DC: CQ Press, 2007).

Thus, while descending into the details of these statewide elections introduces a host of matters peculiar to each election, the task adds an invaluable component to the overall effort to understand electoral change in Pennsylvania because it is vital to know the players and what they did.

Several illustrations quickly provide useful summaries of the overall partisan situation in Pennsylvania from 1960 to 2004 and in the process offer important contextual information for understanding these elections. First, Figure 3.1 presents an abbreviated version of the Pennsylvania Democratic party–strength figure introduced in chapter 1 (Figure 1.1). This figure portrays Pennsylvania Republican party strength in reverse by pointing out, among other things, the relative weakness of the state's Democrats from 1994 to 2004 (the solid line in the figure) alongside of the relatively strong Democratic presidential showing in the state during this period (the dotted line). (Incidentally, although this Democratic party–strength figure has been extended to cover the amazing result of the 2006 election, my full discussion of the Democratic surge in that most recent Keystone State election is located in this book's final chapter.)

Highlighting the post-1960 portion of the full Pennsylvania party-strength figure introduced in chapter 1, which I do in Figure 3.1, calls attention to a key question this chapter and the next one seek to answer: Why did Pennsylvania Republicans do so well in a period of impressive national Democratic strength in the state?

Further, Figures 3.2 and 3.3 recapitulate the main statewide election outcomes via line charts that speedily convey the trends found in more comprehensive form

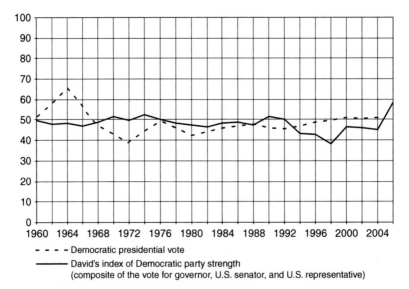

Fig. 3.1. Democratic Party Strength in Pennsylvania, 1960–2006

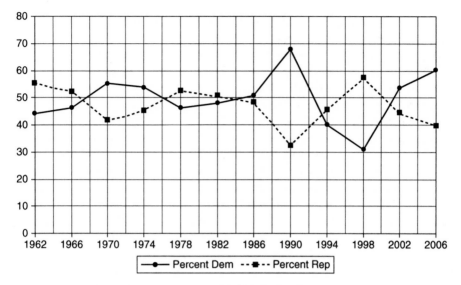

Fig. 3.2. Line Chart of Pennsylvania Vote for Governor, 1962–2006

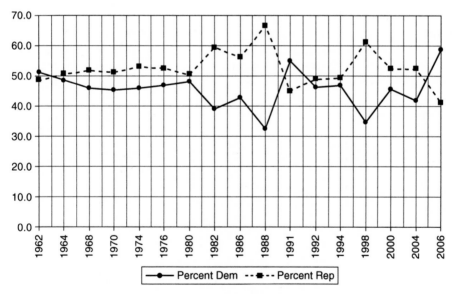

Fig. 3.3. Line Chart of Pennsylvania Vote for Senator, 1962–2006

in Tables 3.1 and 3.2. For example, Figure 3.2 shows how the Republicans and Democrats alternated in their control of the governorship every eight years since 1962. And Figure 3.3 underscores the remarkable success the GOP had in the senatorial elections, winning fourteen of the seventeen!

Finally, Figure 3.4 charts voter registration trends since 1960, demonstrating the advantage Democrats held throughout most of the post-1960 period. This figure also traces the steady rise during the last fifteen years of those voters choosing not to affiliate with a political party when registering to vote, a trend I address in more detail in chapter 5. (Incidentally, Table 5.5 in chapter 5 presents complete state party registration figures from 1926 to 2007.)

The partisan results of elections for the U.S. House of Representatives from Pennsylvania and for both houses of the state legislature are shown in Tables 3.3 and 3.4. After 1964, Democrats held a slight edge in the U.S. House delegation, widening their lead significantly in several post-Watergate elections and then losing their advantage appreciably after a controversial GOP-drafted redistricting plan went into effect in the early twenty-first century. Republicans controlled the Pennsylvania Senate for much of the post-1960 period. On the other hand, the Pennsylvania House alternated party control from 1960 until the late 1970s; then, close divisions continued for two decades until the GOP widened its advantage in the last few years before the 2006 election. Both of these summary tables of federal and state legislature results are useful guides as Pennsylvania's partisan development unfolds below.

Embedded in these tables and figures is a dramatic story of change that can be glimpsed by briefly comparing several benchmark election years. When the balloting in the 1960 elections had been concluded, Democrats in Pennsylvania had much to be pleased about. The party's presidential standard-bearer, John Kennedy, carried the state's thirty-two electoral votes with 51.1 percent, which were important votes in the Massachusetts Democrat's thin electoral college victory margin that

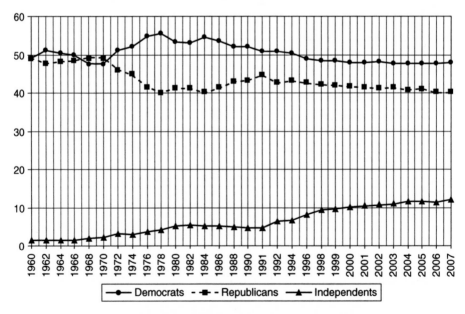

Fig. 3.4. Line Chart of Party Registration in Pennsylvania, 1960–2007

year.[1] It was the first time the Democratic national ticket had won the Keystone State since Franklin D. Roosevelt's third victory in the commonwealth in 1944. Governor David L. Lawrence, a Democrat, had two years remaining in his term, although he was constitutionally ineligible to run for reelection.[2] One U.S. senator, Joseph S. Clark, was a Democrat, having been elected narrowly in 1956. The other U.S. senator was a Republican, Hugh Scott, who had been narrowly elected in 1958. There were fourteen Democrats in the state's thirty-member U.S. House delegation, and Democrats held a 51.9 percent majority in the Pennsylvania House of Representatives while the Pennsylvania Senate was split evenly among Democrats and Republicans. Further, David's index of Democratic party strength, as shown in Figure 3.1, registered 49.6 percent in 1960.

Looking back to 1928 on all these measures reveals that the Democratic party had come a very long way in just thirty-two years, or to put it another way, the long-dominant Pennsylvania GOP had descended a considerable distance. To be precise, David's index of Democratic strength stood at 31.4 percent in 1928 (see Figure 1.1 in chapter 1), and in that year's election, Democrats won only 7.7 percent of the state House seats and held only 12.0 percent of the state Senate seats. There was not a single Democrat in the state's thirty-six-member U.S. House delegation! Finally, as mentioned in chapter 1, the Democratic presidential nominee that year, Al Smith, received only 33.9 percent of the vote.

Looking forward to the end of the forty-four years under study in this chapter and the next one, in 2004 another Massachusetts Democrat, John Kerry, again carried Pennsylvania's electoral votes. This time, however, the Democrat's 51.0 percent of the vote in 2004 yielded only twenty-one electoral votes because the state's slow population growth had been outstripped by rapid growth in other parts of the nation, resulting in the state's loss of seats in the U.S. House after each U.S. census from 1940 to 2000 and thus giving Pennsylvania a diminished role in the electoral college.[3] A Democrat, Edward G. Rendell, had been elected governor in 2002. Both U.S. senators were Republicans: Arlen Specter, who won his fifth term fairly handily in the 2004 general election, although he was nearly defeated in the Republican primary, and Rick Santorum, who was reelected to a second term in 2000 by a comfortable margin. There were seven Democrats in the state's nineteen-member U.S. House delegation after the 2004 elections. Republicans remained in control of the state legislature with 60.0 percent of the seats in the state Senate and 54.2 percent in the state House. Democrats had not controlled the Senate since the early 1980s, nor the state House since the 1994 elections. David's index of Democratic party strength in 2004 was 45.1 percent.

1. Kennedy won 303 electoral votes, just 35 more than the 1960 required majority of 268.

2. It wasn't until the early 1970s that Pennsylvania governors were permitted to seek reelection.

3. Of course, a state's electoral votes are determined by the number of representatives it is allotted in the U.S. House plus two votes for the number of U.S. senators every state has. The allocation of House seats is based on population and shifts after a new census is completed every ten years.

Table 3.3 Partisan Composition of Pennsylvania's U.S. House Delegation, 1928–2006

Election Year	Democratic #	Democratic %	Republican #	Republican %	Total
1928	0	0.0%	36	100.0%	36
1930	3	8.3%	33	91.7%	36
1932	12	35.3%	22	64.7%	34
1934	23	67.6%	11	32.4%	34
1936	27	79.4%	7	20.6%	34
1938	14	41.2%	20	58.8%	34
1940	19	55.9%	15	44.1%	34
1942	14	42.4%	19	57.6%	33
1944	15	45.5%	18	54.5%	33
1946	5	15.2%	28	84.8%	33
1948	15	45.5%	18	54.5%	33
1950	13	39.4%	20	60.6%	33
1952	11	36.7%	19	63.3%	30
1954	14	46.7%	16	53.3%	30
1956	13	43.3%	17	56.7%	30
1958	16	53.3%	14	46.7%	30
1960	14	46.7%	16	53.3%	30
1962	13	48.1%	14	51.9%	27
1964	15	55.6%	12	44.4%	27
1966	14	51.9%	13	48.1%	27
1968	14	51.9%	13	48.1%	27
1970	14	51.9%	13	48.1%	27
1972	13	52.0%	12	48.0%	25
1974	14	56.0%	11	44.0%	25
1976	17	68.0%	8	32.0%	25
1978	15	60.0%	10	40.0%	25
1980	13	52.0%	12	48.0%	25
1982	13	56.5%	10	43.5%	23
1984	13	56.5%	10	43.5%	23
1986	12	52.2%	11	47.8%	23
1988	12	52.2%	11	47.8%	23
1990	12	52.2%	11	47.8%	23
1992	11	52.4%	10	47.6%	21
1994	11	52.4%	10	47.6%	21
1996	11	52.4%	10	47.6%	21
1998	11	52.4%	10	47.6%	21
2000	10	47.6%	11	52.4%	21
2002	7	36.8%	12	63.2%	19
2004	7	36.8%	12	63.2%	19
2006	11	57.9%	8	42.1%	19

Source: For 1964 to 2006, biennial volumes of Richard M. Scammon, Alice V. McGillivray, and Rhodes Cook, *America Votes: 1964–2006*, vols. 5–27 (Washington, DC: CQ Press), and, for 1928 to 1962, Edward F. Cooke and Edward G. Janosik, *Pennsylvania Politics*, rev. ed. (New York: Holt, Rinehart and Winston, 1965).

How and why Pennsylvania arrived at this complex partisan configuration by 2004, not to mention the many twists and turns along the way, is the story told in detail in the rest of this chapter and in chapter 4.[4]

One additional general comparison is useful before embarking on our journey through forty-four years of Pennsylvania electoral change. This is done by examining county-by-county correlations among the candidates. In the analytical narrative that follows, I examine individual elections at various points. In fact, scattergrams of particularly intriguing correlation coefficients are displayed and analyzed with good effect. However, at the outset, it is instructive to view the larger picture by examining correlation matrices for all Democratic candidates for governor and U.S. senator from 1938 to 2004 along with the Democratic presidential nominees of the era, which is done in Tables 3.5, 3.6, and 3.7. These matrices reveal that the New Deal realignment by 1938 had ushered in a stable period of statewide two-party competition that persisted through the early 1970s. The correlations among the various Democratic candidates remained consistently high during this period—mostly above or slightly below 0.90.

Then, from the early 1970s until the elections of 2000, 2002, and 2004, much more inconsistency appears in the correlations. Some are still high, but more than a few drop quite low. For example, the Democratic U.S. Senate nominee in 1976 and the Democratic gubernatorial nominee in 1978 correlate at 0.31, and the Democratic gubernatorial nominees in 1986 and 2002 correlate at 0.40. To fully appreciate the reasons for those weak correlations, one needs to be familiar with the candidates—both Democrats and Republicans—involved in those elections. Unlike the situation at the presidential level, where the main players are familiar figures, major statewide politicians in the Keystone State are generally not as well known except to those who closely follow Pennsylvania politics on a regular basis. The same is true of the details of the state elections they contested.

For example, in regard to the 1976 and 1978 elections just mentioned, clearly Pennsylvania's voters were not showing a consistent partisan pattern when two major statewide candidates of the same party, just two years apart, receive county-level voting results that correlate at a weak 0.31. In the 1986 and 2002 instance, it is obvious from the 0.40 correlation coefficient that considerable partisan change had occurred during the sixteen years separating those two gubernatorial elections. What caused the discontinuities in these major statewide elections? Some of the reasons become apparent when the particulars of each of those four elections are explored. Other puzzling correlation patterns are also illuminated in a similar fashion. Then, in the latter part of chapter 4 at the end of the two-chapter analytical narrative of 1962 to 2004, I offer my overall explanation for the discordant correlation patterns found in Tables 3.4 and 3.5 as well as reasons for the consistent ones. All this is done with the aim of making sense of the myriad elections covered in this chapter.

---

4. Incidentally, less space is devoted to the early elections in an effort to move more quickly into the fascinating contests of the more unsettled period of the last three decades. Still, the elections of the 1960s and early 1970s are mined for all major developments even though fewer details from these earlier contests are offered.

Table 3.4 Partisan Composition of Pennsylvania's State Senate and House, 1928–2006

Election	Senate						House					
	Democratic		Republican				Democratic		Republican			
Year	#	%	#	%	Vac.	Total	#	%	#	%	Vac.	Total
1928	6	12.0%	44	88.0%		50	16	7.7%	192	92.3%		208
1930	4	8.0%	46	92.0%		50	22	10.7%	184	89.3%		206
1932	7	14.0%	43	86.0%		50	65	31.7%	140	68.3%		205
1934	19	38.0%	31	62.0%		50	88	42.7%	118	57.3%		206
1936	34	68.0%	16	32.0%		50	154	74.0%	54	26.0%		208
1938	24	49.0%	25	51.0%		49	79	38.0%	129	62.0%		208
1940	18	36.0%	32	64.0%		50	126	60.6%	82	39.4%		208
1942	18	36.0%	32	64.0%		50	76	36.5%	132	63.5%		208
1944	18	36.0%	32	64.0%		50	99	47.6%	109	52.4%		208
1946	16	32.0%	34	68.0%		50	37	18.0%	168	82.0%		205
1948	15	30.0%	35	70.0%		50	91	44.0%	116	56.0%	1	207
1950	20	40.0%	30	60.0%		50	87	42.0%	120	58.0%	1	207
1952	18	36.0%	32	64.0%		50	98	47.1%	110	52.9%		208
1954	23	46.0%	27	54.0%		50	112	53.6%	97	46.4%	1	209
1956	23	46.0%	27	54.0%		50	84	40.0%	126	60.0%		210
1958	22	44.0%	28	56.0%		50	108	51.4%	102	48.6%		210
1960	25	50.0%	25	50.0%		50	109	51.9%	101	48.1%		210
1962	23	46.0%	27	54.0%		50	102	48.6%	108	51.4%		210
1964	22	44.9%	27	55.1%	1	49	116	55.5%	93	44.5%		209
1966	20	43.5%	26	56.5%	4	46	99	48.8%	104	51.2%		203
1968	23	46.9%	26	53.1%	1	49	106	52.5%	96	47.5%	1	202
1970	26	52.0%	24	48.0%		50	113	55.7%	90	44.3%		203
1972	26	52.0%	24	48.0%		50	94	46.8%	107	53.2%		201
1974	29	59.2%	20	40.8%	1	49	114	56.2%	89	43.8%		203
1976	28	58.3%	20	41.7%	2	48	118	58.4%	84	41.6%	1	202
1978	27	54.0%	23	46.0%		50	100	49.5%	102	50.5%	1	202
1980	25	50.0%	25	50.0%		50	100	49.3%	103	50.7%		203
1982	23	46.0%	27	54.0%		50	103	50.7%	100	49.3%		203
1984	23	46.0%	27	54.0%		50	103	50.7%	100	49.3%		203
1986	23	46.9%	26	53.1%	1	49	103	50.7%	100	49.3%		203

Table 3.4 *(continued)*

Senate						House					
Election	Democratic		Republican				Democratic		Republican		
Year	#	%	#	%	Vac.	Total	#	%	#	%	Vac.	Total
1990	24	48.0%	26	52.0%		50	107	53.2%	94	46.8%	2	201
1992	24	48.0%	26	52.0%		50	105	51.7%	98	48.3%		203
1994	21	42.0%	29	58.0%		50	101	49.8%	102	50.2%		203
1996	20	40.0%	30	60.0%		50	99	48.8%	104	51.2%		203
1998	20	40.0%	30	60.0%		50	100	49.3%	103	50.7%		203
2000	20	41.7%	28	58.3%	2	48	99	48.8%	104	51.2%		203
2002	21	42.0%	29	58.0%		50	94	46.3%	109	53.7%		203
2004	20	40.0%	30	60.0%		50	93	45.8%	110	54.2%		203
2006	21	42.0%	29	58.0%		50	102	50.2%	101	49.8%		203

Source: Annual volumes of *The Book of the States, 1964–2006* (Lexington, KY: Council of State Governments), and Edward F. Cooke and Edward G. Janosik, *Pennsylvania Politics*, rev. ed. (New York: Holt, Rinehart and Winston, 1965).

Elections from 1962 to 1974

The state Republican party's conservative "old guard" and its more pragmatic, moderate faction led by Senator Scott pushed separate candidates for governor and U.S. senator in 1962. According to an account by Philip S. Klein and Ari Hoogenboom, they reached a compromise after "a severe factional fight."[5] The more conservative faction got to have a candidate for the Senate seat, U.S. Representative James E. Van Zandt of Altoona in Blair county, and Scott's moderates got William W. Scranton, a scion of a wealthy Scranton family, for their gubernatorial candidate. (The city of Scranton was named for his great-grandfather.)

A national columnist, Robert Novak, described Scranton as a moderate liberal with "an instinctive talent for ingratiating himself with the conservative party chieftains."[6] Paul B. Beers, a veteran Pennsylvania journalist, characterized Scranton and his place in the state's GOP as follows: "An authentic conservative could neither have won Pennsylvania nor governed it very well in the 1960s. Similarly, a true-believing liberal could have never been the Republican standard-bearer. If ever a

---

5. Philip S. Klein and Ari Hoogenboom, *A History of Pennsylvania*, 2nd ed. (University Park: Pennsylvania State University Press, 1980), 513. See also the account in Paul B. Beers, *Pennsylvania Politics Today and Yesterday: The Tolerable Accommodation* (University Park: Pennsylvania State University Press, 1980), 291–93.

6. Beers, *Pennsylvania Politics*, 276.

Table 3.5 Correlations of the Democratic Vote for President, Governor, and Senator, 1938–1958

	Gov 1938	Sen 1938	Pres 1940	Sen 1940	Gov 1942	Pres 1944	Sen 1944	Sen 1946	Gov 1946	Pres 1948	Sen 1950	Gov 1950	Pres 1952	Sen 1952	Gov 1954	Pres 1956	Sen 1956	Gov 1958	Sen 1958
G1938	1																		
S1938	0.99	1																	
P1940	0.91	0.90	1																
S1940	0.92	0.91	1.00	1															
G1942	0.91	0.89	0.89	0.90	1														
P1944	0.86	0.84	0.96	0.95	0.87	1													
S1944	0.87	0.86	0.95	0.96	0.88	0.99	1												
S1946	0.90	0.88	0.91	0.93	0.95	0.90	0.91	1											
G1946	0.89	0.86	0.89	0.91	0.94	0.87	0.89	0.99	1										
P1948	0.86	0.82	0.91	0.91	0.88	0.95	0.95	0.92	0.90	1									
S1950	0.88	0.86	0.91	0.92	0.92	0.91	0.92	0.94	0.93	0.95	1								
G1950	0.87	0.84	0.91	0.93	0.92	0.92	0.93	0.94	0.93	0.95	0.99	1							
P1952	0.83	0.81	0.90	0.90	0.84	0.96	0.95	0.87	0.85	0.95	0.92	0.92	1						
S1952	0.83	0.81	0.92	0.92	0.84	0.96	0.96	0.88	0.86	0.95	0.92	0.92	0.99	1					
G1954	0.86	0.81	0.89	0.90	0.89	0.90	0.91	0.92	0.92	0.95	0.95	0.95	0.92	0.92	1				
P1956	0.81	0.79	0.87	0.87	0.82	0.91	0.92	0.86	0.84	0.92	0.90	0.90	0.97	0.96	0.91	1			
S1956	0.84	0.81	0.90	0.90	0.85	0.92	0.93	0.88	0.87	0.93	0.92	0.92	0.97	0.96	0.95	0.97	1		
G1958	0.85	0.84	0.88	0.89	0.85	0.93	0.93	0.88	0.86	0.92	0.90	0.90	0.95	0.94	0.90	0.95	0.93	1	
S1958	0.87	0.86	0.90	0.91	0.88	0.91	0.92	0.92	0.90	0.93	0.92	0.92	0.92	0.93	0.93	0.93	0.92	0.97	1

Table 3.6 Correlations of the Democratic Vote for President, Governor, and Senator in Pennsylvania, 1960–1982

	Pres 1960	Gov 1962	Sen 1962	Pres 1964	Sen 1964	Gov 1966	Pres 1968	Sen 1968	Gov 1970	Sen 1970	Pres 1972	Sen 1974	Gov 1974	Pres 1976	Sen 1976	Gov 1978	Pres 1980	Sen 1980	Gov 1982	Sen 1982
P1960	1	0.92	0.93	0.87	0.80	0.89	0.93	0.89	0.82	0.63	0.90	0.69	0.76	0.90	0.66	0.73	0.86	0.72	0.70	0.87
G1962		1	0.96	0.90	0.86	0.94	0.90	0.94	0.83	0.64	0.87	0.67	0.82	0.92	0.71	0.73	0.86	0.71	0.75	0.90
S1962			1	0.92	0.86	0.96	0.93	0.94	0.88	0.67	0.89	0.78	0.78	0.93	0.60	0.81	0.90	0.81	0.74	0.88
P1964				1	0.85	0.93	0.96	0.93	0.92	0.69	0.90	0.67	0.77	0.93	0.67	0.73	0.86	0.75	0.70	0.83
S1964					1	0.84	0.82	0.86	0.81	0.63	0.76	0.59	0.75	0.86	0.68	0.67	0.74	0.65	0.75	0.82
G1966						1	0.93	0.92	0.93	0.68	0.88	0.77	0.77	0.91	0.59	0.83	0.89	0.84	0.75	0.86
P1968							1	0.94	0.91	0.66	0.93	0.71	0.77	0.94	0.65	0.77	0.90	0.79	0.71	0.86
S1968								1	0.86	0.61	0.90	0.64	0.80	0.92	0.71	0.68	0.86	0.70	0.72	0.86
G1970									1	0.71	0.85	0.76	0.78	0.87	0.52	0.82	0.82	0.80	0.68	0.78
S1970										1	0.61	0.53	0.51	0.66	0.45	0.56	0.63	0.57	0.52	0.66
P1972											1	0.65	0.79	0.92	0.69	0.69	0.88	0.71	0.68	0.85
S1974												1	0.48	0.70	0.20	0.94	0.77	0.91	0.60	0.70
G1974													1	0.77	0.67	0.55	0.68	0.48	0.62	0.69
P1976														1	0.74	0.78	0.93	0.79	0.81	0.94
S1976															1	0.31	0.55	0.26	0.57	0.72
G1978																1	0.84	0.95	0.69	0.77
P1980																	1	0.88	0.79	0.88
S1980																		1	0.71	0.76
G1982																			1	0.88
S1982																				1

Table 3.7 Correlations of the Democratic Vote for President, Governor, and Senator in Pennsylvania, 1982–2004

	Gov 1982	Sen 1982	Pres 1984	Gov 1986	Sen 1986	Pres 1988	Sen 1988	Gov 1990	Sen 1991	Pres 1992	Sen 1992	Gov 1994	Sen 1994	Pres 1996	Gov 1998	Sen 1998	Pres 2000	Sen 2000	Gov 2002	Pres 2004	Sen 2004
G1982	1																				
S1982	0.88	1																			
P1984	0.75	0.85	1																		
G1986	0.86	0.88	0.83	1																	
S1986	0.79	0.89	0.92	0.87	1																
P1988	0.74	0.84	0.99	0.84	0.91	1															
S1988	0.67	0.86	0.83	0.72	0.85	0.82	1														
G1990	0.71	0.60	0.61	0.74	0.62	0.61	0.82	1													
S1991	0.73	0.86	0.95	0.82	0.89	0.94	0.84	0.56	1												
P1992	0.64	0.80	0.96	0.74	0.87	0.96	0.87	0.48	0.95	1											
S1992	0.64	0.82	0.83	0.73	0.83	0.84	0.85	0.42	0.90	0.87	1										
G1994	0.70	0.76	0.79	0.77	0.79	0.77	0.83	0.52	0.82	0.82	0.73	1									
S1994	0.73	0.83	0.89	0.79	0.85	0.88	0.86	0.57	0.93	0.93	0.85	0.90	1								
P1996	0.59	0.77	0.87	0.67	0.79	0.86	0.88	0.42	0.92	0.95	0.88	0.81	0.95	1							
G1998	0.69	0.84	0.83	0.74	0.81	0.82	0.91	0.41	0.89	0.88	0.85	0.86	0.89	0.88	1						
S1998	0.67	0.78	0.77	0.75	0.77	0.77	0.79	0.51	0.75	0.75	0.71	0.77	0.77	0.72	0.74	1					
P2000	0.49	0.69	0.80	0.58	0.72	0.78	0.83	0.33	0.87	0.89	0.84	0.77	0.90	0.97	0.86	0.65	1				
S2000	0.61	0.78	0.90	0.71	0.82	0.89	0.87	0.47	0.92	0.95	0.84	0.83	0.92	0.96	0.90	0.77	0.95	1			
G2002	0.36	0.57	0.63	0.40	0.60	0.60	0.76	0.12	0.73	0.75	0.73	0.69	0.78	0.85	0.79	0.51	0.92	0.83	1		
P2004	0.37	0.59	0.71	0.47	0.63	0.70	0.76	0.23	0.79	0.83	0.79	0.68	0.83	0.92	0.79	0.58	0.98	0.90	0.93	1	
S2004	0.47	0.67	0.79	0.56	0.73	0.76	0.85	0.28	0.84	0.88	0.83	0.78	0.87	0.93	0.87	0.69	0.96	0.93	0.91	0.96	1

man fitted the political times and his party's needs, Bill Scranton did."[7] Scranton had worked in the State Department during President Eisenhower's administration and had been elected in 1960 to the U.S. House, where he became know as a centrist who backed President Kennedy's social agenda, including civil rights and the Peace Corps. Scranton labeled himself as follows: "I'm apt to be quite liberal on civil rights, conservative on fiscal policy and generally a middle-of-the-roader."[8]

The Democratic gubernatorial nominee was Mayor Richardson Dilworth of Philadelphia, an independently wealthy liberal from another prominent Pennsylvania family. (His great-grandfather had been a pioneer in Pittsburgh.)[9] Dilworth, along with Senator Clark, who was seeking reelection in 1962, pioneered in liberal politics in Philadelphia in the late 1940s and 1950s, as I mentioned in the discussion of the "programmatic liberals" in chapter 1. In the gubernatorial campaign, according to one account, Dilworth "cut up Scranton in two public debates, but his concrete program to promote industrial development, tourism, school district consolidation, and community colleges hurt him, particularly when he forthrightly admitted that if necessary he would call for new taxes."[10] Another account of the two 1962 gubernatorial debates, provided to the author by A. James Reichley, concludes that "the first debate was no better than a tie for Dilworth and the second a disastrous defeat."[11] Scranton won with 55.4 percent of the vote to Dilworth's 44.3 percent, the victor amassing a plurality of 486,291 votes.

7. Ibid.

8. Klein and Hoogenboom, *History of Pennsylvania*, 513.

9. Ibid.

10. Ibid.

11. January 24, 2007, letter to the author from A. James Reichley, a distinguished political scientist and writer who was Scranton's speechwriter in 1962 and then became the governor's legislative secretary. Here is Reichley's full account: "Going into the first debate Scranton was ahead in the polls but Dilworth was a slashing debater who had cut up a number of past opponents in Philadelphia. Dilworth was confident that he would polish off Scranton in the debates and go on to win the election. This view was widely shared by the press and both Republican and Democratic politicians. Scranton was highly nervous. The outcome of the first debate might fairly be described as a draw, which was a major victory for Scranton. After the debate the press, both state and national, flocked to Scranton's dressing room. Both they and we knew who was likely to be the next governor of Pennsylvania. Scranton's lead in the polls grew and Dilworth became desperate. Only one TV debate had been scheduled, but Dilworth paid for another and said he would debate an empty chair if Scranton did not show up—a favorite device at the time. Scranton did not respond but at the last minute entered the studio and took his place. Dilworth was visibly shaken and went off his game—at one point the moderator (who had been paid for by Dilworth) had to reprimand him for referring to notes, which was against the rules. When the debate ended, Dilworth followed Scranton into the hall and began shouting insults at him, saying among other things, that he was anti-Semitic, antiblack, and 'had never heard shots fired in anger' (Dilworth was an authentic hero in both world wars; Scranton had flown the hump in the Burma-India theatre in World War II)—all eagerly taken down by the press. It was really the end of the election, which up until then had been fairly close." Incidentally, in their account of the 1962 gubernatorial campaign, Klein

In the Senate race, Clark defeated the conservative Van Zandt, whom Beers described as an "inept" campaigner despite having served in Congress for eleven terms.[12] Clark received 51.9 percent of the vote to Van Zandt's 48.8 percent and had a plurality of 103,734 votes, or as Klein and Hoogenboom put it, "an enormous number of split ballots enabled Clark to triumph."[13]

Clark and Dilworth's county-level patterns correlate closely at 0.96, showing that, despite Dilworth's weakness in the governor's race, partisan patterns remained stable. Both candidates correlate closely with President Kennedy's winning pattern in 1960—at 0.93 for Clark and 0.92 for Dilworth. Figure 3.5, a scattergram of the close Clark–Dilworth correlation, conveniently arrays Pennsylvania's sixty-seven counties in a rough 1962 ranking from the most Republican, starting with Union County at the bottom of the best-fit line, to Philadelphia at the top. Later, toward the end of chapter 4, I present a scattergram of the Dilworth pattern with that of the next Philadelphia mayor to run for governor, Ed Rendell in 2002. Its depiction of a 0.62 correlation coefficient of the two Democratic candidates' county-level performance offers a striking picture of the change that had occurred in partisan patterns in Pennsylvania forty years later.

In 1964, President Lyndon Johnson crushed his Republican opponent, Barry Goldwater, the archconservative U.S. senator from Arizona, in Pennsylvania as well as nationally. Johnson won the state with 64.9 percent of the vote and with a whopping plurality of 1,457,297 votes. Still, in what might be a ticket-splitting record for the state, Senator Scott was able to win reelection with a plurality of 70,635 votes, or 50.6 percent to 49.1 percent for his Democratic opponent, Genevieve Blatt, state secretary of internal affairs since 1954 and a politician with impeccable liberal credentials.[14] While Scott said that he supported the entire Republican ticket, he went out of his way to distance himself from Goldwater, staying away from the national nominee when he visited Pennsylvania and actively seeking the support of Senator Jacob K. Javits of New York, a liberal Republican who refused to back Goldwater.[15]

---

and Hoogenboom noted without elaboration that Dilworth's "hot temper . . . cost him votes" (ibid., 513–14). Reichley added the following postscript to his account of the 1962 election: "Dilworth, whom I later got to know fairly well when he became president of the Philadelphia school board, a selfless act if ever there was one, and used to come up to Harrisburg to meet with us on school matters, was a distinguished public servant and an excellent mayor of Philadelphia."

12. Beers, *Pennsylvania Politics,* 295.

13. Klein and Hoogenboom, *History of Pennsylvania,* 514. The victory catapulted Scranton into presidential speculation for 1964. See William G. Weart, "Gov.-Elect Scranton, in National G.O.P. Spotlight, Denies Presidency Aim," *New York Times,* November 7, 1962.

14. For example, in 1947, she was a founder of Americans for Democratic Action. Beers, *Pennsylvania Politics,* 267.

15. Weart, "Outlook Cloudy in Pennsylvania," *New York Times,* October 24, 1964.

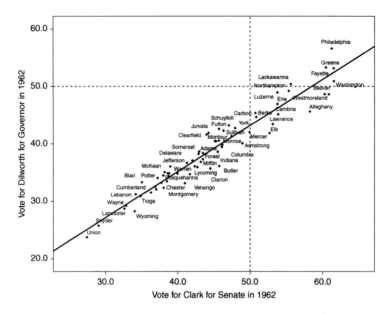

Fig. 3.5. Scattergram of the Democratic Vote for Senator and Governor in 1962

Blatt suffered from bitterness toward her on the part of supporters of her primary election opponent, state Supreme Court Justice Michael A. Musmanno, a prominent Italian American who had wide backing among party leaders. The primary was so close that it required five months of recounts and litigation before Blatt was declared the winner by 491 votes.[16] Klein and Hoogenboom concluded that she "never fully recovered from the internecine struggle."[17] In Allegheny County, she lost by just over 17,000 votes, while President Johnson won there by nearly 234,000, and she carried Philadelphia by only 140,000 to Johnson's nearly 431,000 plurality. Her strongest backer was Senator Clark. The *New York Times* reported that both Blatt and Clark accused Scott "of being a 'political two-timer,' who manages to get 'on both sides of everything.'"[18] Scott contended that Blatt lacked the experience to be a U.S. senator and "would only do the bidding of a party boss [presumably Clark]."[19] "Scott is behaving like a crybaby", the *Times* quoted Clark as saying. "He says he is running on his record, but complains when we honestly expose that record."[20]

The Democratic gubernatorial primary in 1966 featured the rise to statewide prominence of two dominant figures in the party's recent history, even though both were losers that year, one in the primary, the other in the general election.

16. Beers, *Pennsylvania Politics*, 269.
17. Klein and Hoogenboom, *History of Pennsylvania*, 518.
18. Weart, "Outlook Cloudy in Pennsylvania."
19. Ibid.
20. Ibid.

The primary loser was a thirty-four-year-old state senator, Robert P. Casey, a coal miner's son from Scranton who would eventually win the governorship in 1986 on his fourth try and become a legendary figure in Pennsylvania politics. Casey, a Catholic with a progressive record, had the unenthusiastic endorsement of Democratic leaders. He was beaten for the nomination by a maverick, millionaire electronics manufacturer from Philadelphia, Milton J. Shapp, who was described this way by Klein and Hoogenboom:

> A self-made man who started work at 22 cents an hour, Shapp had established a scholarship fund to place Negro and Puerto Rican youth in college, and he claimed to have suggested the Peace Corps to John F. Kennedy. Both the ADA [Americans for Democratic Action] and the Pennsylvania AFL-CIO (which had named him 1963 man of the year) supported Shapp, who proved to be an attractive candidate.[21]

Shapp spent lavishly on the campaign from his own money (eight times more than Casey),[22] filling "the airwaves with thousands of radio and television spots and thirty-four half-hour telecasts at prime time."[23] Shapp's theme was "Man Against the Machine," highlighting Casey's leadership endorsements. Casey said his opponent's theme more accurately should be "Man With a Money Machine."[24] Shapp prevailed narrowly with 543,057 votes to Casey's 493,886.

Governor Scranton's lieutenant governor, Raymond P. Shafer of Meadville in Crawford County, was the Republican nominee. Shafer benefited from his association with Scranton, whose four years in office were marked by progressive, energetic measures aimed at improving the state's weak economy. As Klein and Hoogenboom wrote, "It was [Scranton's] single-minded devotion to industrial development and to creating jobs, his willingness to utilize Federal and state funds and agencies to those ends, and his ability to engender enthusiasm that halted Pennsylvania's sickening decline."[25] Shafer's theme was straightforward: "Keep the good things happening to Pennsylvania." According to a *New York Times* report, Shafer ran on a platform that "was regarded as the most liberal Republican campaign document ever written in Pennsylvania."[26]

Shapp, who continued to spend heavily in the general election campaign, put forward bold ideas that generated considerable attention. For example, he proposed to establish a state human resources authority that would sell $5.5 billion in bonds to provide all Pennsylvanians a free college education, among other things, arguing

21. Klein and Hoogenboom, *History of Pennsylvania*, 521.

22. Beers, *Pennsylvania Politics*, 336.

23. Klein and Hoogenboom, *History of Pennsylvania*, 520.

24. Beers, *Pennsylvania Politics*, 336.

25. Klein and Hoogenboom, *History of Pennsylvania*, 520.

26. Ben A. Franklin, "Shafer Is Victor in Pennsylvania," *New York Times*, November 9, 1966.

that better-educated citizens would eventually generate tax revenue to pay off the bonds. He also urged replacing the state sales tax with an income tax.[27]

Shafer won with 52.1 percent of the vote to Shapp's 46.1 percent. The favorable public view of the performance of Governor Scranton coupled with Shafer's skillful identification with the successes of the outgoing Republican governor were key factors in the GOP win. Also, Shafer won about a third of the African American vote, a high figure for a Republican in the wake of the 1964 Goldwater campaign, which had alienated blacks nationwide.[28] Further, a CBS Vote Profile Analysis, cited by the *New York Times*, found evidence of "a white backlash—apparently focused on Mr. Shapp's Democratic party identification rather than on any statement or policy of his—in the Philadelphia and Pittsburgh areas."[29]

Also, Shapp, the first Jew to seek the Pennsylvania governorship, may have been hurt by anti-Semitic sentiment. The CBS analysis, according to the *Times*, noted that Shapp "appeared to have lost significantly in some areas of strongly Protestant mid-central Pennsylvania in what amounted to a religious backlash."[30] While Clark in 1962 and Blatt in 1964 had won Berks, Cambria, Carbon, Lawrence, and Mercer counties (and, for Blatt only, Clinton, Schuylkill, and York), Shapp did not carry any of them.

In the 1968 presidential election, the Democratic nominee, Hubert H. Humphrey, carried the state with 47.6 percent to 44.0 percent for Richard M. Nixon, the Republican standard-bearer and the national winner. George Wallace, the segregationist former Alabama governor, received 8.0 percent, roughly what he received in Illinois but 2 percentage points below his Michigan vote. As discussed in chapter 2, this was the first of three elections in the post-1960 period in which Pennsylvania would go with the losing national Democratic nominee—2000 and 2004 are the other two.

Despite Humphrey's success, Pennsylvania voters turned out of office another liberal Democrat, Senator Clark. Clark, termed by the veteran journalist Beers as "unquestionably . . . Pennsylvania's most unreconstructed liberal to reach high office,"[31] was a vocal critic of the Vietnam war, an advocate of strong gun-control legislation, and, in general, outspoken on his view of the social responsibilities of government. For example, when asked a question about taxes during the 1968 campaign, he responded: "Look, my friend, you can't sit on your rear end in Lebanon County and let the rest of the world go round. I'm not going to do anything to reduce your taxes. . . . The needs of the cities are too desperate."[32]

Clark was defeated by an ambitious, forty-two-year-old, four-term member of the U.S. House from a well-to-do Montgomery County family, Richard Schweiker,

27. Klein and Hoogenboom, *History of Pennsylvania*, 522.

28. Goldwater voted against the 1964 Civil Rights Act and supported senators from the South in their filibuster against the bill by voting against a cloture motion to shut off debate.

29. Franklin, "Shafer Is Victor." Shapp's pluralities in Philadelphia and Allegheny counties were anemic—109,816 and 35,872, respectively.

30. Ibid.

31. Beers, *Pennsylvania Politics*, 195.

32. Ibid., 196–97.

who received 51.9 percent of the vote to the incumbent's 45.8 percent. Schweiker had a liberal record on many issues; as a congressman, he voted for Medicare, federal rent subsidies, civil rights, and repeal of the right-to-work provision of the Taft-Hartley Act. On the other hand, he was a strong opponent of gun control, and as a U.S. senator opposed abortion, busing, and deficit spending.[33] Clark was able to hold on to only eight counties this time. He increased his margin of victory in Philadelphia to 194,203, but it wasn't enough to offset his losses in Allegheny (by almost 8,000 votes) and in eight other counties he had carried in 1962.[34]

Incidentally, Beers characterized Schweiker as "out of the Scott school of Pennsylvania politics, willing to sacrifice the complaints of the Old Guard and some of its votes in exchange for the support of ticket-switching Pennsylvanians tired of party labels. Some called this 'New Breed Republicanism.' Others, with greater accuracy, said it was probably the only way a Republican could win high office in contemporary Pennsylvania."[35] Beers also applied this comment to another Republican who would come to prominence in the mid-1970s—H. John Heinz.

The 1970 Democratic gubernatorial primary looked like a replay of 1966. Once again, the Democratic state organization endorsed Casey, and once again, Shapp would run against him, calling Casey's selection "old machine politics" from "the puppet show in Harrisburg."[36] Countering, Casey dubbed himself "the unbossed candidate," but events beyond his control would cause him to be seen as the candidate of a powerful Democratic leader. Mayor James H. J. Tate of Philadelphia was an old friend of Casey's from Scranton. In 1969, when Casey was being sworn in as auditor general, a post he won overwhelmingly in the 1968 elections, Tate was in the audience. The oath ends with the words "if you shall so long behave yourself well." Apparently, "behave yourself" was a common Pennsylvania Irish greeting. So, when U.S. District Court Judge William J. Nealon, an Irishman who was administering the oath, said those words, he raised his voice in a humorous manner. Casey, who is also an Irishman, smiled as he repeated them. The strange part of the story came a month later when someone asked Tate if he was going to support Casey. He replied, "If he behaves himself," jokingly referring to the oath. He proceeded to use these same words a couple of more times. However, people interpreted them to mean that Casey was the candidate of the "Philadelphia machine." Confronted by Tate's words on several occasions, Casey finally blurted, "I am no one's man. It is unfortunate the Mayor made that statement. It was demeaning." Still, Casey was unable to shake the impression that he was, in fact, the "machine" candidate, even after Tate said he favored an "open primary" and would vote for Shapp.[37]

---

33. Ibid., 436.
34. The eight counties were Berks, Cambria, Carbon, Elk, Erie, Lawrence, Mercer, and Westmoreland.
35. Beers, *Pennsylvania Politics*, 434.
36. Ibid., 374.
37. This episode of the primary campaign is related in ibid.

Shapp, while declining Tate's support, did seek and receive the help and endorsement of Mayor Pete Flaherty of Pittsburgh, a popular Democratic maverick. And, while Casey was liberal, Shapp was more so, or, as Klein and Hoogenboom put it: "Although Casey took a liberal stance, Shapp, who wished to substitute a graduated income tax for the 6 percent sales tax, who wanted state legislation to prevent Pennsylvanians from serving in undeclared wars, and who favored a liberal abortion reform, went considerably beyond him."[38] Shapp defeated Casey for the nomination by only 38,217 votes statewide. Shapp carried only twenty-seven counties, but his victory in Philadelphia put him over the top.

The Republican gubernatorial nominee was Shafer's lieutenant governor, Raymond J. Broderick, who had broken with the governor in 1969 over the issue of a state income tax. Faced with a major fiscal crisis midway through his term, Governor Shafer in 1969 had unsuccessfully pushed for an income tax. At that time, Pennsylvania was the largest state without an income tax. During the 1970 campaign, Broderick remained steadfast in his opposition to an income tax, claiming he could make up the projected shortfall of half a billion dollars by cutting state government employees and eliminating waste. Saying the state's fiscal "mess" called for a businessman rather than a politician to deal with it as governor, Shapp said that an income tax was needed and that it could be accompanied by a reduction in the 6 percent sales tax. (In office the following year, Shapp was able to enact the income tax along with a measure that exempted common household necessities like clothing from the sales tax.)[39]

The income tax debate was overshadowed late in the campaign when Broderick ran an ad campaign that attempted to portray Shapp as an enemy of "law and order" and a supporter of "rock-throwing" radicals at the 1968 Democratic National Convention in Chicago. In addition to radio and television ads that focused on this theme, Broderick purchased space in 105 newspapers across the state to run a cartoon of Shapp at the Chicago convention. It was widely known that Shapp had marched peacefully with other delegates one day and had contributed to a fund to pay bail for demonstrators arrested that week. However, in the cartoon, which portrayed some of the demonstrators throwing stones, Shapp was shown carrying a sign that read: "Bail money here for arrested demonstrators."[40] The *Philadelphia Bulletin* refused to print the cartoon. Shapp called it a "complete distortion," and after it appeared, he refused to shake Broderick's hand and turned down invitations to debate him. Broderick defended the ad as "symbolic" of "poor judgment" rather than, in the words of a *New York Times* report, "factually definitive." In the final week of the campaign, Shapp responded with his own ads on the air and in newspapers that denounced

---

38. Klein and Hoogenboom, *History of Pennsylvania*, 525.

39. Ibid., 526.

40. Donald Janson, "Shapp, Democrat, Elected Governor of Pennsylvania," *New York Times*, November 4, 1970.

Broderick's claims as misrepresentations and proclaimed his own commitment to law and order.[41]

Shapp defeated Broderick decisively with 55.2 percent of the vote to the Republican's 41.7 percent, amassing a plurality of 500,175 votes, the largest ever for a twentieth-century Democratic gubernatorial candidate up to that time. (Casey would later far exceed that showing when he won reelection in 1990.) Shapp took thirty-six counties, winning Allegheny by over 126,000 and Philadelphia by over 180,000.

Also in 1970, Senator Scott, who ran unopposed in the Republican primary, was challenged in the general election by Democratic state Senator William Sesler, a little known, forty-two-year-old Erie attorney. Sesler drew attention to Scott's age, 69, and hammered away at him for supporting Nixon's decision to send troops into Cambodia while vacillating himself on the Vietnam war issue. For his part, Scott, who had become the Senate's minority leader, ran ads proclaiming himself, "The most powerful Senator Pennsylvania ever had."[42] Scott won with 51.4 percent to Sesler's 45.4 percent.

The only major statewide contest in 1972 was for Pennsylvania's twenty-seven electoral votes. In Pennsylvania, President Nixon crushed his Democratic challenger, Senator George McGovern, an anti-Vietnam war liberal, with 59.1 percent of the vote to McGovern's 39.1 percent. Nationally, Nixon won with 60.7 percent to his opponent's 37.5 percent.

By 1974, when Pennsylvanians would go to the polls again to decide on the governorship and a U.S. Senate seat, the political environment would be quite different than it was when President Nixon won a forty-nine-state landslide victory just two years earlier. American involvement in the divisive Vietnam war virtually ended after the Paris peace accords were reached in early 1973, and, most important of all on the national scene, President Nixon had been forced to resign in August 1974 in the wake of the Watergate scandal.

Incumbents of both parties—Governor Shapp and Senator Schweiker—won second terms in 1974. Shapp, who had received high marks for his handling of the devastating floods that hit Pennsylvania as a result of Hurricane Agnes in June 1972 and for his energetic leadership in general, faced a relatively unknown Republican, Andrew (Drew) L. Lewis Jr., state GOP treasurer and president of a large employment agency. A year and a half before the election, it looked like Shapp might be opposed by Frank L. Rizzo, the self-proclaimed "toughest cop in America" who rode the white racial backlash to victory in the 1971 Philadelphia mayoral election. Rizzo, a high school dropout from Little Italy in south Philadelphia, rose through the city's police ranks to become "a volatile and charismatic" police commissioner. As Klein and Hoogenboom reported, "Rizzo's attitude toward blacks was the [1971] campaign's main issue, and Philadelphians knew that his shrewd slogan 'Rizzo

---

41. The account of the "law-and-order" campaign ad dispute is drawn from Janson, "Shapp, Democrat."

42. Ibid.

means business' referred to race relations rather than the economy.... Campaigning primarily in white, working-class areas, Rizzo promised to end permissiveness, to emphasize the three R's in the public schools, and not to raise taxes."[43] A Democrat, albeit a conservative one who supported Nixon's reelection in 1972, Rizzo vowed to oppose Shapp even if it meant switching parties. But, a series of setbacks tarnished his image by early 1974, and he didn't make the race.[44]

Lewis focused on scandals in the Shapp administration and vowed to eliminate graft and corruption. Shapp dismissed the scandals, saying that he was not involved and that he had fired anyone who was.[45] Lewis, who like many other Republicans that year was hurt by Watergate, received 45.2 percent of the vote to Shapp's 53.8 percent.

Senator Schweiker was opposed by the popular mayor of Pittsburgh, Peter Flaherty, who had been overwhelmingly reelected in Pittsburgh in 1973 with his " 're-Pete' " campaign. "By combining reform, economy, lower taxes, and sound fiscal management, Flaherty was popular with all but black voters," Klein and Hoogenboom observed.[46] A New York Times report stressed the similarities between Flaherty and Schweiker in the campaign: "The Senate contest . . . seemed almost devoid of issues, with both candidates taking firm stands against inflation, recession, big spending by the Federal Government and abortion on demand. Moreover, both men proposed tax cuts and the reinstitution of capital punishment for certain crimes.... Each described himself as an independent 'maverick' who stands outside his party's machinery."[47] Schweiker, who was supported by the political committee of the state AFL-CIO, touted his record in Washington and distanced himself from Watergate by emphasizing his cool relations with the Nixon White House, including his early call for the President to resign and the fact that he had been on Nixon's

43. Klein and Hoogenboom, *History of Pennsylvania*, 535.

44. Ibid., 530. For more on Rizzo, see Joseph R. Daughen and Peter Binzen, *The Cop Who Would Be King: Mayor Frank Rizzo* (Boston: Little, Brown and Company, 1977); and S. A. Paolantonio, *Frank Rizzo: The Last Big Man in Big City America* (Philadelphia: Camino Books, 2003). Interestingly, as early as 1968, Richard Nixon had his eye on Rizzo as a possible Republican candidate for mayor of Philadelphia. Paolantonio relates the substance of a July 1968 meeting between Nixon and Rizzo, which the former had sought during a campaign visit: "Nixon later told reporters that the two men talked about law enforcement, about the crisis confronting America's cities. What Nixon didn't say was that he approached Rizzo about running for mayor of Philadelphia—as a Republican. By then it was no secret, in or out of the city, that Rizzo had his sights on a political career. Nixon thought that the police commissioner's approach and ideals were perfectly suited for the new Republican majority which [Nixon] wanted to forge, a majority built with two constituencies that could be pried loose from the Democratic Party—southern whites and northeastern ethnics in the cities and suburbs" (ibid., 97).

45. James T. Wooten, "Shapp and Schweiker Win Contests in Pennsylvania," *New York Times*, November 6, 1974.

46. Klein and Hoogenboom, *History of Pennsylvania*, 530.

47. Wooten, "Shapp and Schweiker Win."

"enemies list."[48] Schweiker won with 53.0 percent of the vote to Flaherty's 45.9 percent. Schweiker captured only fifty-three counties this time, down from fifty-nine in 1968. In 1968, he won Allegheny County by 8,000 votes, but he lost it in 1974 by almost 93,000 to the Pittsburgh mayor. Flaherty took Philadelphia by a mere 4,491 compared to Shapp's nearly 223,000 vote margin there in the same election. The result in this Senate race exhibited a sharp east–west divide that reflected the regional identifications of Flaherty and Schweiker. In fact, the statewide patterns of the two 1974 Democratic candidates, Shapp and Flaherty, correlate at a weak 0.48.

The 1976 Election

Jimmy Carter, the Democratic presidential nominee in 1976, won Pennsylvania's twenty-seven electoral votes with 50.4 percent to President Gerald Ford's 47.7 percent in a close national election. Nationwide Carter had 50.1 percent to Ford's 48.0 percent. Without the Keystone State's electoral votes, Carter's victory margin would have been reduced to a single electoral vote.[49] Carter's pattern of support was similar to McGovern's in 1972, although McGovern was a big loser in the state. Carter and McGovern correlate at 0.93.

The victor in the U.S. Senate race that year, however, amassed an atypical victory pattern that broke with past patterns for reasons peculiar to the candidates running that year. The winner was Republican H. John Heinz III, an attractive, thirty-eight-year-old, multimillionaire Pittsburgh-area congressman with a moderate-to-liberal voting record; he was heir to the huge H. J. Heinz ketchup fortune. He defeated William J. Green III, a Democratic congressman from Philadelphia who in the mid-1960s had captured the U.S. House seat held for many years by his father. Heinz received 52.4 percent of the vote to Green's 46.8 percent in capturing the seat vacated by Senator Scott's retirement.

A major issue in the campaign became the several million dollars of his own money that Heinz was spending in the campaign. Green ran a barrage of newspaper and television advertisements highlighting Heinz's lavish personal spending. As a Green aide put it, "Bill sees [the election] as a battle of power and wealth against talent. He knows he could eat John Heinz for breakfast every morning, and it galls him to see the election so close."[50] A *Philadelphia Inquirer* reporter wrote that Green "bitterly mocked his millionaire Republican opponent for the U.S. Senate: 'I'm John Heinz . . . I'm wonderful and compassionate and I love children . . . that's why I voted with Richard Nixon to impound federal funds for education.'"[51]

---

48. Klein and Hoogenboom, *History of Pennsylvania*, 531.

49. Carter won 297 electoral votes; 270 were needed for victory.

50. Paul Critchlow, "A Good Mood and Big Lead Fade as Fortune Tells on Green," *Philadelphia Inquirer,* October 24, 1976.

51. Ibid.

For his part, Heinz met the personal spending issue head on, telling a *Washington Post* reporter the following:

> Listen, I'm John Heinz and there's nothing I can do about it. I'm not ashamed of being wealthy. I'm a Republican in a predominantly Democratic state, and I need to attract independently minded voters. I can't do that with a smile. Maybe there's a point to be made about money and politics, but not by Mr. Green. He inherited his congressional seat. . . . If I didn't spend this much money, I wouldn't stand a chance. . . . It's necessary to take my message through the media to the people.[52]

Heinz did extraordinarily well in western Pennsylvania, winning Allegheny County by nearly 212,000 votes and doing much better than statewide Republican candidates had previously done in surrounding southwestern counties. He lost Philadelphia overwhelmingly—by nearly 306,000 votes—but he did very well in the greater Philadelphia area, taking Montgomery, Chester, Delaware, Lehigh, and Lancaster by wide margins. The pattern was so different from the standard GOP winning configuration that Heinz's race, for example, correlates at a remarkably weak 0.19 with the victory pattern just two years earlier of his fellow Republican, Senator Schweiker, a Philadelphia-area politician. A scattergram of this correlation is displayed in Figure 3.6 to highlight the partisan discontinuity found between these two elections. Notice Allegheny and the southwestern counties prominently displayed in the upper left-hand corner, illustrating a very low level of support for Schweiker but a very high level of support for "favorite son" Heinz. Also, notice Philadelphia, where Heinz did markedly worse than Schweiker.

Obviously, this election highlighted the classic "friends-and-neighbors" influence that V. O. Key Jr. pointed out decades ago in studying state elections in the American South, that is, the tendency of voters to favor candidates from their home county or region.[53] The Philadelphia–Pittsburgh rivalry makes its way into more than a few statewide elections in some fashion because these two large metropolitan areas frequently are the homes of major state politicians.[54] Keep in mind, however, that when Key isolated the phenomenon, he did so within the context

---

52. William Claiborne, "Heinz Media Cost Is the Biggest Issue in Pa. Senate Race," *Washington Post,* October 30, 1976.

53. V. O. Key Jr., *Southern Politics in State and Nation* (New York: Alfred A. Knopf, 1949), 37–41.

54. Jack M. Treadway wrote: "The dominance of the two major cities and their respective metropolitan areas is manifested most clearly in U.S. Senate elections. Seven senators each came from Philadelphia and Allegheny Counties [during the twentieth century], and all seventeen individuals elected during the century resided in the Philadelphia or Pittsburgh metropolitan areas." Treadway also reported that, of the twenty men elected governor in the twentieth century, eleven came from these two metropolitan areas. Jack M. Treadway, *Elections in Pennsylvania: A Century of Partisan Conflict in the Keystone State* (University Park: Pennsylvania State University Press, 2005), 197–98.

of Democratic primaries in a one-party region. In the Pennsylvania two-party context, the "friends-and-neighbors" factor is tempered in varying degrees by the pull of partisan attachment. Thus, although Heinz in 1976 ran well behind his fellow Republican from the Philadelphia area, Schweiker, in 1974, in Philadelphia itself, Heinz matched Schweiker in most of the then heavily Republican Philadelphia suburban counties.[55]

An interesting side note to the 1976 election occurred in the auditor general's race to replace the now forty-four-year-old Robert P. Casey, who was stepping down. A sixty-six-year-old Robert E. Casey from Cambria County ran to replace him and won against two more widely known Democratic politicians while spending only $750. Of this election, the "real" Casey complained: "This confirms a positive name recognition I knew was there. The unfortunate thing is I think the people were fooled. Unfortunately, this fellow from Johnstown is the unwitting, undeserving beneficiary, and frankly, I don't like being used."[56]

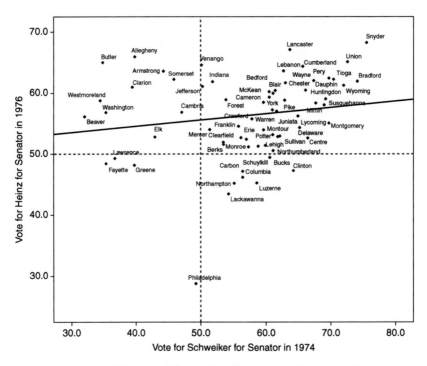

Fig. 3.6. Scattergram of the Republican Vote for Senator in 1974 and 1976

55. Of course, further complicating the process of sorting out the "friends-and-neighbors" influence in the 1974 and 1976 Senate elections is the fact that Schweiker's Democratic opponent was the mayor of Pittsburgh and Heinz's Democratic opponent was a Philadelphia congressman.

56. Beers, *Pennsylvania Politics*, 412.

The 1978 Election

Republican Richard L. Thornburgh, a former federal prosecutor from Pittsburgh with a stellar reputation for fighting political corruption, captured the governorship in 1978 with 52.5 percent of the vote. He defeated another Pittsburgher, Mayor Peter Flaherty, the maverick Democrat who trimmed taxes in Pittsburgh and ran a reform-oriented, corruption-free administration.[57] Flaherty received 46.4 percent of the vote in an election full of atypical alliances, especially Thornburgh's successful courting of African Americans in Philadelphia.[58]

Corruption formed the backdrop of the election. As Paul Beers wrote, outgoing Governor Shapp, who was constitutionally barred from seeking a third term, "concluded his tenure with the reputation, justified or not, of presiding over one of the most corrupt administrations in the Commonwealth's modern history."[59] For this reason, among others, Flaherty repudiated any support from Shapp, writing him a public letter saying so.[60] Thornburgh, who served as head of the Justice Department's criminal division under President Ford, had played a critical role in aiding the successful anticorruption investigations and prosecutions of U.S. Attorney David W. Marston of Philadelphia. In January 1978, a Democratic congressman under investigation, U.S. Representative Joshua Eilberg of Philadelphia, convinced President Carter to fire Marston; Eilberg was indicted later in the year and lost his bid for reelection.[61] As Klein and Hoogenboom put it, "[The Marston/Eilberg affair] enabled Thornburgh to capitalize on his career as a fighter of crime and corruption."[62] William W. Scranton III, the son of the former governor, was the Republican nominee for lieutenant governor, strengthening the GOP effort by associating Thornburgh with the accomplishments of Governor Scranton's administration.[63]

Also on the ballot in November in Philadelphia was a proposed change to the city's charter to allow Mayor Rizzo to run for a third term. The city's blacks,

---

57. Flaherty won the Democratic nomination in a hotly contested three-way race against Lieutenant Governor Ernest P. Kline, who finished a distant third, and former state auditor Robert P. Casey, who lost his third gubernatorial bid with 445,146 votes to Flaherty's 574,889. See ibid., 411–12, for more on the 1978 Democratic primary, which featured another Robert P. Casey on the ballot as a candidate for lieutenant governor. This Casey was a biology teacher from Monroeville in Allegheny County who spent $4,000 on his campaign and yet won the nomination over thirteen other candidates!

58. Klein and Hoogenboom, *History of Pennsylvania*, 535.

59. Beers, *Pennsylvania Politics*, 402.

60. Ibid., 446. The letter read in part: "I do not seek nor do I accept your endorsement for my candidacy. I also request that you make no statements on behalf of my candidacy."

61. Robert E. Taylor, "Eilberg Loses Reelection Bid," *Philadelphia Evening Bulletin,* November 8, 1978.

62. Klein and Hoogenboom, *History of Pennsylvania*, 535.

63. Ibid.

who had poor relations with the mayor, vehemently opposed the charter change and turned out in record numbers, helping to defeat the measure by a two-to-one margin. Thornburgh, who opposed the charter change and vigorously campaigned for black support in Philadelphia, was a major beneficiary of the charter fight. As a *Philadelphia Evening Bulletin* reporter, Mark Manoff, put it, "Much of Thornburgh's support [in Philadelphia] came from black voters attracted to the polls in record numbers to vote against Mayor Rizzo's campaign to change the city's charter; Thornburgh carried 17 of the city's 25 predominantly black wards."[64] An Associated Press–NBC News Election Day poll, as cited by Manoff, estimated that Thornburgh won 56 percent of the black vote statewide. Beers further explained Thornburgh's success in attracting African Americans in Philadelphia and elsewhere this way: "[B]lacks went to Thornburgh in droves, partly because he sought their vote and partly because of Flaherty's close identification with white working-class neighborhoods and antibusing positions."[65] In explaining why "traditionally Democratic blocs of urban voters" rebuffed Flaherty, Klein and Hoogenboom noted: "While Thornburgh courted blacks and wooed labor, Flaherty failed to return calls from union leaders and took the black vote for granted, despite the fact that blacks were cool to him in Pittsburgh and hostile to Rizzo (a fellow Democrat) in Philadelphia."[66] Or, as a Reading state senator said, "Pete Flaherty spent his entire campaign running away from the Democratic Party. On election day, the Democratic Party ran away from him."[67]

Thornburgh's winning plurality was 228,154 votes. In Philadelphia, where Democrats outnumbered Republicans by 572,506 registered voters, Thornburgh lost by only 34,875 votes, and, in Allegheny County, where Democrats outnumbered Republicans by 299,398, the Republican lost by just 17,870 votes. Thornburgh also won by substantial margins in the counties surrounding Philadelphia, and he even captured the Democratic strongholds of Lackawanna and Luzerne. The unusual alliances and events of this election are reflected in the correlation data. Flaherty's 1978 county-level pattern correlates with Governor Shapp's 1974 reelection pattern at a relatively weak 0.55, or, to look at it from the Republican side, Thornburgh's pattern correlates with the 1974 GOP gubernatorial nominee, Lewis, at 0.57 and with Republican Heinz's 1976 U.S. Senate victory at 0.30. The latter amazing GOP correlation is depicted in Figure 3.7. On the other hand,

64. Mark Manoff, "Flaherty Loses in Upset," *Philadelphia Evening Bulletin*, November 8, 1978.

65. Beers, *Pennsylvania Politics*, 447.

66. Klein and Hoogenboom, *History of Pennsylvania*, 536. Beers reported further on Flaherty's problem with African Americans, a core Democratic constituency, quoting a University of Pittsburgh authority: "Pitt Professor James V. Cunningham, a Democratic ward leader, traced Flaherty's trouble with black voters to the 1973 Pittsburgh mayoralty primary. Flaherty didn't reverse the situation in his 1974 losing bid for the U.S. Senate. By 1978, said Cunningham, college educators and independents joined blacks in being fearful of what they perceived as Flaherty's intransigence"(ibid., 447).

67. Ibid., 447.

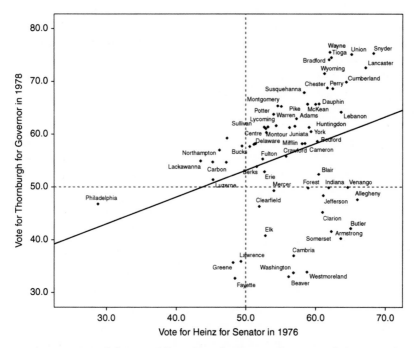

Fig. 3.7. Scattergram of the Republican Vote for Senator in 1976 and Governor in 1978

Flaherty, the "maverick," as he was regularly referred to in the press, exhibited a degree of personal consistency in 1978—he correlates at a high 0.94 with his own losing pattern in the 1974 Senate election.[68]

The 1980 Election

Ronald Reagan, the Republican presidential nominee in 1980, carried Pennsylvania with 49.6 percent of the vote to President Carter's 42.5 percent; the independent John B. Anderson received 6.4 percent. The Pennsylvania result mirrored the national outcome except that, in the Keystone State, Reagan, a former two-term governor of California, ran a percentage point below his 50.7 percent national average.

---

68. Flaherty, who died in April 2005, was described by Terry Nichols Clark, an urban politics scholar at the University of Chicago, as "a brilliant pioneer in the new fiscal populist mayoral style," adding: "He invented a whole style of politics . . . he came from a left Democratic Party background and he combined it with fiscal conservatism, fighting business, fighting labor unions, fighting interests groups of all sorts." James O'Toole, "Pete Flaherty Dies at 80," *Pittsburgh Post-Gazette*, April 19, 2005. O'Toole noted that Flaherty, in his efforts to win state-wide office, "traveled a bumpier political road [compared to] his successes as mayor."

In the U.S. Senate race, former Mayor Flaherty made his third and final bid for statewide office since 1974. The Republican nominee to replace the retiring Senator Schweiker was Arlen Specter, a former Philadelphia district attorney who won his first elective office as a Democrat. Specter, a moderate who ran unsuccessfully for the GOP nomination for U.S. senator in 1976 and for governor in 1978, outspent Flaherty two-to-one aiming to overcome the Democrat's edge in name recognition.[69] A *Philadelphia Evening Bulletin* reporter, Philip Lentz, wrote: "[Specter] is counting on his moderate image to attract Democrats turned off by Flaherty and [on] his popularity in Philadelphia and its suburbs to offset Flaherty's vote in the west."[70] On the race in general, Lentz continued: "The battleground has been the traditional Democratic voting blocs—blacks, labor, liberals and party regulars. Flaherty ignored these voters in the past, but this time he shelved his image as 'nobody's boy' and tried to portray himself as a regular Democrat."[71]

The results of Flaherty's outreach efforts were mixed. Flaherty did receive support from Philadelphia's black ward leaders and from the head of Pittsburgh's NAACP branch; he also won the endorsements of a handful of unions and was backed by most party leaders. Specter, however, also received some key endorsements from labor and from well-known, popular black leaders in Philadelphia.[72] Central to this election, of course, was the simple fact that Specter was popular in his home base of Philadelphia, as was Flaherty in his base of western counties around Pittsburgh. Thus, it is not surprising that there was a strong east–west component in the election's county patterns.

On Election Day, Flaherty turned in his strongest performance of his three statewide races, but he still came up short, getting 48.0 percent of the vote to Specter's 50.5 percent. The Republican's statewide plurality was 108,013. Flaherty carried twenty-three counties, winning the west as expected, even capturing some Republican-leaning counties there. However, despite a voter registration edge of 281,465 in Allegheny, Flaherty did not do as well as anticipated in his home county; he won there by a margin of only 151,494. While he did win by rather large margins in Beaver, Butler, Cambria, Erie, Fayette, Lackawanna, Lawrence, Washington, and Westmoreland, in the remainder of the counties he took, he won by only slight margins. Specter, on the other hand, carried forty-four counties with the big prize being Philadelphia. Despite a Democratic registration edge of 539,553, Specter won "the City of Brotherly Love" by 11,923 votes, even though Reagan lost there by 177,145 votes. Specter won strong pluralities in the southeastern counties surrounding Philadelphia.

Not surprisingly given their different geographic bases in this Senate election, Specter's victory pattern bore little resemblance to fellow Republican Heinz's winning pattern of four years earlier. Their pattern yields a correlation coefficient of 0.26.

69. Philip Lentz, "Senate Race: Tight to the Wire," *Philadelphia Evening Bulletin*, November 2, 1980.

70. Ibid.

71. Ibid. See also Kathy Kiely, "East Again Costs Pete the Election," *Pittsburgh Press*, November 5, 1980.

72. Ibid.

Similarly, Heinz and Thornburgh were weakly correlated at 0.30 because Thornburgh, a Pittsburgh politician, did exceptionally well in Philadelphia due to the odd circumstances of that 1978 election; that correlation was depicted in Figure 3.7. Thornburgh and Specter, however, correlate at a very high 0.95. Of course, both Republicans ran against the same Democrat, Flaherty, who managed in his three straight statewide defeats to turn in three very consistent county-level patterns. The strong Thornburgh-Specter relationship is illustrated in the scattergram in Figure 3.8.

The 1982 Election

The 1982 election was a major national setback for President Reagan and the Republican party caused mainly by a sharp economic recession blamed on the President's economic policies. The Republican party lost twenty-six seats in the U.S. House, although the partisan balance in the U.S. Senate did not change. Pennsylvania was hit hard by the recession. Unemployment reached 11 percent in 1982, one of the highest in the nation, and the health of many of Pennsylvania's key industries (steel, coal mining, and manufacturing) was not good. Despite the economic woes, neither Republican incumbent up for reelection in 1982—Governor Thornburgh nor Senator Heinz—drew one of the state's more prominent Democrats as a challenger.

Senator Heinz's GOP opponent was Cyril Wecht, an Allegheny County commissioner and former county coroner, who was not widely known outside of the Pittsburgh area. He lacked the money to change that situation and was not taken seriously. A *Philadelphia Inquirer* headline near Election Day said it all: "The Race for Senator That No One Seemed to Notice."[73] Heinz won with 59.3 percent of the vote to Wecht's 39.2 percent. Taking no chances, Senator Heinz buttressed his image as a moderate at every turn in 1982, distancing himself from Reagan's fiscal policies, the President's cuts in education programs, his increases in defense spending, and his deficit spending, among other issues.[74]

Governor Thornburgh's opponent, three-term U.S. Representative Allen Ertel of Lycoming County in central Pennsylvania, was a credible challenger with several assets, although he was not widely known. A former prosecutor, he was a moderate with a reputation for fairness and honesty. He won endorsements of the state AFL-CIO and the Pennsylvania State Education Association (PSEA). PSEA had backed Thornburgh in 1978, but the organization contended that the governor had gone back on his word to raise state funds for education.[75]

---

73. Larry Eichel and Howard S. Shapiro, "The Race for Senator That No One Seemed to Notice," *Philadelphia Inquirer*, October 31, 1982. Wecht was a compelling public speaker, according to Eichel and Shapiro. Of him they wrote: "Few candidates anywhere delivered more blistering attacks this fall against President Reagan's economic policies and priorities."

74. Ibid.

75. Robert Kilborn Jr., "Pennsylvania Governor's Race: Incumbent's Chief Foe: The Economy," *Christian Science Monitor*, May 13, 1982.

Thornburgh once again outraised and outspent his rival, this time by four to one.[76] David Broder of the *Washington Post* assessed the election as follows in early October: "In this year of embattled Republican governors, Pennsylvania's Richard L. Thornburgh sticks out like a well thumb." One reason Broder pointed to was the Governor's leadership during the Three Mile Island nuclear power plant accident in April 1979. "With public uncertainty about the danger verging on panic," Broder wrote, "Thornburgh drew widespread praise for striking the necessary note of calm and control. When President Carter visited the state, he praised Thornburgh for 'a superlative job.' "[77] Broder added that Thornburgh cracked down on corruption, submitted all of his budgets on time, and avoided an increase in taxes.

And, perhaps most importantly, according to Broder, Thornburgh is a skillful politician. Friends and enemies alike depict Thornburgh as "a wooden public speaker who generates little electricity in a room and conveys little warmth on television. He is surrounded, they say, by a tightly knit circle suspicious of outsiders." Broder quoted

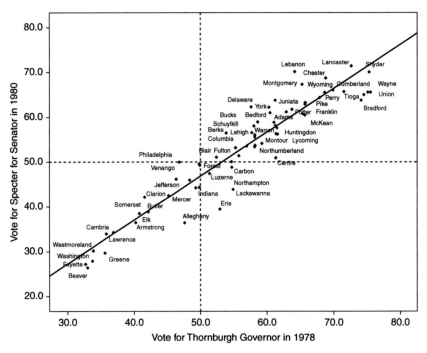

Fig. 3.8. Scattergram of the Republican Vote for Governor in 1978 and Senator in 1980

76. William Robbins, "Key Pennsylvania Race Dominated by Optimism," *New York Times*, October 6, 1982.

77. David S. Broder, "The 1982 Elections: Pennsylvania Governor's Race; GOP Ebb Tide Hasn't Caught Thornburgh," *Washington Post*, October 6, 1982.

one Republican elected official's view of Thornburgh: "There is a dark underside to Dick's personality. He can be mean and vindictive. When you're around him, you sense there's still a lot of prosecutor in his makeup. I'm surprised his personality defects haven't hurt him politically, but they haven't. He's been very skillful politically."[78]

During the campaign, Thornburgh took credit for increasing spending on human services and education and improving the business climate. Ertel disputed these claims, asserting that Thornburgh was responsible for higher property taxes, rising utility costs, and doing nothing to alleviate the economic crisis facing Pennsylvanians.[79] Thornburgh also drew complaints from black leaders. K. Leroy Irvis, a prominent African American state legislator, criticized Thornburgh for cuts in welfare and unemployment insurance that, he said, could result in the death of blacks who are not able to buy food or find shelter. Irvis recounted an encounter Thornburgh had with an unemployed Erie woman who was complaining to the Governor about not being able to find a job or pay her bills. Apparently, Thornburgh offered an unsympathetic reply: "Things are tough all over."[80] For his part, Thornburgh said he anticipated significant African American support. "Black voters have proved before that they are not led around by the nose by a bunch of Democratic politicians."[81]

A few days before the election, Thornburgh encountered a small group of hecklers outside of his New Castle headquarters. One detractor shouted: "We're gonna put you in the unemployment line."[82] As a *Philadelphia Inquirer* reporter wrote in a postelection analysis, the remark seemed "an empty threat."[83]

When the votes came in, the threat was a lot more real that most people realized. Ertel came within 100,431 votes of pulling off an upset. The Democrat won 48.1 percent to Thornburgh's 50.8 percent. The morning after the election, Republicans were shell-shocked by Thornburgh's slim margin. A *New York Times* reporter, William Robbins, began his postelection article this way: " 'Let's everyone take a deep breath,' Gov. Dick Thornburgh told his supporters this morning at a delayed celebration of a victory that had not come as early or as handily as the experts had expected. It was a victory that fell considerably short of the margin his supporters

---

78. Ibid.

79. Ertel made his share of mistakes, including refusing to release his income tax returns as Thornburgh had done. Ertel said he didn't want to be "whipsawed" by charities. Among other blunders, Ertel criticized Thornburgh for using his twenty-two-year-old son in a campaign ad touting himself as sponsoring education programs for the mentally retarded. Thornburgh's son had endured brain damage since a car accident in 1960 in which Thornburgh's first wife, Ginny, had died. David Morrison, "The Victory Recipe for Thornburgh," *Philadelphia Inquirer*, November 7, 1982.

80. Paul Nussbaum, David Morrison, and Steve Stecklow, "Blacks at Issue in Pa. Race," *Philadelphia Inquirer*, October 25, 1982.

81. Ibid.

82. David Morrison, "Victory Recipe for Thornburgh."

83. Ibid.

and other experts here had looked for. . . ."[84] Robbins continued: "It now appears that a Democratic tide, with some crosscurrents, was running as strongly here in Pennsylvania, a state hit hard by the recession, as anywhere else in the country."[85]

Thornburgh carried Allegheny County by 6,445 votes this time, but he lost Philadelphia by 150,131 votes, in sharp contrast to his Philadelphia performance in 1978. His support among African Americans dropped from over 50 percent in 1978 to an estimated 18 percent in 1982.[86] Overall, the sharp contrast with Thornburgh's first gubernatorial victory is indicated by the tepid correlation between the county-level patterns of his two elections—coefficient of 0.70. Thornburgh got caught up in, as a *Philadelphia Inquirer* reporter put it, "the effectiveness in some areas of the Democratic appeal for straight-ticket voting as a protest against Reaganomics."[87] Pennsylvania Democrats were also able to increase their percentage of U.S. House seats in 1982 and to take back control of the state House of Representatives, which they had lost in 1978, by capturing four Republican seats in 1982. The Democrats kept their state House majority until 1994, a year in which the electoral tide was even stronger for the Republicans than 1982 was for the Democrats.

The 1986 Election

There were no major Pennsylvania statewide contests in the presidential election year of 1984. President Reagan, who rebounded in popularity after the economy improved in 1983, was overwhelmingly reelected, carrying all states except the home state of his Democratic opponent, former Vice President Walter Mondale of Minnesota. Nationwide Reagan received 58.8 percent to Mondale's 40.6 percent. However, in Pennsylvania it was much closer: Reagan 53.3 percent; Mondale 46.0 percent.

In 1986, Pennsylvania made up in a big way for sitting out the 1984 election at the statewide level. It was a banner election year with a titanic, down-to-the wire contest for the governorship along with the relatively easy first reelection of Senator Specter.

The Republican party avoided a primary fight by coalescing around Lieutenant Governor William W. Scranton III as their candidate for governor and, in the words of a *New York Times* reporter, "sat back united and flush with money" while a pair of candidates waged an aggressive, rancorous primary battle for the Democratic gubernatorial nomination.[88] The two were Robert P. Casey, the former two-term state auditor general from Scranton who lost hard-fought, close races for the Democratic gubernatorial nomination in 1966, 1970, and 1978, and Ed Rendell, Philadelphia's popular two-term district attorney.

84. William Robbins, "G.O.P. Shaken in Pennsylvania," *New York Times*, November 4, 1982.

85. Ibid.

86. Larry Eichel, "Overall, the Day Was Democratic in Penna.," *Philadelphia Inquirer*, November 4, 1982.

87. Ibid.

88. William K. Stevens, "Pennsylvania Democrats Divided in Sharp Primary," *New York Times*, May 18, 1986.

Casey, now 54, had virtually retired from politics after his third loss eight years earlier, returning to his home town to practice law in the Scranton office of a major Philadelphia law firm and to raise his eight children. This time he campaigned as "the real Bob Casey" after other men with the same name piggybacked off of him in the 1970s to run low-budget campaigns, one of them actually winning the Democratic nomination for lieutenant governor in 1978, the year the "real" Casey lost the gubernatorial nomination to Pete Flaherty. Rising from the politically dead to give it one last shot, Casey made economic revitalization the central theme of his campaign and attracted to him a talented campaign staff, including James Carville, his campaign manager, and speechwriter Paul Begala (Carville and Begala became famous as political consultants in the 1990s for their role in Bill Clinton's 1992 presidential victory).[89] Described in a *New York Times* article as "a liberal who built a reputation as a tough law-enforcement official," Rendell, forty-two, also made economic development the center of his campaign. In addition, he attacked public utilities for charging excessively high rates.[90]

The race was marked by negative television ads portraying Rendell as corrupt and Casey as a "tool of the interests."[91] According to a political consultant, Thomas E. (Doc) Schweitzer, "What you've got is two of the most honest pols in the state running the most vicious campaigns."[92] Rendell, although well known in Philadelphia, battled low name recognition across the rest of the state, whereas Casey had already run in five statewide elections prior to this one, two successful ones for auditor general and his three previously unsuccessful bids for governor. Casey won by 160,000 votes with victory margins of at least two to one in virtually all of the counties outside of the Philadelphia area and four to one in some western Pennsylvania counties. Likewise, Rendell carried Philadelphia and its surrounding counties by a two-to-one margin.[93] Casey's choice as his running mate, state Senator Mark Singel of Johnstown in Cambria County, narrowly won the lieutenant governor's nomination in the primary.[94] Incidentally, Scranton selected state Senator Mike Fisher of

---

89. Thomas Ferrick Jr., "Casey Beats Rendell in Primary," *Philadelphia Inquirer*, May 21, 1986. Casey's team also included Pat Caddell, President Carter's pollster, and Robert Shrum, a well-known media consultant.

90. Stevens, "Pennsylvania Democrats Divided."

91. Ibid.

92. Ferrick, "Casey Beats Rendell."

93. Ferrick, "Region Was Good to Rendell, Better to Edgar," *Philadelphia Inquirer*, May 22, 1986. The regional nature of the voting prompted Ferrick, in an opinion article, to assert that "years from now, Rendell's defeat will be held up as an example of how a Philadelphian cannot win statewide," adding "not to put too fine a point on it, the tribes in the other areas of the state do not like Philadelphia." After Governor Rendell won relatively easy reelection in 2006 after a successful first term as Pennsylvania's chief executive, one cannot help but wonder what Ferrick thinks today of his 1986 postprimary election assertion. Ferrick, "Raising Some Primary Considerations," *Philadelphia Inquirer*, May 25, 1986.

94. In Pennsylvania, a political party's candidates for governor and lieutenant governor run as a team in the general election, but they are selected separately in the primaries. Thus, Casey's endorsement of Singel did not insure he would have him as a running mate.

suburban Pittsburgh as his running mate. (Democrat Singel and Republican Fisher would both secure gubernatorial nominations in their own right, the former in 1994 and the latter in 2002. Both would lose in the general election.)

The day after the primary, Scranton, thirty-eight, hit the ground running, asserting, "We cannot go back to the old politics or the old ways of doing business in a state that time has changed." Casey quickly termed Scranton's comments "ill considered and immature."[95] And so the campaign of charge and countercharge began. By fall, Casey had launched a character assault on Scranton in an attempt to depict him as a dilettante, floating carelessly from one lifestyle to the next. Scranton's biography made him vulnerable, as Paul Taylor, a *Washington Post* reporter, wrote as the fall campaign was about to begin:

> En route to assuming the mantle [of the governorship] from his father, Scranton took a few detours. He admits to smoking marijuana and using harder drugs in the 1960s and early 1970s. In 1972, as the pony-tailed publisher of a few Northeastern Pennsylvania weeklies his family had bought for him, he endorsed George McGovern for president. He eventually got unhooked from drugs by getting heavily involved in the Transcendental Meditation movement, serving as an associate of TM founder Maharishi Mahesh Yogi. In the mid 1970s, Scranton went straight and Republican.[96]

Casey, a Catholic with a large family, presented himself as the more conservative of the two on social issues, in particular on the abortion issue: Casey was pro-life while Scranton was prochoice.[97] When buttons began circulating at Democratic events that proclaimed "We Need a Governor, Not a Guru," the Casey campaign denied having anything to do with them and generally stayed away from the issue of Scranton's earlier adult life until the final weekend of the campaign, a development covered below. Instead, Casey's television attack ads criticized Scranton for being absent 80 to 100 percent of the time from meetings he was to chair as lieutenant governor, saying, "They gave him the job because of his father's name. The least he could do is show up for work."[98] Scranton countered with attacks on Casey's stint as auditor general, charging that he didn't crack down on corruption enough during the Shapp administration. In addition, Governor Thornburgh criticized Casey, asserting that his "20-year lust" for the post of governor has caused him "to run a campaign so negative it was a 'virus on the body politic.' "[99]

95. Ferrick, "Raising Some Primary Considerations."

96. Paul Taylor, "Democrats Hope to Overturn Tradition with Strong Ticket," *Washington Post,* August 25, 1986.

97. Paul Taylor, "Scranton Drops Ads and His Mitts; Opponent Casey Keeps Punching; Candidates Clash Over Class, Life Style in Bruising Campaign," *Washington Post,* October 24, 1986. Incidentally, the city of Scranton was home to both men, although their family origins there diverged significantly. Scranton's family owned the anthracite coal mines around the city that bears his family name, while Casey's father worked in them. Taylor, "Scranton Drops Ads."

98. Ibid.

99. Gary A. Warner, "Casey Savors Win After 3 Defeats," *Pittsburgh Press,* November 5, 1986.

While Scranton tried to tag Casey as a political relic unable to transform Pennsylvania from a manufacturing to a service economy, Casey argued that Scranton was the one who had been in office for the past eight years as Thornburgh's lieutenant governor and that made him the candidate hitched to old tactics. Although the Philadelphia area was handling the transition to a postindustrial era reasonably well, much help was still needed, Casey argued, in the Pittsburgh, Scranton, and the Wilkes-Barre areas and the Lehigh Valley.[100]

Polls showed the race tight throughout October with the lead changing hands several times. Entering the last week, Casey's internal polls indicated the contest was dead even with a large number of voters still undecided. Just three days to go before Election Day, the Casey campaign unleashed one of the most famous television commercials in recent Pennsylvania political history, the so-called "guru ad," aimed at tapping into the Republican conservative base and pulling ahead of Scranton.[101] The thirty-second ad played sitar music and featured images of Maharishi Mahesh Yogi and old photos of a long-haired, bearded Scranton. The ad, which ran in every media market except Philadelphia's (where liberal voters, it was thought, might be more open to transcendental meditation), asked:

> Is Bill Scranton qualified to be governor? After college he bought three newspapers with family money, but he stopped going to work and the papers failed. Scranton joined transcendental meditation and became a disciple of the Maharishi Mahesh Yogi. *Time* magazine said Scranton traveled the world evangelizing for transcendental meditation. And he said his goal was to bring transcendental meditation to state government. His only real job was lieutenant governor, and they gave him that because of his father's name.[102]

With no time to launch an ad answering the attack, Scranton, who was campaigning in Pittsburgh and Philadelphia, denounced it as an assassination of his character, saying that he sold the newspapers, which are still operating, and that he had no secret agenda. He added that in his eight years as lieutenant governor, he never talked to anyone about transcendental meditation.[103] In addition to the ad, the Casey campaign sent a last-minute mass mailing to the state's Republican voters, urging them to stay home instead of voting for Scranton.[104] The Casey camp defended the ad by arguing that Scranton's past was fair game because he had attacked Casey's record as auditor general. In a postelection article about the ad, headlined "How the Late 'Guru Ad' Turned Things Casey's Way," three *Philadelphia*

100. Stevens, "Governor's Race Upends the War of Generations," *New York Times*, October 20, 1986.

101. Ferrick, "How the Late 'Guru Ad' Turned Things Casey's Way," *Philadelphia Inquirer*, November 6, 1986.

102. Russell E. Eshleman Jr., Dan Meyers, and Thomas Ferrick Jr., "Casey Makes Meditation an Issue," *Philadelphia Inquirer*, November 2, 1986.

103. Ibid.

104. Ferrick, "Casey and Specter Are Winners," *Philadelphia Inquirer*, November 5, 1986.

Inquirer reporters described the ad as "the political equivalent of a two-by-four" and credited it with eroding Scranton's support among conservative Republican voters in the central part of the commonwealth.[105]

On his fourth try, "the real Bob Casey" won the governorship with 50.7 percent of the vote to Scranton's 48.4 percent. Of the nearly 3.4 million votes cast, Casey's margin of victory was only 79,216 votes. Casey took twenty-four of the sixty-seven counties with solid leads in Scranton, Philadelphia, and Pittsburgh. And his socially conservative stance also stood him well in the Republican strongholds of central and northern Pennsylvania. In those areas, he did lose but with less of a losing margin than the normal seven-to-three ratios of other Democratic candidates.[106]

In summing up the gubernatorial election, Thomas Ferrick Jr. of the *Philadelphia Inquirer* wrote that the 1986 gubernatorial election offered several rules. First, he wrote, "It pays to be the candidate who is the straightest arrow." Here he argued that Scranton's past hurt him and that when the Scranton camp looked into Casey's past, they found that "beneath that image of integrity lay more integrity." A second rule: "It pays to be aggressive." The reporter contended that the "guru ad" apparently worked and that perhaps Casey won "because he wanted to be governor more than any one else did."[107] Apparently, rule one is not in conflict with rule two.

Meanwhile, Senator Specter coasted to a second term by handily defeating his Democratic challenger, U.S. Representative Bob Edgar, with 56.4 percent of the vote to Edgar's 42.9 percent. While Casey's negative ads seemed to have worked, Edgar could not get his negative ads to stick to Specter. Edgar was a liberal Democrat who had won six terms in an overwhelmingly Republican suburban Philadelphia district; he had first run for Congress indignant over President Nixon's conduct in Watergate. Despite a vigorous, if underfunded, campaign attacking the incumbent, Edgar had difficulty demonizing his skillful, moderate Republican opponent, who prided himself on his independence from his own party.[108]

Edgar was able to carry only six counties, one of which was Westmoreland, where he won by only 844 votes. He could not hold onto his home county of Delaware, losing

105. Ferrick, "How the Late 'Guru Ad' Turned Things."

106. Ferrick, "Casey and Specter Are Winners."

107. Ferrick, "In Penna., a Year of the Incumbent," *Philadelphia Inquirer*, November 9, 1986.

108. Stevens, "Specter Turns Back Challenger; Governorship Taken by Democrat," *New York Times*, November 5, 1986; Sherley Uhl, "Specter Keeps Seat in Senate," *Pittsburgh Press*, November 5, 1986. Although Senator Specter won renomination in the Republican primary handily, his opponent, Richard Stokes, a thirty-six-year-old schoolteacher from central Pennsylvania, took in a surprising 24 percent of the vote statewide and 38 percent in some central Pennsylvania counties. The vote for Stokes, a born-again Christian and a conservative, was seen as a protest to show dissatisfaction with Specter's liberal stances on abortion and school prayer. In 2004, Senator Specter would barely survive a similar challenge from the right in the GOP primary, but in 2004, his opponent was a well-financed, articulate, three-term congressman.

it by 24,143 votes. And he took Philadelphia by only 60,566. Specter beat his Democratic challenger by nearly 8,500 votes in heavily Democratic Allegheny County.

Since Casey carried twenty-four counties, eighteen counties voted for both Casey and Specter.[109] That large number of split counties coupled with the fact that Senator Specter had a plurality of 458,318 votes, as compared to Casey's narrow margin of nearly 80,000 votes, led a *Pittsburgh Press* reporter to remark that Pennsylvanians in 1986 had "indulged in a ticket-splitting orgy,"[110] which no one could deny.

The 1988 Election

As it had in 1984, Pennsylvania continued to give a stronger percentage of its vote to the losing Democratic presidential nominee than the national Democrat received in the nation as a whole. Michael Dukakis, the liberal Massachusetts governor, won 48.4 percent of the vote in the state to Vice President George H. W. Bush's winning percentage of 50.7 percent. In the nation, Bush won 53.4 percent to Dukakis's 45.6 percent, as discussed in chapter 2. In fact, Bush's plurality of 105,143 votes was the lowest plurality of any winning presidential candidate in the state from 1960 to 2004.

Senator Heinz was overwhelmingly reelected to a third term in 1988, winning 66.5 percent of the vote to 32.4 percent for his Democratic opponent, Joe Vignola, a former Philadelphia city controller. It was the most lopsided two-party outcome since 1960. Vignola, who was outspent ten to one by Heinz, was viewed by political analysts as the Democrat's "sacrificial lamb" to the popular Republican senator.[111] Heinz's plurality was a staggering 1,484,951 votes.

The 1990 Election

Governor Casey, who enjoyed high public approval of his conduct in office,[112] was overwhelmingly reelected in 1990. He defeated the Republican state auditor general, Barbara Hafer, a former Allegheny County commissioner and a public health nurse. Casey won 67.7 percent of the vote to Hafer's 32.3 with a plurality of 1,077,728 votes.[113] (Incidentally, Casey topped Heinz's record-winning percentage of two years earlier.)

The abortion issue figured prominently in the 1990 campaign, starting with the May primaries. Casey, a vehement prolife Democrat, was challenged for

109. The eighteen "swing" counties were Allegheny, Armstrong, Carbon, Clearfield, Clinton, Columbia, Elk, Greene, Indiana, Lackawanna, Luzerne, Mercer, Montour, Northampton, Northumberland, Schuylkill, Somerset, and Washington.

110. Uhl, "Specter Keeps Seat."

111. Edward Colimore, Michael Vitez, and Carol Morello, "Heinz Soundly Defeats Vignola to Capture Third Term in Senate," *Philadelphia Inquirer*, November 9, 1988.

112. Casey's approval rating never dipped below 65 percent in his first term. Michael deCourcy Hinds, "Pennsylvania Campaign Fizzles, but Not Quietly," *New York Times*, October 11, 1990.

113. In her unsuccessful general election campaign, Hafer even lost her home county, Allegheny, by nearly 172,000 votes.

renomination by Philip Berg, a Montgomery County attorney who favored legalized abortion. Casey crushed him, winning over 77 percent of the Democratic primary vote. On the Republican side, Hafer, a strong prochoice Republican, received a jolt when a politically unknown antiabortion activist, Marguerite (Peg) Luksik, came within 51,000 votes of defeating her for the Republican gubernatorial nomination; Hafer received 54 percent of the GOP primary votes to 46 percent for Luksik. Luksik had only joined the Republican party in March in order to run against Hafer.[114] (By way of a preview, in the hotly contested 1994 gubernatorial election, described in chapter 4, Luksik ran as the Constitution party nominee and garnered 12.8 percent of the vote.)

In her only televised debate with Governor Casey during the campaign, Hafer did her best to highlight their differences on the abortion issue. "This man would condemn women in Pennsylvania to going to the back alley and having an illegal abortion. I was a public health nurse; I have held women in my arms that have died from botched abortions."[115] A *New York Times* reporter wrote the following concerning Casey's debate response on abortion. "[H]e did not back down from his strong anti-abortion position. He was asked whether he would sign a law, presuming it had the blessing of the United States Supreme Court, that banned all abortions and provided criminal penalties for doctors and hospitals that violated the law. 'If the legislature passed such a law and it had an exception for the health of the mother, I will sign it,' he said."[116] Earlier in the year Casey had dismissed Hafer as a single-issue candidate, saying: "I never thought that voters in either party vote on the basis of a single issue. The voters in Pennsylvania vote on a wide range of important issues. Abortion is certainly an important issue. But it's not the only important issue."[117]

With Casey's easy reelection as governor in 1990, Pennsylvania Democrats reached a high point in party strength not attained since the first half of the 1970s. As shown in Figure 3.1, David's Democratic party-strength index peaked at 51.4 percent in 1990. The percentage dipped slightly two years later, then dropped off considerably to around 43 percent in 1994 and 1996, finally bottoming out at 38.0 percent in 1998. The Democrats rebounded to a little over 46 percent in 2000 and 2002, going up to 49.0 percent in 2004. Chapter 4 tells the story of the elections of these years and their implications for both parties, ending with my overview of the entire 1962 to 2004 period.

Figure 3.1 also previews the amazing Democratic forward leap in 2006, when David's index of Democratic party strength registered a whopping 58.7 percent, its highest mark since the start of Professor David's calculations in 1872![118] The story of that remarkable election and its relevance for my analysis of Pennsylvania electoral change is told in this book's concluding chapter.

114. Dennis B. Roddy and Don Wolf, "Unknown a Shocker for GOP," *Pittsburgh Press*, May 16, 1990.
115. Hinds, "Pennsylvania Campaign Fizzles."
116. Ibid.
117. Roddy and Wolf, "Unknown a Shocker."
118. Unlike Figure 3.1, Figure 1.1 plots Democratic party strength in Pennsylvania back to 1872, substantiating the record-breaking nature of the 2006 Democratic performance.

4

Electoral Competition in Pennsylvania from 1991 to 2004: An Examination of Gubernatorial and U.S. Senate Elections

This chapter tells the fascinating story of recent Pennsylvania elections through 2004, completing the analytical narrative begun in chapter 3. In the latter part of this chapter, after the conclusion of the narrative, I offer my overview of all of these post-1962 elections and seek to answer the question posed at the outset of our two-chapter journey through four decades of major Keystone State elections: In a period of impressive national Democratic strength in the state, why did Pennsylvania Republicans do so well through the 2004 election?

The story picks up in 1991 with a tragic accident that took the life of a popular Pennsylvania politician, resulting in a surprising special election victory that stunned political observers and was the talk of the nation.

The 1991 Special Senate Election

On April 4, 1991, Senator John Heinz was killed when his small private plane collided with a helicopter over a Philadelphia suburb, cutting short the life of a rising political star in the GOP. The tragedy, which necessitated a special election in November to choose the person to fill out the remaining three years of Heinz's term, precipitated an astonishing upset victory and generated extensive national media coverage of the fall campaign and its outcome.

Pennsylvania Republicans quickly had their candidate, former Governor Richard Thornburgh, who had gone to Washington to become President Reagan's attorney general in 1988 and continued as head of the Justice Department under President Bush. Thornburgh, who left his post in mid-August to launch his Senate campaign, immediately became the odds-on favorite, maintaining a lead of 25 to 40 percent in the polls until early October.[1]

In May, Governor Casey named his secretary of industry and labor, Harris Wofford, to serve as senator in the interim before the special election and to be the Democratic candidate in November. Virtually unknown to the Pennsylvania electorate at the time of his Senate appointment, Wofford, then 65, had a long, varied, and distinguished career in public affairs. He worked as a civil rights aide in John Kennedy's presidential campaign and was instrumental in an important phone call of concern that Kennedy made to Dr. Martin Luther King's wife when the civil rights leader was imprisoned in Georgia in October 1960. The episode is credited with galvanizing black support for Kennedy in that close election. A New York City native and a graduate of the University of Chicago, he wrote a book in 1951 with his wife, Clare, about Gandhi's nonviolent campaigns, entitled *India Afire*. Later in the 1950s, he took Dr. King to India to learn more about nonviolent protests.

Within the Kennedy administration, he assisted with the founding of the Peace Corps and served as its associate director until 1966, when he became the first president of the State University of New York's College at Old Westbury on Long Island. In 1970, he was named the first male president of Bryn Mawr College, in suburban Philadelphia. A Yale Law School graduate, who had taught law at Howard University and Notre Dame University earlier in his career, he practiced law with a Philadelphia firm after leaving Bryn Mawr in 1978 and became active in Pennsylvania politics in support of his longtime friend Casey, who named him state Democratic party chair before appointing him to his cabinet in 1986. In his role as secretary of labor and industry, Wofford was credited with bringing labor and management together and creating a statewide system of job centers.[2] Described by a *Washington Post* reporter as "soft-spoken and courtly" and "an engaging, worldly man of ideas and ideals," Wofford had never run for public office. As a worried Senate aide who admired Wofford put it: "He is everyone's idea of a senator and no one's idea of a candidate."[3]

Thornburgh hired Roger Ailes and Greg Stevens to handle his media relations; the former had been associated with President Reagan's campaigns, and the latter was known as the architect of the attack ads used by George Bush in his 1988 presidential campaign. Wofford took a page out of Casey's playbook and hired partners James Carville and Paul Begala to be his campaign managers.[4]

1. Michael deCourcy Hinds, "Democrats Look to the Senate Race in Pennsylvania for Lessons and Hope," *New York Times*, October 23, 1991.

2. Hinds, "Low-Profile Pennsylvanian Seeks Long Run as Senator," *New York Times*, May 21, 1991; and Helen Dewar, "From 'Politics of Service' to the Real Thing; Pennsylvania's New Sen. Wofford, Facing First Electoral Test, Strives to Define His Candidacy," *Washington Post*, June 9, 1991.

3. Ibid.

4. Michel Marriott, "Pennsylvania Senate Race Kicks Off, Signals Issues in '92 Presidential Race," *New York Times*, August 30, 1991. Thornburgh termed Carville a "pretty nasty guy." Responding to the comment, Begala said, "There is a reason for the little beads of sweat on Thornburgh's brow. It is because of his record and not because of a consultant. He cares only for protecting the powerful and privileged, and cares nothing about working families." Both are quoted in Marriott, "Pennsylvania Senate Race Kicks Off."

Citing his experience as governor, Thornburgh said he would fight for economic growth, jobs, tougher measures against crime and violence, and good government. He labeled Wofford a "60's liberal" and a "tax-and-spend Democrat" who was out of touch with Pennsylvanians.[5] In general, he ran the race, in the words of Michael deCourcy Hinds, a *New York Times* reporter, "as though he were the incumbent running unopposed." Then came the gaffe. On September 20, Thornburgh's campaign manager, Michele Davis, told the Associated Press, "Dick Thornburgh is the salvation of this sorry-assed state." Thornburgh apologized for the insult, but as Hinds observed, he "could not control the damage as the statement was repeated across the state in newspapers and talk shows." On October 1, the *Pittsburgh Post-Gazette* and WTAE-TV released a poll they commissioned that showed Thornburgh's huge lead had shrunk to 12 percentage points.[6]

For his part, Wofford, calling himself a progressive Democrat, went on "an angry populist offensive," to again quote Hinds, "saying that he has had it with Washington's corruption and failure to revive the economy, stem the flow of jobs overseas and enact a national health care policy."[7] Alluding to Thornburgh's boast about the Republican's Washington influence, Wofford agreed "that his opponent has, indeed, walked the corridors of power and knows Washington inside out. But he [Wofford] prefers to 'clean up the corridors of power and turn Washington upside down.' "[8] Although Wofford talked about various issues, from helping the middle class send their children to college to making the environment right for job growth, his advocacy of a national health care plan became the centerpiece of his campaign and received the most attention.

Haynes Johnson and David Broder relate how Wofford hit upon the health care approach he used in the campaign:

> Early in his campaign, Wofford met with Dr. Bob Reinecke, a Philadelphia ophthalmologist and potential contributor. After an hour-long conversation, Reinecke picked up from his desk a copy of the U.S. Constitution. "Take this Constitution, Senator," the doctor said, "and tell people that the Constitution says if you're charged with a crime, you have a right to a lawyer. Every American, if they're sick, should have the right to a doctor."
>
> Wofford was so impressed he tried out the argument in a campaign appearance that night. The response was immediate. Loud applause. He tried the line in black churches. Loud amens. . . .
>
> When he went to film the first of his political ads, Wofford told his consultants he had found a strong applause line. One who was skeptical was James Carville. . . . "Senator," Wofford remembers

5. Ibid.

6. Both the quote and the poll result are from Hinds, "Democrats Look to the Senate Race."

7. Ibid.

8. Marriott, "Pennsylvania Senate Race Kicks Off."

Carville drawling, "that's so theoretical, only you academics would think something like that would make sense."

But Carville humored his candidate. The TV spot was made. Wofford looked earnestly into the camera and proclaimed: "If criminals have a right to a lawyer, I think working Americans should have the right to a doctor."[9]

On the stump, after making his policy proposals, Wofford gave his standard tag line: "It's time to take care of our own."[10] The slogan tied into the post–Cold War shift in American attention toward long-neglected domestic issues as the Soviet Union collapsed, a development that in 1992 would catch up with President Bush, who was much better known for his mastery of foreign affairs than his interest in domestic policies.

In the final seventy-two hours of the campaign, the polls depicted the candidates running even. Wofford's national health care platform was working, and even his Republican opponent came to realize it. Late in the game, the Thornburgh campaign started running ads attacking Wofford on his national health insurance plan. The thirty-second ad asserted: "Harris Wofford. Hand-picked by Bob Casey. Together they gave us the biggest tax hike in history [Governor Casey's popularity had declined earlier in 1991 after he successfully pushed through a tax increase on businesses and on gasoline and cigarettes.] Now Wofford wants to give us government-run health care. Just like the failed Canadian plan, where people are forced to wait in line for surgery."[11] The ad noted that, as senator, Thornburgh would make health care more affordable by containing costs. In response to the negative spot, Begala said, "We're all too happy to see Thornburgh go on the air and tell people they don't want national health insurance. They want health insurance, and they know they want it. This issue is strong enough to turn goat spit into gasoline."[12]

"Wofford Stuns Thornburgh" proclaimed the *Philadelphia Inquirer*'s lead headline the morning after the election.[13] Wofford won 55.0 percent of the vote to the former governor's 45.0 percent with the Democratic victor amassing a plurality of 338,774 votes. The 10-percentage point margin of victory was breathtaking considering how far behind Wofford had been just two months earlier.

9. Haynes Johnson and David S. Broder, *The System: The American Way of Politics at the Breaking Point* (Boston: Little, Brown and Company, 1996), 59–60.

10. Rhodes Cook, "Wofford's Win Lifts Democrats, Who See Wider Implications," *Congressional Quarterly Weekly Report*, November 9, 1991, 3302.

11. Hinds, "Pennsylvania Senate Race Full of Bare Knuckles and Nail Biting," *New York Times*, November 3, 1991.

12. Ibid.

13. Katharine Seelye, "Wofford Stuns Thornburgh: Sends Message to DC," *Philadelphia Inquirer*, November 6, 1991.

Although Pittsburgh had been Thornburgh's home base, his popularity there was not enough to offset rising unemployment figures and labor's organized support of Wofford. Wofford took Allegheny County by 89,601 votes. Thornburgh carried the central part of the state, but by only about half the margin he did in 1982.[14] And, though he tried to pick up some of the black vote by pointing out that Wofford voted against Clarence Thomas's Supreme Court nomination, Wofford captured the black vote in Philadelphia by more than ten to one and won the city by margins of three to one, even outpacing Democrat Ed Rendell in his successful race for mayor.[15]

Wofford carried three of the four suburban counties surrounding Philadelphia, Montgomery, Delaware, and Bucks, losing only Chester. The map in Figure 4.1 depicts the 1991 county-level partisan result. In 1982, Thornburgh's combined margin of victory in these four counties was 200,260. And in 1988, Bush's margin of victory here was 205,732. In 1991, with Wofford's total in these four counties of 314,065, he lost by only 694 votes. The executive director of the Republican party in Bucks County was astounded, saying, "If you find someone who says they saw

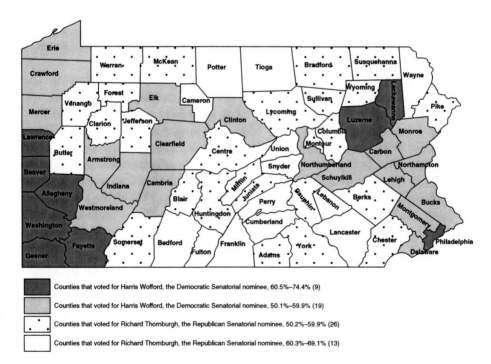

Counties that voted for Harris Wofford, the Democratic Senatorial nominee, 60.5%–74.4% (9)

Counties that voted for Harris Wofford, the Democratic Senatorial nominee, 50.1%–59.9% (19)

Counties that voted for Richard Thornburgh, the Republican Senatorial nominee, 50.2%–59.9% (26)

Counties that voted for Richard Thornburgh, the Republican Senatorial nominee, 60.3%–69.1% (13)

Fig. 4.1. Map of the Vote for Senate in 1991

14. Not surprisingly, Thornburgh in 1991 correlates with his 1982 county-level gubernatorial victory pattern at 0.74.

15. Cook, "Wofford's Win Lifts Democrats," 3305.

this coming, they're lying."[16] Even Begala remarked that he did not think many Democrats would be able to imitate Wofford's success in the Philadelphia suburbs, explaining that Montgomery County is and will continue to be Republican. Begala added: "It takes an extraordinary candidate to break through that."[17] Dave Sanko, the executive director of the Republican party in Bucks County, said: "I think what Harris Wofford did was deliver a wake-up call that may have saved the White House for the Republicans."[18] Both Begala and Sanko were wrong: The White House didn't get the alert or didn't fully understand it, and subsequent Democratic candidates did do well in those suburban Philadelphia counties, starting the next year.

The 1992 Election

In the 1992 presidential election, Democrat Bill Clinton won Pennsylvania's twenty-three electoral votes with 45.1 percent of the vote to President Bush's 36.1 percent; Ross Perot's strong independent candidacy received 18.2 percent. Clinton's Pennsylvania percentage was 2.1 points above his national average of 43.0 percent; nationally Bush received 37.4 percent and Perot 18.9 percent. Clinton's Pennsylvania plurality of 447,323 votes was the highest Democratic presidential plurality since Johnson's 1964 landslide.

Philadelphia gave Clinton a 301,576-vote margin, and, like Wofford the previous year, Clinton carried Montgomery, Delaware, and Bucks counties but lost Chester. His combined vote in all four of these Philadelphia suburban counties was actually a few thousand votes (2,450 to be exact) more than Bush.[19] The Clinton and Wofford winning county-level patterns correlate at a very high 0.95.

Senator Specter's path to a third term in 1992 encountered an unexpected obstacle. It appeared that his Democratic opponent would be Lieutenant Governor Mark Singel, the best-known Democrat in the primary field. But, in a remarkable turnaround, Lynn Yeakel, a political unknown, catapulted to the nomination with powerful television ads attacking Senator Specter for his aggressive, even arrogant, interrogation of Anita Hill during the U.S. Supreme Court confirmation hearings of Clarence Thomas the previous fall. Hill had testified that Thomas sexually harassed her when she worked with him in government. Yeakel's ads, which showed Specter's overbearing manner at the hearings before the all-male Senate Judiciary Committee, pictured Yeakel forcefully asking, "Did this make you as angry as it made me?" In less than a month, Yeakel, 50, the founder and executive director of Women's Way, a Philadelphia-based, fund-raising coalition that aids

16. Ibid.

17. Ibid.

18. Ibid., 3304.

19. To be precise, in the four suburban Philadelphia counties, Clinton won 405,327 votes to President Bush's 402,877 with Perot getting 185,933.

battered women, went from being a political unknown to defeating an established Democratic leader with 44 percent of the vote to Singel's 33 percent.[20]

In an election year that featured a number of women candidates nation-wide—it was called the "year of the woman"—Yeakel's Senate nomination generated considerable excitement and posed Specter with his strongest challenge since he had won his seat in 1980. Yeakel ran a spirited, anti-Washington, outsider campaign that stressed the need for a national health care plan. Given Wofford's success with similar themes the previous year, her prospects in November seemed reasonably good. When the votes were counted, however, she came up short. Specter won with 49.1 percent to Yeakel's 46.3 percent; the incumbent's plurality was 133,159 votes.

Specter won by avoiding several of the pitfalls that did in Thornburgh in 1991. He distanced himself from President Bush, stressing his "independence." Unlike Thornburgh, "Specter hit the airwaves two months before Yeakel and attacked first, often criticizing Yeakel's character," to quote from a *Harrisburg Patriot-News* article that compared and contrasted the two Senate elections. The reporters added: "Wofford caught Thornburgh by surprise. Specter knew what to expect and hunkered down, courting every Democratic vote he could get." Also important for Specter were televised endorsements from Teresa Heinz, Senator Heinz's widow, something Thornburgh didn't get.[21]

In Bucks, Chester, Delaware, and Montgomery counties, where Wofford lost by only 694 and Clinton won by 2,450, Yeakel lost by 91,885. She won Philadelphia, but by only 121,553 votes. Specter also took Allegheny County by nearly 16,000 votes. There were eleven counties that went for Clinton but not Yeakel, including, Luzerne, Bucks, Lehigh, Westmoreland, and Armstrong. The county-level correlation of Clinton's victory pattern in 1992 with Yeakel's losing one in the same election is 0.87. By contrast, Clinton and Wofford, as mentioned previously, correlate at 0.95.

The 1994 Election

Pennsylvania elected both a governor and a U.S. senator in 1994, and both races were fiercely contested affairs, full of fascinating insights into the state's partisan politics. I start with the Senate election.

U.S. Representative Rick Santorum, a thirty-six-year-old conservative Republican from Pittsburgh, defeated Senator Wofford's 1994 bid for a full six-year term with 49.4 percent of the vote to the incumbent's 46.9 percent. Santorum's

20. Nathan Gorenstein, "The Surprise Rapid Rise of Lynn Yeakel," *Philadelphia Inquirer*, April 30, 1992. See also Mitchell Locin, "Hill Hearings Spark a 2nd Primary Upset," *Chicago Tribune*, April 29, 1992.

21. Joseph J. Serwach and David S. Martin, "Specter's Standing, Strategies Paid Off, *Harrisburg Patriot-News*, November 5, 1992.

plurality was 87,210 votes, the narrowest Republican Senate margin in Pennsylvania since Hugh Scott's close first reelection win in 1964.

In the House, Santorum, in the words of columnist Jack Germond, "earned a name for himself as part of an aggressive group of young, tough conservatives, who rigidly resist taxes and big government."[22] In his first term, he was one of a "gang of seven" Republican freshmen who pursued the House bank and post office scandals, which tarnished the House Democratic leadership as well as individual members of both parties. An aggressive, attractive campaigner, he unapologetically championed the conservative Republican agenda, which in the 1994 election was being spearheaded by U.S. Representative Newt Gingrich of Georgia, his former House colleague. Gingrich was then second in command in the House GOP hierarchy and would become speaker after the Republicans stunned the political establishment in November 1994 by capturing fifty-five additional seats to take control of the U.S. House for the first time in forty years. Clearly, Santorum benefited from the strong tide running in favor of the GOP in 1994.

Santorum's message, to again quote from Germond's column, "is clearly directed at voters who are fed up with government's growing more powerful and controlling more aspects of American lives—what he calls 'the whole concept of government taking their freedom away.' Or, as he put it to people who heckled him [at a recent rally], 'I know you want to be antagonistic . . . but we can all agree that the federal government takes too much of your money and makes too many decisions.'" [23] Santorum also stressed his youth. For example, in announcing in October 1993 that he was running against the sixty-eight-year-old Democratic senator, who worked in President Kennedy's administration over three decades earlier, Santorum chose to do it at John F. Kennedy Park in McKeesport, a blue-collar town in Allegheny County. That day, he attacked Wofford's health care proposal as "to the left of Clinton," arguing that his opponent's plan was a threat to jobs and that Wofford's vote for President Clinton's budget will raise the taxes of retired steel workers. Then, standing beneath a large statue of President Kennedy, he asserted: "If John Kennedy were alive today, he would be 76 years old and he would say it's time to pass the torch to a new generation of leaders." Santorum added that he is committed "to a mission to restore the energy, drive, and responsibility that Pennsylvania lost in 1991."[24]

A chief difficulty Wofford faced in the campaign stemmed from the failure in Congress of the Clinton heath care plan, a major part of the new President's domestic agenda, as well as the falling public approval ratings of the President. Clinton, who would go on to have remarkably high public approval in 1996 and during much of his second term, went into a slump in the fall of 1994, averaging

22. Jack W. Germond, "In Pennsylvania, a Question of Message," *Baltimore Sun*, October 1, 1994.

23. Ibid.

24. Dennis B. Roddy, "Santorum Starts Drive for Senate; GOP Congressman Attacks Wofford's Health-Care Proposal," *Pittsburgh Post-Gazette*, October 2, 1993.

national approval in the low 40 percent range.[25] A Keystone Poll in October 1994 put Clinton's job approval in Pennsylvania at 30 percent.[26]

Still, Wofford conducted an aggressive campaign. "Have you ever heard Hubert Humphrey scorch the kind of Republicans I'm running against?" he said to a *Minneapolis Star Tribune* reporter. "When I am running against someone who is a menace to this country, as Rick Santorum is, you have to fight." He added: "Santorum . . . has the simple message of the radical right, which is 'The government is the enemy.' I don't want government to take over, but I want it to take action.' " [27]

A *Washington Post* reporter conveyed the different approaches of the two candidates this way:

> Wofford calls the 1994 race even more portentous than the last. He said he believes Pennsylvanians want a government that actively responds to their needs. "If the signal out of this election is that a Republican congressional leadership is the solution," he warned, the result will be government for the rich, a mushrooming deficit and a return to "trickle-down Reaganomics that landed Pennsylvania on its back."
>
> Santorum makes a mirror-imaged point: "If Harris Wofford wins, it will be a shot in the arm for very classic, big government, 1960s-style solutions. If he loses, his health reform plan, now dead, will be buried. Permanently."[28]

The campaign ended with a flurry of accusations over Social Security. With less than three weeks before the balloting, Santorum, in the words of a reporter, "tripped over the third rail of American politics—Social Security—by suggesting that the retirement age be moved back to 70."[29] Santorum had made the comment at La Salle University in Philadelphia in answer to a student's question about the long-term future of the Social Security system. He called the current retirement age of sixty-five "ridiculous" and suggested changing it to seventy to be phased in gradually over several years. The Wofford campaign quickly attacked him with an ad containing "sound bites" from Santorum's remarks, warning: "Rick Santorum

25. Lynn Ragsdale, *Vital Statistics on the Presidency: Washington to Clinton* (Washington, DC: Congressional Quarterly Press, 1998), 214–16.

26. G. Terry Madonna and Berwood Yost, "Santorum/Wofford—1994 Senate Race," research paper issued by the Center for Politics and Public Affairs, Millersville University of Pennsylvania, November 1999.

27. Tom Hamburger, "Pennsylvania Race Is a Muddy Slugfest," *Minneapolis Star Tribune*, November 6, 1994.

28. Dale Russakoff, "Torchbearer for Clinton Struggling to Keep Senate Seat," *Washington Post*, October 15, 1994.

29. Robert Shogan, "Wofford Foe Is Forced on the Defensive," *Los Angeles Times*, November 4, 1994.

says it's time to change the rules. . . . He wants to delay Social Security until you're 70." The Santorum campaign labeled the commercial "a recklessly false ad" because it omitted Santorum's idea for phasing the change in so as not to affect current or near-term beneficiaries.[30]

Then there was the flap involving Teresa Heinz, who served on the board supervising President Clinton's new National Service Corps. During a debate with Wofford, who was a major backer of the program, Santorum disparaged what came to be called AmeriCorps, saying "These are old solutions and they don't work. Someone's going to pick up trash in a park and sing 'Kumbayah' around a campfire and you're going to give them 90 percent of the benefits of the GI Bill."[31] As a *Los Angeles Times* reporter put it: "The late senator's widow more than got even in a lecture [at the University of Pittsburgh the next week]. She described Santorum as an 'unfortunate example' of negative trends in American politics—'a challenger who is short on public service and even shorter on accomplishments [but] overflowing with glib ideology.' " [32] In an interview after the speech, she characterized Wofford as "a dignified, noble human being" and said she would not vote for Santorum, whom she had referred to in the speech as "the antithesis of John Heinz."[33]

When asked about Mrs. Heinz's comments during a radio interview in Erie, Santorum caused a minor stir by saying that her criticism of him may have come about because she is dating "a Democratic senator from Massachusetts," referring to Senator John Kerry, whom she later married.[34] The long-distance exchange of words continued when Heinz released a statement accusing Santorum of using "innuendo and gossip as a tool for election."[35]

When the results were counted, Wofford had lost seventeen of the twenty-eight counties[36] he had carried in 1991. This time he also lost the four-county area surrounding Philadelphia by 71,758. In one bright spot for the defeated senator, he managed to steal Santorum's home turf, winning Allegheny by 22,099 votes.

30. Ibid.

31. Ibid.

32. Ibid.

33. Roddy, "GOP Chief Shows Heinz the Door in Santorum Flap," *Pittsburgh Post-Gazette*, October 29, 1994. The article reported that, as a result of her comments, the Allegheny County GOP chairman sent Heinz a party registration form and suggested that she consider switching to the Democratic party.

34. Hamburger, "Pennsylvania Race Is a Muddy Slugfest."

35. "Teresa Heinz Hits Santorum for 'Innuendo,' " Allentown *Morning Call*, November 4, 1994. The newspaper attributed the story to its staff and wire reports. Wofford entered the fray as well: "In Rick's world, even the courageous widow of a distinguished statesman is fair game for sleazy attacks and cheap-shot comments. We don't appreciate the politics of fear and smear." Hamburger, "Pennsylvania Race Is a Muddy Slugfest."

36. The counties Wofford lost in 1994 were Armstrong, Bucks, Carbon, Clearfield, Crawford, Delaware, Elk, Erie, Indiana, Lehigh, Mercer, Monroe, Montgomery, Northampton, Northumberland, Schuylkill, and Westmoreland.

In the 1994 gubernatorial election, a personable, prochoice moderate Republican from Erie, U.S. Representative Thomas J. (Tom) Ridge, defeated Lieutenant Governor Mark Singel, a prochoice Democrat who lacked the active support of outgoing Governor Casey. The race also featured the strongest Pennsylvania third-party gubernatorial candidate in over eight decades, Peg Luksik, the prolife activist who had done so well in the 1990 GOP senatorial primary. Luksik ran as the nominee of the Constitution party and won 12.8 percent of the vote. Ridge's victory percentage was 45.4 compared to his Democratic opponent's 39.9 percent of the vote.

When Ridge announced his candidacy in February 1993, earlier than any other candidate, he laughingly called himself the man "nobody ever heard of, from a town [Erie, tucked away in the northwest corner of the state on Lake Erie] that nobody ever visited."[37] His chief Republican rival for the nomination was state Attorney General Ernie Preate. Ridge, who was endorsed by the state party committee, depicted himself as a moderate, while Preate vigorously catered to the more conservative wing of the party, even advertising on the Rush Limbaugh show. Because Preate at the time of the primary campaign was being investigated by the Pennsylvania Crime Commission and a federal grand jury, Ridge, in the words of a *Philadelphia Inquirer* reporter, "suggested to Republicans that Preate was damaged goods and would hurt the party's chances in November."[38] (In fact, in 1995, Preate was indicted on corruption charges, pleaded guilty, and was sentenced to fourteen months in federal prison.)[39] Ridge won the hard-fought primary with 35 percent of the vote to Preate's 29 percent. Trailing in third place was Mike Fisher, who would later be elected attorney general and become the GOP's candidate for governor in 2002.

In the Democratic primary, Singel prevailed over five candidates with 31 percent of the vote. Lynn Yeakel, the party's 1992 U.S. Senate nominee, ran a distant fourth. The primary victory was particularly sweet for Singel because he had been denied the Senate nomination by Yeakel two years earlier, overlooked by Casey when he wanted to fill the late Senator Heinz's seat, and insulted when the state Democratic party refused to endorse any of the Democrats running for governor in 1994.[40]

Singel tried to capitalize on the six months he served as acting governor while Governor Casey was recuperating from a heart and liver transplant in 1993. His

---

37. Robert Zausner, "Ridge and Santorum Victors in Pennsylvania, *Philadelphia Inquirer*, November 9, 1994.

38. Zausner, "Democrats Choose Singel; GOP Race Still Too Close to Call," *Philadelphia Inquirer*, May 11, 1994.

39. The *Philadelphia Inquirer* reported: "Preate pleaded guilty to a mail-fraud charge stemming from his failure to report $20,000 in illegal cash contributions from operators of illegal video-poker machines in Lackawanna County" when he was the county's district attorney in the mid-1980s. The federal judge who accepted the plea said the operators believed, by giving Preate the money, they lessened their likelihood of being prosecuted. Robert Moran, "Preate Gets 14-Month Term, $25,000 Fine," *Philadelphia Inquirer*, December 15, 1995.

40. Zausner, "Democrats Choose Singel."

campaign theme was "Ready Right Now."[41] Ridge ran ads focusing on his working-class background, which included a period during his childhood when his family lived in public housing in Erie, his service in Vietnam (he earned a Bronze Star), and his experience as a prosecutor before he was elected to Congress in 1982.[42]

Both campaigned as prochoice on abortion, for increased jail time for violent offenders, for capital punishment, on treating juveniles who commit serious crimes as adults, for reducing welfare dependency, for decreasing government spending, and on stimulating the economy. Their many similarities led two Allentown *Morning Call* reporters to begin a summary article they wrote on the eve of the election as follows: "Come Wednesday, Pennsylvania will have elected its first Baby Boomer governor from a county that's never before produced the state's chief executive. They will have chosen a man of working-class roots. A man of moderate views. A man of extensive political experience. They will have elected Tom Ridge . . . or Mark Singel."[43]

The candidates, of course, did everything they could to differentiate themselves from each other. At a campaign rally in Allegheny County, Singel, the grandson of a coal miner, told supporters, "[This campaign] is about working families. It's not about the wealthy. It's not about the rich who can take care of themselves. It's not about a backbench Republican congressman who hasn't done a thing in 12 years."[44] Singel focused on Ridge's years in Congress, picking out instances in which he said the Republican voted against working families, such as opposing the family leave act, voting against extending unemployment benefits, voting for President Bush's capital gains tax cut for the wealthy, and bailing out the savings and loan industry.

For his part, Ridge termed Singel a flip-flopper on such issues as abortion and capital punishment.[45] Further, Ridge reached out to supporters of Governor Casey, who, it was revealed after the election, was purposely snubbing his lieutenant governor because he believed Singel misled him into thinking that he opposed abortion.[46] At a campaign rally in late October in "Casey country" in northeastern

---

41. Megan O'Matz and Mario Cattabiani, "2 Governor Candidates Share Similar Views, Backgrounds," *Allentown Morning Call*, November 6, 1994.

42. Incidentally, Ridge spent at least $11 million during his entire campaign, while Singel spent over $8 million. Taken together, the two candidates spent around $19 million on the primary and general elections, the most spent on a Pennsylvania campaign to date, up from the $13.8 million spent by Casey and Scranton in 1986. O'Matz and Cattabiani, "2 Governor Candidates Share Similar Views."

43. Ibid.

44. Ibid.

45. Ibid.

46. Associated Press, "Casey Explains Rift With Singel," *Philadelphia Inquirer*, November 14, 1994; and Associated Press, "Singel Mulls Loss, Lashes Out at Casey," *Philadelphia Inquirer*, November 16, 1994. Regarding the disagreement with Casey over abortion, Singel explained that he was personally against abortion but that he never actually had to stake out a public position until his run for the Senate. "There was never enough communication between us on the subject," Singel added.

Pennsylvania, Ridge was careful not to disparage Governor Casey, saying: "I'm trying to get Casey Democrats, there's no denying that. Singel is a Clinton Democrat, and there's a big difference. Any candidate that doesn't seek Democratic support statewide will never win because the last time I checked there were 420,000 more Ds than Rs."[47] In the closing week of the campaign, Ridge ran an ad containing his most direct appeal for Casey supporters. The ad's announcer says: "Democrats and Republicans disagree on many issues, but we all admire Governor Casey for his commitment to principle. Now Mark Singel wants to fill Governor Casey's shoes. But on issues of principle, Singel's been on both sides of the abortion issue. Casey called it 'a question of high principle.' . . ." The announcer concludes: "Mark Singel. He's no Bob Casey."[48]

Then came the Reginald McFadden episode. As chairman of the state's Board of Pardons, Singel voted in 1992 to recommend to Governor Casey that McFadden's life sentence for a 1969 murder be commuted. At age sixteen, McFadden had been convicted in the suffocation death of a Philadelphia woman. Believing McFadden had been rehabilitated, Casey agreed, and McFadden was paroled during the summer of 1994. On October 7, McFadden was arrested in New York on rape and kidnapping charges; at the end of October, he was indicted in the September death of a 78-year-old Long Island woman.[49] Ridge, who had previously made combating crime a major issue in his campaign, quickly aired television ads on the episode, with the tag line: "Mark Singel: Bad Judgment. Too Liberal on Crime."[50]

Apart from the late-breaking McFadden issue, a wild card in the race was Luksik, a mother of six from Johnstown and the prolife Constitution party nominee, who was registering support in double-digits in October polls. She was the founder of Mom's House, a nonprofit organization that gives pregnant single women another choice besides abortion and also helps single parents to escape welfare by providing them with necessary support services, such as childcare, so they can complete their education. Singel highlighted her importance to the race in the view of his campaign by airing an ad in the last week that asserted she is the best candidate for those with antiabortion views, presumably an attempt to get prolife Republicans to vote for Luksik instead of Ridge. His ad starts with photos of the three candidates. Then, the narrator says: "Mark Singel is prochoice. Singel believes in a woman's right to choose. Tom Ridge says he's prochoice but supports all of the severe restrictions put on women by the Pennsylvania Abortion Control Act, which also requires a burdensome waiting period. Peg Luksik is the prolife candidate.

47. Ibid.

48. Tim Reeves, "Singel's Ad Strategy Spotlights Abortion; Tries to Shift Votes from Ridge by Touting Luksik," *Pittsburgh Post-Gazette*, November 5, 1994.

49. Cattabiani, "Reginald McFadden Indicted in N.Y. Murder Case; Pardoned Lifer Could Become Turning Point of Pa. Governor Race," *Allentown Morning Call*, November 1, 1994. The incident that led to his arrest in early October was different from the one involved in the indictment.

50. Ibid.

Luksik is totally opposed to abortion and would abolish it if elected governor." The ad concludes with the narrator saying: "It's our choice. It's your decision."[51]

Correlating Luksik's county-level pattern of support with all the other candidates in the 1990s turns up no notable relationship. For example, her pattern correlates with Perot in 1992 at 0.11 and Perot in 1996 at –0.12. She ran again for governor in 1998, and her pattern that year, not unremarkably, was related to her 1994 one—coefficient of 0.76. Incidentally, her candidacy probably played a role in Santorum's relatively narrow Senate victory in 1994 by bringing to the polls conservative prolife voters who might not otherwise have voted. An exit poll suggests that two-thirds of Luksik's supporters voted for Santorum over Wofford.[52]

When considering what the two major party candidates stood for in the election, plus adding in the Luksik wild card, it is no wonder that the 1994 gubernatorial pattern is one of the least consistent in a period when consistent partisan patterns among the gubernatorial and U.S. Senate elections in Pennsylvania are not easy to find.

Finally, Figure 4.2 displays a scattergram of the 0.77 correlation of Santorum and Ridge in 1994. Some notable "outliers" can easily be accounted for, such as

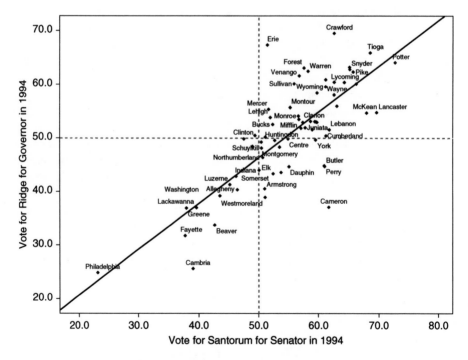

Fig. 4.2. Scattergram of the Republican Vote for Senator and Governor in 1994

51. Reeves, "Singel's Ad Strategy Spotlights Abortion."
52. Madonna and Yost, "Santorum/Wofford—1994 Senate Race."

Ridge's home county of Erie and several Pittsburgh-area counties that were part of Santorum's House district. In general, the loose Ridge–Santorum pattern illustrates well a broad, county-by-county Republican victory configuration when the party's standard is carried by two very different kinds of Republicans. Incidentally, one prominent Democrat was not shy in 1994 about expressing his opinion on the two GOP victors in 1994. Of the new governor, Mayor Rendell of Philadelphia said: "I believe Tom Ridge is a very decent, honorable, and caring man who I think will try to help the city. He's a good man." As for Santorum, the mayor "had not a kind word," to use the phrase of a *Philadelphia Inquirer* reporter. "I think he's a well-packaged Ollie North [referring to the polarizing, right-wing figure from the Iran-contra scandal in the Reagan administration]. I hope I'm wrong. I hope he proves me wrong. I think he's a better-packaged Ollie North. And that better packaging allowed him to slip through."[53]

The 1996 Election

President Clinton was easily reelected in 1996 over Senator Bob Dole of Kansas, the Republican nominee. Clinton won 49.2 percent of the vote in Pennsylvania, which was also his exact percentage in the nation. Dole received 40.0 percent in the Keystone State, just slightly under his national percentage of 40.7. Perot won 9.6 percent in the state and 8.4 percent nationally, less than half of his record-breaking 1992 performance. Clinton had rebounded from the huge Democratic congressional loss in 1994, aided by the negative public reaction to the federal government shutdowns forced by Speaker Gingrich and his conservative Republican allies in a budget confrontation with Clinton. Dole, who was the oldest person ever to seek the presidency, trailed Clinton in the polls throughout 1996, even though the Kansas Republican had led Clinton throughout much of 1995. Clinton's county-level victory pattern in 1996 was similar to his 1992 pattern; the correlation coefficient of his two races was 0.95.

Two politicians who would figure prominently in the 2002 gubernatorial election were elected in 1996 to "down-ticket" offices, generally called state constitutional offices but known in Pennsylvania as "row offices."[54] Robert P. Casey Jr., the son of the former governor, won the office of auditor general, which had been an important stepping-stone office for his father. In 2002, he and Mayor Rendell would wage a spirited contest for the Democratic gubernatorial nomination. State Senator Mike Fisher of Allegheny County, who had run unsuccessfully for the Republican gubernatorial nomination in 1994, won the office of attorney general,

---

53. Amy Rosenberg, " 'It's Not a Total Disaster'; Rendell Takes GOP Surge in Stride," *Philadelphia Inquirer*, November 10, 1994.

54. John J. Kennedy devotes over a quarter of his *Pennsylvania Elections: Statewide Contests from 1950–2004* (Lanham, MD: University Press of America, 2006) to these row office elections. See his chapter 4, "Pennsylvania Row Office Elections," 117–66.

which had been held by a fellow Republican, Ernie Preate, who went to prison in 1995. Fisher became the GOP gubernatorial nominee in 2002.[55]

The 1998 Election

Both Republican incumbents, Governor Ridge and Senator Specter, won decisively in their 1998 reelection bids. Prominent Democrats admitted that they had no serious candidates in line for governor or U.S. senator. The most viable Democratic contenders had removed themselves from the race over a year before the general election, citing the fact that Specter and Ridge already had $2.4 million and $6 million, respectively, in the bank by early fall 1997.[56]

In a *Pittsburgh Post-Gazette* editorial just before the Democratic primary, the newspaper, after interviewing the two "serious" Democratic candidates for governor, Ivan Itkin, a twenty-six-year veteran state representative from the Pittsburgh area, and Don Bailey of Greensburg, a former state auditor general and congressman, had this to say about the candidates:

> This is not an easy call for the *Post-Gazette* to make, nor one in which we take particular pride. Although no longer a majority party in Pennsylvania, Democratic voters account for about 49 percent of the electorate. We wish, for their sake, that the party had put forth better candidates. But it didn't, and just because they are on the ballot doesn't mean they merit support.[57]

Itkin won the primary, but most people counted him and the Democratic party out from the beginning, making it very difficult for him to raise money. As an *Allentown Morning Call* reporter, Mario F. Cattabiani, put it: "In political terms, Tom Ridge has a war chest; Itkin has a piggy bank."[58] Itkin raised only

---

55. Finally, several of those involved in a third 1996 election for a state row office were also active in 2002. Republican Barbara Hafer, the term-limited auditor general, was elected state treasurer, defeating Mina Baker Knoll, the daughter of the incumbent treasurer, Catherine Baker Knoll. Hafer, a prochoice moderate Republican who was never comfortable with her party's conservative wing, endorsed the 2002 Democratic gubernatorial nominee, Rendell, and Catherine Baker Knoll, then seventy-two, became Rendell's running mate in 2002 when she won a multifield Democratic primary for lieutenant governor.

56. The figures were cited in an *Allentown Morning Call* editorial, "Democrats Let Down the Process," September 21, 1997. The editorial concluded: "How disappointing, then, that the party with the highest voter registration statewide, with an edge of almost 500,000 voters over the Republicans, can't get viable candidates to the starting line."

57. Editorial, *Pittsburgh Post-Gazette*, May 21, 1998.

58. Cattabiani, "Outgunned, Unknown and Undaunted: Ivan Itkin's Dogged Run for the Gubernatorial Seat," *Allentown Morning Call*, September 20, 1998.

$420,000 to Ridge's $14 million.[59] Many donors chose to give their money to those running for the legislature in the hopes they could regain control, which they did not accomplish. And it seemed that there was not much the state Democratic party organization could do to help. Many Democrats saw this as a disturbing downward spiral. Democratic state representative Mike Veon of Beaver Falls complained, "There's no long-term strategy, no plan, no vision. We are in very difficult and challenging times for the Democratic party in Pennsylvania. There's no magic answer or easy answer for us to get back to where we should be. . . . We have to put it together at the county level, at the grass-roots level. We have to do the grunt work that we have ignored for the last 10 years."[60] He went on to explain that the state party lacks an up-to-date voter database from which to make phone calls and send targeted mailings, adding: "That's a very significant tool in the '90s. If you talk to the Republican operatives, they'll tell you. . . . If you walk into Democratic headquarters today, we have no voter file. We have to do a much better job at raising money; we have to do a better job at the grass roots. The Republican Party has been much better at that than us in the last few years."[61]

But Neil Oxman, a long-time Democratic consultant, contended that there isn't anything wrong with the party. He argued:

> Modern campaigns are personality-driven, not party-driven. The Democratic party has a lot of terrific candidates. Bob Casey Jr. is going to be a terrific candidate. Rendell is a terrific candidate. Rendell would beat Specter; he'd give Santorum a terrific race. It just happens that Rendell made a pledge not to run while he's mayor. . . . The Democrats have plenty of strong candidates. The problem is that a lot of these people are choosing not to run right now. . . . All of this stuff is cyclical, like baseball or anything else.[62]

For his part, Itkin tried to chip away at Ridge's popularity by suggesting that he wasted four years of prosperity on tax cuts for business. "He looks good," Itkin said, "but that's a façade."[63] With a master's degree in nuclear engineering and a Ph.D. in mathematics, Itkin was considered "one of the smartest men in Harrisburg and an honest, hard worker who genuinely cares about his constituents."[64] But he never gained traction. Ridge won with 57.4 percent of the vote to Itkin's 31.0 percent, a margin of 798,099 votes, the largest GOP gubernatorial

59. James O'Toole, "Ivan Itkin," *Pittsburgh Post-Gazette*, October 25, 1998.

60. O'Toole, "Democrats Face Gubernatorial Mountain; Recent Statewide Elections Suggest Tough Proposition to Unseat Ridge," *Pittsburgh Post-Gazette*, January 11, 1998.

61. Ibid.

62. Ibid.

63. Cattabiani, "Outgunned, Unknown and Undaunted."

64. Ibid.

plurality since World War II. Peg Luksik ran again, receiving 10.4 percent of the vote.[65] Ridge lost only Philadelphia. His victory was so overwhelming that Ridge's county-level pattern in 1998 yielded only a 0.77 correlation coefficient with his own pattern in 1994.

At sixty-eight, Senator Specter crushed his Democratic opponent, state Representative Bill Lloyd, an eighteen-year veteran from Somerset County, to win a fourth term. Specter received 61.3 percent of the vote to Lloyd's 34.8 percent, winning with a plurality of 785,341 votes.

The incumbent outspent his challenger by twenty to one, $4 million to $200,000, conducting a vigorous campaign despite having had open-heart surgery in May.[66] He was endorsed by the state AFL-CIO as he had been in previous campaigns, but this time he became the first Republican Senate candidate in Pennsylvania to be endorsed by the United Steelworkers of America, which was appreciative of his efforts to block imports of foreign steel.[67] Specter stressed the clout for Pennsylvania that he had amassed in Washington as well as his effort to visit all of the state's sixty-seven counties at least once a year. He took all but Philadelphia and Somerset counties. Like Ridge, Specter's county-level pattern in his last election, 1992, correlates with his 1998 race at only 0.72. Interestingly, Ridge and Specter correlate at only 0.75, suggesting that even under landslide conditions, these two major Pennsylvania moderate Republican politicians had somewhat different bases of support.

Of course, nationally these campaigns took place at the same time President Clinton was battling impeachment proceedings flowing from the Monica Lewinsky scandal. Republicans tried to make this election a referendum on the President just as they had done in 1994 during their "Contract with America" campaign, confident that off-year elections following a president's reelection almost always go against the president's party. However, 1998 was to be an exception. Democrats gained five seats in the U.S. House and maintained their position in the Senate. Apparently, this result didn't surprise Governor Ridge, who commented shortly after the election: "If you make it a referendum on a president with a 67 percent approval rating, you shouldn't be surprised if the election goes against you."[68]

65. Luksik generated considerably less interest and publicity this time, mainly because the race between the two major candidates was not viewed as close in contrast to the 1994 election. For more on the media-savvy Luksik, see her Web site: www.constitutional.net/Luksik/main. html.

66. Pete Leffler, "Specter Easily Retains Seat in U.S. Senate," *Allentown Morning Call*, November 4, 1998.

67. Casey Combs, "Sen. Specter Wins Steelworkers' Endorsement," Associated Press dispatch, October 29, 1998.

68. "Election Had Lots of Mud, Bright Spots," *Allentown Morning Call*, November 5, 1998. The story did not carry a byline.

The 2000 Election

Democratic Vice President Al Gore defeated Texas Governor George W. Bush, the Republican nominee, to capture Pennsylvania's twenty-three electoral votes in the national cliff-hanger presidential election of 2000. In the state, Gore received 50.6 percent of the vote to Bush's 46.4 percent. Ralph Nader, running as the Green party candidate, received 2.1 percent. Gore's Pennsylvania plurality was 204,840.

Demonstrating once more the strength of the national Democratic appeal in Pennsylvania, Gore ran 2.2 percentage points ahead of his national percentage of 48.4, while Bush finished 1.5 percent behind his national percentage of 47.9. Nader also lagged in Pennsylvania, running 0.6 of a percentage point behind his national average of 2.7 percent. Gore's winning county-level pattern in 2000 was almost identical with Clinton's in 1996. The two Democrats correlate at 0.97.

Senator Santorum won reelection over Ron Klink, a four-term Democratic congressman from the Pittsburgh suburbs. The Republican incumbent received 52.4 percent of the vote to Klink's 45.5 percent, amassing a 327,054 vote plurality. The final vote was much closer than the preelection polls had indicated. A Keystone Poll at the end of October had Santorum ahead by 21 percentage points with a quarter of the respondents saying they were undecided.[69]

Santorum and Klink took positions similar to those of the presidential candidates of their parties. On prescription drugs, for example, Klink favored a benefit built into the Medicare program, but Santorum favored a larger role for private providers to increase seniors' choices, contending that Klink wanted a "one-size-fits-all" government-run program.[70] At the last of their five debates, Klink, to quote from a *Pittsburgh Post-Gazette* account, "accused Santorum of spending millions of dollars on campaign ads intended to soften his image as one of the Senate's most conservative members." Later, "Klink repeatedly accused Santorum of voting against relief for Pennsylvania flood victims and against child nutrition programs. When Santorum said he had 'grown' during his six years in the Senate, Klink snapped, 'Some falsehoods are so great that they take your breath away.' "[71] Santorum, who raised $8.8 million to Klink's $3 million, benefited, in the words of an Associated Press reporter, "from an image transformation that began in early 1999. Santorum started his term as an outspoken conservative. . . . [He] later moderated his tone . . . and emerged as a leading player on such issues as welfare reform and the effort to ban the procedure opponents call 'partial-birth' abortion."[72]

69. Claude R Marx, "Klink, Santorum Take Different Approaches One Week Out," Associated Press dispatch, November 1, 2000.

70. O'Toole, "No Klink in Santorum's Armor," *Pittsburgh Post-Gazette*, October 31, 2000.

71. Jack Torry, "Santorum and Klink Slug It Out, Blame Each for Campaign Rancor," *Pittsburgh Post-Gazette*, October 25, 2000.

72. Marx, "Santorum and Klink Face Off in U.S. Senate Race," Associated Press dispatch, November 7, 2000.

Klink, who was prolife and an avid hunter skeptical of gun-control restrictions, had difficulty raising money in liberal Democratic circles. These difficulties led him a few days before the election to lash out at some Philadelphia Democratic party donors, calling them "fair weather friends" who "only want to invest with a winning team." An Associated Press dispatch said Klink's "financial shortfall resulted from the failure of cultural liberals, who fund a substantial portion of Democratic candidates, to help because of his conservative views on abortion and gun control."[73] At the end of the campaign, Klink was still not widely known outside of southwestern Pennsylvania.

The county-level patterns of both Senate candidates roughly reflected those of the presidential candidates of their party: Gore and Klink at 0.95 and Bush and Santorum at 0.88. The slight fall-off in the GOP coefficient probably reflected the considerable ticket-splitting that went on in favor of Santorum. For example, while Gore won Philadelphia by 348,223, Klink's margin in the city was 277,323. And of the four suburban Philadelphia counties, Gore won three (Chester being the holdout) and received 54,346 more votes from them than Bush. Klink lost all four by a total vote margin of 151,644. And in Allegheny, Klink actually won the county by 59,005 votes, but Gore won by more, 94,602.

The 2002 Election

Ed Rendell, the former Philadelphia mayor, won the governorship in 2002, returning the Democratic party to the most important office in the state. He defeated Mike Fisher, the Republican attorney general, with 53.4 percent of the vote to Fisher's 44.4 percent. The general election, however, was not Rendell's toughest assignment that year. He first needed to win the Democratic nomination against a formidable rival, Auditor General Robert P. Casey Jr.

A *Washington Post* reporter captured the flavor of the intra-Democratic contest in an excellent preprimary article:

> As the national Democratic Party's traveling salesman in 2000, former Philadelphia mayor Ed Rendell was pitch-perfect. Here was a big-city Democrat who had faced down powerful unions to rescue a dying city from the brink of bankruptcy, then revived its historic downtown so smashingly that even the Republican Party came there for its 2000 convention.
>
> Rendell as national chairman sought to personify a party that remained true to its blue-collar and disadvantaged base without being run by it—a party that could speak for both rich and poor, city and suburb.

73. Marx, "Fingerpointing Already Starting about Klink's Campaign," Associated Press dispatch, November 6, 2000.

But back in Pennsylvania . . . it is not at all clear who speaks for Democrats. [P]olls show him running even with state Auditor General Robert Casey, Jr., 41, an antiabortion, pro-gun populist who champions organized labor, the elderly and the poor. . . .

It is as if the diverse constituencies Bill Clinton twice stitched together nationally have split asunder here. Rendell, an earthy Ivy Leaguer who says he will do for stagnant Pennsylvania what he did for Philadelphia, advertises his disdain for the old Democratic establishment. "I don't owe the unions a thing. I don't owe the politicians a thing. I'm going to work for the people," he rasped to retired teachers near [Pittsburgh].

Casey, a carbon copy of his father from his politics to his strikingly thick, black eyebrows, exudes reverence for his elders and Pennsylvania's past.

Endorsed by every major union and the state party, he promises expanded health care, job training and a governor who will "not just stand up for working families, but stand in their shoes."[74]

The two men raised $35 million between them, making this the most expensive gubernatorial primary in the state's history. Rendell started running ads in January, in the western part of the state where he was not well known, nearly three months before Casey. When Casey did start his ads, they had a sharply negative tone. Some analysts contended that one of Casey's biggest mistakes was going too negative, too soon. A Keystone Poll found that 51 percent of respondents thought Casey's ads were more negative as opposed to 23 percent who thought Rendell's were. The poll also showed that Casey's unfavorable rating had nearly doubled between April and May.[75]

A *Philadelphia Inquirer* reporter summed up the contrasting versions of reality offered in television commercials by each side on one topic, Rendell's mayoral record:

In the Casey version of his tenure, Rendell drove away people and jobs; he failed to fight crime; he left the schools in crisis. And, oh, by the way, he'll do that to Pennsylvania, too.

In Rendell's version, he turned around a city in crisis, producing surpluses where there were only deficits; attracted jobs after years of decline; slowed the population loss; and reduced the murder rate. And, oh, by the way, "Bobby" Casey never did much of anything.[76]

---

74. Dale Russakoff, "In Pa. Governor's Race, a Democratic Divide," *Washington Post*, April 3, 2002.

75. Debbie Goldberg, "Rendell Seen as Leading Pa. Race," *Washington Post*, May 18, 2002.

76. Tom Infield, "Casey, Rendell Spar on Taxes, Nasty TV Ads," *Philadelphia Inquirer*, April 22, 2002.

Expecting a close primary, Rendell urged Republicans who supported him to switch their party registration so they could vote for him in the primary. His strategy may have proven successful, because at least 19,000 Republicans, dubbed "Rendellicans," in the five-county Philadelphia area switched their party registration before the filing deadline.[77]

And there were other differences. On abortion, Rendell was prochoice, while Casey was prolife like his father, the former governor. Rendell favored limiting the sale of guns, while Casey, who had close ties with the gun lobby, was opposed. Both wanted to improve education but were split on how to do it. Rendell was gregarious, even charismatic. Casey was more reserved. Casey was a defender of the coal and steel industries, while Rendell was more interested in luring high-tech industry to Pennsylvania.[78]

Rendell defeated Casey with 56.6 percent of the vote to Casey's 43.5 percent, a margin of 162,648 votes out of 1.2 million cast. As Figure 4.3 shows, Rendell carried only ten counties: Philadelphia, the four inner suburban counties, the next four counties out from Philadelphia—Northampton, Lehigh, Berks, and Lancaster—and Centre County, the home of Penn State's main campus. The figure also shows that the strongest Casey counties were in the central region and northern tier of the

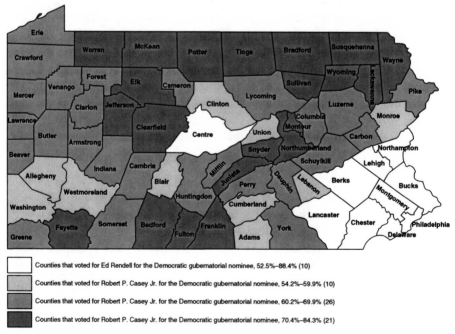

Counties that voted for Ed Rendell for the Democratic gubernatorial nominee, 52.5%–88.4% (10)

Counties that voted for Robert P. Casey Jr. for the Democratic gubernatorial nominee, 54.2%–59.9% (10)

Counties that voted for Robert P. Casey Jr. for the Democratic gubernatorial nominee, 60.2%–69.9% (26)

Counties that voted for Robert P. Casey Jr. for the Democratic gubernatorial nominee, 70.4%–84.3% (21)

Fig. 4.3. Map of the Vote for Rendell and Casey in the 2002 Democratic Primary

77. "Handshaking Ed Rendell Gets 'Rendellicans' into His Camp," Associated Press dispatch, May 4, 2002.

78. Germond, "Pa. Governor's Race Divides Democrats," *Baltimore Sun*, May 1, 2002.

state, counties that reliably go Republican in general elections. Casey also cleaned up in the western part of the state, and although he carried Allegheny and nearby Westmoreland and Washington, they were part of his weaker majority counties.[79]

The general election campaign between Rendell and Fisher featured a series of televised debates that highlighted their policy differences. For example, at one debate, as reported by the *Pittsburgh Post-Gazette*: "Rendell argued that it was time to bring change to Harrisburg after a decade in which Pennsylvania's growth had lagged behind the nation's. Fisher argued that the state's recent economic history would not look so disappointing were it not dragged down by the net job loss that Philadelphia experienced in the 1990s."[80] The candidates also clashed repeatedly over opposing plans to increase school funding and to cut property taxes, among other issues.[81]

Fisher lagged behind in the polls throughout the fall, often by double digits. Thus, when Rendell won with a plurality of 323,827, it was no surprise. What did catch some political observers by surprise were the huge margins Rendell had piled up in the Philadelphia suburban counties. Rendell received a total of 508,129 votes in Montgomery, Delaware, Bucks, and Chester to Fisher's 273,153, giving the Democrat a margin of 234,967 votes there. In Philadelphia, he surpassed Fisher by 280,474 votes and carried eight other counties in the eastern part of the state. Then, he won Allegheny by 40,294 along with five other southwestern counties.

This eighteen-county Democratic victory pattern is displayed in Figure 4.4, the county-level map of the 2002 gubernatorial election. It contrasts sharply with the winning Democratic pattern of Bob Casey in the 1986 gubernatorial election, portrayed in Figure 4.5. The 1986 map shows that Casey was much stronger than Rendell in the Pittsburgh metro area and throughout the northern tier and central region of the state. By contrast, Rendell was much stronger than Casey in the southeastern inner and outer arc of counties surrounding Philadelphia. Thus, these two winning Democrats—Casey with 50.7 percent of the vote in 1986 and Rendell with 53.4 percent in 2002—are tapping very different electoral bases of support, a point made even more precisely in Figure 4.6, a scattergram of their respective county-level support patterns. The 1986–2002 Democratic gubernatorial correlation yields a coefficient of 0.40!

Finally, in the 2002 election, the Republican party expanded its edge over the Democrats in U.S. House seats from Pennsylvania. After the 2000 census found that Pennsylvania's population growth continued to lag behind other parts of the country, the state lost two more House seats, dropping its total to nineteen. The Republican-controlled state legislature then redrew the House district lines in such a way as to give the GOP a decided edge in the 2002 election, the first to

79. Thomas Fitzgerald, Matthew P. Blanchard, and Tom Infield, "Rendell Wins Democratic Nomination for Governor," *Philadelphia Inquirer*, May 22, 2002.

80. O'Toole, "Governor Candidates Get a Tad Nasty in Last Debate," *Pittsburgh Post-Gazette*, October 30, 2002.

81. John M. R. Bull, "Property Taxes, School Aid Liven Fisher-Rendell Debate," *Pittsburgh Post-Gazette*, October 25, 2002.

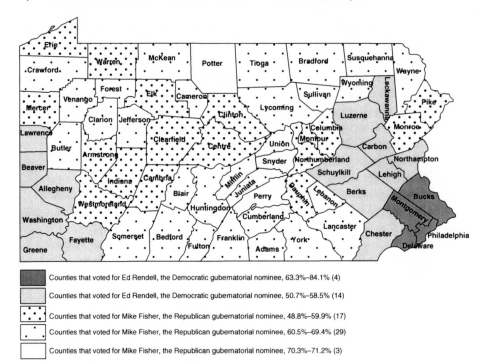

Counties that voted for Ed Rendell, the Democratic gubernatorial nominee, 63.3%–84.1% (4)

Counties that voted for Ed Rendell, the Democratic gubernatorial nominee, 50.7%–58.5% (14)

Counties that voted for Mike Fisher, the Republican gubernatorial nominee, 48.8%–59.9% (17)

Counties that voted for Mike Fisher, the Republican gubernatorial nominee, 60.5%–69.4% (29)

Counties that voted for Mike Fisher, the Republican gubernatorial nominee, 70.3%–71.2% (3)

Fig. 4.4. Map of the Vote for Governor in 2002 with Five Levels of County Support

use the new districts. U.S. Representative Robert Borski, a ten-term Democrat from northeast Philadelphia, decided to retire rather than compete with a fellow Democratic incumbent after their districts were dismembered and merged. He called the Republican redistricting effort "extraordinarily unfair," blasting it as "immoral, if not unconstitutional."[82]

After the 2002 elections were contested using the new lines, the state's U.S. House delegation went from eleven Republicans and ten Democrats in 2000 to twelve Republicans and seven Democrats, a partisan ratio that did not change through the 2004 election.[83] Starting in 2002, state Democrats mounted a legal challenge to the redistricting scheme, attacking it as an unconstitutional partisan gerrymander. By a five-to-four majority, the United States Supreme Court ruled in favor of the Republican plan in April 2004. Justice Antonin Scalia, in an opinion joined by three of his colleagues in the majority, wrote that no "judicially manageable standards for adjudicating political gerrymandering claims have emerged" by which to void plans such as the Pennsylvania one.

82. "Dems Feel Redistricting Squeeze," Associated Press dispatch, March 5, 2002.

83. As will be covered fully in chapter 7, the Democrats gained four congressional seats in the 2006 election, giving their party eleven seats from Pennsylvania compared to eight for the Republicans.

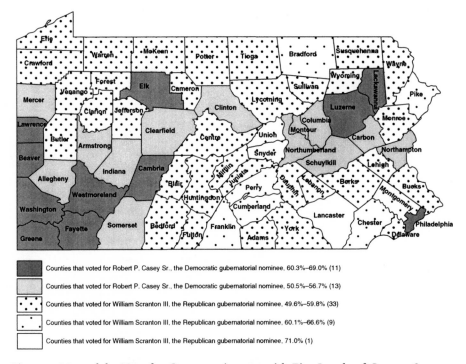

Counties that voted for Robert P. Casey Sr., the Democratic gubernatorial nominee, 60.3%–69.0% (11)

Counties that voted for Robert P. Casey Sr., the Democratic gubernatorial nominee, 50.5%–56.7% (13)

Counties that voted for William Scranton III, the Republican gubernatorial nominee, 49.6%–59.8% (33)

Counties that voted for William Scranton III, the Republican gubernatorial nominee, 60.1%–66.6% (9)

Counties that voted for William Scranton III, the Republican gubernatorial nominee, 71.0% (1)

Fig. 4.5. Map of the Vote for Governor in 1986 with Five Levels of County Support

Four dissenting justices argued that courts could draw up sensible definitions of excessively partisan redistricting.[84]

The 2004 Election

In 2004, with the Democratic voter registration advantage at its highest point[85] since 1986, John Kerry became the fourth straight Democratic presidential nominee to carry Pennsylvania, but, like Al Gore four years before, he did it in a losing bid for the White House. Senator Kerry won Pennsylvania with 51.0 percent of the vote to President Bush's 48.5 percent, a statewide plurality of 144,248 votes.

In the nation, the President won reelection with 50.7 percent to the Democratic senator's 48.3 percent. Thus, Bush finished 2.2 percentage points behind his national average in the Keystone State, slipping slightly from 2000, when the Republican ran 1.5 percentage points behind his national average in Pennsylvania. I return to the

---

84. Charles Lane, "Supreme Court Upholds GOP Redistricting in Pa.," *Washington Post*, April 29, 2004.

85. Registered Democrats outnumbered Republicans in 2004 by 580,208 voters. See Table 5.5 in chapter 5 for Pennsylvania party registration figures from 1926 to 2007.

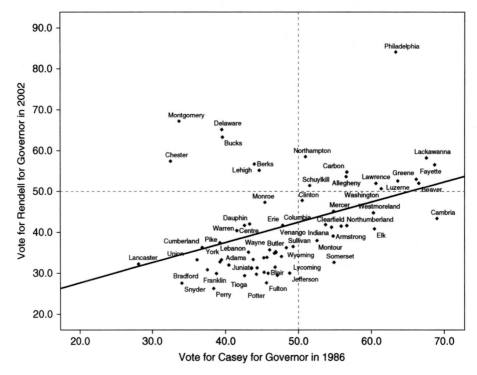

Fig. 4.6. Scattergram of the Democratic Vote for Governor in 1986 and 2002

2004 presidential results in Pennsylvania shortly when I compare recent trends at this level with changes at the statewide level.

One final election must be covered to conclude this two-chapter analytical narrative of major Pennsylvania elections from 1962 to 2004: the U.S. Senate race in 2004. In the general election, Senator Specter easily defeated his Democratic challenger, three-term U.S. Representative Joseph M. Hoeffel of Montgomery County, to earn an unprecedented fifth term. Specter received 52.7 percent of the vote to Hoeffel's 41.9 percent with the rest going to two minor party candidates.[86] In achieving this victory, Specter carried the four large suburban counties nearest to Philadelphia with a total margin of 147,120 votes. By contrast, Kerry's margin there was 87,124.

This part of the 2004 election was the easy part for Specter. To get to a November victory, however, he had to beat back his strongest Republican primary challenge since he won the seat in 1980, and he just barely managed to do it. If roughly nine thousand Republicans had cast their votes differently, out of the over 1 million GOP votes cast in the late April 2004 primary, Specter would have been defeated. The

86. The Constitution party's James N. Clymer won 3.9 percent, and the Libertarian party's Betsy Summers received 1.4 percent.

story of that remarkable, divisive GOP senatorial primary is quite instructive for understanding current Pennsylvania partisan dynamics.

Being cast as a moderate-to-liberal Republican nearly cost Specter the Republican nomination. And that is exactly what Specter's primary opponent, U.S. Representative Patrick Toomey, an unabashed conservative, tried to do at every turn. As Neil Oxman, Hoeffel's campaign manager, put it: "Every time Toomey called Specter a liberal, it was bad for Specter in the primary but good for him against Joe."

Toomey was a three-term congressman from a district that encompassed Lehigh and Northampton counties. He had come from a working-class family, attended Harvard on scholarships, worked in international finance, and opened a restaurant before capturing an open U.S. House seat in 1998.[87] In this primary campaign, Toomey was running against the united advice of the Pennsylvania Republican party establishment, whose leaders urged him to drop out of the race in an effort to conserve resources.[88]

Different factions of the national conservative right, never enamored with Specter's prochoice stance on abortion, his position on school choice and taxes, and his specific Senate votes that they perceived as liberal, teamed up to put their resources and financial support behind Toomey in the hopes of teaching moderate and liberal Republicans a lesson, namely, that there is no place for them in the Republican party. These groups included the Club for Growth; the National Right to Life Committee; the National Taxpayer's Union Campaign Fund; Dr. James Dobson, the director of Focus on the Family; and other conservatives who saw Specter as a "RINO"—"Republican in Name Only."[89] The Club for Growth ran about $1 million in ads disparaging Specter, and its members contributed $800,000 to Toomey's campaign. According to Stephen Moore, who was president of the Club for Growth: "If we beat Specter, we won't have any trouble with wayward Republicans anymore. It serves notice to [Lincoln] Chafee [of Rhode Island], [Olympia] Snowe [of Maine], [George] Voinovich [of Ohio], and others who have been problem children that they will be next."[90] While campaigning for Toomey, Dobson, who does not usually endorse candidates, said: "We see this time as the climax of the civil war of values that's been raging for 35 years. This is the Gettysburg. This is the D-Day, the Stalingrad. We must oppose those who have done so much to create the mess that we're in."[91] In one ad from the Club for Growth, the announcer said, "He is rated one of the Senate's most wasteful spenders. John Kerry? No, Arlen Specter."[92]

87. James Dao, "Conservative Takes on Moderate G.O.P. Senator in Pennsylvania," *New York Times*, April 3, 2004.

88. "Toomey Within Striking Distance in Senate Primary," Associated Press dispatch, April 22, 2004.

89. Ibid.

90. Dao, "Conservative Takes on Moderate."

91. Dao, "G.O.P. Senate Race in Pennsylvania Heats Up," *New York Times*, April 23, 2004.

92. Dao, "Conservative Takes on Moderate."

In order to combat these charges, Specter moved to the right in the primary, appearing with President Bush, and touting his record and commitment to the National Rifle Association and other conservative groups. Bush campaigned for Specter in Pennsylvania, saying, "I'm here to say it as plainly as I can: Arlen Specter is the right man for the United States Senate."[93] Bush added that Specter was "a little bit independent-minded sometimes, but there's nothing wrong with that." He proclaimed that Specter is "a firm ally when it matters most."[94] Senator Santorum, showing his practical side, endorsed Specter, appearing in some television commercials for him.

Noting that prominent conservatives were supporting Specter prompted Moore, of the Club for Growth, to say: "For 25 years, they have complained about Specter. Now we've got this guy cornered and we can actually replace him, and yet there are some conservatives that are sitting on the sidelines."[95] During the primary, Toomey was fond of saying, "I represent the Republican wing of the Republican party," while Specter would declare that Toomey was "not far right, he's far out."[96] Capitalizing on his greatest strength, his seniority in the Senate, and his clout in Washington, Specter raised about $10 million, outspending Toomey three to one.[97]

With a little over three weeks to go in the primary, polls showed that Toomey had pulled to within 13 points of Specter.[98] With only six days left, another poll showed Toomey within striking distance, 5 points, and it appeared that conservative Republicans throughout the state were deserting Specter in droves. According to that last poll, 51 percent agreed that Specter was "too liberal," while only 14 percent thought that Toomey was "too conservative."[99] Specter warned his supporters that he had a fight on his hands. To a reporter, he commented, "The biggest problem I have is that my supporters think I have no problem."[100] On the evening of the election, just before the polls closed, Specter remarked: "I have covered all of Pennsylvania's 67 counties. We have met the people, we have analyzed the projects, we have dealt with the issues. And there's nothing more that I could have done."[101]

When the primary votes were counted, Specter barely eked out a win with 50.8 percent of the votes to Toomey's 49.2 percent, a plurality of 17,146 votes out of the 1,044,532 votes cast. Toomey was able to take twenty counties; see Figure 4.7, which

93. Elisabeth Bumiller, "Bush and Specter on Same Page When It Comes to Re-Election," *New York Times*, April 20, 2004.

94. Ibid.

95. Dao, "Conservative Takes on Moderate."

96. Ibid.

97. Charles Babington, "Specter Survives Primary Challenge," *Washington Post*, April 28, 2004.

98. Dao, "Conservative Takes on Moderate."

99. Patrick Kerkstra, "Toomey Cuts Deeply into Specter Lead, Poll Shows," *Philadelphia Inquirer*, April 21, 2004.

100. "Toomey Within Striking Distance in Senate Primary," Associated Press dispatch, April 22, 2004.

101. Babington, "Specter Survives Primary Challenge," *Washington Post*, April 28, 2004.

identifies the counties carried by each man. In addition to his home counties of Lehigh and Northampton, some other counties that Toomey took with rather large margins were Allegheny, Beaver, Butler, Lancaster, Washington, and Westmoreland. There were seven counties that he lost by less than one hundred votes (in Pike he lost by only eight, and in Somerset he lost by only twenty), and there were thirty-two counties where he lost by less than a thousand votes. Shortly after the primary, Toomey announced his support for Specter in the general election.

The fall campaign was almost an afterthought for Specter following his near-death political experience in April. Hoeffel tried to paint Specter as being too close to Bush, but Specter distanced himself from the President. As always, Specter ran a superb campaign, capitalizing on his superior name recognition, coffers of cash, and seniority. In fact, he claimed to have brought $400 million home to Pennsylvania's schools, hospitals, and highways.[102] In general, during the fall campaign, Specter adopted his typical moderate-to-liberal stance. According to Hoeffel's campaign manager, Oxman, the strategy worked extremely well: "[Specter] shut us down with the unions, with endorsements and financially. . . . Arlen Specter is the heavy-weight champ. He ran a tremendous campaign."[103]

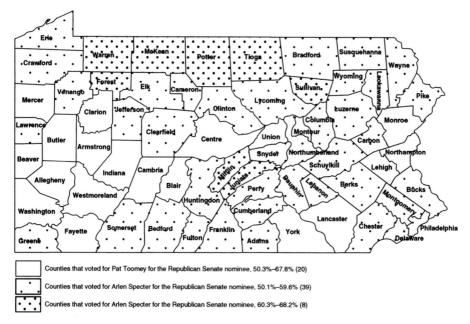

☐ Counties that voted for Pat Toomey for the Republican Senate nominee, 50.3%–67.8% (20)

Counties that voted for Arlen Specter for the Republican Senate nominee, 50.1%–59.6% (39)

Counties that voted for Arlen Specter for the Republican Senate nominee, 60.3%–68.2% (8)

Fig. 4.7. Map of the Vote for Specter and Toomey in the 2004 Republican Primary

102. Steve Goldstein, "Specter Shows Power of Incumbency," *Philadelphia Inquirer*, November 3, 2004.

103. Ibid. When it was all said and done, Specter had raised $20 million, half of which he spent on the primary. This was compared to the $4 million that Hoeffel was able to scrape together.

On election night, Specter told his supporters: "This victory tonight is important as a symbol for the moderate wing of the Republican party. This is a party of inclusion . . . that reaches out to minorities, women, gays, and labor."[104]

Specter's victorious county-level victory pattern in the general election in November is portrayed in the scattergram in Figure 4.8 along with President Bush's Pennsylvania pattern in 2004. The two Republicans correlate at 0.88, which, while certainly a strong relationship, was loose enough to allow a veteran Pennsylvania Republican, who knows how to skillfully maneuver around all factions of the GOP, to stay a safe distance from his party's national loser in Pennsylvania in 2004.

Likewise, a scattergram of Kerry's victorious Pennsylvania pattern in 2004 with Rendell's in 2002 (correlation coefficient of 0.93) offers a fairly recent partisan display from the Democratic perspective, one that is comparable to the Bush–Specter scattergram. See Figure 4.9.

The merger of the presidential and statewide levels exhibited in these two scattergrams comes appropriately at the conclusion of our long journey through

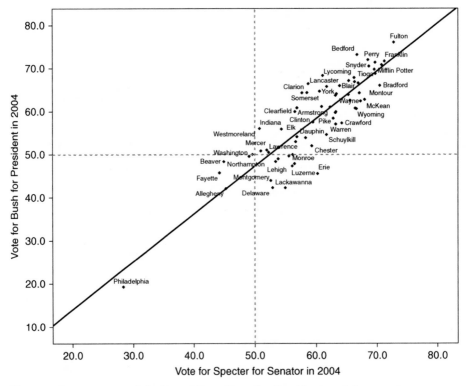

Fig. 4.8. Scattergram of the Republican Vote for President and Senator in 2004

104. Carrie Budoff, Amy Worden, and Kellie Patrick, "Specter Survives Challenge by Hoeffel," *Philadelphia Inquirer*, November 3, 2004.

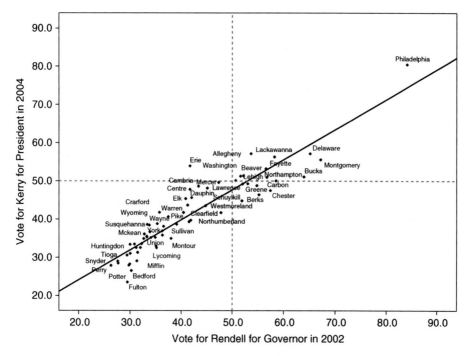

Fig. 4.9. Scattergram of the Democratic Vote for Governor in 2002 and President in 2004

the details of Pennsylvania's major elections from 1962 to 2004. The task remaining in this chapter's final section is to highlight several important statewide trends.

An Examination of Overall Statewide Trends

In the next two chapters, I examine a wealth of aggregate and survey data in an effort to shed further light on the behavior of the post-1960 Pennsylvania electorate. As I embark on these analytical tasks, there are several trends that call out for mention at the conclusion of this two-chapter journey through twenty-seven major statewide elections from 1962 to 2004.

Why did Republican candidates for governor and U.S. senator do so well in a state that consistently supported Democratic presidential candidates at a higher rate than the nation as a whole and in a state where Democratic party registration continued to outstrip Republican registration by several hundred thousand voters? The ideas of Robert Speel, as presented in his *Changing Patterns of Voting in the Northern United States* and as mentioned in chapter 1, are valuable for understanding these Pennsylvania GOP successes in a Democratic-trending state. In Speel's view, if a political party at the state level regularly nominates and elects candidates for high office who hold views in line with the majority of the state's voters but whose views differ from the party's position at the national level, the party and the voters who support the party's candidates are acting rationally. Or, to quote him directly: "While the national Republican party increasingly projects an image that is more popular in the South than in the North, Northern Republicans are free to set their own agendas at the state level, where they rarely emphasize cultural conservatism or patriotism. . . . It is perfectly rational for an electorate to vote Republican at the state level while rejecting that party at the national level."[105]

Pennsylvania Republicans have been exceedingly savvy at adjusting and accommodating themselves to the partisan realities they confronted. Consider the way a *Washington Post* reporter, Paul Taylor, summed up the state's partisan record in August 1986, just a few months before Democrat Robert Casey's gubernatorial victory that year. Impressed with the many Republican statewide victories over the previous two decades or so, especially for the state's U.S. Senate seats, Taylor wrote: "Keystone Democrats have established a record of election-day futility second to none—and done so with their feet planted on some of the most Democratic sod in the country."[106] Among the explanations Taylor pointed to was this one: "[S]mart Republicans . . . have figured out that in a state where the old FDR coalition is alive, the way a Republican wins is by preaching the Democratic gospel." Taylor then recounted his observations from the campaign trail on his trip to the state for the article:

> The state is well into its second generation of moderate-to-leftish Republican leaders. Its gubernatorial candidate, Lt. Gov. William W. Scranton III, 39, is son of former governor William Scranton, a man who symbolized the species in the 1960s. This summer, the younger Scranton is showing that in Pennsylvania, the apple does not fall far from the tree.
>
> Let the New and Christian Right Republicans make their head-lines in other states, Scranton was busy last week campaigning in a black church just outside Pittsburgh, telling a town meeting that he is "very much" for affirmative action, opposes tuition tax credits, supports divestment of state pension funds from companies doing business in South Africa, favors state-funded abortion in certain cases, and finds the Reagan administration "incredibly naïve" for failing to take action against the predatory pricing schemes of foreign steel competitors.
>
> The next morning, Sen. Arlen Specter (R), who is seeking reelection, was at a labor meeting in Harrisburg, spelling out all the times he had

---

105. Robert W. Speel, *Changing Patterns of Voting in the Northern United States: Electoral Realignment, 1952–1996* (University Park: The Pennsylvania State University Press, 1998), 197.

106. Paul Taylor, "Democrats Hope to Overturn Tradition with Strong Ticket," *Washington Post*, August 25, 1986.

"bucked" President Reagan and the GOP Senate leadership, and wearing
recent conservative denunciations of him like a badge of honor.
The two, in short, have a steely grip on the center.[107]

Looking back over the elections I just covered, many other examples besides
the two used in the newspaper article appear to fit the pattern. Republican Tom
Ridge said it well in his 1994 gubernatorial campaign: "Any [Republican] candidate
that doesn't seek Democratic support statewide will never win because the last time
I checked there were 420,000 more Ds than Rs."[108] The account of Arlen Specter's
2004 reelection to a fourth term demonstrates this phenomenon extremely well.
Specter, whose independence from GOP orthodoxy is legendary, was assailed in a
tough primary fight by a conservative Republican congressman as a RINO. After
he eked out a narrow renomination victory, Specter returned to his moderate-to-
liberal stances and easily defeated his Democratic challenger, a veteran congressman and a strong campaigner.

To explore this explanation of GOP success further, I examined the congressional voting records of the successful post-1960 statewide Pennsylvania politicians in
an effort to gauge how liberal or conservative they were. Since many of them were
senators and even two of the governors had previously served in Congress, I was
able to find an abundance of detailed interest-group ratings for nine of the fourteen.
I then averaged the liberal and conservative ratings that these various organizations,
such as Americans for Democratic Action and the American Conservative Union,
employ. The results are exhibited in Table 4.1. (Appendix B contains a lengthy table
listing the year-by-year scores of each of the nine men for all of the eight interest
groups doing the rating.) Figure 4.10 displays the average liberal and conservative
ratings for the nine politicians in bar-graph form. Not surprisingly, the lone two
Democratic senators of the post-1960 era, Clark and Wofford, top the liberal scale.
Three Republican senators, Heinz, Schweiker, and Specter, received liberal scores of
61 percent, 58 percent, and 57 percent respectively, confirming the impression one
forms of their political positioning on the basis of the accounts of their election
campaigns and other information about their careers. Scranton's 53 percent rating
is based on a single term in the U.S. House, but it appears to fit his reputation. With
a score of 49 percent, Senator Scott demonstrates that he well deserves his universal
characterization as a moderate. The relatively low 44 percent liberal rating for Ridge
rings true as well on the basis of his career path and strong ties to conservative
national leaders such as President George W. Bush.

The GOP far outlier, of course, is Rick Santorum who, with an 18 percent
liberal rating and an 89 percent conservative score, represented a departure for
the Pennsylvania GOP. A skillful and attractive campaigner who proved himself in
statewide elections in 1994 and 2000, Santorum was by far the most conservative,

107. Ibid.

108. Associated Press, "Singel Mulls Loss, Lashes Out at Casey," *Philadelphia Inquirer*, November 16,
1994.

Table 4.1 Liberal and Conservative Ratings of Pennsylvania Politicians

Liberal Rating		Conservative Rating	
Clark	96	Santorum	89
Wofford	80	Ridge	62
Heinz	61	Specter	54
Schweiker	58	Heinz	43
Specter	57	Scott	42
Scranton	53	Schweiker	39
Scott	49	Clark	25
Ridge	44	Wofford	16
Santorum	18		

These liberal and conservative scores are an average of ratings done on members of Congress by the following interest groups: Americans for Democratic Action, the American Civil Liberties Union, the Consumer Federation of America, the Committee on Political Education (AFL-CIO), the League of Conservation Voters, the National Education Association, the Chamber of Commerce of the U.S., and the American Conservative Union. The ratings are for all of Pennsylvania's U.S. senators since 1957 and include their ratings if they also served in the U.S. House. In addition, two governors, Tom Ridge and William Scranton, are rated above for their U.S. House service. Appendix B contains a detailed table listing the scores of each member by each interest group that rated him. These ratings range from 0 to 100.

Source: J. Michael Sharp, *Directory of Congressional Voting Scores and Interest Group Ratings* (Washington, DC: CQ Press), 2000; and Jackie Koszczuk and H. Amy Stern, *CQ's Politics in America 2006: The 109th Congress* (Washington, DC: CQ Press), 2006.

successful Republican statewide leader in Pennsylvania politics in the post-1960 era. That he lacked the moderate-to-liberal image of his many statewide Republican predecessors made his 2006 reelection effort a high-priority target of the Democratic party, which recruited a strong, seasoned challenger, Robert Casey Jr., to oppose him. The resulting high-profile 2006 Senate election battle, which generated significant national attention in the fall of 2006, receives full coverage in chapter 7.

The interest-group ratings summarized in Table 4.1 and Figure 4.10 buttress my effort in Table 4.2 to present a classification of all fourteen of Pennsylvania's victors in the gubernatorial and U.S. Senate elections from 1962 to 2004. Three of the Democratic governors, Shapp, Casey, and Rendell, and two of the Republican governors, Shafer and Thornburgh, did not serve in Congress and thus were not part of the interest-group ratings. Still, they have extensive records in public life, both as campaigners and in office, and are known well enough to

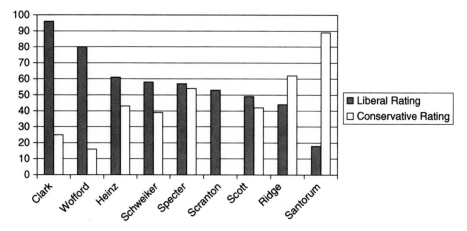

Fig. 4.10. Liberal and Conservative Ratings of Pennsylvania Politicians
Note: There was no conservative rating of Scranton.

justify my placing them as I did in the Table 4.2 typology. The three Democratic governors are easy cases. Shapp was known as an outspoken liberal throughout his political career. Casey's conservative positions on the issues of the culture wars were also well known, as was his economically liberal stance on the old New Deal–style issues. Rendell prided himself on his moderate "New Democrat" approach on noneconomic issues like welfare reform; yet he is clearly in the liberal mainstream of his party on bread-and-butter economic issues. Likewise, governors Shafer and Thornburgh were closely associated with the moderate wing of their party.

Table 4.2 categorizes the political positioning of each man (no woman won an election for governor or U.S. senator during the 1960 to 2006 period)[109] as it appeared from the perspective of the old issues of the New Deal realignment and the new issues of the culture-wars realignment. Six of the nine successful Republican nominees in elections for governor or U.S. senator from 1960 to 2006 fall into the dead center of the typology—moderate on both sets of issues.[110] Two Republicans classify as liberal on the culture-wars issues and moderate on the New Deal economic issues. And, as with the interest-group ratings, the lone GOP dissenter occupying the conservative polar position on both spheres was Senator

109. Only two women won major party nominations during the period: Barbara Hafer, the Republican nominee for governor in 1990, and Lynn Yeakel, the Democratic nominee for U.S. senator in 1992. Both lost the general election.

110. In seeking to classify Governor Scranton, I was aided by the following assessment of A. James Reichley: "The hot button cultural issues were not really much of a factor in Scranton's time. The religious right had not been invented, and the churches were focused on preserving Sunday closing laws and fighting booze, as well as to some extent [supporting] civil rights. Scranton was liberal on civil rights but no more than moderate on the rest." Letter to the author, January 24, 2007.

Table 4.2 Classification of Pennsylvania's U.S. Senatorial and Gubernatorial Victors on the Political Spectrum, 1960–2004

		Issues of the Culture-Wars Realignment		
		Liberal	Moderate	Conservative
Issues of the New Deal Realignment	Liberal	Joseph S. Clark (D) Milton Shapp (D) Harris Wofford (D)	Edward G. Rendell (D)	Robert P. Casey (D)
	Moderate	H. John Heinz (R) Arlen Specter (R)	Hugh Scott (R) William W. Scranton (R) Raymond P. Shafer (R) Richard S. Schweiker (R) Richard L. Thornburgh (R) Thomas J. Ridge (R)	
	Conservative			Rick Santorum (R)

Santorum, even though in his statewide campaigns he downplayed his conservative voting record and issue advocacy or stressed his nonideological constituency service. The five successful Democrats all occupy the liberal position on New Deal issues, as those issues resonated in their time, but on the newer cultural issues they range from the conservative, prolife positioning of Casey to Rendell's moderate stances to Wofford, Shapp, and Clark, who were viewed as classic liberals on both sets of issues.

This political positioning of the moderate-to-liberal Republicans made it difficult for Pennsylvania voters to sort themselves out along the same lines as their national preferences, resulting in the type of ticket-splitting behavior Speel pointed out.

Whether future statewide Pennsylvania Republicans will follow the lead of Senator Specter and the other moderate-to-liberal Republicans or Senator Santorum's conservative direction is yet to be determined. In either case, the fortunes of both parties will be affected. Yet, those partisan fortunes will also be determined by other changes underway in the Pennsylvania electorate. I conclude this chapter with a quick preview of some of those changes and then pick them up again in greater detail in chapters 5 and 6, the first one using aggregate data and the second chapter solely based on survey data.

As the correlation matrices in chapter 3, Tables 3.6 and 3.7, indicate, from the early 1970s through much of the 1990s, the county-by-county electoral patterns of Democratic (and Republican) candidates for governor and U.S. senator exhibited notable discontinuities, signaling that rampant ticket-splitting was going on. I have just addressed the question of how moderate-to-liberal Republicans managed to do well in this shifting partisan environment. Now, I turn more broadly to the meaning of these discordant partisan patterns.

A rough way to isolate this ticket-splitting is to calculate the number of times the Democratic and Republican nominees have carried each county from 1962 to 2002 for the governor's seat and from 1962 to 2004 for one U.S. Senate seat and from 1964 to 2000 for the other Senate seat. The results of these calculations are presented in the county-level composite maps in Figures 4.11, 4.12, and 4.13. Incidentally, Figure 4.12 displays the county pattern for the seat held by Senator Clark in 1962 and later won five times by Senator Specter; Figure 4.13 is for the seat held by Senator Scott in 1964 and won by Senator Santorum in 1994 and 2000.

The gubernatorial map is more diverse than the two maps for the Senate seats, which is not surprising given the long-term dominance of the Senate seats by

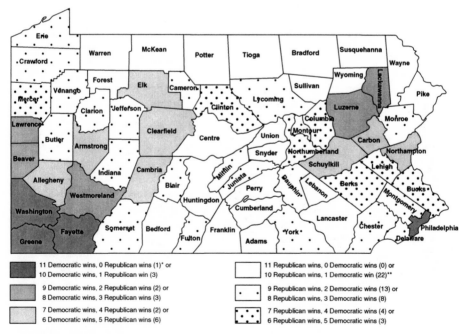

11 Democratic wins, 0 Republican wins (1)* or 10 Democratic wins, 1 Republican win (3)

9 Democratic wins, 2 Republican wins (2) or 8 Democratic wins, 3 Republican wins (3)

7 Democratic wins, 4 Republican wins (2) or 6 Democratic wins, 5 Republican wins (6)

11 Republican wins, 0 Democratic wins (0) or 10 Republican wins, 1 Democratic win (22)**

9 Republican wins, 2 Democratic wins (13) or 8 Republican wins, 3 Democratic wins (8)

7 Republican wins, 4 Democratic wins (4) or 6 Republican wins, 5 Democratic wins (3)

* Philadelphia was the only county that had eleven Democratic wins
** The one Democratic victory in every one of these twenty-two counties was for Casey in 1990.

Fig. 4.11. Map of Democratic and Republican Victories by County in the Gubernatorial Elections, 1962–2002

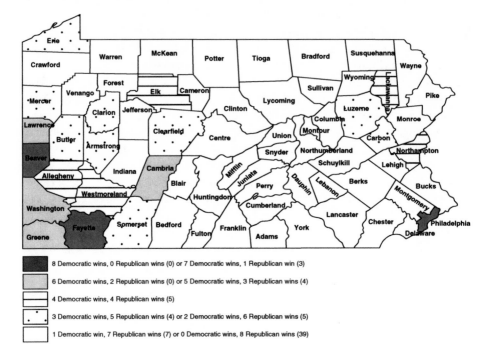

Fig. 4.12. Map of the Vote for Pennsylvania U.S. Senate, Seat One, 1962–2004

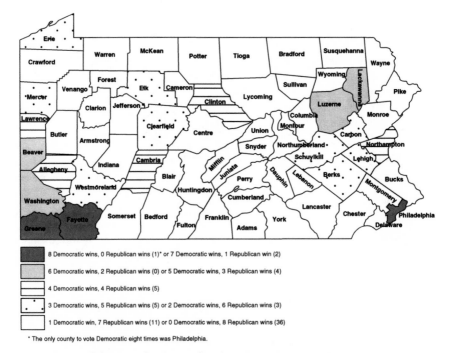

Fig. 4.13. Map of the Vote for Pennsylvania U.S. Senate, Seat Two, 1964–2000

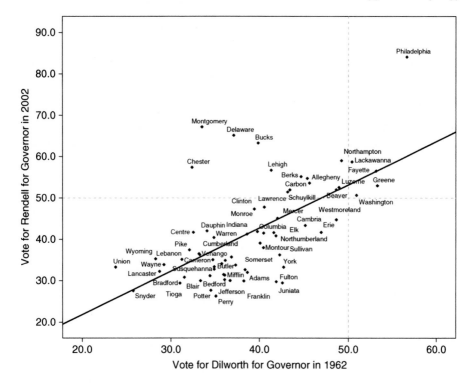

Fig. 4.14. Scattergram of the Democratic Vote for Governor in 1962 and 2002

several Republican incumbents. Still, a dozen or so swing counties stand out in the Senate maps. The gubernatorial map indicates that many more localities were up for grabs during the eleven elections for governor. In chapter 5, when I present an analysis of the shifting county patterns in recent elections, these important "swing" counties play a key role in the new partisan configuration that emerged in the first years of the twenty-first century.

A good way to preview the discussion of these new patterns in statewide elections, the topic that begins the next chapter, is to compare the two book-end gubernatorial elections covered by the two-chapter electoral narrative—the gubernatorial elections of 1962 and 2002. The Democratic nominees, Richardson Dilworth in 1962 and Ed Rendell in 2002, had both been mayor of Philadelphia. Of course, Dilworth lost to William Scranton that year, 44.3 percent to 55.4 percent, and Rendell defeated Mike Fisher in 2002, 53.4 percent to 44.4 percent.

Although the county-level patterns of these two Philadelphia Democrats running forty years apart correlate with each other at a modest 0.61, the scattergram of this correlation is quite revealing. See Figure 4.14. Counties that were weak for Dilworth but strong for Rendell are found in the upper, left-center portion of the figure. An extreme far outlier is Montgomery County along with Delaware, Bucks, and Chester, the four suburban Philadelphia counties that drew considerable attention in the chapter 2 section on presidential election patterns in

Pennsylvania. Nearby in the scattergram are other eastern Pennsylvania counties that were much stronger for Rendell than they were for Dilworth. Then, of course, there are counties, like York and Armstrong (right, lower-center part of the figure) and Erie and Westmoreland, that gave Rendell a lower percentage than they gave Dilworth.

An important trend is tied up in the patterns of change revealed in this scattergram. Much more will be said about these patterns in the next two chapters as attention shifts to ways of tapping voter behavior demographically and attitudinally.

5

Post-1960 Electoral Patterns in the Keystone State: A Detailed Analysis of Voting Trends

I n this chapter, I turn to a variety of aggregate data sources to further analyze Pennsylvania electoral patterns since 1960. In the first section, I employ another valuable statistical technique to provide a more precise view of overall electoral change at the county level in the post-1960 era and earlier. Like the correlations and scattergrams already used, this technique, known as factor analysis, is a valuable analytical tool once its basic purpose is explained in nontechnical language. Next, I examine census data in an effort to explore in more detail the demographic and electoral changes taking place in the state and, specifically, in the Philadelphia and Pittsburgh metropolitan areas. Finally, I investigate party registration data and voter turnout figures to further understand important changes going on at the county level.

Exploring County-Level Electoral Change Using Factor Analysis

At the end of my analysis of Pennsylvania's presidential-election patterns in chapter 2 and at the end of my overview of major statewide elections in chapter 4, I presented two revealing scattergrams that traced the movement of the state's counties between the 1960 and 2004 presidential elections (Figure 2.24) and between the 1962 and 2002 gubernatorial elections (Figure 4.14). Notable county-level shifts were found in these two scattergrams depicting these bookend elections of the post-1960 era, one at the presidential level and one at the gubernatorial level. Prominent among the changes was a dramatic transformation of the populous Philadelphia suburban counties away from their previously strong Republican voting trends and toward the Democratic party. In addition, the scattergrams detected a weakening of Democratic voting patterns in the counties of the Pittsburgh metropolitan region, apart from the core county of Allegheny. Less startling, yet still significant, changes were also visible in other parts of the commonwealth, as careful study of Figure 2.24 and Figure 4.14 reveals.

In order to investigate further the county-level changes isolated by those two important scattergrams, I turned to factor analysis, a statistical technique that enables one to find common patterns in large quantities of data. In that sense, factor analysis is like the correlation/scattergram technique introduced in chapter 2 and used extensively in the last three chapters. However, the factor-analysis technique does more than show relationships among pairs of individual elections. It takes many elections over time and groups them on the basis of how all of their county-by-county patterns relate to each other. As one published guide to factor analysis put it, the procedure is used in "exploratory data analysis [to study] the correlations among a large number of interrelated quantitative variables by grouping the variables into a few factors [hence the name of the technique]. . . . [A]fter grouping, the variables within each factor are more highly correlated with variables in that factor than with variables in other factors."[1] Thus, the technique allows one to uncover broad patterns of electoral change and continuity in a manner different from examining correlation matrices.

To begin the process, I ran a factor analysis of the county-by-county Democratic percentage of the vote for all of the eighty-nine elections for president, governor, and U.S. senator in Pennsylvania from 1896 to 2004. The factor-analysis report grouped the elections into several related components, the top three of which accounted for 83.4 percent of the variance. This means that, cumulatively, the first three factors explain 83.4 percent of the relationship among all of the variables used in the factor analysis, that is, the county-level Democratic votes in the eighty-nine elections. (See Appendix C for numerous tables displaying all the detailed tabulations of the three factor analyses used in this chapter.) In fact, the first factor accounted for 54.9 percent of the variance, the second factor for 23.4 percent, and the third factor for 5.0 percent. Considering that so much of the variance is explained by the first three factors, I decided to focus on them.

My next step was to investigate the relationship of all eighty-nine elections within each of the three factors. In factor analysis terminology, this is called examining the component matrix. (Incidentally, the term *component* is used as a synonym for *factor* in this type of analysis.) The component matrix for the second factor shows that the twenty-two elections between 1896 and 1926 are more closely related to each other than to any of the other later elections. Thus, the factor-analysis technique confirms the major changes that started in the 1928 and 1932 elections, the "Al Smith Revolution" and the New Deal "earthquake," the causes of which were discussed in chapters 1 and 2.

The new and exciting part of using factor analysis in this chapter is that I can examine the post-1928 and post-1932 elections in search of other, more recent

---

1. "Factor Analysis" in *SPSS Base 8.0: Applications Guide* (Chicago: SPSS, Inc., 1998), 317. Chapter 16 of this manual (pp. 317–57) was my chief guide in doing factor analysis for this book.

electoral changes, since, as just demonstrated, this high-powered statistical tool is capable of uncovering big changes if they exist. Examination of the first factor in the component matrix reveals that all of the elections after 1932 are very closely related to each other through 1968 and reasonably closely related through 2004. Thus, it appears that there has been no major disruption in county-level electoral patterns since 1932. This was also indicated in the correlation analysis in the second part of chapter 2 and in the first part of chapter 3.

Interestingly, however, in the elections after 1994, the relationship of these latest elections with those back to 1932 appears weaker, signaling a degree of discontinuity. In fact, the third factor that broke out suggests that something significant was occurring in the elections from 2000 to 2004 that had not happened earlier. This was especially interesting because the common relationship in the third factor held together over the course of nearly all of the twenty-first-century elections. Further, as noted previously, in the correlations and scattergrams of recent individual elections, I had found a series of highly correlated elections. Therefore, the findings in the third factor were particularly intriguing.

To look more closely at patterns found in a factor analysis, one must examine what are called the case summaries. Case summaries report how individual cases, which, in my study, are Pennsylvania's sixty-seven counties, relate to the overall pattern in each factor. The higher a county's score, the more consistent is its voting pattern with the dominant Democratic pattern represented by the factor. If the county's score is 1.0 or higher, it is appropriate, by convention, to say that it is demonstrating Democratic voting consistency on the particular factor being examined. On the other hand, a county with a negative number shows a tendency to vote Republican.

For example, on the second factor, which grouped together the elections from 1896 to 1926, as highly related, Monroe County posts a score of 2.52 and Fulton County registers 2.07, meaning that these counties were voting very consistently Democratic through 1926. Other counties that exhibited strong Democratic consistency, that is, scoring above 1.0, were Adams (1.60), Berks (1.20), Clarion (1.15), Columbia (1.84), Cumberland (1.18), Greene (1.38), Montour (1.56), Pike (1.95), and York (1.40). Nearly all of these are the counties that were shown to have voted Democratic most often in the composite map of presidential voting in five selected elections between 1896 and 1920 (see Figure 2.14).

After the New Deal shake-up, the first factor shows a different set of counties exhibiting Democratic consistency. Leading the pack is Greene at 2.28, followed by Philadelphia with a score of 2.13 and Fayette at 2.16. The other counties are Allegheny (1.10), Beaver (1.48), Cambria (1.47), Carbon (1.01), Lackawanna (1.51), Luzerne (1.09), Northampton (1.30), Washington (1.71), and Westmoreland (1.37). All of these counties were identified as strongly Democratic in the composite presidential election maps from the New Deal forward (Figures 2.17–2.20).

Finally, in the third factor, which breaks out to help explain the elections from 2000 to 2004, we find a new set of counties rising to a level of Democratic consistency above 1.0: Bucks (1.79), Delaware (1.66), Lehigh (1.49), Monroe (1.48),

Montgomery (2.63), Philadelphia (2.86), Pike (1.79), and Wayne (1.35) with Chester close behind at 0.97.

Because the main focus of this book is the post-1960 period, I decided to narrow my next factor analysis to the elections that occurred between 1960 and 2004 so that I could obtain the list of counties that most consistently voted Democratic during this shortened time period. The component matrix shows that all of these elections are closely related, except that the relationship weakens with the elections of the twenty-first century. For instance, the gubernatorial election of 2002 and the presidential election of 2004 posted relatively low scores of 0.73 and 0.78 respectively. Incidentally, the first factor explained 76.0 percent of the variance.[2] The case summaries of the first factor isolated those counties that showed the strongest Democratic consistency during the 1960 to 2004 period. They are listed in the second column of Table 5.1.

In light of the fact that these two separate factor analyses pointed to something new happening from 2000 to 2004, I decided to run a separate factor analysis encompassing only the five elections held from 2000 to 2004 to get a handle on the counties exhibiting a high level of Democratic consistency during this time frame, and what I found was striking. The first factor explained 94.2 percent of the variance, and the component matrix showed a very high degree of intercorrelation, ranging from 0.95 to 0.99, a finding that, of course, mirrored what I found in the correlations in chapter 3, Table 3.7.

The most consistently Democratic counties identified by the case summaries were many of the same newcomers identified in the third factor of the 1896 to 2004 factor analysis: Delaware (1.45), Montgomery (1.41), and Bucks (1.02). The top Democratic counties also consisted of many of those that had earlier been in this category. They are all displayed in the third column in Table 5.1, a useful comparative visual aid. Keep in mind that Delaware, Montgomery, and Bucks counties break into the Democratic consistency ranks for the first time even though they still have Republican registration pluralities. As mentioned, the first and second columns of Table 5.1 display the most consistently Democratic counties found in the first factor of the two previous factor analyses reported in this chapter: the ones for the 1896 to 2004 and 1960 to 2004 overlapping periods.

Overall, Table 5.1 offers an excellent summary of the major movements of the top Democratic counties over time. Notice that Philadelphia increases from 2.14 in the time frame encompassing 1896 to 2004, to 3.06 in the 1960 to 2004 period, to 4.04 in the 2000 to 2004 period, clearly showing that Philadelphia has progressively become even more Democratic in each period. At the same time, Fayette, in the Pittsburgh metro area, increases from 2.16 in the 1896 to 2004 analysis, to 2.19 in the 1960 to 2004 timeframe, and then falls to 1.61 in the latest period from 2000 to 2004.

---

2. Several elections that featured candidates with unusually strong support in western Pennsylvania caused second, third, and fourth factors to break out, explaining their different support patterns. See the component matrix for the factor analysis of the 1960 to 2004 elections in Appendix C.

Table 5.1 Comparison of Counties Showing Democratic Consistency in the First Component of the Factor Analyses of the Democratic Vote for President, Governor, and U.S. Senator, 1896–2004, 1960–2004, and 2000–2004

| | Pres Gov Sen 1896-2004 | | Pres Gov Sen 1960-2004 | | Pres Gov Sen 2000-2004 | |
	County	Score	County	Score	County	Score
1	Greene	2.28	Philadelphia	3.06	Philadelphia	4.04
2	Fayette	2.16	Fayette	2.19	Fayette	1.61
3	Philadelphia	2.14	Greene	1.97	Allegheny	1.56
4	Washington	1.71	Beaver	1.81	Lackawanna	1.51
5	Lackawanna	1.51	Washington	1.70	Delaware	1.45
6	Beaver	1.48	Lackawanna	1.51	Montgomery	1.41
7	Cambria	1.47	Cambria	1.36	Beaver	1.29
8	Westmoreland	1.37	Lawrence	1.35	Greene	1.20
9	Northampton	1.30	Westmoreland	1.25	Lawrence	1.18
10	Allegheny	1.10	Allegheny	1.24	Washington	1.11
11	Luzerne	1.09	Luzerne	1.24	Bucks	1.02
12	Carbon	1.01	Northampton	1.10	Northampton	1.01

Also, note that Greene, another Pittsburgh-area county, falls from 2.28 to 1.97 to 1.20. Even more striking is that Cambria, Westmoreland, and Luzerne all fall from Democratic consistency between the 1960 to 2004 and the 2000 to 2004 periods.

Clearly, the last two factor analyses were tapping the underlying partisan movements that I have witnessed throughout my study of Pennsylvania's post-1960 elections. Therefore, I thought that a comparison of the county scores from the 1960 to 2004 period with those from the 2000 to 2004 period held the potential for capturing the complex partisan patterns that have emerged in Pennsylvania's sixty-seven counties in recent elections. Thus, I produced a scattergram depicting the relationship between these two factor analyses. The result, pictured in Figure 5.1, more than confirmed my hope that much of the partisan upheaval I had observed could be sorted out in an understandable fashion.

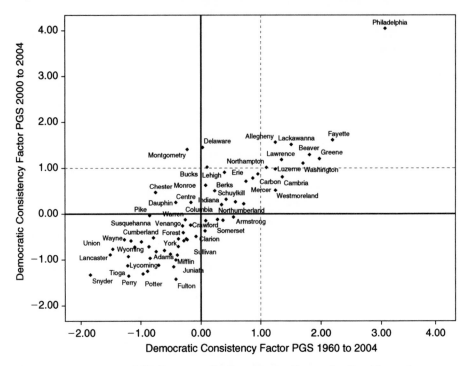

Fig. 5.1. Scattergram of the Democratic Consistency Factor for President, Governor, and Senator, 1960–2004, with the Democratic Consistency Factor for President, Governor, and Senator, 2000–2004

This scattergram is slightly different from the straightforward scattergrams used previously.[3] Every county's Democratic consistency score, that is, the factor score that each county received in the case summaries, is plotted. A reference line is placed at zero for both the *x* and *y* axes to separate the positive and negative scores. The scores in these two factor analyses range from +4.04 to –1.42. As mentioned previously, positive scores represent a Democratic voting tendency in those counties. Negative scores, by definition, represent a Republican voting tendency. The dotted lines are added at the 1.0 position to easily identify those counties that reached the level of Democratic consistency in their voting.

Along the bottom of the plot (on the *x* axis) is the Democratic consistency measure for 1960 to 2004, and along the left side of the plot (on the *y* axis) is the Democratic consistency measure for 2000 to 2004. Each county's point on the plot is determined by the intersection of its two Democratic consistency scores. For example, Chester County, which scored –0.76 in the 1960 to 2004 factor analysis and 0.47 in the 2000 to 2004 factor analysis, is plotted in the upper left-hand quadrant at the spot where those two points intersect.

3. A scattergram displaying factor-analysis scores is technically known as a *factor score* plot in the terminology of factor analysis.

If a county appears on the left side of the vertical zero reference line, then that county exhibited Republican voting tendencies in the 1960 to 2004 time period. If the county is plotted to the right of the vertical zero reference line, that county exhibited Democratic tendencies in the 1960 to 2004 time period. If a county appears below the horizontal zero reference line, that county exhibited Republican tendencies in the 2000 to 2004 period. And, if a county appears above the horizontal zero reference line, that county exhibited Democratic tendencies in the 2000 to 2004 period. The beauty of this plot is that we can see the direction of every county's partisan movement from its position in the 1960 to 2004 period to its position in the 2000 to 2004 period.

Thus, the top right-hand quadrant consists of all counties that have maintained their Democratic consistency over the past forty-four years. Still, within this quadrant, we can pinpoint the movement of each county over the two overlapping time periods. For example, consider Luzerne County. On the x axis, that is, during the 1960 to 2004 period, Luzerne scored a 1.24. However, on the y axis, that is, during the 2000 to 2004 period, Luzerne registered only a 0.98. Consequently, Luzerne's movement in the most recent period is clearly away from Democratic consistency. In the bottom left quadrant are found those counties that have retained their Republican voting tendency over the last forty-four years. For instance, Lancaster posted a –1.51 in the 1960 to 2004 period. However, in the 2000 to 2004 period, it registered only –0.89, demonstrating a decline in Republican consistency, or to put it another way, a movement toward the Democratic party.

The bottom right-hand quadrant is host to those counties that had shown Democratic tendencies but have now fallen below the horizontal zero reference line in the more recent time period. For instance, Armstrong County registered a 0.55 in the 1960 to 2004 period. However, its score fell below zero to –0.07 in the 2000 to 2004 period, demonstrating a decline in Democratic voting. Finally, the top left-hand quadrant represents the counties that were below zero but have moved up above zero. In the case of Montgomery County, it moved all the way from –0.23 on the x axis to 1.41 on the y axis, registering a sizable increase in Democratic voting.

Space limitations preclude labeling every point on the plot, so it is important to introduce Table 5.2 in order to pinpoint the movement of all of Pennsylvania's sixty-seven counties. Just as the scattergram did, this table categorizes the counties into the same quadrants, but unlike the scattergram, all counties and their scores are visible. The bold lines crisscrossing the table are the same as the vertical and horizontal zero reference lines on the scattergram. The dotted lines represent the separation of those counties showing Democratic strength above and below 1.0 and signify those counties showing Republican strength, as displayed in italics, above and below –1.0.

Further, the table displays the two scores for each county side by side, that is, the one for the 1960 to 2004 period and the one for the 2000 to 2004 time period. The number in the third column represents the change between the two scores, that is, a subtraction of the 1960 to 2004 score from the 2000 to 2004 score. Those counties posting a positive score during the 1960 to 2004 time period showed Democratic

Table 5.2 Quadrants Identifying Each County's Democratic Consistency Factor from the Factor Analyses of the Democratic Vote for President, Governor, and U.S. Senator, 1960–2004 and 2000–2004

Counties at or above +1.0

	1960–2004	2000–2004	Change
Philadelphia	3.06	4.04	+0.99
Fayette	2.19	1.61	-0.58
Allegheny	1.24	1.56	+0.32
Lackawanna	1.51	1.51	0.00
Delaware	0.03	1.45	+1.42
Beaver	1.81	1.29	-0.52
Greene	1.97	1.20	-0.77
Lawrence	1.35	1.18	-0.16
Washington	1.70	1.11	-0.60
Bucks	0.10	1.02	+0.92
Northampton	1.10	1.01	-0.08

Counties maintained position above 0

	1960–2004	2000–2004	Change
Luzerne	1.24	0.98	-0.27
Lehigh	0.40	0.91	+0.51
Carbon	0.95	0.87	-0.08
Cambria	1.36	0.81	-0.55

Counties moved from below 0 to above +1.0

	1960–2004	2000–2004	Change
Montgomery	-0.23	1.41	+1.63

Counties moved from below 0 to above 0

	1960–2004	2000–2004	Change
Chester	-0.76	0.47	+1.22
Centre	-0.17	0.25	+0.42
Dauphin	-0.42	0.25	+0.67

Counties maintained position below 0

	1960–2004	2000–2004	Change
Pike	-0.85	-0.04	+0.82
Warren	-0.26	-0.13	+0.13
Crawford	-0.17	-0.24	-0.07
Venango	-0.30	-0.26	+0.04
Forest	-0.29	-0.41	-0.11
Butler	-0.08	-0.49	-0.41
Susquehanna	-0.79	-0.52	+0.27
York	-0.37	-0.54	-0.17
Clarion	-0.24	-0.54	-0.30

Mercer	0.87	0.78	-0.09
Erie	0.75	0.71	-0.04
Monroe	0.08	0.63	+0.55
Westmoreland	1.25	0.51	-0.73
Berks	0.23	0.50	+0.27
Schuylkill	0.42	0.32	-0.11
Clinton	0.58	0.26	-0.32
Elk	0.72	0.22	-0.50
Indiana	0.35	0.20	-0.15

Counties moved from above 0 to below 0

	1960–2004	2000–2004	Change
Armstrong	0.55	-0.07	-0.62
Northumberland	0.28	-0.12	-0.40
Clearfield	0.37	-0.14	-0.51
Columbia	0.08	-0.15	-0.23
Somerset	0.07	-0.37	-0.44

No counties moved from above 0 to -1.0

Montour	-0.23	-0.56	-0.33
Wayne	-1.27	-0.56	+0.71
Sullivan	-0.28	-0.58	-0.30
Wyoming	-1.16	-0.59	+0.58
Cumberland	-0.99	-0.61	+0.38
Cameron	-0.38	-0.71	-0.33
McKean	-0.86	-0.71	+0.15
Lebanon	-1.10	-0.72	+0.38
Union	-1.47	-0.76	+0.70
Adams	-0.61	-0.79	-0.18
Blair	-0.75	-0.82	-0.07
Lycoming	-0.51	-0.87	-0.37
Lancaster	-1.51	-0.89	+0.62
Jefferson	-0.39	-0.89	-0.50
Bradford	-1.21	-0.93	+0.28
Huntingdon	-0.85	-0.97	-0.12

Counties at or below -1.0

	1960–2004	2000–2004	Change
Mifflin	-0.42	-1.01	-0.59
Franklin	-0.71	-1.12	-0.42
Tioga	-1.22	-1.13	+0.09
Juniata	-0.45	-1.15	-0.70
Bedford	-0.89	-1.25	-0.36
Potter	-0.96	-1.31	-0.35
Snyder	-1.84	-1.33	+0.51
Perry	-1.20	-1.35	-0.15
Fulton	-0.42	-1.42	-1.01

consistency, while those counties posting a negative score during that time period exhibited some level of Republican strength. For example, Montgomery County, as mentioned previously, scored −0.23 in the 1960 to 2004 period but surged to 1.41 in the 2000 to 2004 period. Thus, Montgomery posted a huge change in the direction of Democratic voting of +1.63, which, in fact, was the largest change recorded by any of the sixty-seven counties. When this measure of change is calculated for all the counties, the table comprehensively displays the most recent partisan direction of each county and becomes the first research device that afforded me the opportunity to present such an all-inclusive picture of recent Pennsylvania electoral change, one that makes sense of the disparate election patterns spanning these years.

Notable movements can be seen throughout the state. Although Montgomery was the only county in the top left-hand quadrant to rise above 1.0, Chester, Dauphin, and Centre made significant advances of +1.22, +0.67, +0.42 respectively. In the top right-hand quadrant, Philadelphia and Allegheny became more consistently Democratic, posting gains of +0.99 and +0.32 respectively.

Conversely, Fayette's and Greene's Democratic consistency scores fell by −0.58 and −0.77. Also, notice how Luzerne, Cambria, and Westmoreland counties experienced movement from above the 1.0 dotted line to below it. Luzerne registered a decrease of −0.27, nearly resting it right on the line at 0.98. Cambria is not that much farther down (at 0.81), posting a loss of −0.55. And Westmoreland dropped by −0.73. Also, in the upper right-hand quadrant, Delaware and Bucks moved from 0.03 and 0.10, respectively, to 1.45 and 1.02, posting large increases of +1.42 and +0.92. Lehigh, Monroe, and Berks are also moving toward the 1.0 line, recording gains of +0.51, +0.55, and +0.27 respectively.

In the bottom right-hand quadrant, Armstrong, Northumberland, Clearfield, Columbia, and Somerset, counties that were once above zero and thus showed some mild Democratic tendency, descended below zero and are now exhibiting Republican tendencies. For example, Armstrong, which led the move, went from 0.55 to −0.07 for a net loss of −0.62. Of the thirty-four counties in the bottom left-hand quadrant, twenty became stronger in their Republican vote, such as York and Huntingdon. Conversely, fourteen posted Democratic gains, moving them closer to the zero mark. For example, Pike and Lancaster moved from −0.85 to −0.04 (gain of +0.82) and −1.51 to −0.89 (gain of +0.62) respectively. Warren County moved from −0.26 to −0.13, posting a gain of +0.13 and inching closer to the zero line, or moving closer to a Democratic voting tendency. Also, Wayne County, which was located at −1.27, inched up to −0.56, posting an increase of +0.71. Nine counties, led by Fulton, went or remained below −1.0 in the 2000 to 2004 period. In fact, Fulton became the state's most Republican county by posting a net Democratic loss of −1.01.

Table 5.2 provides a precise illustration of the movement of Pennsylvania's counties. Thirty-nine counties register below zero and twenty-eight counties, above zero. Forty-one counties are moving away from Democratic consistency, twenty-five are increasing or moving toward Democratic consistency, and one county—Lackawanna—remained unchanged. Of course, regardless of the direction of movement, a county's score on the hierarchy of Democratic consistency is important in and of itself because it reveals the strongest and weakest Democratic counties, or to put it the other way, the weakest and strongest Republican counties.

The geographic dimension of these movements can best be seen in the map in Figure 5.2. This map displays the positive or negative Democratic consistency "direction-of-change" figure for each county, or the third column of numbers from Table 5.2. The county is shaded gray if the county's 2000 to 2004 Democratic consistency score is above zero; the county is white if the score is below zero. Thus, the map acts as a quick summary of my findings concerning the partisan direction of Pennsylvania's counties, as displayed in Figure 5.1 and Table 5.2. All three capture the increasing Democratic consistency of the Philadelphia metro area, the decreasing Democratic strength in the Pittsburgh metro area, the declining Democratic vote in the southern border counties except for Lancaster, the rise in Democratic voting in the rapidly growing northeastern counties in the region of the Pocono Mountains, and the relative partisan stability of the northern and central regions.

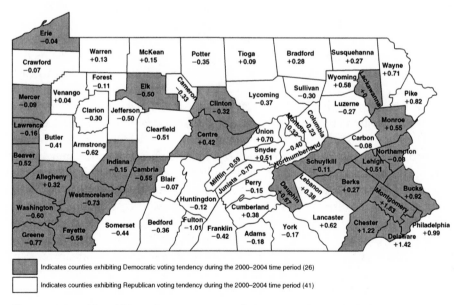

Fig. 5.2. Map Identifying the Increases and Decreases in Democratic Consistency via a Comparison of the Factor Analyses of the 1960 to 2004 Democratic Vote for President, Governor, and Senator and the 2000 to 2004 Democratic Vote for President, Governor, and Senator

Note: Positive numbers (increases) indicate movement toward Democratic consistency; negative numbers (decreases) indicate movement away from Democratic consistency.

I now turn to census data in an effort to shed light on the reasons for these county-level partisan movements.

Analysis of Census Data: Insights into Pennsylvania Electoral Change

In this section, I use census data to add to our understanding of the Pennsylvania electorate in two ways. First, I examine various demographic variables and relate them to voting patterns. This is done by correlating several census variables with a composite variable that captures recent Democratic county-level voting trends. Then, I concentrate my census-data analysis on the Philadelphia and Pittsburgh metropolitan counties in order to better understand voting trends there in the context of the fascinating, diverse political and demographic changes that have taken place in these two key population centers.

Before examining the relationship of specific demographic variables and voting trends, it is useful to look at the state's overall general population trend. Between the 1960 and 2000 censuses, Pennsylvania's population grew by only 8.5 percent, to 12,281,054 in 2000 from 11,319,366 in 1960, a slow enough growth rate relative to other parts of the country to result in Pennsylvania losing eleven of its thirty U.S. House seats during the four decades after the 1960 census.[4] The map in Figure 5.3 presents the percentage gain or loss in population experienced by each of the state's counties from 1960 to 2000.[5] The big losers have been the counties in western Pennsylvania, led by Allegheny, which lost 21.3 percent of its population over the four decades. Two northeastern Pennsylvania counties—Lackawanna and Luzerne—also lost population along with Philadelphia, which declined 24.2 percent over the forty-year period. The Philadelphia-area suburban counties were big population gainers, as Figure 5.3 indicates. Big percentage increases were also posted in many south-central counties like the populous Lancaster and York counties and in the three far northeastern counties of Monroe, Pike, and Wayne. In fact, Pike and Monroe counties posted huge population increases of 405.6 percent and 250.5 percent respectively between 1960 and 2000. The rapid growth in these three counties is transforming them politically, as evidenced by an increase in Democratic party registration and in the Democratic vote for president in recent years. (See Appendix D for the actual population figures used to calculate these change percentages.)

---

4. In 1960, two years before the results of the 1960 census were applied to the apportionment of seats in the U.S. House, Pennsylvania had thirty members of the House. Starting in 2002, it had nineteen members. The state lost three seats after the 1960 census and two seats after every census since then.

5. See Appendix D for a county-by-county presentation of the state's population for 1960, 1980, and 2000.

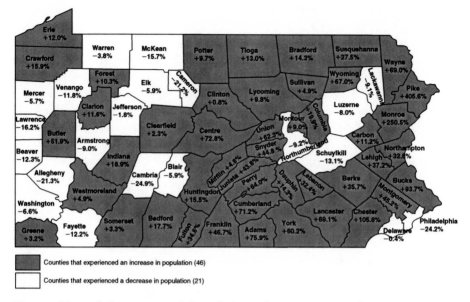

Fig. 5.3. Map of Percentage of Population Change in Pennsylvania by County Between 1960 and 2000

Statewide Demographic Comparisons

Examination of several demographic variables statewide sheds further light on Pennsylvania political patterns. First, the state's black population in 2000 was 1,211,669, or 9.9 percent, up from 8.8 percent in 1980. Philadelphia contained 653,364 African Americans in 2000, accounting for 53.9 percent of the state's total. Allegheny had 158,002 African Americans (13.0 percent of the state total); Delaware, 79,260 (6.5 percent); Montgomery, 55,190 (4.6 percent); Dauphin, 41,439 (3.4 percent); Chester, 26,421 (2.2 percent); and Bucks, 18,454 (1.5 percent). Together these six counties plus Philadelphia accounted for 80.5 percent of the state's black population in the 2000 census. Most of the state's rural, small-town counties had hardly any African Americans living there at all. For example, Adams County, with a population of 91,292, had 1,126 blacks, or 1.2 percent of the county's population.

This pattern, of course, is not atypical for large industrial states of the North, where blacks were attracted from the South by the lure of job opportunities in the larger cities. Since African Americans have been wedded to the Democratic party dating back to the civil rights era of the 1960s, and in many cases, to the New Deal era, the concentration of large numbers of blacks in a few urban settings has important implications for politics in those localities. One cannot understand Philadelphia politics, for example, without a full appreciation of the politics of race there.[6]

6. See Miriam Ershkowitz and Joseph Zikmund II, eds., *Black Politics in Philadelphia* (New York: Basic Books, 1973); Judith Goode and Jo Anne Schneider, *Reshaping Ethnic and Racial Relations in Philadelphia: Immigrants in a Divided City* (Philadelphia: Temple University Press, 1994);

Figure 5.4 is a scattergram of the correlation of the percentage of African Americans in Pennsylvania's sixty-seven counties with a composite of Democratic voting strength in each county between 2000 and 2004, that is, the Democratic consistency factor for president, governor, and U.S. senator derived in the 2000 to 2004 factor analysis used profitably in the first section of this chapter and fully explained there.[7] The figure shows that the relationship between the two variables is by no means random; the correlation coefficient is 0.65. The figure also highlights the concentration pattern of Pennsylvania's African American population. In chapter 6, which is devoted to survey research analysis, I use the far more precise polling tool to demonstrate the heavily Democratic voting behavior of the state's black population.

Of course, the results of the correlation depicted in Figure 5.4 and others employed in this section are limited by the nature of aggregate data, which do not directly tap individuals.[8] Yet, sensible, cautious inferences about individual voter behavior can be made from correlations of data grouped into aggregates as I have done throughout this book by following a venerable tradition in political science election studies, that is, by examining the relationship of county-level voting patterns in various elections. However, one must go beyond such correlations in the search for complete understanding,[9] as I have also done with the election accounts, the composite county-level maps, and other data sources and as I do in the rest of this chapter and, via survey data, in chapter 6.

Pennsylvanians with a Latino/Hispanic background numbered 394,088, or 3.2 percent of the state's population in 2000. Lehigh County had the largest percentage of Latinos in 2000—10.2 percent of the county's population. Philadelphia's Latino population was next in percentage terms, 8.5 percent of the city's population. Given Philadelphia's size, this meant that there were about 130,000 Latinos in the city, not an inconsiderable presence. By contrast, the number of Latinos in Allegheny County was negligible, only 0.9 percent of the county's population. The state had a relatively small population of persons from

and Joe William Trotter Jr. and Eric Ledell Smith, eds., *African Americans in Pennsylvania: Shifting Historical Perspectives* (University Park: Pennsylvania State University Press and the Pennsylvania Historical and Museum Commission, 1997).

7. By the way, the Democratic consistency factor used in Figure 5.4 correlates at 0.99 with the county-level vote of the Democratic presidential nominee in 2000, Al Gore, and at 0.98 with the Democratic nominee in 2004, John Kerry. Each county's 2000 to 2004 Democratic consistency factor can be found in Appendix C.

8. This problem, known as the ecological fallacy, is discussed by W. Phillips Shively, *The Craft of Political Research*, 6th ed. (Upper Saddle River, NJ: Pearson/Prentice Hall, 2005), 127.

9. Consider the advice of V. O. Key Jr., a pioneer in election studies: "In work relating to the electoral behavior of geographical units, for example, one needs to bring into the analysis every scrap of evidence to be had. In fact, experience develops a two-way working pattern. Correlation of statistical data points to inquiries to be made [via other sources]. In turn, such information gives substance to the correlation-centered analysis." *A Primer of Statistics for Political Scientists* (New York: Thomas Y. Crowell, 1954), 125.

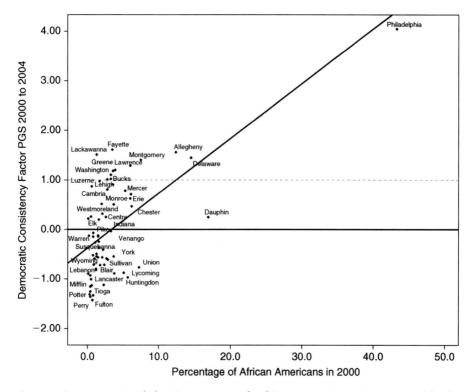

Fig. 5.4. Scattergram of the Percentage of African Americans in 2000 with the 2000–2004 Democratic Consistency Factor

Asia, 219,813, or 1.8 percent of the total population in 2000, mainly concentrated in the greater Philadelphia area. (See Appendix D, Table 2, for county-by-county data on the state's African American, Latino, and Asian populations.)

Between 1980 and 2000, Pennsylvania became an even more urban state, going from 69.3 percent urban to 77.0 percent, a 7.7 percentage point gain. The percentage of urban population yields a moderately positive relationship (correlation coefficient of 0.66) with a county-by-county measure of Democratic voting consistency in the 2000 to 2004 period. See Figure 5.5, the scattergram of this relationship.

Not surprisingly, the percentage of rural population correlates at the same 0.66 with a comparable Republican consistency factor. An intriguing variable is the percentage of the population engaged in agriculture, forestry, fishing, and hunting, which dropped from 1.6 in 1980 to 1.0 in 2000. This variable in 2000 yields a correlation coefficient of −0.72 with the Democratic consistency factor. See Figure 5.6 for a scattergram of the relationship.

The changing reality of Pennsylvania's economy is captured in the percentage of the population engaged in manufacturing variable. The U.S. census calculates the percentage at 28.4 in 1980; by 2000, it had dropped to 16.0 percent. The county-by-county figures for both census years in this category point to countless

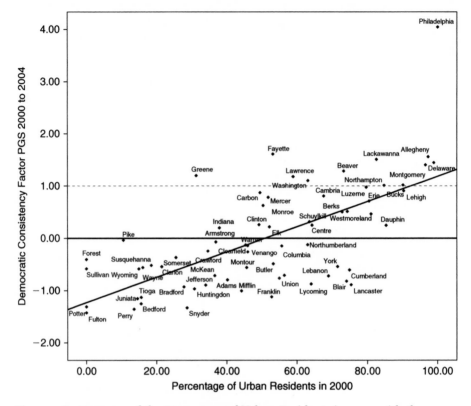

Fig. 5.5. Scattergram of the Percentage of Urban Residents in 2000 with the 2000–2004 Democratic Consistency Factor

stories of plant closings and joblessness, qualifying parts of the state for inclusion in the nation's industrial "rust belt." Erie County, for example, had 36.9 percent of its workforce engaged in manufacturing in 1980; in 2000, the figure stood at 23.8 percent. In Lackawanna County, the comparable percentages were 30.0 and 15.7. This variable for 2000 correlated with the Democratic consistency factor at –0.45. (See Appendix D, Table 3, for county-by-county population percentage engaged in manufacturing plus the percentage of urban population and the percentage of persons engaged in the agriculture, forestry, fishing, and hunting industries.)

Trends in the Philadelphia and Pittsburgh Areas

As the analysis of county-level voting patterns in chapters 2 and 4 and the factor analysis in the first section of this chapter showed, fascinating, divergent trends are underway in the populous Philadelphia suburban counties and in the counties surrounding Pittsburgh. I recap these trends in two pairs of charts. The first, Figures 5.7 and 5.8, trace the Democratic presidential voting results in the counties of both areas from 1960 to 2004. The second, Figures 5.9 and 5.10, trace Democratic

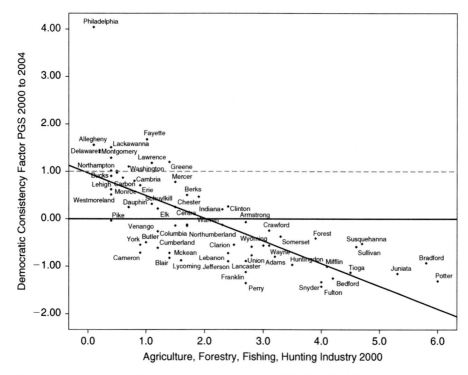

Fig. 5.6. Scattergram of Percentage of People Employed in the Agriculture, Forestry, Fishing, and Hunting Industries with the 2000–2004 Democratic Consistency Factor

party registration in both metro areas. The pro-Democratic voting patterns in the Philadelphia suburban counties are clearly shown in Figure 5.7. Note that the Democratic vote for president has been steadily increasing since 1980 in each of these counties. Conversely, Figure 5.8 demonstrates the weakening of the Democratic presidential vote since 1988 in the counties surrounding Pittsburgh, although this is not the case for Pittsburgh's own county of Allegheny, which did trend downward in 1988 but has been on the rise since 1992. These movements over time are also revealed in the factor analysis.

Similar trends are depicted in Figures 5.9 and 5.10 for Democratic party registration. While Figure 5.9 demonstrates an increase in the percentage of voters registered as Democrats since 1988 in Philadelphia and its surrounding counties, Figure 5.10 illustrates a declining percentage of registered Democrats in the Pittsburgh area since 1988. (Bucks is an exception in the Philadelphia area because its share of Democrats dipped in 1988; however, in raw numbers, Democratic registration has been on the rise there since 1960.)

As explained in chapter 1, the ideas of John B. Judis and Ruy Teixeira are helpful in understanding the political behavior of these populous areas. In *The Emerging Democratic Majority*, Judis and Teixeira write that many American postindustrial

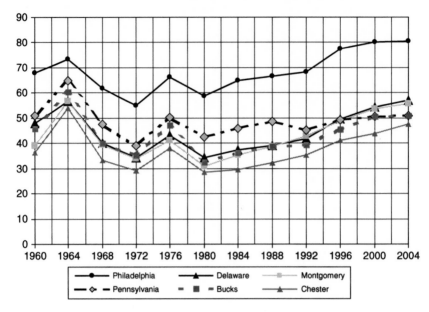

Fig. 5.7. Democratic Vote for President in the Philadelphia Metro Area, 1960–2004

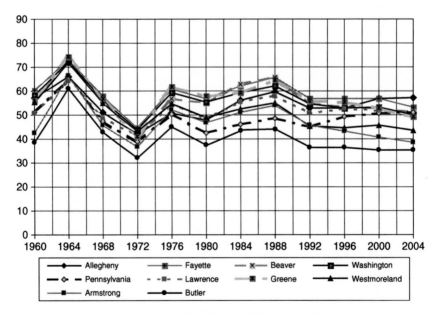

Fig. 5.8. Democratic Vote for President in the Pittsburgh Metro Area, 1960–2004

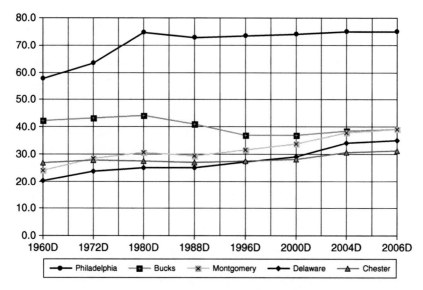

Fig. 5.9. Democratic Party Registration in the Philadelphia Metro Area, 1960–2006

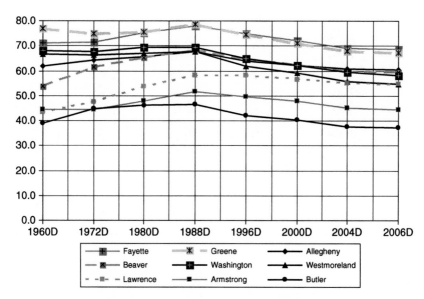

Fig. 5.10. Democratic Party Registration in the Pittsburgh Metro Area, 1960–2006

metropolitan areas have become "headquarters for the production of ideas" peopled by new professionals who hold socially liberal views. They call these places "ideopolises" and point to Chicago and San Francisco along with Philadelphia as prime examples of the phenomenon. In the past, these cities were surrounded by Republican suburbs, they write, but no more: "Now the entire metropolitan area in many of these locations has become strongly Democratic."[10]

Comparing the Philadelphia and Pittsburgh metro areas makes clear that the former deserves the ideopolis label, but the Pittsburgh area is some distance away from meeting the criteria sketched by Judis and Teixeira. In their description, an ideopolis is one that has attracted highly educated people, many in professional occupations, with high incomes. Further, these vibrant places are experiencing significant population growth as they become meccas for young, upwardly mobile men and women. In fact, they point to the strong presence of women professionals as a key ingredient.[11] Also, the authors mention the growth of minorities as part of the overall mix.

Using census data, I have constructed a series of illustrations that support my classification of the Philadelphia area, but not the Pittsburgh area, as an ideopolis. First, Figures 5.11 and 5.12 trace the percentage of persons in both places who have completed four years of college or more from 1960 to 2000. Then, Figures 5.13 and 5.14

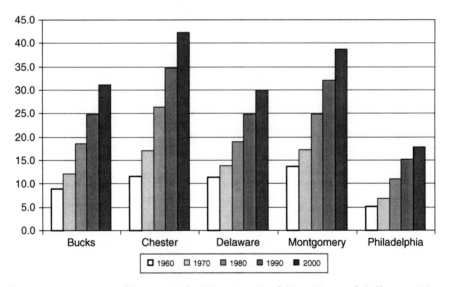

Fig. 5.11. Percentage of Persons Who Have Attained Four Years of College or More in Each County in the Philadelphia Metropolitan Area, 1960–2000, as Reported by the U.S. Census

10. John B. Judis and Ruy Teixeira, *The Emerging Democratic Majority* (New York: Scribner, 2002), 8–9.

11. Judis and Teixeira's ideas from *The Emerging Democratic Majority* are summarized in considerable detail in my chapter 1.

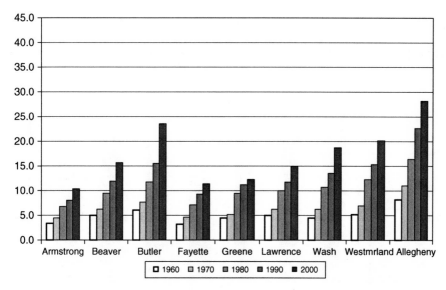

Fig. 5.12. Percentage of Persons Who Have Attained Four Years of College or More in Each County in the Pittsburgh Metropolitan Area, 1960–2000, as Reported by the U.S. Census

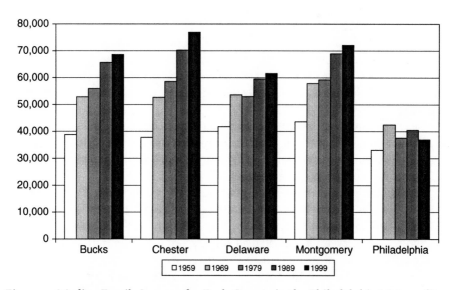

Fig. 5.13. Median Family Income for Each County in the Philadelphia Metropolitan Area, 1960–2000, as Reported by the U.S. Census

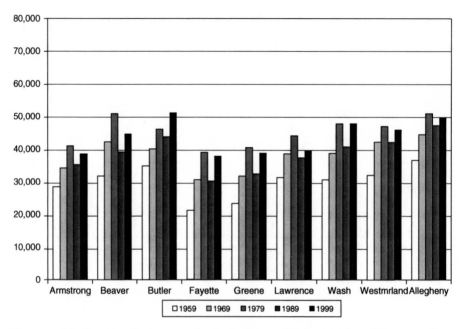

Fig. 5.14. Median Family Income for Each County in the Pittsburgh Metropolitan
Area, 1960–2000, as Reported by the U.S. Census

compare the median family income (in 1999 dollars) for each county in both regions,
demonstrating much larger incomes in the counties surrounding Philadelphia than
in those in the Pittsburgh region.

Next, Figures 5.15 and 5.16 trace overall population trends for both areas,
indicating two very different trends—one of growth in the Philadelphia region and
one of stagnation in the Pittsburgh area. Of course, in both regions, the two central
counties—Philadelphia and Allegheny—are declining in population, as Figure 5.17
indicates.

Table 5.3 shows that African Americans play a much larger role in the Philadelphia
area than in the Pittsburgh area. Further, the modest increases of African Americans
in the Philadelphia suburbs, shown in Table 5.3, cannot alone account for the surge
in Democratic strength in those counties.

Finally, Table 5.4 compares the percentage of professionals in each region,
showing that the Philadelphia area outstrips the Pittsburgh area in overall professionals and in female professionals. For example, Bucks, Chester, Delaware,
Montgomery, and even Philadelphia all surpassed the average state percentage for
female professionals of 16.4. On the other hand, with the exception of Allegheny
County itself at 18.5 percent, the eight counties surrounding Pittsburgh all fell
below the state average.

All these figures and tables demonstrate the very real underlying demographic
differences between these two regions. In chapter 6, I analyze survey data that reveal
a core attitudinal difference between the regions: that residents in the Pittsburgh

area are more socially conservative than those in the Philadelphia ideopolis. Of course, as stated in chapter 1, I view the differentiation taking place between these regions as reflective of the aftershocks of the culture-wars realignment. The ideas of Judis and Teixeira are especially valuable for helping to explain why those aftershocks played out differently in these two key Pennsylvania population centers.

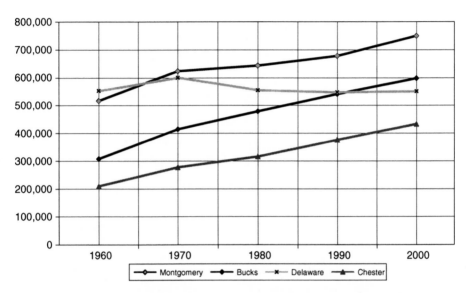

Fig. 5.15. Population of Each County in the Philadelphia Metropolitan Area, 1960–2000, as Reported by the U.S. Census

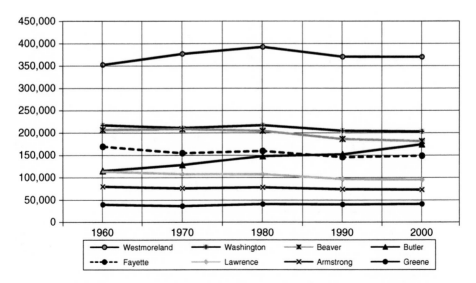

Fig. 5.16. Population of Each County in the Pittsburgh Metropolitan Area, 1960–2000, as Reported by the U.S. Census

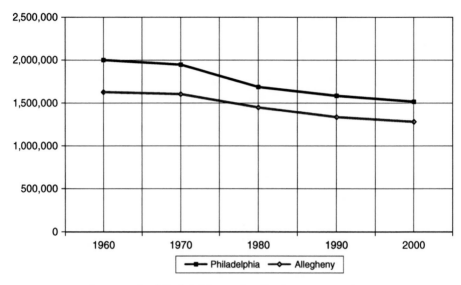

Fig. 5.17. Population of Philadelphia and Allegheny Counties, 1960–2000, as Reported by the U.S. Census

Table 5.3. Percentage of African Americans in the Philadelphia and Pittsburgh Metropolitan Areas, 1960–2000

	Philadelphia Metro Area				
	1960	1970	1980	1990	2000
Bucks	1.9	2.3	2.5	2.9	3.3
Chester	8.4	8.0	7.3	6.5	6.2
Delaware	7.1	7.6	9.0	11.4	14.5
Montgomery	3.8	4.0	4.8	5.8	7.5
Philadelphia	26.7	34.4	37.8	40.4	43.2

	Pittsburgh Metro Area				
	1960	1970	1980	1990	2000
Armstrong	1.1	1.1	0.9	0.8	0.8
Beaver	5.4	5.7	5.6	5.7	6.0
Butler	0.5	0.5	0.5	0.5	0.8
Fayette	4.8	4.4	3.8	3.5	3.5
Greene	1.0	1.0	0.8	1.0	3.9
Lawrence	2.5	2.7	2.8	3.1	3.6
Washington	4.2	3.7	3.5	3.3	3.3
Westmoreland	2.1	1.8	1.6	1.9	2.0
Allegheny	8.3	9.3	10.4	11.3	12.4

Table 5.4. Percentage of Professionals in the Philadelphia and Pittsburgh Metro Areas, 2000

Professionals	Philadelphia Metro Area						
	Employed Civilians 16+	Professionals	%Prof	Male Prof	%Male	Fem Prof	%Fem
Bucks	308,281	118,482	38.4	61,870	20.1	56,612	18.4
Chester	221,255	99,985	45.2	53,859	24.3	46,126	20.8
Delaware	258,782	101,646	39.3	50,129	19.4	51,517	19.9
Montgomery	384,688	171,063	44.5	88,729	23.1	82,334	21.4
Total	1,173,006	491,176	41.9	254,587	21.7	236,589	20.2
Philadelphia	584,957	184,361	31.5	79,975	13.7	104,386	17.8
Total w/Philly	1,757,963	675,537	38.4	334,52	19.0	340,975	19.4

Professionals	Pittsburgh Metro Area						
	Employed Civilians 16+	Professionals	%Prof	Male Prof	%Male	Fem Prof	%Fem
Armstrong	30,308	6,709	22.1	2,998	9.9	3,711	12.2
Beaver	82,493	21,625	26.2	10,004	12.1	11,621	14.1
Butler	82,534	26,394	32	13,511	16.4	12,883	15.6
Fayette	59,017	14,111	23.9	6,474	11.0	7,637	12.9
Greene	15,168	3,770	24.9	1,599	10.5	2,171	14.3
Lawrence	41,035	10,897	26.6	5,142	12.5	5,755	14.0
Washington	90,861	26,658	29.3	13,250	14.6	13,408	14.8
Westmoreland	167,853	51,777	30.8	26,402	15.7	25,375	15.1
Total	569,269	161,941	28.4	79,380	13.9	82,561	14.5
Allegheny	591,905	223,974	37.8	114,406	19.3	109,568	18.5
Total w/ Allegheny	1,161,174	385,915	33.2	193,786	16.7	192,129	16.5
Pennsylvania	5,653,500	1,841,175	32.6	913,636	16.2	927,539	16.4

Analysis of Party Registration Data and Turnout

An examination of Pennsylvania party registration data and turnout adds another dimension to our understanding of the state's electoral system. As I noted in chapter 1 and as can be seen in Table 5.5, the Republican party had a tremendous edge in party registration in the late 1920s and maintained a huge plurality of about 900,000 registered voters as late as 1954. By November 1960, however, Democrats surpassed the GOP narrowly for the first time in the twentieth century and, with the exception of a few years, have continued to far outstrip Republican registration, maintaining a half million voter plurality in the early years of the twenty-first century.

To be specific, in 1960, 49.3 percent of Pennsylvania's registered voters were Democrats, 49.3 percent were Republicans, and 1.4 percent were in the "others" category. In 2004, 47.6 percent of the state's registered voters were Democrats, 40.7 percent were Republicans, and 11.7 percent were in the others category. (The remarkable growth of the others category is discussed below along with its definition.)

This final section of chapter 5 goes far beyond those statewide totals in Table 5.5 to examine party registration at the county level, especially changes between 1960 and 2004. A quick way to gauge change over the recent forty-four-year period is to examine a scattergram of the correlation of the 1960 and the 2004 Democratic registration percentages (coefficient of 0.75). This is done in Figure 5.18, which reveals many fascinating county trends over the period. For example, Philadelphia and York provide contrasting examples. In Philadelphia, Democratic registration went from 57.7 percent in 1960 to 74.9 percent in 2004. The raw numbers add more to the story.[12] Although only about 45,000 more people were registered in 2004 than in 1960, there was an increase of almost 210,000 Democratic registrants and a decrease of about 233,000 Republicans, meaning that the Democrats went from having a plurality of 178,463 in 1960 to having a huge edge of 620,599 in 2004. Keep in mind, however, that between 1960 and 2000, Philadelphia's total population, as measured by the census, went from 2,002,512 to 1,517,550, a 24.2 percent decline.

In contrast to the Philadelphia pattern, Figure 5.18 isolates York as a county in which Democratic registration fell from 57.2 percent in 1960 to 33.9 percent in 2004, going from a Democratic plurality of 17,200 to a Republican plurality of 47,021. Unlike Philadelphia, York had a population increase of 60.2 percent from 1960 to 2000, from 238,336 people to 381,751.

The net gain in Democratic and Republican party registration for each county from 1960 to 2004 is displayed in the map in Figure 5.19. If the Democratic party had a party registration plurality in 2004, the county is shaded gray on the map; if the GOP had a plurality, the county is white. Then, under each county's name on the map is exhibited the net partisan-percentage gain, followed by a D if the Democratic party experienced a net gain or an R if the Republican party experienced a net gain. For instance, Montgomery County had 268,755 registered Republicans in 2004, up 41.8 percent over the 1960 total of 189,550 Republicans. But Democratic registration rose from 61,654 in 1960 to 214,233 in 2004, a Democratic

---

12. The raw figures supporting the percentages in the scattergram are in Appendix E, Table 2.

Table 5.5 Pennsylvania Party Registration Statistics, 1926–2007

Year	Democrats	Republicans	Others	Total	Plurality	% Dem	% Rep	% Other
1926	657,329	2,279,031	287,766	3,224,126	1,621,702 R	20.4	70.7	8.9
1928	867,391	2,861,919	242,566	3,971,876	1,994,528 R	21.8	72.1	6.1
1930	675,584	2,659,850	187,076	3,522,510	1,984,266 R	19.2	75.5	5.3
1932	833,977	2,911,068	167,626	3,912,671	2,077,091 R	21.3	74.4	4.3
1934	1,401,005	2,624,386	166,509	4,191,900	1,223,381 R	33.4	62.6	4.0
1936	2,065,697	2,665,902	184,747	4,916,346	600,205 R	42.0	54.2	3.8
1938	2,209,276	2,372,528	65,703	4,647,507	163,252 R	47.5	51.1	1.4
1940	2,161,307	2,782,890	70,513	5,014,710	621,583 R	43.1	55.5	1.4
1942	1,948,372	2,603,104	60,812	4,612,288	654,732 R	42.2	56.4	1.3
1944	1,854,111	2,645,263	60,057	4,559,431	791,152 R	40.7	58.0	1.3
1946	1,854,080	2,737,279	61,735	4,653,094	883,199 R	39.9	58.8	1.3
1948	1,810,517	2,864,029	62,427	4,736,973	1,053,512 R	38.2	60.5	1.3
1950	1,930,916	2,772,778	57,966	4,761,660	841,862 R	40.6	58.2	1.2
1952	2,136,511	3,130,078	75,381	5,341,970	993,567 R	40.0	58.6	1.4
1954	2,088,857	2,995,971	69,906	5,154,734	907,114 R	40.5	58.1	1.4
1956	2,450,396	2,897,307	74,447	5,422,150	446,911 R	45.2	53.4	1.4
1958	2,554,007	2,771,613	71,787	5,397,407	217,606 R	47.3	51.4	1.3
1960	2,805,202	2,802,237	80,398	5,687,837	2,965 D	49.3	49.3	1.4
1962	2,896,099	2,700,164	77,234	5,673,497	195,935 D	51.1	47.6	1.4
1964	2,884,396	2,759,565	84,398	5,728,359	124,831 D	50.4	48.2	1.5
1966	2,759,524	2,678,934	80,543	5,519,001	80,590 D	50.0	48.5	1.5
1968	2,715,507	2,775,456	108,401	5,599,364	59,949 R	48.5	49.6	1.9
1970	2,627,130	2,680,411	112,010	5,419,551	53,281 R	48.5	49.5	2.1
1972	2,993,092	2,697,694	181,116	5,871,902	295,398 D	51.0	45.9	3.1
1974	2,884,523	2,479,802	164,722	5,529,047	404,721 D	52.2	44.9	3.0
1976	3,152,450	2,387,197	210,013	5,749,660	765,253 D	54.8	41.5	3.7

Table 5.5 (continued)

Year	Democrats	Republicans	Others	Total	Plurality	% Dem	% Rep	% Other
1978	3,224,953	2,321,807	249,750	5,796,510	903,146 D	55.6	40.1	4.3
1980	3,072,700	2,374,303	307,284	5,754,287	698,397 D	53.4	41.3	5.3
1982	3,035,523	2,357,448	309,586	5,702,557	678,075 D	53.2	41.3	5.4
1984	3,380,675	2,487,552	325,475	6,193,702	893,123 D	54.6	40.2	5.3
1986	3,128,265	2,422,385	296,325	5,846,975	705,880 D	53.5	41.4	5.1
1988	3,069,234	2,518,282	288,427	5,875,943	550,952 D	52.2	42.9	4.9
1990	2,976,547	2,458,426	270,106	5,705,079	518,121 D	52.2	43.1	4.7
1991	2,693,644	2,363,810	242,911	5,300,365	329,834 D	50.8	44.6	4.6
1992	3,043,757	2,567,643	381,602	5,993,002	476,114 D	50.8	42.8	6.4
1994	2,955,594	2,534,087	389,412	5,879,093	421,507 D	50.3	43.1	6.6
1996	3,336,933	2,910,614	558,065	6,805,612	426,319 D	49.0	42.8	8.2
1998	3,514,970	3,072,299	671,553	7,258,822	442,671 D	48.4	42.3	9.3
1999	3,615,197	3,128,333	716,809	7,460,339	486,864 D	48.5	41.9	9.6
2000	3,736,304	3,250,764	794,929	7,781,997	485,540 D	48.0	41.8	10.2
2001	3,733,739	3,233,171	806,631	7,773,541	500,568 D	48.0	41.6	10.4
2002	3,768,316	3,235,172	832,287	7,835,775	533,144 D	48.1	41.3	10.6
2003	3,677,488	3,204,440	828,673	7,710,601	473,048 D	47.7	41.6	10.8
2004	3,985,486	3,405,278	975,899	8,366,663	580,208 D	47.6	40.7	11.7
2005	3,836,701	3,294,568	934,267	8,065,536	542,133 D	47.6	40.9	11.6
2006	3,900,685	3,300,894	981,297	8,182,876	599,791 D	47.7	40.3	12.0
2007	3,872,018	3,259,243	976,172	8,107,433	612,775 D	47.8	40.2	12.0

All figures are from November except the 2005 and 2007 statistics, which are from May.

Source: Bureau of Commissions, Elections, and Legislation, Department of State, Commonwealth of Pennsylvania.

gain of 247.5 percent. Subtracting the Republican gain from the Democratic gain yields a net percentage gain of 205.7 percent for the Democrats. Thus, on the map, Montgomery County is white to signify that Republican registrants still outnumber Democrats, but +205.7%D appears under Montgomery in Figure 5.19 to represent this astounding Democratic advance.

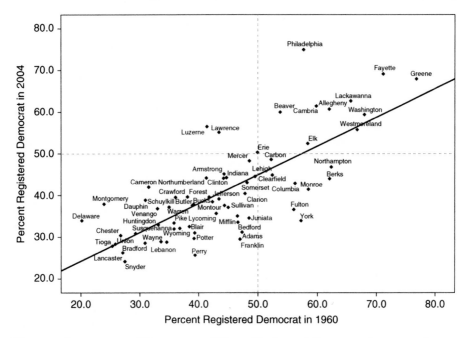

Fig. 5.18. Scattergram of Percentage of Voters Registered Democrat in 1960 and 2004

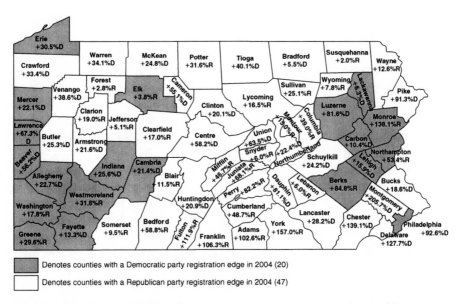

Fig. 5.19. Map of Percentage of Net Gain in Democratic and Republican Party Registration, 1960–2004

Westmoreland, the largest Pittsburgh-area suburban county, is shaded gray because there were 142,979 registered Democrats there in 2004 compared to 88,727 registered Republicans. But Republican registration in Westmoreland advanced 52.8 percent since 1960, when 58,078 Republicans were registered there. Democratic registration has only increased 21.1 percent since 1960, when there were 118,024 Democrats registered in Westmoreland. After the subtraction, Westmoreland has a net Republican gain of 31.6 percent since 1960. Thus, under Westmoreland on the map, a +31.6%R appears. This is an excellent way to capture overall partisan registration change county by county. Of course, the Montgomery and Westmoreland examples reflect broader substantive trends already discussed at several places in this book. For instance, note the other white counties with net gains for the Democrats surrounding Montgomery, indicating that the Republicans still hold the registration edge but that it is the Democrats who are gaining ground. This is also the case with Lancaster and Dauphin. The former is one of the counties mentioned previously as having benefited from enormous population growth of 69.1 percent, gaining 192,299 people since 1960.

Between 1960 and 2004, the Democrats experienced a net gain in thirty-five counties. Of those, thirteen have a Democratic registration edge, and twenty-two have a Republican registration edge. The Republican party experienced a net gain in thirty-two counties, seven of which have a Democratic registration edge and twenty-five of which have a Republican registration edge. (Incidentally, the raw numbers and the percentage calculations of the change in party registration for each county that I used to construct Figure 5.19 appear in Appendix E, Table 2.)

Another way to gauge the Pennsylvania party registration trends, apart from scrutinizing the revealing map in Figure 5.19, is to study the maps in Figures 5.20 and 5.21, which show Democratic and Republican registration percentages in 1960 and 2004, respectively, by six shaded and patterned categories. Shades of gray, from light to dark, are used to indicate three ascending percentage ranges for the Democratic plurality, and white and dotted patterns do the same thing for the Republican plurality. The six percentage categories isolate several general trends. There were twenty counties with Democratic pluralities in 1960 and again in 2004; thus, Republican registration surpassed Democratic registration in the remaining forty-seven counties in both years.

The overall change depicted in the maps for the Philadelphia-area counties is striking and confirms patterns already familiar from previous analyses. Keep in mind that the registration changes in the four suburban Philadelphia counties have to be considered in the context of their recent pro-Democratic voting trends. Obviously, party registration in Bucks, Chester, Delaware, and Montgomery counties is lagging behind voting behavior. Note also that Philadelphia itself over the forty-four-year period went from light gray, the color denoting the lowest Democratic registration percentage, to dark gray, the highest Democratic percentage category. Fulton, Columbia, and Clearfield, to point to three others as examples, also left their light gray status behind, but to go in the opposite direction of Philadelphia. Fulton moved to light dots (the second highest Republican percentage range), and Columbia and Clearfield went to heavy dots (the lowest GOP range). Erie County,

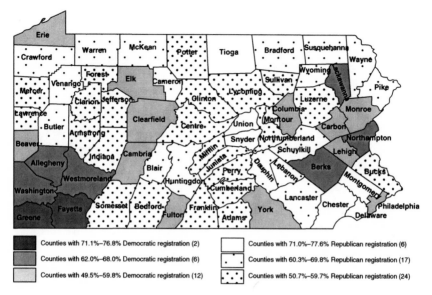

Fig. 5.20. Map of Pennsylvania Voter Registration by County in 1960

recently something of a bellwether county on registration, moved in the opposite direction from those three GOP-trending counties, going from light gray in 1960 to medium gray in 2004.[13] A large part of the reason for this was a decrease in Republican registration that was accompanied by a 9 percent increase in those classifying themselves as independents. (See Appendix E for a full listing of the registration numbers and percentages for all counties in 1960 and 2004.)

An important story in the overall registration numbers is the growth of those who chose not to affiliate with either of the two major parties. Table 5.5 shows the year-by-year rise in this category, which is also displayed in a line chart in chapter 3 (see Figure 3.4). In 1960, the others category was 1.4 percent; in 1970, it was 2.1 percent; in 1980, 5.3 percent; in 1990, 4.7 percent; in 1996, 8.2 percent; in 2000, 10.2 percent, and in 2004, it reached 11.7 percent. In May 2007, it reached 12 percent. The vast majority of these people are telling registration officials that they have "no affiliation" with a political party.[14] The Pennsylvania Department of State's

13. In 1960, Erie's party registration closely resembled the Pennsylvania totals: 49.9 percent registered Democrats, 49.0 percent registered Republicans, and 1.1 percent others. The raw numbers were 59,559 Democrats, 58,391 Republicans, and 1,308 others. By 2004, Erie Democrats outnumbered Republicans by 50.3 percent to 39.7 percent with others at 10.0 percent, or, in raw numbers, 92,922 Democrats, 73,308 Republicans, and 19,614 others. Incidentally, Erie's population grew 12.0 percent from 1960 to 2000, going from 250,682 people to 280,843. The Erie party registration percentages were still reasonably close to the statewide totals in 2004, although Erie was 2.7 percent more Democratic than the state as a whole and had 1 percent fewer voters in the others category.

14. To make sure I understood the registration mechanics correctly, I examined the 2004 Pennsylvania Voter Registration Application Form. In Box 9, the form states: "In which party do you wish to register?" Then, it lists the following: "Democratic, Republican, Libertarian,

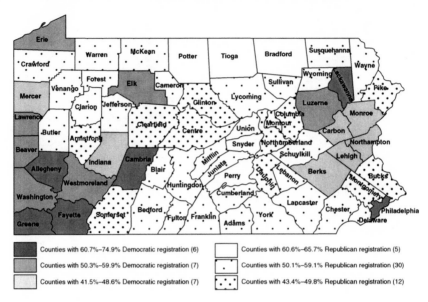

Counties with 60.7%–74.9% Democratic registration (6)

Counties with 50.3%–59.9% Democratic registration (7)

Counties with 41.5%–48.6% Democratic registration (7)

Counties with 60.6%–65.7% Republican registration (5)

Counties with 50.1%–59.1% Republican registration (30)

Counties with 43.4%–49.8% Republican registration (12)

Fig. 5.21. Map of Pennsylvania Voter Registration by County in 2004

semiannual sheet listing party registration by county has used various reporting categories over the decades in regard to those registrants who say they are not affiliated with the two major parties.[15] In recent years, the department has reported county and state totals of those who choose an officially recognized third party

---

Green, Constitution, No affiliation, Other: Please Specify." The instructions that accompany the form state: "Box 9. Political Party: Select a political party or no affiliation. You must register with a party if you want to take part in that party's primary." That last sentence on the form is in red ink!

15. Getting the story straight as to exactly how Pennsylvania handles the reporting of those who do not affiliate with the Republican or Democratic party required some investigation. Allison Deibert, the voter registration coordinator in the Bureau of Commissions, Elections, and Legislation in the Pennsylvania Department of State, who kindly and cheerfully responded to my many requests for registration data, wrote me the following in response to my questions concerning the "no affiliation/other parties" labeling issue after she sought staff guidance concerning the policy. She wrote: "Basically, in PA we report voter registration stat[istic]s on major and minor political parties. The major political parties are D's and R's. But the minor political parties can change every year because the definition is based on a percentage of votes. To qualify, a party must receive 2% of the highest entire vote total for any elected candidate in the preceding General or Municipal Election. Anybody that doesn't qualify as a party is considered a political body. For reporting purposes all these political bodies are lumped together and called 'Others.' In PA we use Independent, No affiliation, and No party interchangeably with others because we do not track their registration, only report their numbers in total. Honestly, we do this because someone can write down whatever they want on their voter registration application and register whatever party they want and we have to tally it. So we can have 3 people registered in the Birthday Party. We're not going to keep track of the Birthday Party's registrations, just report that there are 3 people registered in a party other

along with an "other parties" category. The vast majority of those in the depart-ment's other parties category have circled the "no affiliation" choice when asked the standard party registration question.[16]

Examining this category further in a scattergram reveals where the nearly one million Pennsylvanians in the others grouping in 2004 are located as well as where the biggest growth in this category has occurred over forty-four years. See Figure 5.22, which depicts the correlation of the county-by-county others percentages in 1960 with the 2004 percentages (coefficient of 0.59). Of course, with such a dramatic increase in this category, from 80,398 people statewide in 1960 to 975,899 people in 2004, there is hardly an area in the state that is not involved in a big way in the trend. Thus, even the counties with the lowest percentages of others in 2004, such as Forest (6.0 percent) and Greene (6.3 percent), have moved a considerable distance from where they were in 1960 (Forest was at 2.0 percent then and Greene at 0.2 percent).

As the scattergram reveals, eleven counties are at the top of the list of registered voters in the others category, having over 14 percent. All of them are located in the eastern third of the state except Centre, the home of Penn State's main campus. They are Monroe (18.8 percent), Pike (18.2 percent), Centre (18.0 percent), Chester (17.1 percent), Northampton (15.6 percent), Lehigh (15.3 percent), Bucks (15.4 per-cent), Lancaster (14.7 percent), Montgomery (14.5 percent), York (14.3 percent), and Berks (14.2 percent). The leaders, Monroe and Pike, have also undergone dramatic population increases since 1960, involving the influx of outsiders to this rapidly developing Pocono Mountains region.

Overall, there is no doubt that the large increase across the state of people who want no affiliation with the Democratic or Republican party is an important new factor to add to the electoral mix in the state. However, Pennsylvania is not alone in having a large increase in voters who choose not to affiliate with one of the two major political parties. In 2002, Rhodes Cook, a noted political analyst, reported the following after studying party-registration trends in the nation:

> The big story of the last decade was the dramatic growth in the number of voters not affiliated with either party. [In 1992] nearly

---

than a reportable one. Bottom line, there is not an Independent Party (at least a reportable one) in the state." E-mail to the author from Deibert, November 10, 2005.

16. For example, the November 2004 official Pennsylvania voter registration sheet reports there were 34,258 people affiliated with the Libertarian party, 15,788 affiliated with the Green party, and 925,853 listed as other parties. The other parties category in the report does not include the Green and Libertarian parties. Thus, for my others category, I add in the separately reported "third parties," knowing full well that my others category, and even the department's other parties category, is made up mostly of people who have chosen not to affiliate with a political party; that is, they have circled or checked the "no affiliation" choice on the regis-tration form. Incidentally, the term *others*, which is my term, reflects better the reality than does the department's *other parties* label. Of course, the best term for the category would be *no affiliation*, but that would require the department to keep separate those who choose no affiliation from those who specified something in the form's other category, whether it is the Birthday Party or something else.

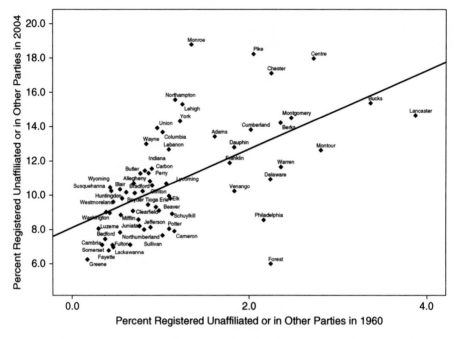

Fig. 5.22. Scattergram of Percentage of Voters Registered Other in 1960 and 2004

half (48%) of the 67.7 million voters in party registration states were Democrats, 34% were Republicans, and 17% were not affiliated with either party. (This latter figure includes voters registered with third parties, but is overwhelmingly comprised of independents.)

Eight years later, during the last primary season in 2000, 44% of the 83.7 million voters in party registration states were Democrats, 33% were Republicans, and 23% were not affiliated with either party. In short, while both the Democratic and Republican share of the voter pie shrank a bit from 1992 to 2000, the unaffiliated portion increased significantly.[17]

Obviously, which registered voters turn out to vote on Election Day has an important impact on the results. Political scientists regularly calculate turnout by dividing the number of people who voted in a particular election into the total voter age population (VAP). State election officials and even some journalists often use the number of registered voters instead of VAP. Calculating turnout both ways

17. *The Rhodes Cook Letter*, May 2002. For example, Cook reported that in Maryland, the unaffiliated category was 12.6 percent in February 2000, up from 8.1 percent in March 1992. In North Carolina, he wrote, the unaffiliated category stood at 15.5 percent in April 2000, up from 6.3 percent in May 1992. And, according to Cook, in West Virginia, unaffiliated registered voters were at 8.5 percent in May 2000, but they had been only 3.2 percent in May 1992.

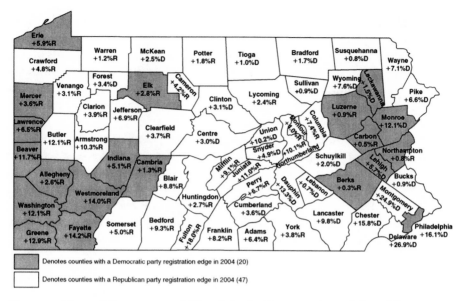

Fig. 5.23. Map of Percentage of Net Gain in Democratic and Republican Party Registration, 2000–2004

for the last presidential election, I found that VAP turnout in Pennsylvania was 60.3 percent in 2004. The turnout of registered voters was 68.9 percent. Overall, 87.4 percent of the statewide VAP was registered to vote in 2004. My calculations of this basic turnout information for Pennsylvania's sixty-seven counties in the 2004 election are displayed in Appendix E, Table 4.

In order to determine which of the two major parties is better at getting its registered voters to the polls, I divided the state's counties into quartiles sorted by the percentage of Democratic and Republican registered voters. Then, I totaled up the percentage by quartile of registered voters in each party who actually voted. The results are displayed in Appendix E, Tables 5 and 6, which use only registered voter turnout. The counties in the highest quartile of Democratic registered voters turned out at a rate of 67.1 percent. On the other hand, counties in the highest quartile of Republican registered voters turned out at 70.0 percent. The lowest Democratic quartile counties had a turnout of 71.2 compared to the GOP's lowest quartile counties with turnout at 68.8 percent. Thus, these calculations suggest that Republicans do a better job than Democrats in turning out their registered voters.

Before ending this section on party registration, I present one more party-registration map in Figure 5.23. It is constructed exactly like Figure 5.19 except that the net partisan-registration gain calculated and displayed for each county covers only the four-year period from 2000 to 2004. Thus, this map captures very recent partisan trends.[18] Note that throughout western Pennsylvania the net gain favors

18. Appendix E, Table 3, contains the raw numbers and percentage calculations used to construct Figure 5.23.

the Republican party with double-digit figures recorded in seven of the eight counties surrounding Pittsburgh. In much of eastern Pennsylvania, the net gains favor the Democratic party. These recent county-level party registration trends visible in Figure 5.23 echo the Democratic registration trends illustrated in Figures 5.9 and 5.10. Remarkably, these trends are quite similar to the recent voting patterns revealed by my factor analysis in the first section of this chapter and depicted in summary form in the map in Figure 5.2.

Together these two maps—Figures 5.2 and 5.23—complement each other and strongly suggest that the aggregate-data analysis in this chapter has uncovered key developments that have occurred in recent Pennsylvania partisan politics.

Now that this profitable journey through a wealth of aggregate data is at an end, I leave behind aggregates of data and the analytical inferences they require, and in chapter 6, I establish direct links with individual Pennsylvanians via their responses given in public opinion surveys and Election Day exit polls.

6

The Pennsylvania Electorate: Insights from Public Opinion Surveys and Exit Polls

I use public opinion surveys and Election Day exit polls in this chapter to better understand the behavior of the Pennsylvania electorate. The county-level voting patterns analyzed in the last chapter, based as they are on aggregate data, can only hint at what is motivating voters in casting their ballots. Sometimes the inferences that can be drawn from the data are quite powerful when the trends are strong and the different characteristics of the counties are quite distinct. But one always runs up against the reality that no individuals are being tapped directly when aggregate data are used. With surveys, we have the ability to reach individuals directly.

Of course, a chief drawback of surveys is they are not as widely available as aggregate data. In fact, reliable national surveys date back only to the 1940s, and those conducted in the early decades of survey research were rarely at the state level. Indeed, the first Pennsylvania survey that I could make use of was a Harris poll in 1964. Still, at the national level, great advances have been made in survey research since the late 1940s. The National Election Studies (NES), conducted at the University of Michigan for every national election since 1952, lead this forward movement. In fact, the NES surveys have evolved into highly sophisticated instruments that are invaluable for our understanding of national electoral change.

Unfortunately, when one descends to the state level, even today, the sophistication of the surveys falls off greatly in most states, and Pennsylvania is not an exception. However, in addition to the 1964 Harris poll, I was able to secure two other fine, relatively early surveys, a 1968 Pennsylvania survey done as part of the Comparative State Elections Project at the University of North Carolina and a 1972 Yankelovich survey.

Starting in 1982, we enter the era of the Election Day exit polls. For Pennsylvania, they are available every two years from then on with the exception of 2002, which was conducted at the polls but never reported because of technical failures.[1] Although the exit-poll instruments are not as far-reaching as the NES surveys, they do contain valuable data, and I make extensive use of them in this chapter.

In the first section of this chapter, I draw on a regional subsample of the fine NES surveys along with the various Keystone State surveys mentioned above in a comparative effort to understand changes in party identification and presidential voting patterns in Pennsylvania.

Then, in the second and last section of this chapter, I rely exclusively on the exit polls in an effort to understand further why Pennsylvanians voted as they did. I employ a valuable geographical division of the state into five regions, the *geocode,* in the terminology of those who constructed the exit polls that used this valuable device for getting at the diverse intrastate trends already examined using county-level aggregate data. This section ends with a survey-based overview of the Pennsylvania electorate in the early twenty-first century in comparison with the national electorate.

Presidential Voting and Party Identification Trends in Pennsylvania and the North

Electoral trends as well as changes in the social composition of the major parties can be traced via survey data using two key variables: party identification and the presidential vote. I rely extensively in the first section of this chapter on both of these to compare Pennsylvania with a comparable portion of the nation, as is explained shortly.

Table 6.1 presents the percentage of voting-age Americans from 1960 to 2004 who identified with either the Democratic or Republican party or chose independent when asked the standard party identification question: "Generally speaking, do you usually think of yourself as a Republican, a Democrat, an Independent, or what?"[2] A striking trend in the table is the decline of the national Democratic party from its commanding lead in party identifiers in the 1960s to rough parity with

---

1. News accounts from the 2002 election report that serious sampling problems were discovered on Election Day. These led the Voter News Service, which conducted the exit poll that year, to take the unprecedented step of not reporting its state-by-state results that night or since. Beth Gillin, "Media Organizations Discuss What Went Wrong with Exit-Poll Service," *Philadelphia Inquirer,* November 6, 2002.

2. All the NES and other survey results reported in this chapter were calculated by the author using SPSS. Many political scientists make good use of these NES data, and I profited by studying their works. Especially useful were the seven volumes in the *Change and Continuity* series written by Paul R. Abramson, John H. Aldrich, and David W. Rohde after every presidential election since 1980, a recent volume of which I cited in chapter 1.

Table 6.1   Party Identification in the Nation, 1960–2004

	1960	1964	1968	1972	1976	1980	1984	1988	1992	1996	2000	2004
Democrats	46	52	46	41	40	42	38	36	36	39	35	32
Republicans	30	25	25	24	24	23	28	28	26	28	25	29
Independents	23	23	30	35	36	35	35	36	39	33	40	39
Total Percent	99	100	101	100	100	100	101	100	101	100	100	100
N =	1864	1536	1531	2656	2825	1577	2198	1999	2447	1694	1776	1195

Because of rounding, column percentages range from 99 to 101 percent.

Wording of the NES party identification question is as follows: "Generally speaking, do you usually think of yourself as a Republican, a Democrat, an Independent, or what?" The independents include those who, when asked a follow-up question, said they lean toward one of the major parties.

Source: Calculations done by the author using SPSS on the American National Election Studies (www.electionstudies.org). The 1948–2004 ANES Cumulative Data File [dataset]. Stanford University and the University of Michigan [producers and distributors], 2005. This is the source for all of the national and regional surveys used in this chapter.

the Republican party by the early twenty-first century. A second trend is the rise of those who claim to be independents.[3]

There is a heated debate among political scientists concerning the meaning of the independent figures. NES follows up its initial question to all those respondents who say they are independent by asking them if they lean toward one or the other of the two major parties. When those who say they lean one way or the other are stripped away, the core independents who are left have not shown sustained growth over the decades. This is demonstrated by the percentages in the "Independent Independent" category in Table 6.2 and is also displayed in the line chart in Figure 6.1 in which the Democratic and Republican leaners are included in their respective parties.

As I confirm below with the introduction of the Pennsylvania party identification data, those identifying as independents in the Keystone State have risen considerably as well, although not as much as the independents shown in the NES figures when the leaners are included with the so-called pure independents, as I do in Table 6.1 and elsewhere in this section.[4] Further, as we saw in chapter 5, the

3. Answering a party self-identification question in a survey is not to be confused with actual party registration. The two, of course, are very different. The latter requires an act that has consequences; the former is merely a response given to someone taking a survey. When registering to vote, if a Pennsylvanian does not choose a political party, he or she cannot vote in that party's primary elections.

4. One reason for the higher numbers of self-identifying independents in the NES surveys than in the exit polls is that the NES samples the entire adult population, while the exit polls tap only voters. While there is no conclusive evidence, this may indicate that self-identified Democrats and Republicans turn out to vote at a higher rate than independents.

Table 6.2 Party Identification 7-Point Scale in the Nation, 1960–2004

	1960	1964	1968	1972	1976	1980	1984	1988	1992	1996	2000	2004
Strong Democrat	20	27	20	15	15	18	17	17	18	19	19	17
Weak Democrat	25	25	25	26	25	23	20	18	18	20	15	15
Independent Democrat	6	9	10	11	12	11	11	12	14	13	15	18
Independent Independent	10	8	10	13	15	13	11	11	12	9	11	10
Independent Republican	7	6	9	10	10	10	12	13	12	11	13	12
Weak Republican	14	14	15	13	14	14	15	14	14	15	12	13
Strong Republican	16	11	10	10	9	8	12	14	11	12	13	16
Apolitical	2	1	1	1	1	2	2	2	1	1	1	0
Total Percent	100	101	100	99	101	99	100	101	100	100	99	101
N =	1911	1550	1553	2694	2850	1612	2236	2032	2474	1710	1797	1197

Because of rounding, column percentages range from 99 to 101 percent.

Wording of the NES party identification question is as follows: "Generally speaking, do you usually think of yourself as a Republican, a Democrat, an Independent, or what?"

If respondent answers Republican or Democrat, questioner follows up with:

"Would you call yourself a strong Republican/Democrat or a not very strong Republican/Democrat?"

If respondent answers Independent, other, or no preference, questioner follows up with:

"Do you think of yourself as closer to the Republican or Democratic party?"

Source: The American National Election Studies (www.electionstudies.org). The 1948–2004 ANES Cumulative Data File [dataset]. Stanford University and the University of Michigan [producers and distributors], 2005.

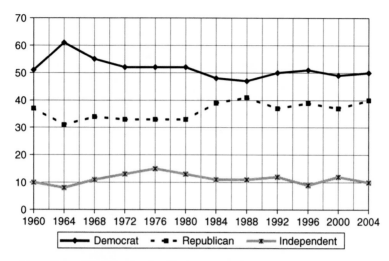

Fig. 6.1. Party Identification in the Nation, 1960–2004

Note: The Democratic and Republican leaners are included with their respective parties. Please refer to Table 6.1 for source.

percentage of Pennsylvanians who choose to remain independent of the two major parties when they register to vote has risen considerably in recent years as well. Thus, there is no denying that the loosening of partisan attachments is an important feature of the current American party system. With that recognition affirmed once again, the survey analysis continues the important task of understanding the voting behavior of both those who identify with the major parties as well as the self-identified independents.

As was emphasized in the first section of chapter 2, the political paths followed by the North and the South have been quite different until just recently (that is, when nationalizing trends in Dixie brought that region once more within the national mainstream), necessitating a separate examination of each region. In chapter 2, a comparison of the party strength figures for the South and the North made this point. Using survey data, we again see the value of this regional distinction; see Table 6.3, which presents the NES party identification figures for both regions. The percentage of southerners identified with the Democratic party in the 1960s far outstrips the percentage in the North. Again, the reasons for these differences were explained in chapter 2, but I emphasize them here to justify my reliance solely on the northern trend figures for comparison with Pennsylvania. It makes no sense to cloud the Keystone State analysis by lumping in results clearly tied to a major regional transformation in Dixie that was only partly connected to national or nonsouthern developments, at least, not until the two-party South really took hold in the last decade or so.

Furthermore, an important truth about American politics since the early 1960s is that African Americans overwhelmingly identify with the Democratic party, North and South, as is shown in Table 6.4.

Table 6.3 Party Identification in the North and the South, 1960–2004

	The North											
	1960	1964	1968	1972	1976	1980	1984	1988	1992	1996	2000	2004
Democrat	42	47	42	38	37	39	35	33	34	37	34	31
Republican	33	29	29	26	25	24	31	31	27	30	25	28
Independent	25	24	29	36	38	37	34	36	39	33	41	41
Total Percent	100	100	100	100	100	100	100	100	100	100	100	100
N =	1395	1184	1155	1968	2113	1118	1567	1370	1685	1102	1134	820

	The South											
	1960	1964	1968	1972	1976	1980	1984	1988	1992	1996	2000	2004
Democrat	60	69	58	51	50	49	44	42	40	43	36	34
Republican	22	13	11	17	18	20	20	22	22	24	26	32
Independent	19	19	31	33	32	32	36	37	38	33	38	34
Total Percent	101	101	100	101	100	101	100	101	100	100	100	100
N =	469	352	376	688	713	459	631	629	763	591	642	375

Because of rounding, column percentages range from 99 to 101 percent.

Wording of the NES party identification question is as follows: "Generally speaking, do you usually think of yourself as a Republican, a Democrat, an Independent, or what?"

Source: The American National Election Studies (www.electionstudies.org). The 1948–2004 ANES Cumulative Data File [dataset]. Stanford University and the University of Michigan [producers and distributors], 2005.

Even those blacks who identify as independents vote overwhelmingly for Democratic candidates. This reality has not changed markedly in four decades. Thus, in order to understand electoral change, it is essential to limit the analysis to those who are changing, namely whites or other identifiable racial or ethnic groups: Hispanic/Latino Americans, Asian Americans, and American Indians/Native Americans. For Pennsylvania, because Hispanics/Latinos and Asian Americans make up only small percentages of the state's population and are concentrated in just a few urban locations, as discussed in chapter 5, I do not analyze their separate partisan trends. If mine were a study of California or Texas, obviously those groups would be included.

With a sensible national subsample for comparison with Pennsylvania established, that is, northern whites, I turn next to Keystone State party identification figures, then to the changing composition of the parties in both Pennsylvania and the North. Unfortunately, I could not get Pennsylvania survey data for three general elections within the period of this study: 1960, 1976, and 1980. Also, the

Table 6.4 Party Identification by Race in the North and the South, 1960–2004

	Northern Whites											
	1960	1964	1968	1972	1976	1980	1984	1988	1992	1996	2000	2004
Democrat	42	46	39	35	33	35	32	28	30	35	31	27
Republican	35	30	31	28	28	28	34	35	31	33	28	33
Independent	24	25	30	37	39	38	34	37	39	33	41	40
Total Percent	100	101	100	100	100	101	100	100	100	101	100	100
N =	1290	1095	1057	1786	1864	965	1344	1135	1397	897	898	626

	Northern Blacks											
	1960	1964	1968	1972	1976	1980	1984	1988	1992	1996	2000	2004
Democrat	48	72	80	71	73	74	63	69	66	66	70	61
Republican	13	10	3	9	4	5	2	3	2	5	0	0
Independent	40	18	18	20	23	21	36	29	32	30	30	39
Total Percent	100	100	101	100	100	100	101	101	100	101	100	100
N =	88	79	80	122	146	104	112	118	133	88	70	82

	Southern Whites											
	1960	1964	1968	1972	1976	1980	1984	1988	1992	1996	2000	2004
Democrat	60	66	50	47	45	42	36	34	30	33	28	25
Republican	21	15	13	20	22	23	26	28	27	34	34	45
Independent	19	20	37	34	32	35	38	38	43	33	38	30
Total Percent	0	0	100	101	99	100	100	100	100	100	100	100
N =	410	281	310	528	499	347	396	382	464	365	418	210

	Southern Blacks											
	1960	1964	1968	1972	1976	1980	1984	1988	1992	1996	2000	2004
Democrat	54	83	97	67	70	76	64	60	66	67	66	63
Republican	27	4	2	7	5	5	7	10	6	5	5	3
Independent	19	13	2	27	25	18	30	30	27	29	29	35
Total Percent	0	0	101	101	100	99	101	100	99	101	100	101
N =	59	70	64	139	142	76	137	144	175	132	137	104

The categories of whites and blacks exclude Hispanics/Latinos, Asians, American Indians, and others. Please refer to Table 6.3 for the question wording and the source of the survey.

same questions were not asked in every survey, resulting in data gaps, especially involving the 1972 and 1984 surveys.[5]

Based on the available Pennsylvania surveys and exit polls, the first panel in Table 6.5 presents party identification in Pennsylvania from 1964 to 2004. As the table shows, Democrats maintained a statewide edge from 1964 to 2004, although their margin over the Republicans has decreased slightly in the last decade. Overall, both the Democratic party and the Republican party have lost identifiers as the percentage of Pennsylvanians opting to identify themselves to exit-poll takers as independents has increased.

The second and third panels of Table 6.5 present the party identification percentages broken down by race, first for Pennsylvania's whites, then for the state's blacks. These important party-identification trends in the Keystone State are charted in

Table 6.5 Party Identification in Pennsylvania, Overall and by Race, 1964–2004

	All Pennsylvanians								
	1964	1968	1972	1984	1988	1992	1996	2000	2004
Democrat	49	47	50	43	42	43	43	41	43
Republican	45	40	42	38	40	38	40	41	41
Independent	6	13	8	19	19	19	17	17	17
Total Percent	100	100	100	100	101	100	100	99	101
N* =	473	467	682	2031	1513	1512	1553	1682	1914

*In addition to whites and African Americans, this table includes Hispanics/Latinos, Asians, American Indians, and others.

	Whites								
	1964	1968	1972	1984	1988	1992	1996	2000	2004
Democrat	45	45	47	40	39	41	39	38	37
Republican	49	43	44	42	43	40	44	44	46
Independent	7	13	9	19	19	19	18	18	17
Total Percent	101	101	100	101	101	100	101	100	100
N =	418	434	621	1806	1355	1393	1385	1519	1562

	African Americans								
	1964	1968	1972	1984	1988	1992	1996	2000	2004
Democrat	82	76	85	76	75	75	81	81	79
Republican	12	10	8	7	9	5	8	9	9
Independent	6	14	8	17	16	21	11	11	12
Total Percent	100	100	101	100	100	101	100	101	100
N =	51	29	53	192	131	83	133	103	239

Because of rounding, column percentages range from 99 to 101 percent.

5. I have placed a reminder about these data gaps at the bottom of each chart containing missing survey years.

Table 6.5 *(continued)*

1964	Regardless of how you may vote, what do you usually consider yourself a Republican, a Democrat, or what?
1968	Regardless of how you vote, when it comes to national politics, do you usually think of yourself as a Republican, a Democrat, an Independent, or what?
1972	Are you a Democrat, a Republican, or what?
1984–1988	Do you usually think of yourself as a Republican, a Democrat, or an Independent?
1992–2004	No matter how you voted today, do you usually think of yourself as a Democrat, a Republican, an Independent, or something else?

Source Note: The author analyzed the following polls to gather these data: Louis Harris 1964 presidential election survey in Pennsylvania, no. 1357. Chapel Hill: University of North Carolina, The Odom Institute [distributor]. David M. Kovenock, and James W. Prothro. Comparative State Elections Project, 1968 Chapel Hill: University of North Carolina, Institute for Research in Social Science, 1970 [producer]. Ann Arbor, MI: Inter-University Consortium for Political and Social Research (ICPSR) [distributor], 1977. Yankelovich Voter Study, 1972 [Computer file]. ICPSR ed. Ann Arbor, MI: ICPSR [distributor]. CBS News Election Day Surveys, 1984: State Surveys ICPSR ed. Ann Arbor, MI: ICPSR [producer and distributor]. ABC News "Good Morning America" Five State Poll, October–November 1988. Radnor, PA: Chilton Research Services [producer], 1989. Ann Arbor, MI: ICPSR [distributor]. Voter Research and Surveys (VRS) General Election Exit Polls, 1992. New York: VRS [producer]. 2nd ICPSR release. Ann Arbor, MI: ICPSR [distributor]. Voter News Service (VNS) General Election Exit Polls, 1996 & 2000. ICPSR version. New York: VNS [producer]. Ann Arbor, MI: ICPSR [distributor]. National Election Pool, Edison Media Research, and Mitofsky International. General Election Exit Polls, 2004. ICPSR version. Somerville, NJ: Edison Media Research/New York: Mitofsky International [producers], 2004. Ann Arbor, MI: ICPSR [distributor]. These are the sources for all of the Pennsylvania surveys used in this chapter.

Figures 6.2 and 6.3. Like African Americans all over the country, blacks in Pennsylvania are wedded to the Democratic party. There has been virtually no change over the four decades, as Figure 6.3 and the third panel of Table 6.5 demonstrate. On the other hand, the state-level surveys show that white identification with the Democratic party in the state has declined appreciably, going from about 45 percent in the 1960s to 37 percent in 2004. From 1996 to 2004, the Republican party maintained a consistent lead over Democrats among Pennsylvania's whites, as Figure 6.2 and the second panel of Table 6.5 confirm.

What do the surveys tell us about who is shifting? First, I examine religion, and the findings are striking. As shown in Figures 6.4a and 6.4b, Democratic party identification of white Catholics has plummeted in Pennsylvania and in the North. In 1964, 63 percent of Pennsylvania's white Catholics identified with the Democratic party. By 2004, that percentage had dropped to 41 percent. In fact, by 2004, the Republican party in Pennsylvania, at 43 percent, had a larger percentage of Pennsylvania's white Catholics identifying with it than with the Democratic party, a remarkable turnabout considering that in 1964 only 30 percent of the state's white Catholics called themselves Republicans. As Figures 6.4a and b also show, the Pennsylvania trend is found in the North as a whole, although independent identifiers are much more numerous in the

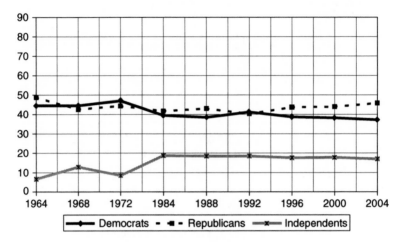

Fig. 6.2. Party Identification of Whites in Pennsylvania, 1964–2004

Note: Because there are data gaps in the availability of post-1960 Pennsylvania surveys, several years are omitted in this chart. Please refer to Table 6.5 for source.

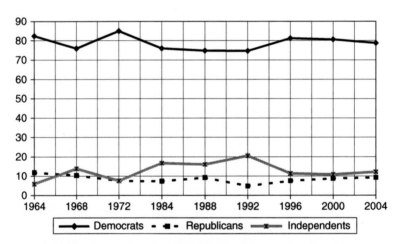

Fig. 6.3. Party Identification of African Americans in Pennsylvania, 1964–2004

Note: Because there are data gaps in the availability of post-1960 Pennsylvania surveys, several years are omitted in this chart. Please refer to Table 6.5 for source.

NES regional data than in the Pennsylvania polls. Incidentally, the state surveys indicate that the Catholic population of the state is about 38 percent, a figure that remained fairly consistent in all of the 1964 to 2004 polls.

Like party identification, the voting behavior of white Pennsylvania Catholics is also becoming more Republican in presidential elections, as is shown in Figure 6.5a. In fact, by the 2004 presidential election, the Republican nominee, George W. Bush, beat the Democratic nominee, John Kerry, by 52 percent to 48 percent among white Pennsylvania Catholics, according to that year's exit poll. The GOP performance is even more impressive when you consider that Kerry is a Catholic.

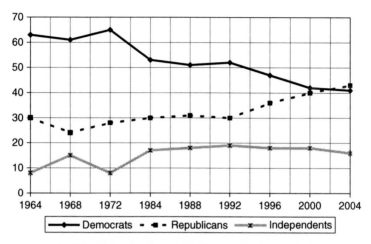

Fig. 6.4a. Party Identification of White Catholics in Pennsylvania, 1964–2004

Note: Because there are data gaps in the availability of post-1960 Pennsylvania surveys, several years are omitted in this chart. Please refer to Table 6.5 for source.

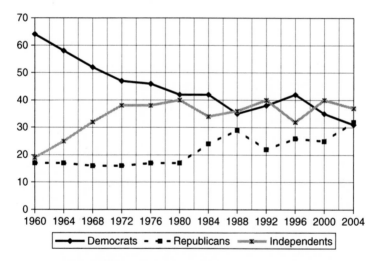

Fig. 6.4b. Party Identification of White Catholics in the North, 1960–2004

Note: Please refer to Table 6.1 for source.

Figure 6.5a also shows that President Nixon in 1972 was the first Republican in the post-1960 era to win a majority among the state's white Catholics, although it is possible that Reagan may have done so in 1980, a year for which I do not have a general election exit poll. As the chart for white northerners in Figure 6.5b indicates, the Republican presidential nominees received larger percentages of Catholics regionwide than Democratic nominees in all three elections in the 1980s. Then, by 2000 and 2004, the northern and Pennsylvania trends track closely.

Why did this big change in partisanship allegiance and voting behavior among Catholics occur? William B. Prendergast, in his book *The Catholic Voter in American*

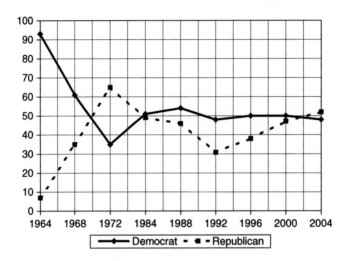

Fig. 6.5a. Presidential Vote of White Catholics in Pennsylvania, 1964–2004

Note: Because there are data gaps in the availability of post-1964 Pennsylvania surveys, several years are omitted in this chart. Please refer to Table 6.5 for source.

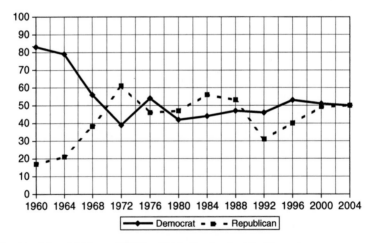

Fig. 6.5b. Presidential Vote of White Catholics in the North, 1960–2004

Note: Please refer to Table 6.1 for source.

Politics: The Passing of a Democratic Monolith, offered an interpretation that supports my culture-wars realignment thesis, at least in regard to this one important segment of the electorate.[6] He wrote the following in his concluding chapter:

> Cultural considerations have played an important part in bringing about a changed political alignment of Catholic voters. Particularly

---

6. The surveys show that Pennsylvania Catholics made up about 38 percent of the state's electorate, a figure that remained reasonably steady in all the Pennsylvania surveys and exit polls studied.

in the years when it was directed by the forces that George McGovern relied on in 1972, the Democratic Party seemed to reject a set of values held by most Catholics. . . .

In the estrangement of Catholics from the Democratic Party, two modifications of party policy made in the 1980s should not be over-looked, for they suggested an indifference to the Catholic constituency. One involved the question of abortion, on which an absolute and uncompromising pro-choice position was adopted. . . . The second was the abandonment in the 1988 platform of a pledge of assistance to children in nonpublic schools.

In the 1970s and 80s the Republican party exploited "the social issue." On both abortion and aid to non-public schools, it took a stand opposed to that adopted by the Democrats.[7]

Although Prendergast stressed the cultural explanation in his book's conclu-sion, he also pointed to the rise in socioeconomic status experienced by Catholics in American society over the last half century as another reason for their shift away from the Democratic party. He wrote: "[Catholics] are better educated, richer, more secure. They hold better jobs, more power, and more influence." The author added that the Democratic party did not adjust its program to appeal to "the interests of this upwardly mobile socio-economic group [prospering American Catholics]."[8]

As Figure 6.6a confirms, Pennsylvania's white Protestants remained over-whelmingly Republican, although the GOP's majority among this religious group has declined somewhat, going from 62 percent in 1964 to 54 percent in 2004. Figure 6.6b illustrates that white northern Protestants differ to some extent from those in the Keystone State chart, again, partly because of the larger indepen-dent contingent in the NES survey. As Figure 6.7a demonstrates, Pennsylvania Republicans maintained a substantial advantage in the voting behavior of the state's white Protestants, a pattern that is similar to the regional configuration in Figure 6.7b.

Considering the overall Catholic and Protestant trends, it is notable that even after the sizable growth of white Republican Catholics, the Democratic party in Pennsylvania and in the North still does better among white Catholics than it does among white Protestants both in terms of party identification and in presidential elections.[9]

---

7. William B. Prendergast, *The Catholic Voter in American Politics: The Passing of a Democratic Monolith* (Washington, DC: Georgetown University Press, 1999), 223.

8. Ibid., 222.

9. Incidentally, Pennsylvania Jews, who register in the state exit polls at about 3 to 4 percent of the electorate, identify overwhelmingly with the Democratic party and vote Democratic for president in the 70 percent range. Since the numbers are so small, one cannot be confident about the exact percentages, but the overall pro-Democratic trend is clear and did not appear to be changing in 2004.

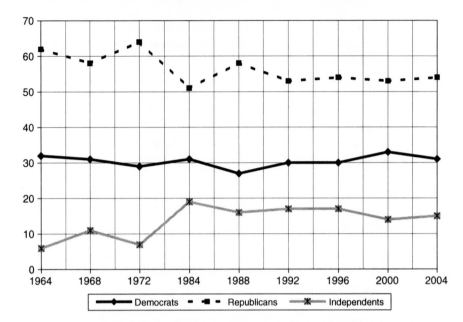

Fig. 6.6a. Party Identification of White Protestants in Pennsylvania, 1964–2004

Note: Because there are data gaps in the availability of post-1960 Pennsylvania surveys, several years are omitted in this chart. Please refer to Table 6.5 for source.

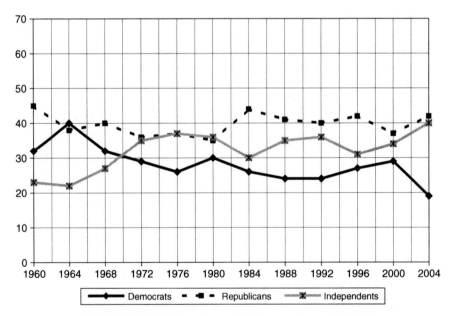

Fig. 6.6b. Party Identification of White Protestants in the North, 1960–2004

Note: Please refer to Table 6.1 for source.

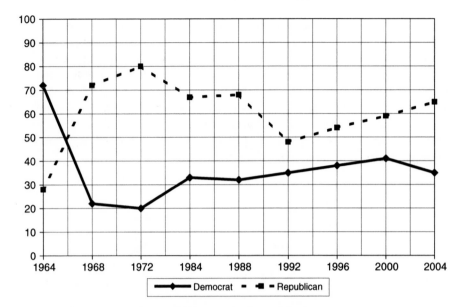

Fig. 6.7a. Presidential Vote of White Protestants in Pennsylvania, 1964–2004

Note: Because there are data gaps in the availability of post-1960 Pennsylvania surveys, several years are omitted in this chart. Please refer to Table 6.5 for source.

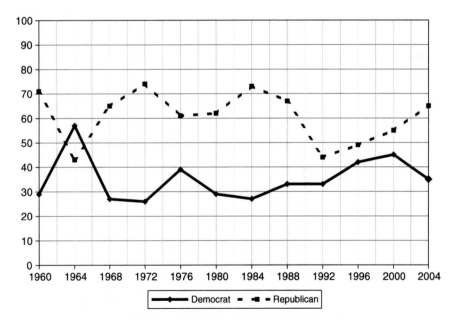

Fig. 6.7b. Presidential Vote of White Protestants in the North, 1960–2004

Note: Please refer to Table 6.1 for source.

Another way to differentiate voters is to look at their level of religiosity as measured, for lack of a better way, by church attendance. Although NES has asked respondents about church attendance since the 1950s, only three of my Pennsylvania surveys included that question. I'll start with the results for northern whites broken into four categories: regularly (once a week or more), often (a few times a month), seldom (a few times a year), and never. Cross-tabulating church attendance with political party identification results in the following breakdown by party as displayed in Figure 6.8a for white northern Democrats and Figure 6.8b for white northern Republicans.

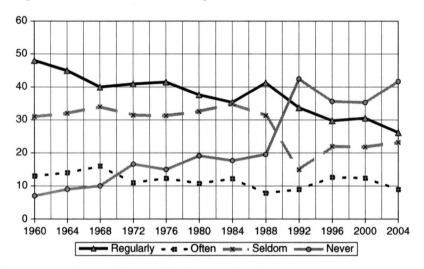

Fig. 6.8a. Church Attendance of Northern White Democrats, 1960–2004

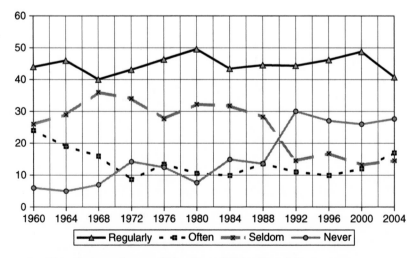

Fig. 6.8b. Church Attendance of Northern White Republicans, 1960–2004

Note: Please refer to Table 6.1 for source.

The results of a similar cross-tabulation with those who voted Democratic or Republican for president are in Figures 6.9a and 6.9b. For the Democrats, the trends are unmistakable. Over the forty-four-year period, those whites in the North who attend church regularly have become far less likely to identify as Democrats or to vote for Democratic presidential candidates. This is another indication of the effect of the culture-wars realignment because more than a few of the issues of this recent partisan reshuffling involved religious issues, from prayer in the public schools to abortion to euthanasia and even to gay rights.

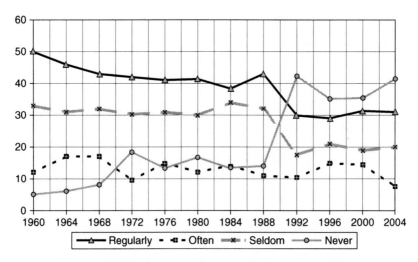

Fig. 6.9a. Church Attendance of Northern Whites Who Voted Democratic for President, 1960–2004

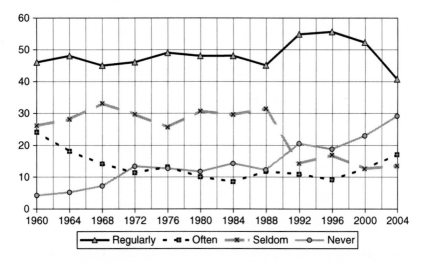

Fig. 6.9b. Church Attendance of Northern Whites Who Voted Republican for President, 1960–2004

Note: Please refer to Table 6.1 for source.

Notice the upward path of those who answer "never" to the church attendance question, a trend that includes Republicans as well as Democrats, the latter, of course, getting more of the nonattenders. Some of the noticeable rise that occurred in 1992 resulted from an unfortunate change in the way NES asked the question as well as the ordering of the question in the survey instrument, but that technical problem can be credited with only part of the pronounced general movement.[10] One reality affecting the trends in both parties shown in these church attendance figures is that overall church attendance is down among whites in the North. Those attending services regularly declined from an average of 42 percent in the 1960s to 33 percent in the early twenty-first century. Those who said they never attended church services shot up from 8 percent to 36 percent over the same period. Those who selected "seldom" went down by half, from 33 percent in the 1960s to 17 percent in the 2000 to 2004 period. The "often" category was the most stable, going from 15 to 13 percent overall.

Analysis of three Pennsylvania surveys reflects these same trends. For example, Figure 6.10a shows that in 1968, 59 percent of white Pennsylvania Democrats attended church regularly. By 2004, the percentage was 36! At the same time, the level of those who seldom or never attend church rose. As Figure 6.10b indicates, the Republicans have experienced a similar trend, although they have more regular churchgoers and less of those who attend seldom or never.

Similarly, in Figure 6.11a, of those white Pennsylvanians who voted Democratic for president in 1968 (and helped Hubert Humphrey carry the Keystone State while he was losing the nation), 64 percent attended church regularly. Of those white Pennsylvanians who voted Democratic in 2004 (and helped John Kerry carry the state in his losing bid for the White House), only 31 percent attended church regularly. The "never" category for both Democrats and Republicans is smaller than the regional NES figures. Figure 6.11b shows that of those Pennsylvania whites who voted Republican for president in 1968, 61 percent attended church regularly, whereas in 2004, only 47 percent attended regularly.

An examination of education and party identification reveals much fluctuation but also a fair amount of similarity between the two parties in recent years in the composition of their adherents by educational attainment. Figures 6.12 and 6.13 tell the party identification story for the Democratic and Republican parties

10. Starting in 1990, NES changed the wording of its church attendance question. The old question had been the following, if any religious preference had been indicated by the respondent in answer to previous religious affiliation questions: "Would you say you go to church or synagogue every week, almost every week, once or twice a month, a few times a year, or never?" The new wording is: "Lots of things come up that keep people from attending religious services even if they want to. Thinking about your life these days, do you ever attend religious services, apart from occasional weddings, baptisms, or funerals?" If the answer is yes, then this next question is asked: "Do you go to religious services every week, almost every week, once or twice a month, a few times a year, or never?" Further, beginning in 1990, NES reversed its question order so that the church attendance question precedes its religious affiliation questions. Incidentally, to get a four-part division for the church attendance variable, I classify the first two choices—every week and almost every week—as "regularly."

among whites in the North. However, before examining this regional pattern, it is important to recognize that educational attainment among voting-age Americans has advanced significantly from 1960 to 2004. Specifically, the overall education levels for whites in the North in 1960 were as follows for the five categories used in Figures 6.12 and 6.13: 46 percent had not graduated high school; 32 percent had graduated high school; 13 percent attended some college; 7 percent were college graduates; and 2 percent held postgraduate degrees. Forty-four years later, in 2004, the percentage reflected a heavy national investment in education: 7 percent had not graduated high school; 29 percent had graduated high school; 31 percent attended some college; 19 percent were college graduates; and 13 percent held

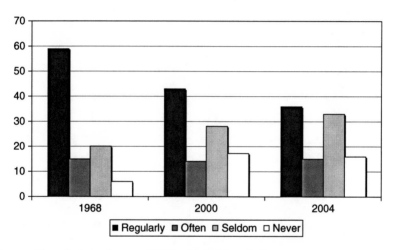

Fig. 6.10a. Church Attendance of White Pennsylvania Democrats

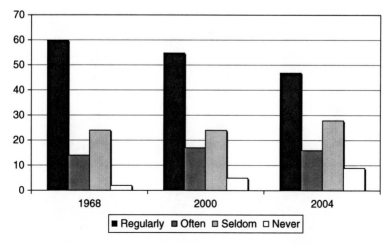

Fig. 6.10b. Church Attendance of White Pennsylvania Republicans

Note: Please refer to Table 6.5 for source.

postgraduate degrees. The bar chart in Figure 6.14 reduces those ten percentages just listed to an amazing illustration of educational change, at least as measured by years of school completed.

With that trend in mind, the path of the two parties in party identification among white northerners is less shocking. In 1960, 52 percent of Democratic party identifiers among white northerners had less than a high school education. For the Republicans, the percentage was 38. In 2004, those without a high school education made up only 8 percent of the Democratic identifiers and just 3 percent of the Republican identifiers. Both parties advanced in the category of those with

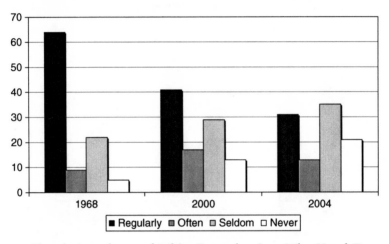

Fig. 6.11a. Church Attendance of White Pennsylvanians Who Voted Democratic for President

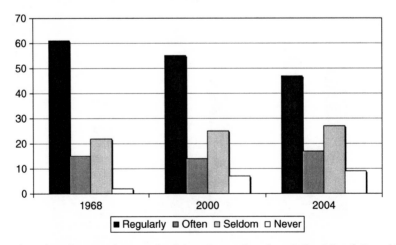

Fig. 6.11b. Church Attendance of Whites Pennsylvanians Who Voted Republican for President

Note: Please refer to Table 6.5 for source.

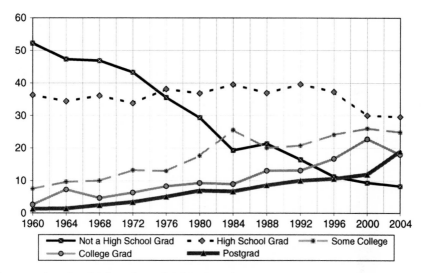

Fig. 6.12. Levels of Education of White Northern Democrats, 1960–2004

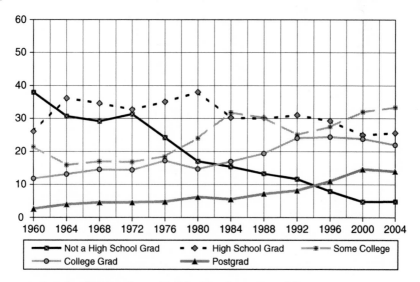

Fig. 6.13. Levels of Education of White Northern Republicans, 1960–2004

Note: Please refer to Table 6.1 for the source for these figures.

postgraduate degrees: the Democrats from 1 percent to 19 percent; the GOP from 3 percent to 14 percent.

Of course, these changes have to be viewed in light of the overall level of change in educational attainment pictured in Figure 6.14. Although one can see clear differences in the end points each party reached by 2004, such as in the two extreme educational categories just mentioned, overall the two figures show that both major parties in the North are much more similar in the education attainment of their white adherents in 2004 than they were forty-four years earlier.

Turning to education and the Pennsylvania party-identification patterns for whites of both parties, as shown in Figures 6.15 and 6.16, we see a configuration that resembles the overall northern one with a few exceptions. By 2004, college graduates are several percentage points higher for both the Pennsylvania Republican and Democratic parties compared to their northern counterparts. Also by 2004, Pennsylvania Democrats were doing better among whites with some college than were regional Democrats. Still, the similarity between the Keystone State patterns for both parties and their regional parties stands out.

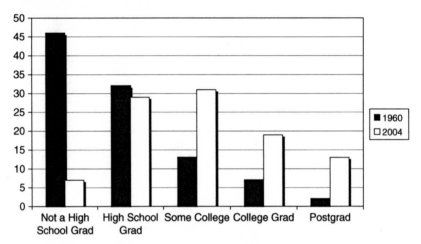

Fig. 6.14. Levels of Education of Northern Whites in 1960 and 2004

Note: Please refer to Table 6.1 for source.

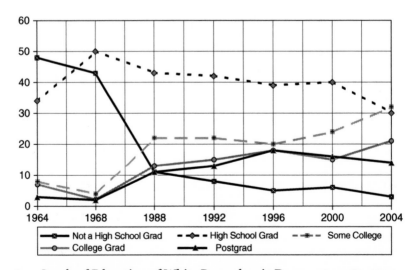

Fig. 6.15. Levels of Education of White Pennsylvania Democrats, 1964–2004

Note: Because there are data gaps in the availability of post-1960 Pennsylvania surveys, several years are omitted in this chart. Please refer to Table 6.5 for source.

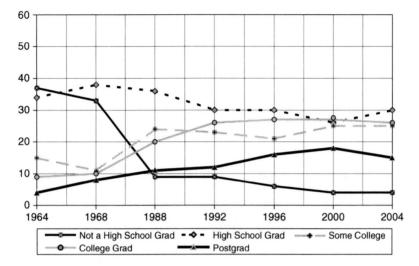

Fig. 6.16. Levels of Education of White Pennsylvania Republicans, 1964–2004

Note: Because there are data gaps in the availability of post-1960 Pennsylvania surveys, several years are omitted in this chart. Please refer to Table 6.5 for source.

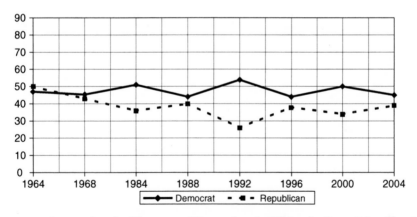

Fig. 6.17a. Lowest Level of Income of Pennsylvania Whites by Party Identification, 1964–2004

Investigating income with our two chief variables—party identification and the vote for president—sheds further light on Pennsylvania's partisan configuration in comparison to the North. Looking first at the Keystone State, Figures 6.17a through e present Democratic and Republican party identification at five levels of income. Incidentally, after Figure 6.17e, I describe the various dollar levels used in the disparate state surveys to divide respondents into five income categories. Also, I provide two samples of what the dollar figures from those earlier years would be equivalent to in 2004 dollars using a Consumer Price Index (CPI) adjustment formula.

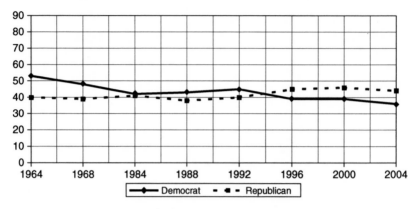

Fig. 6.17b. Second-Lowest Level of Income of Pennsylvania Whites by Party Identification, 1964–2004

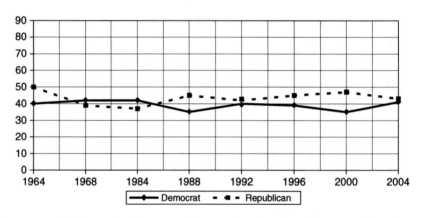

Fig. 6.17c. Middle Level of Income of Pennsylvania Whites by Party Identification, 1964–2004

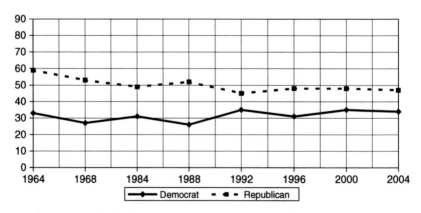

Fig. 6.17d. Second-Highest Level of Income of Pennsylvania Whites by Party Identification, 1964–2004

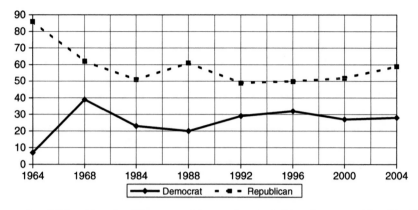

Fig. 6.17e. Highest Level of Income of Pennsylvania Whites by Party Identification, 1964–2004

Note: Because there are data gaps in the availability of post-1960 Pennsylvania surveys, several years are omitted in these charts. Please refer to Table 6.5 for source.

Income Categories Used in Disparate State Surveys				
	Lowest Level	Second-Lowest Level	Middle Level	Second-Highest Level	Highest Level
1964	Under 5K	5–7K	7–10K	10–20K	20K or more
1968	Under 5K	5–10K	10–15 K	15–20K	20K or more
1984	Under 12.5K	12.5–25K	25–35K	35–50K	50K or more
1988	Under 25K	25–35K	35–50K	50–100K	100K or more
1992	Under 15K	15–30K	30–50K	50–75K	75K or more
1996	Under 30K	30–50K	50–75K	75–100K	100K or more
2000	Under 30K	30–50K	75–100K	50–75K	100K or more
2004	Under 30K	30–50K	50–75K	75–100K	100K or more

Two Examples of CPI-Adjusted Dollars for 2004			
1964	$5,000	$7,000	$10,000	$20,000
2004	30,468	42,655	60,935	121,871
1992	$15,000	$30,000	$50,000	$75,000
2004	20,804	41,608	69,347	104,020

Figures 6.17d and 6.17e confirm that the old New Deal–style economic class cleavages in the party system can still be found among white Pennsylvania partisans in the two highest income levels. Those with the highest incomes preferred the Republican party by at least 20 to 30 percentage points throughout. The 1964 survey placed the gap at 70 percentage points. In 2004, 59 percent of those in the highest income level identified with the GOP compared to 28 percent who opted for the Democratic party. The second-highest income level showed a smaller but still distinct gap. In this category in

1964, 59 percent were Republicans compared to 33 percent who were Democrats, while in 2004, 47 percent were Republicans, and 34 percent were Democrats.

In the middle-income level, Figure 6.17c, the percentages were close with the GOP, holding a slight edge in most years. For the second-lowest level of income, Figure 6.17b, the percentages are again close, but the two parties switched the lead in the early 1990s, when the Republican party attained the edge. Among those in the lowest level of income, shown in Figure 6.17a, Democrats generally maintained an advantage in nearly all years with margins running from a few percentage points to nearly 30 in 1992. In the last year sampled, 45 percent of white Pennsylvanians in the lowest income group identified with the Democratic party compared to 39 percent favoring the GOP.

Figures 6.18a through e make a similar income-level comparison for white partisan identifiers in the North. White northerners in the highest percentile of income, shown in Figure 6.18e, also identified with the GOP by sizable margins, although not as large

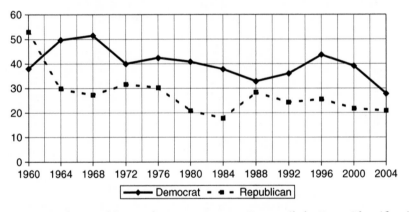

Fig. 6.18a. Northern Whites at the 0 to 16 Income Percentile by Party Identification, 1960–2004

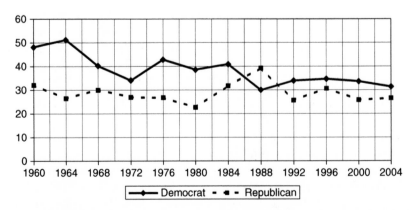

Fig. 6.18b. Northern Whites at the 17 to 33 Income Percentile by Party Identification, 1960–2004

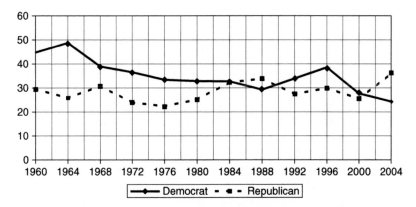

Fig. 6.18c. Northern Whites at the 34 to 67 Income Percentile by Party Identification, 1960–2004

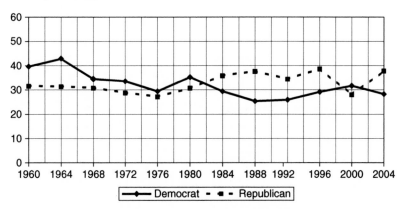

Fig. 6.18d. Northern Whites at the 68 to 95 Income Percentile by Party Identification, 1960–2004

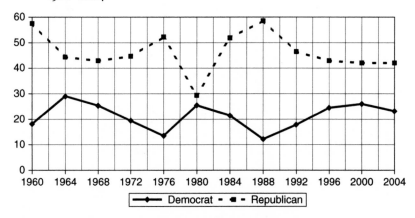

Fig. 6.18e. Northern Whites at the 96 to 100 Income Percentile by Party Identification, 1960–2004

Note: Please refer to Table 6.1 for source.

as in Pennsylvania in most years. Differing somewhat from the Pennsylvania trend, the second-highest income level for the region, Figure 6.18d, shows a Democratic edge in the earlier years with the GOP taking the lead among these identifiers in 1984 and maintaining the lead except for 2000. Figures 6.18b and 6.18c illustrate that the next two levels were reasonably close with the Democrats having an advantage in most years. Finally, northern white Democratic identifiers in the lowest income percentile, Figure 6.18a, were ahead of the GOP as they were in Pennsylvania.

Turning to income and the vote for president, the trend lines in the state are more volatile than was the case for party identification. See Figures 6.19 and 6.20. The same volatility was present in the region as well except for Bill Clinton's two presidential victories in 1992 and 1996. Figure 6.20e shows that in 1996, northern whites with the highest incomes supported Clinton with 50 percent of the vote to his GOP opponent's 48 percent. In 2000 and 2004, however, the GOP returned to its sizable advantage among these wealthy voters.

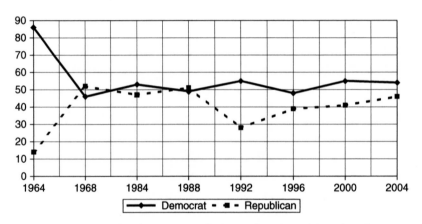

Fig. 6.19a. Lowest Level of Income of Pennsylvania Whites by the Vote for President, 1964–2004

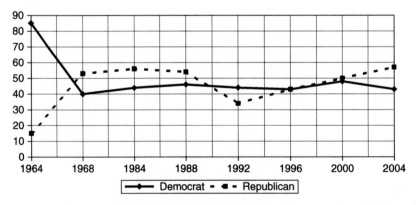

Fig. 6.19b. Second-Lowest Level of Income of Pennsylvania Whites by the Vote for President, 1964–2004

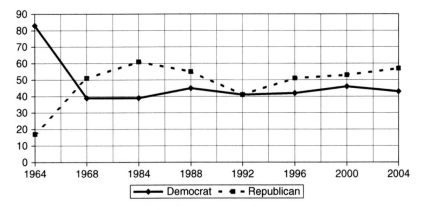

Fig. 6.19c. Middle Level of Income of Pennsylvania Whites by the Vote for President, 1964–2004

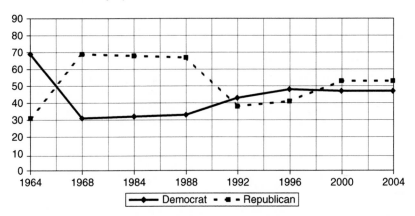

Fig. 6.19d. Second-Highest Level of Income of Pennsylvania Whites by the Vote for President, 1964–2004

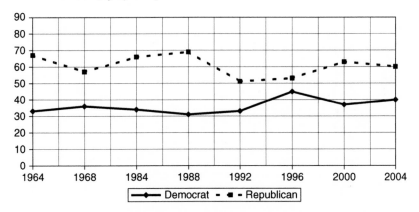

Fig. 6.19e. Highest Level of Income of Pennsylvania Whites by the Vote for President, 1964–2004

Note: Because there are data gaps in the availability of post-1960 Pennsylvania surveys, several years are omitted in this chart. Please refer to Table 6.5 for source.

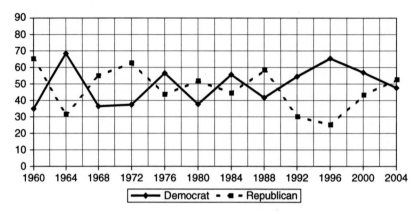

Fig. 6.20a. Northern Whites at the 0 to 16 Income Percentile by the Vote for President, 1960–2004

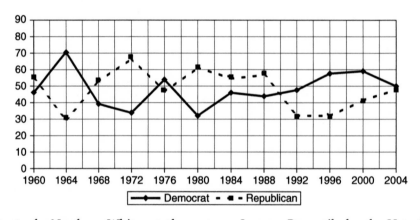

Fig. 6.20b. Northern Whites at the 17 to 33 Income Percentile by the Vote for President, 1960–2004

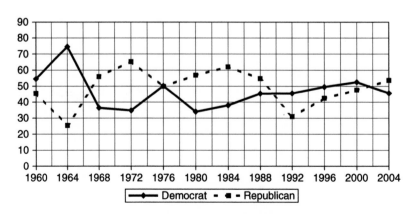

Fig. 6.20c. Northern Whites at the 34 to 67 Income Percentile by the Vote for President, 1960–2004

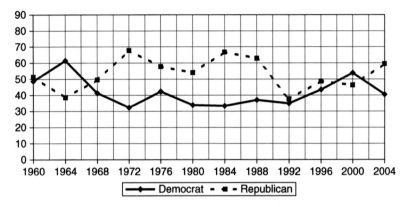

Fig. 6.20d. Northern Whites at the 68 to 95 Income Percentile by the Vote for President, 1960–2004

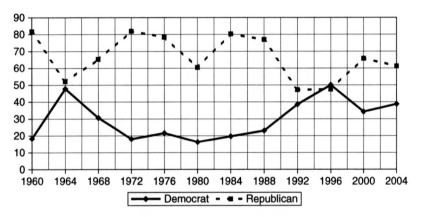

Fig. 6.20e. Northern Whites at the 96 to 100 Income Percentile by the Vote for President, 1960–2004

Note: Please refer to Table 6.1 for source.

Another way to learn more about what is motivating white partisans in Pennsylvania is to cross-tabulate party identification with responses to a standard political philosophy question, such as this one used in the state exit polls: "On most political matters, do you consider yourself: Liberal, Moderate, or Conservative?"[11] See Figure 6.21. Of the white Pennsylvanians in 1964 who called themselves liberals, shown in Figure 6.21a, 49 percent identified with the Democratic party. In that same year, white Pennsylvania Republicans made up 40 percent of the self-identified liberals. By 2004, the percentage of white Pennsylvania Democrats making up the liberal category had increased to 68, and white Republicans had dropped to 11 percent. Likewise, white Pennsylvanians who called themselves conservatives have undergone a transformation, vis-

11. This is the wording used in all of the Pennsylvania exit polls examined in this study.

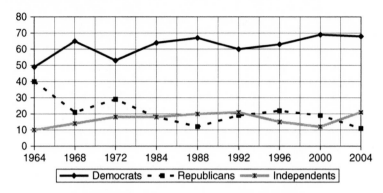

Fig. 6.21a. Party Identification of Pennsylvania White Liberals, 1964–2004

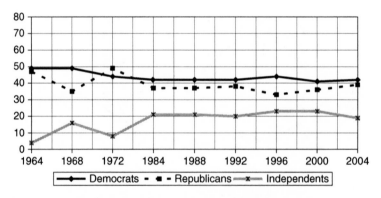

Fig. 6.21b. Party Identification of Pennsylvania White Moderates, 1964–2004

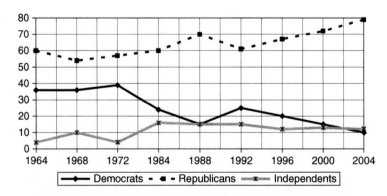

Fig. 6.21c. Party Identification of Pennsylvania White Conservatives, 1964–2004

Note: Because there are data gaps in the availability of post-1960 Pennsylvania surveys, several years are omitted in this chart. Please refer to Table 6.5 for source.

ible in Figure 6.21c. In 1964, 36 percent of the self-identified conservatives were Democrats. By 2004, that percentage had declined to 10 percent. Of the Republicans in 1964, 60 percent were self-identified conservatives, while in 2004 that number had risen to 79 percent.[12]

Another way to capture the effect of changing political philosophies on the major parties is to chart the percentage of self-identified liberals, moderates, and conservatives who claim identification with a major party. This is done for white Pennsylvanians in Figure 6.22. The plot for the Democrats, in Figure 6.22a, depicts the demise of the conservatives in the party; they declined 21 percentage points between 1964 and 2004. Likewise, Figure 6.22b indicates that liberal Republicans fell 13 percentage points, while the conservatives climbed from 43 to 54 percent.

This change sends a strong message to Republican moderates in the Keystone State. It was a message that Congressman Pat Toomey, a conservative Republican, tried to deliver to Senator Arlen Specter, the epitome of the moderate-to-liberal

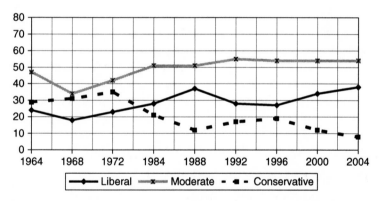

Fig. 6.22a. Political Philosophy of Pennsylvania White Democrats, 1964–2004

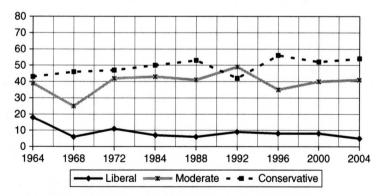

Fig. 6.22b. Political Philosophy of Pennsylvania White Republicans, 1964–2004

12. Incidentally, these Pennsylvania patterns concerning partisanship and political philosophy are also visible in the survey data for whites in the North.

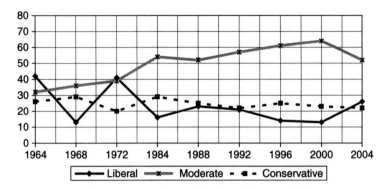

Fig. 6.22c. Political Philosophy of Pennsylvania White Independents, 1964–2004

Note: Because there are data gaps in the availability of post-1960 Pennsylvania surveys, several years are omitted in this chart. Please refer to Table 6.5 for source.

wing of the state's GOP, in the 2004 Republican primary, when Toomey very nearly ended Specter's twenty-four-year U.S. Senate career.

With this comparative analysis of party identification and the vote for president among whites in Pennsylvania and the North at an end, I continue to employ survey data in the second half of this chapter to shed light on the political behavior of the Pennsylvania electorate.

Pennsylvania Voting Behavior: Further Survey Findings from Presidential and Major Statewide Elections in the Keystone State

Using survey data in the first section of this chapter, I provided an overview of four decades of partisan change in Pennsylvania in comparison to the North. To do this, I examined the changing relationship of religion, church attendance, education, income, and political philosophy with party identification and the vote for president.

In this second and final part of the chapter, I probe more deeply into Pennsylvania voting behavior by investigating differences among voters in five geographical divisions of the state using 2004 survey data. Then, I turn to several major statewide elections for governor and U.S. senator in search of survey data insights into those contests. Lastly, I shift my focus to a comparison of Pennsylvania with the rest of the nation by examining the 2004 national exit poll along with the Pennsylvania exit poll conducted at the same time. This final activity returns attention to an important topic in chapter 2, the task of evaluating the Keystone State's political direction in the national context.

In the first section of this survey chapter, I restricted my analysis to Pennsylvania and northern white voters because, as I stated above, African Americans have been virtually united in their support for the Democratic party throughout the post-1960 period and to include them in that analysis would have obscured whatever change was occurring. However, by looking only at whites, a false impression is conveyed, among other things, about overall party strength in Pennsylvania. Thus, since my purpose in the first section of showing change involving several key variables has been accomplished, the analysis in this section is done for all voters, allowing me now to present the partisan reality in a more inclusive fashion.

To begin that task, Table 6.6 presents a cross-tabulation of the vote for president in 2004 by race, which includes Hispanics/Latinos, Asians, and others along with whites and blacks. Among white voters, President Bush is the victor with

Table 6.6 Cross-Tabulation of the 2004 Vote for President in Pennsylvania by Race

			Vote for President in 2004		
			Kerry	Bush	Total
Race	White	N	780	926	1706
		% within Race	46%	54%	100%
		% within Vote for President in 2004	72%	91%	82%
	Black	N	228	43	271
		% within Race	84%	16%	100%
		% within Vote for President in 2004	21%	4%	13%
	Hispanic/ Latino	N	44	17	61
		% within Race	72%	28%	100%
		% within Vote for President in 2004	4%	2%	3%
	Asian	N	12	15	27
		% within Race	44%	56%	100%
		% within Vote for President in 2004	1%	1%	1%
	Other	N	13	13	26
		% within Race	50%	50%	100%
		% within Vote for President in 2004	1%	1%	1%
Total		N	1077	1014	2091
		% within Race	52%	48%	100%
		% within Vote for President in 2004	100%	100%	100%

Source: 2004 Presidential Exit Poll in Pennsylvania, conducted by Edison Media Research.

54 percent to 46 percent for his Democratic challenger, Senator Kerry.[13] Among the state's African Americans, Kerry won 84 percent of the vote to Bush's 16 percent. Kerry did very well among the state's small Hispanic/Latino population, and Bush carried the even smaller Asian American vote. Note that 91 percent of Bush's total vote came from whites and that Kerry would have lost Pennsylvania had it not been for his strong support from blacks.

To probe more deeply into Pennsylvania's presidential voting patterns in 2004, I employ a valuable five-part regional division of the state used by the exit-poll takers Edison Media Research. The map in Figure 6.23 shows five regions and the counties included within each. Edison drew its survey sample in such a way that it would have a representative sample for each division, making analysis of the exit poll much more valuable.[14] Having one of the regions made up of the four populous suburban

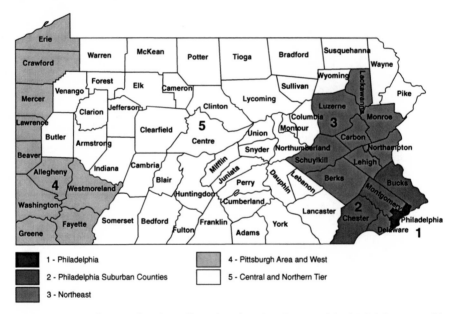

Fig. 6.23. Map of Pennsylvania Delineating the Five Geographical Divisions Used by Edison Media Research

13. Of the 1,978 Pennsylvania voters interviewed in the exit poll, only nine people said they voted for someone other than President Bush or Senator Kerry. To keep the cross-tabulations as simple as possible, I made them "missing values" for the analysis along with the three voters who said they did not cast a presidential ballot when they voted in the general election.

14. Joe Lenski of Edison Media Research, which conducted the 2004 exit poll for ABC, CBS, NBC, CNN, and Fox News, the five major television networks, plus the Associated Press, explained to me the way the survey was conducted in an e-mail message on November 11, 2005. After making the central point about how the samples were drawn in the regions, Lenski added: "However, the sample sizes can be fairly small within each geographic division—perhaps 5 to 10 precincts—so the sample errors can be relatively large for any estimates made within geographic divisions."

counties surrounding Philadelphia—Bucks, Chester, Delaware, and Montgomery—was particularly valuable because it fit well with my strong interest in the political behavior of these pivotal counties.

The Northeast region includes Lackawanna and Luzerne but also Lehigh and other counties just north or west of the Philadelphia suburbs. The Pittsburgh area and other western counties include much of the Pittsburgh metropolitan area plus Erie and several counties in between. The central and northern tier consist of the GOP-trending rural, small-town counties that make up the Republican T, mentioned earlier. The fifth division is, of course, Philadelphia.[15] This five-part regional division is extremely useful because it allows for sorting out voter attitudes and behavior in these regions according to the input of individuals.[16]

Table 6.7 Cross-Tabulation of the 2004 Vote for President in Pennsylvania by Region

| | | | Vote for President in 2004 | | |
			Kerry	Bush	Total
Region	Philadelphia	N	198	46	244
			81%	19%	100%
	Philadelphia suburbs	N	244	207	451
			54%	46%	100%
	Northeast	N	153	148	301
			51%	49%	100%
	Pittsburgh area/West	N	264	229	493
			54%	46%	100%
	Central/northern tier	N	230	395	625
			37%	63%	100%
Total		N	1089	1025	2114
			52%	48%	100%

Source: 2004 Presidential Exit Poll in Pennsylvania, conducted by Edison Media Research.

15. Edison's Joe Lenski sent me the map delineating the regions. No division of the state is perfect; one always wants to take issue at the boundaries. Two counties north of Pittsburgh, Butler and Armstrong, should have been included in the Pittsburgh area. It is always difficult to know where to put Erie, because it clearly does not fit with the GOP-trending central/northern tier region. So, the exit poll's decision to put Erie in with the Pittsburgh area to form a western region is a sensible one. Finally, Lehigh is much closer today to the Philadelphia orbit than to the other Northeast Pennsylvania counties. The placement of Berks and Northampton in the Northeast is also not completely satisfying.

16. The fact that the poll findings I delineate are similar to trends noted in other places in this book via nonsurvey-research methods was a welcomed—and an unexpected—bonus.

Table 6.7, the first to use the exit poll's five geographical divisions, shows the results of a cross-tabulation of the 2004 presidential vote by the regions of the state, results that are not surprising, of course, after the extensive study of the county-level voting patterns presented in other chapters using aggregate data. Philadelphia voted overwhelmingly for Kerry, 81 percent to Bush's 19 percent, the exit poll shows. The Philadelphia suburbs gave Kerry 54 percent to Bush's 46 percent. The Northeast region split almost evenly, Kerry receiving 51 percent to Bush's 49. The Pittsburgh area and western Pennsylvania went for Kerry by 54 percent to Bush's 46 percent. Finally, the central/northern tier region went heavily for Bush, 63 percent to 37 percent for Kerry.

Table 6.8 uses the five regional divisions to examine 2004 party identification more closely. The huge plurality of self-identified Democrats in Philadelphia is no surprise, as is the case for the Northeast and the Pittsburgh/West region. That the respondents from the Philadelphia suburbs were far more likely to identify with the Republican party, 45 percent for the GOP compared to the 35 percent who identified themselves as Democrats (although more than a few of the Republicans there were clearly voting Democratic), is solid confirmation of what the voting and party registration trends show. Whether this voting behavior witnessed in the several major elections of the early twenty-first century is a prelude to a permanent partisan change, that is, a significant switch in party identification (and, more importantly, official party registration) is addressed in chapter 7.

When coupled with the regional divisions, the political philosophy question used in the first section of this chapter is a good one for gauging the political

Table 6.8 Cross-Tabulation of 2004 Party Identification in Pennsylvania by Region

| | | | Party Identification | | | |
			Democrat	Republican	Independent	Total
Region	Philadelphia	N	145	27	27	199
			73%	14%	14%	100%
	Philadelphia suburbs	N	146	189	83	418
			35%	45%	20%	100%
	Northeast	N	123	98	47	268
			46%	37%	18%	100%
	Pittsburgh area/West	N	233	155	72	460
			51%	34%	16%	100%
	Central/northern tier	N	177	307	86	570
			31%	54%	15%	100%
Total		N	824	776	315	1915
			43%	41%	16%	100%

Source: 2004 Presidential Exit Poll in Pennsylvania, conducted by Edison Media Research.

orientation of areas within Pennsylvania. The overall state sample divided as follows: liberal, 22 percent; moderate, 48 percent; conservative, 30 percent. Table 6.9 contains the results. Notice that Philadelphia is the most liberal of the state's regions and that the central/northern tier is the most conservative, neither of which is surprising given my previous analysis of the voting patterns of both regions.

In a further effort to understand what was motivating voters in 2004, Edison Media asked voters the following question: "Which *ONE* issue mattered most in deciding how you voted for *president*?" Then, the respondent was asked to check only one of the following seven items: Taxes, Education, Iraq, Terrorism, Economy/Jobs, Moral values, Health care. The responses, cross-tabulated with the vote for president, are displayed in Table 6.10.

Of the seven issues, four drew the most responses—Iraq, terrorism, the economy/jobs, and moral values, in that order. Of those choosing terrorism (22 percent of the sample), 83 percent voted for the President. Of those choosing Iraq (21 percent), 71 percent voted for Senator Kerry. The third issue (picked by 19 percent) was the economy/jobs, and they supported Kerry with 82 percent. The fourth issue, moral values (chosen by 19 percent), drew much national commentary and controversy after the election because people choosing it throughout the country favored Bush by substantial margins, as was the case in Pennsylvania, where Bush got the votes of 81 percent of those selecting this issue. The controversy stemmed from the vague nature of the term, but in the context of several decades of the "culture wars,"

Table 6.9 Cross-Tabulation of 2004 Political Philosophy in Pennsylvania by Region

| | | | Political Philosophy | | | |
			Liberal	Moderate	Conservative	Total
Region	Philadelphia	N	71	83	48	202
			35%	41%	24%	100%
	Philadelphia suburbs	N	96	216	113	425
			23%	51%	27%	100%
	Northeast	N	74	114	86	274
			27%	42%	31%	100%
	Pittsburgh area/West	N	94	258	120	472
			20%	55%	25%	100%
	Central/northern tier	N	95	269	221	585
			16%	46%	38%	100%
Total		N	430	940	588	1958
			22%	48%	30%	100%

Source: 2004 Presidential Exit Poll in Pennsylvania, conducted by Edison Media Research.

Table 6.10 Cross-Tabulation of the 2004 Vote for President in Pennsylvania
by Top Issue Choice

| | | | Vote for President in 2004 | | |
			Kerry (D)	Bush (R)	Total
Issue	Taxes (8%)	N	66	60	126
			52%	48%	100%
	Education (5%)	N	65	23	88
			74%	26%	100%
	Iraq (21%)	N	248	102	350
			71%	29%	100%
	Terrorism (22%)	N	64	305	369
			17%	83%	100%
	Economy/jobs (19%)	N	265	58	323
			82%	18%	100%
	Moral values (19%)	N	60	259	319
			19%	81%	100%
	Health care (7%)	N	93	21	114
			82%	18%	100%
	Total	N	861	828	1689
			51%	49%	100%

Source: 2004 Presidential Exit Poll in Pennsylvania, conducted by Edison Media Research.

perhaps the term served as code for a host of conservative positions from that conflict. Fewer people in the sample picked taxes (8 percent), health care (7 percent),
and education (5 percent) with Kerry having a slight lead in the first (52 percent
to Bush's 48 percent) and an overwhelming edge on the other two (82 percent on
health care and 74 percent on education).

Further using the "issues" question, especially the "moral values" choice, I
cross-tabulated the responses with both the vote for Kerry or Bush as well as with
the respondents' choices on political philosophy. See Table 6.11. Of the 155 conservative respondents who chose moral values as their most important issue, 154 of
them, or 99 percent, voted for Bush! Of those 34 liberals who chose moral values,
79 percent voted for Kerry, suggesting that either moral values meant something
different to them than it did for the conservatives, or they were influenced more by
other factors in their vote choice. The conservatives who chose terrorism as their
top issue were also for Bush by a staggering percentage, 96 percent. Liberals turned
in many very high percentages for Kerry on key issues to them, such as education,
the economy/jobs, and Iraq. Overall in Pennsylvania, liberals voted 88 percent

Table 6.11 Cross-Tabulation of the 2004 Vote for President in Pennsylvania by Respondents' Top Issue Choice and Political Philosophy

Political Philosophy				Vote for President in 2004		Total
				Kerry	Bush	
Liberal	Issue	Taxes	N	27	4	31
				87%	13%	100%
		Education	N	22	1	23
				96%	4%	100%
		Iraq	N	101	9	110
				92%	8%	100%
		Terrorism	N	21	10	31
				68%	32%	100%
		Economy/jobs	N	67	6	73
				92%	8%	100%
		Moral values	N	27	7	34
				79%	21%	100%
		Health care	N	35	4	39
				90%	10%	100%
		Other	N	14	2	16
				88%	13%	100%
	Total		N	314	43	357
				88%	12%	100%
Moderate	Issue	Taxes	N	26	23	49
				53%	47%	100%
		Education	N	29	15	44
				66%	34%	100%
		Iraq	N	117	51	168
				70%	30%	100%
		Terrorism	N	32	115	147
				22%	78%	100%
		Economy/jobs	N	148	26	174
				85%	15%	100%
		Moral values	N	27	83	110
				25%	75%	100%
		Health care	N	41	11	52
				79%	21%	100%

Table 6.11 (*continued*)

Political Philosophy				Vote for President in 2004		
				Kerry	Bush	Total
		Other	N	32	20	52
				62%	38%	100%
	Total		N	452	344	796
				57%	43%	100%
Conservative	Issue	Taxes	N	4	31	35
				11%	89%	100%
		Education	N	9	8	17
				53%	47%	100%
		Iraq	N	13	36	49
				27%	73%	100%
		Terrorism	N	6	161	167
				4%	96%	100%
		Economy/jobs	N	23	18	41
				56%	44%	100%
		Moral values	N	1	154	155
				1%	99%	100%
		Health care	N	9	4	13
				69%	31%	100%
		Other	N	3	17	20
				15%	85%	100%
	Total		N	68	429	497
				14%	86%	100%

Source: 2004 Presidential Exit Poll in Pennsylvania, conducted by Edison Media Research.

for Kerry; conservatives, 86 percent for Bush, and moderates opted for Kerry 57 percent to 43 percent for Bush.

The top-issue question also yields additional insight into the differences among the state's five regions. See Table 6.12, which displays these differences via a cross-tabulation of the issue choices with the regions. For example, moral values was selected by 25 percent of the central/northern tier respondents, but by only 11 percent of those in the Philadelphia suburbs. The Pittsburgh/West area came in at 19 percent, closer to the conservative central/northern tier than to its fellow metropolitan area in the east.

I turn now to the use of survey data to illuminate aspects of several major state-wide elections already covered in chapters 3 and 4. I give special attention to the 1986

Table 6.12 Cross-Tabulation of 2004 Top Issue Choice in Pennsylvania by Region

			Region					
			Philadel-phia	Philadelphia Suburbs	North east	Pittsburgh area/West	Central/ northern tier	Total
Issue	Taxes	N	23	21	10	37	38	129
		% within Issue	18%	16%	8%	29%	29%	100%
		% within Region	11%	7%	3%	9%	6%	7%
	Education	N	30	16	4	18	22	90
		% within Issue	33%	18%	4%	20%	24%	100%
		% within Region	15%	5%	1%	5%	3%	5%
	Iraq	N	24	71	64	61	134	354
		% within Issue	7%	20%	18%	17%	38%	100%
		% within Region	12%	23%	22%	16%	21%	19%
	Terrorism	N	23	71	68	62	146	370
		% within Issue	6%	19%	18%	17%	39%	100%
		% within Region	11%	23%	23%	16%	23%	20%
	Economy/ jobs	N	46	52	59	91	78	326
		% within Issue	14%	16%	18%	28%	24%	100%
		% within Region	22%	17%	20%	23%	12%	18%
	Moral values	N	15	35	44	74	155	323
		% within Issue	5%	11%	14%	23%	48%	100%
		% within Region	7%	11%	15%	19%	25%	18%
	Health care	N	22	19	24	24	27	116
		% within Issue	19%	16%	21%	21%	23%	100%
		% within Region	11%	6%	8%	6%	4%	6%

Table 6.12 *(continued)*

			Region					
			Philadel-phia	Philadelphia Suburbs	North east	Pittsburgh area/West	Central/ northern tier	Total
Issue	Other	N	23	24	17	25	31	120
		% within Issue	19%	20%	14%	21%	26%	100%
		% within Region	11%	8%	6%	6%	5%	7%
	Total	N	206	309	290	392	631	1828
		% within Issue	11%	17%	16%	21%	35%	100%
		% within Region	100%	100%	100%	100%	100%	100%

Source: 2004 Presidential Exit Poll in Pennsylvania, conducted by Edison Media Research.

gubernatorial election in which Democrat Robert Casey, the economically liberal, prolife veteran Democrat, defeated William Scranton, the prochoice Republican lieutenant governor whose father had been governor in the 1960s, by 50.7 percent of the vote to Scranton's 48.4 percent. In the analysis, I make use of the 1986 Pennsylvania exit poll, conducted that November by CBS News and the *New York Times* and which featured the same five-part Pennsylvania regional breakdown used above for the 2004 election. In Table 6.13, I cross-tabulate party identification with the vote for governor.[17] The poll found that party identification in 1986 broke down as follows: Democrats, 43 percent; Republicans, 40 percent; and independents, 18. The table indicates that both major-party nominees had difficulty getting full backing from their parties. In their close contest, Casey received the votes of 23 percent of the Republicans, and Scranton was backed by 19 percent of the Democrats.

There was considerable ticket-splitting going on in that election, which also featured the first reelection of Senator Arlen Specter, the moderate-to-liberal Republican. Specter won his election fairly handily over Bob Edgar, a Democratic congressman, with 56.4 percent of the vote to Edgar's 42.9 percent. By cross–tabulating the vote for governor with the vote for U.S. senator that same year, the extent of the ticket-splitting in the election can be observed. See Table 6.14. Of those who voted for Casey, 29 percent also voted for Specter, or to put it the other way, of those voting for Specter, 26 percent voted for Casey. At any rate, there were 199 respondents who were Casey-Specter ticket-splitters, 15 percent of the sample. There were also 81 respondents, or 6 percent

17. To simplify the display of the gubernatorial vote, the small number of people who said they voted for someone other than Casey and Scranton (twenty-four respondents) or said they didn't cast a ballot in the governor's race even though they voted in the general election (seventeen respondents) were declared "missing values" for the tables using the 1986 vote for governor.

Table 6.13 Cross-Tabulation of the 1986 Vote for Governor of Pennsylvania
by Party Identification

| | | | Vote for Governor in 1986 | | |
			Casey (D)	Scranton (R)	Total
Party Identification	Democrat (43%)	N	444	107	551
			81%	19%	100%
	Republican (40%)	N	115	393	508
			23%	77%	100%
	Independent (18%)	N	103	122	225
			46%	54%	100%
Total		N	662	622	1284
			52%	48%	100%

Source: 1986 Exit Poll in Pennsylvania, conducted by CBS News and the New York Times.

Table 6.14 Cross-Tabulation of the 1986 Pennsylvania Vote for Governor and
U.S. Senator

| | | | Vote for Senator in 1986 | | |
			Edgar (D)	Specter (R)	Total
Vote for Gov in 1986	Casey (D)	N	491	199	690
		% within Gov Vote	71%	29%	100%
		% within Sen Vote	86%	26%	52%
	Scranton (R)	N	81	552	633
		% within Gov Vote	13%	87%	100%
		% within Sen Vote	14%	74%	48%
Total		N	572	751	1323
		% within Gov Vote	43%	57%	100%
		% within Sen Vote	100%	100%	100%

Source: 1986 Exit Poll in Pennsylvania, conducted by CBS News and the New York Times.

of the sample, who were Scranton-Edgar ticket-splitters. Unfortunately, dissecting
such a small subsample for further clues runs up against the problem of having only
very small numbers in any further breakdowns of the already small number of ticket–
splitters, thus providing little confidence in the reliability of such categories.

However, cross-tabulation of the Casey and Scranton voters with several demographic variables illuminated the nature of the partisan conflict witnessed in that

Table 6.15 Cross-Tabulation of the 1986 Vote for Governor of Pennsylvania
by Income

| | | | Vote for Gov in 1986 | | |
			Casey (D)	Scranton (R)	Total
1985 Family Income	Under $12,500	N	143	86	229
			62%	38%	100%
	$12,500–$24,999	N	202	162	364
			55%	45%	100%
	$25,000–$34,999	N	124	138	262
			47%	53%	100%
	$35,000–$50,000	N	109	139	248
			44%	56%	100%
	Over $50,000	N	55	83	138
			40%	60%	100%
Total		N	633	608	1241
			51%	49%	100%

Source: 1986 Exit Poll in Pennsylvania, conducted by CBS News and the New York Times.

interesting election. Table 6.15 presents the 1986 gubernatorial vote broken down by income, revealing partisan cleavages by income similar to those observed in the Pennsylvania figures for presidential elections displayed in the first section of this chapter.[18] As shown in Table 6.16, blacks voted overwhelmingly for Casey, the Democrat. Scranton had the edge among whites, 52 percent to 48 percent for Casey.

For a Democrat, Casey did very well among self-identified conservatives, as is shown in Table 6.17. Of the conservatives, 42 percent voted for Casey compared to 58 percent for Scranton. The account of this election in chapter 3 stressed Casey's campaign tactics aimed at getting conservatives to either support his candidacy or stay away from the polls. On the other hand, Scranton did reasonably well among liberals for a Republican, as the table also shows.

Table 6.18 examines attitudes on abortion and the 1986 gubernatorial vote. The exit-poll question was worded this way: "Should abortion be legal?" and was followed by these three choices: Yes, as it is now; Legal only in extreme circumstances; No. Prolife Democrat Casey received 59 percent of the votes of those who answered no, while Scranton, who was prochoice, won the votes of the 56 percent who said yes, as it is now.

18. Of course, those income percentages for respondents in the presidential elections analyzed in this chapter's first section were for whites only.

Table 6.16 Cross-Tabulation of the 1986 Vote for Governor of Pennsylvania by Race

| | | | Vote for Governor in 1986 | | |
			Casey (D)	Scranton (R)	Total
Race	White	N	574	614	1188
			48%	52%	100%
	Black	N	118	18	136
			87%	13%	100%
	Hispanic	N	3	0	3
			100%	0%	100%
	Other	N	1	7	8
			13%	88%	100%
Total		N	696	639	1335
			52%	48%	100%

Source: 1986 Exit Poll in Pennsylvania, conducted by CBS News and the New York Times.

Table 6.17 Cross-Tabulation of the 1986 Vote for Governor of Pennsylvania by Political Philosophy

| | | | Vote for Gov in 1986 | | |
			Casey (D)	Scranton (R)	Total
Political Philosophy	Liberal	N	155	85	240
			65%	35%	100%
	Moderate	N	308	268	576
			53%	47%	100%
	Conservative	N	187	261	448
			42%	58%	100%
Total		N	650	614	1264
			51%	49%	100%

Source: 1986 Exit Poll in Pennsylvania, conducted by CBS News and the New York Times.

When the Casey-Scranton vote is cross-tabulated with the state's five regions, Casey's success in running much better than Democrats usually do in the central/northern tier is apparent. He received 47 percent there compared to Scranton's 53 percent. See Table 6.19. Also, Casey did well in the Pittsburgh area, offsetting his relative weakness in the Philadelphia suburbs. Casey's weakness in these four large suburban counties—Montgomery, Chester, Bucks, and Delaware—stands in sharp

Table 6.18 Cross-Tabulation of the 1986 Vote for Governor of Pennsylvania by Stance on Abortion

			Vote for Gov in 1986		
			Casey (D)	Scranton (R)	Total
Should abortion be legal?	Yes, as it is now	N	240	306	546
			44%	56%	100%
	Legal only in extreme circumstances	N	238	173	411
			58%	42%	100%
	No	N	194	137	331
			59%	41%	100%
Total		N	672	616	1288
			52%	48%	100%

Source: 1986 Exit Poll in Pennsylvania, conducted by CBS News and the New York Times.

Table 6.19 Cross-Tabulation of the 1986 Vote for Governor of Pennsylvania by Region

			Vote for Gov in 1986		
			Casey (D)	Scranton (R)	Total
Region	Philadelphia	N	169	79	248
			68%	32%	100%
	Philadelphia suburbs	N	86	108	194
			44%	56%	100%
	Northeast	N	73	89	162
			45%	55%	100%
	Pittsburgh industrial area	N	166	133	299
			56%	44%	100%
	Central/northern tier	N	208	236	444
			47%	53%	100%
Total		N	702	645	1347
			52%	48%	100%

Source: 1986 Exit Poll in Pennsylvania, conducted by CBS News and the New York Times.

contrast to Democrat Ed Rendell's strength there in his successful 2002 gubernatorial campaign, as was shown in chapter 4.

Another banner election year in Pennsylvania was 1994, which featured victories by two Republicans with very different political images—Tom Ridge as governor and Rick Santorum as U.S. senator. The details of their elections were presented in chapter 4. Ridge, an Erie congressman, defeated Democrat Mark Singel with 45.4 percent of the vote to Singel's 39.9 percent. Peg Luksik, the prolife nominee of the Constitutional party, won 12.8 percent of the vote. Santorum, a Pittsburgh-area congressman, defeated Senator Harris Wofford with 49.4 percent to the Democratic incumbent's 46.9 percent. Table 6.20 cross-tabulates the vote by the poll's respondents in both elections. The Ridge-Wofford ticket-splitters made up 8 percent of the exit-poll sample, and the Santorum-Singel ticket-splitters were 4 percent of the sample.

In addition, of those who voted for Luksik, 74 percent cast their votes for Santorum, while only 26 percent voted for Wofford. As revealed in Tables 6.21 and 6.22, the two Republicans drew differently among voters arrayed by political philosophy, Santorum doing better among conservatives and Ridge better among liberals. This lack of congruence was previewed by the relatively weak coefficient (0.77) found when their county-level electoral patterns were correlated in chapter 4.

Finally, the patterns in the 1994 gubernatorial and senatorial elections are cross-tabulated with the five Pennsylvania regions. See Tables 6.23 and 6.24. Luksik's relatively strong third-party candidacy makes a straight comparison between Ridge and Santorum somewhat difficult. Still, the tables indicate that in Philadelphia, Ridge ran stronger than Santorum, since Luksik was not much of a factor in the city. In the Philadelphia suburbs, however, Luksik received 19 percent of the vote, according to the exit poll, no doubt reducing the Erie Republican

Table 6.20 Cross-Tabulation of the 1994 Pennsylvania Vote for Governor and U.S. Senator

| | | | Vote for Senator in 1994 | | |
			Wofford (D)	Santorum (R)	Total
Vote for Governor in 1994	Singel (D)	N	685	74	759
		% within Gov Vote	90%	10%	100%
		% within Sen Vote	77%	8%	41%
	Ridge (R)	N	151	726	877
		% within Gov Vote	17%	83%	100%
		% within Sen Vote	17%	77%	48%
	Luksik (C)	N	51	145	196
		% within Gov Vote	26%	74%	100%
		% within Sen Vote	6%	15%	11%
Total		N	887	945	1832
		% within Gov Vote	48%	52%	100%
		% within Sen Vote	100%	100%	100%

Source: 1994 Exit Poll in Pennsylvania, conducted by Voter News Service.

Table 6.21 Cross-Tabulation of the 1994 Pennsylvania Vote for U.S. Senator by Political Philosophy

| | | | Vote for Senator in 1994 | | |
			Wofford (D)	Santorum (R)	Total
Political Philosophy	Liberal	N	190	43	233
			82%	18%	100%
	Moderate	N	380	275	655
			58%	42%	100%
	Conservative	N	107	415	522
			20%	80%	100%
Total		N	677	733	1410
			48%	52%	100%

Source: 1994 Exit Poll in Pennsylvania, conducted by Voter News Service.

Table 6.22 Cross-Tabulation of the 1994 Vote for Governor of Pennsylvania by Political Philosophy

| | | | Vote for Governor in 1994 | | | |
			Singel (D)	Ridge (R)	Luksik (C)	Total
Political Philosophy	Liberal	N	156	55	24	235
			66%	23%	10%	100%
	Moderate	N	335	278	71	684
			49%	41%	10%	100%
	Conservative	N	87	358	99	544
			16%	66%	18%	100%
Total		N	578	691	194	1463
			40%	47%	13%	100%

Source: 1994 Exit Poll in Pennsylvania, conducted by Voter News Service.

congressman's vote in those four populous counties. In the central/northern tier counties, Santorum did better than the prochoice Ridge, 60 percent as compared to 51 percent, while Luksik drew in 14 percent from this area. Interestingly, Wofford received more support than Santorum in the Pittsburgh-area counties, which is surprising because the Pittsburgh region is the conservative Republican's home base. With the vote for senator as close as it was, Luksik was no doubt a force in helping to push Santorum over the top by bringing out conservatives, who, as pointed out previously, favored him overwhelmingly.

Table 6.23 Cross-Tabulation of the 1994 Pennsylvania Vote for U.S Senator by Region

| | | | Vote for Senator in 1994 | | |
			Wofford (D)	Santorum (R)	Total
Region	Philadelphia	N	172	53	225
			76%	24%	100%
	Philadelphia Suburbs	N	155	193	348
			45%	55%	100%
	Northeast	N	118	122	240
			49%	51%	100%
	Pittsburgh area	N	231	216	447
			52%	48%	100%
	Central/northern tier	N	247	375	622
			40%	60%	100%
Total		N	923	959	1882
			49%	51%	100%

Source: 1994 Exit Poll in Pennsylvania, conducted by Voter News Service.

Table 6.24 Cross-Tabulation of the 1994 Vote for Governor of Pennsylvania by Region

| | | | Vote for Governor in 1994 | | | |
			Singel (D)	Ridge (R)	Luksik (C)	Total
Region	Philadelphia	N	151	67	10	228
			66%	29%	4%	100%
	Philadelphia Suburbs	N	113	193	72	378
			30%	51%	19%	100%
	Northeast	N	108	108	28	244
			44%	44%	11%	100%
	Pittsburgh area	N	198	200	51	449
			44%	45%	11%	100%
	Central/northern tier	N	228	332	93	653
			35%	51%	14%	100%
Total		N	798	900	254	1952
			41%	46%	13%	100%

Source: 1994 Exit Poll in Pennsylvania, conducted by Voter News Service.

Overall, this venture into four major statewide elections via exit-poll data has presented individual-level insights not possible when relying solely on aggregate data. The fortuitous division of the state into five reasonably well-constructed regions by those who designed the exit polls was a much-appreciated feature of their work.

That five-part division of the state also offers a way to tap shifting philosophical thinking about politics in Pennsylvania over several decades. I do this by charting the responses to the standard political philosophy question in each of the state's regions in Figures 6.24a through e. (Incidentally, the question is worded this way: "On most political matters, do you consider yourself: liberal, moderate or conservative?") In an ideal world, one would have available a series of issue questions over many polls over many years to draw on to follow changing political attitudes in Pennsylvania. Unfortunately, such an issue series does not exist. But this one political philosophy question has been a regular feature of the exit polls and in fact was also asked in the 1968 Comparative State Elections Project's Pennsylvania poll.[19]

What does Figure 6.24 reveal about changing political attitudes in the Keystone State? Figure 6.24a shows that Philadelphia has become considerably more liberal since 1968; that is, it contains a higher proportion of people who identify themselves as liberals, going from 19 percent in 1968 to 35 percent in 2004. Concurrently, the presence of conservatives has plummeted, dropping from 49 percent in 1968 to 24 percent thirty-six years later while moderates have risen from 32 to 41 percent.

In Figure 6.24b, the political philosophy trend lines indicate that the Philadelphia suburbs have also experienced a sizable drop in the proportion of their citizens who call themselves conservatives, declining from 47 percent in 1968 to 27 percent in 2004. Moderates have advanced to 51 percent from 36 percent. Finally, those calling themselves liberals increased slightly from 17 percent to 23 percent.

Figure 6.24c, which showcases the Allegheny/Southwest counties, also uncovers a significant decline in people who call themselves conservatives, slipping from 42 percent to 25 percent thirty-six years later. Liberals in the greater Pittsburgh area did increase noticeably from 1968 to 1988, rising from 14 percent to 26 percent, but after that year, liberals in this western part of the state slipped into the low 20s, ending up at 20 percent in 2004. Conservatives have also evinced an up-and-down pattern there, finishing 17 percentage points lower in 2004 than where they were in the greater Pittsburgh area in 1968. Moderates, always high in the Pittsburgh area, advanced to 55 percent, marking their largest increase after 1996. Note that conservatives were declining during this same post-1996 period.

Figure 6.24d indicates that the recent pattern in the Northeast counties resembles the one in the Pittsburgh area except that the moderates are less numerous in this eastern section of the state north of Philadelphia. As mentioned, Lehigh and Berks counties have a lot less in common with Luzerne and Lackawanna than they may have had several decades ago when the eastern division was crafted.

---

19. Fortunately, the regional divisions used by the Comparative State Elections Project fit three of the five geocode divisions used by the exit polls—Philadelphia, the Philadelphia suburbs, and the Allegheny/Southwest counties. The other two could not be used with accuracy.

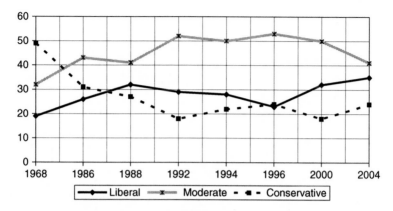

Fig. 6.24a. Political Philosophy of Philadelphia, 1968–2004

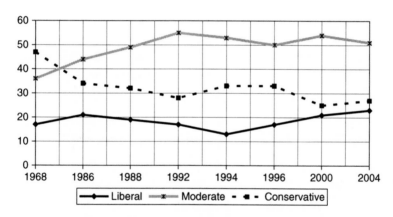

Fig. 6.24b. Political Philosophy of the Philadelphia Suburban Counties, 1968–2004

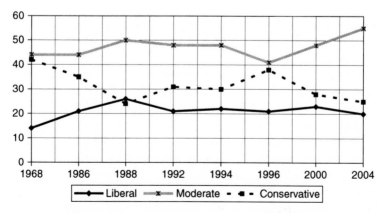

Fig. 6.24c. Political Philosophy of Allegheny and the Southwest Counties, 1968–2004

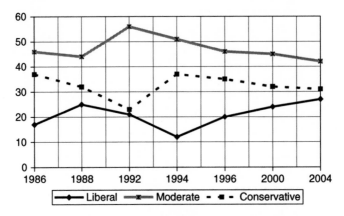

Fig. 6.24d. Political Philosophy of the Northeast Region, 1986–2004

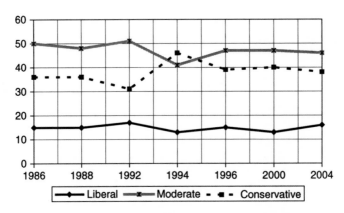

Fig. 6.24e. Political Philosophy of the Central/Northern Tier, 1986–2004

Note: Please refer to Table 6.5 for source.

Also, Monroe, part of the Northeast counties, has more in common with its other rapid-growth neighbors, Pike and Wayne, than with the counties in its current region.

The vast expanses and many counties that make up the central/northern tier present a pattern in Figure 6.24e that confirms what all the other data about this region have shown: it is very conservative, and there has not been a lot of change in the last few decades. Conservatives are holding steady at 38 percent, as are moderates at 46 percent. And the woefully outnumbered liberals register their lowest Pennsylvania regional scores here—only 16 percent of the adults, virtually the same proportion they had eighteen years earlier.

Finally, Figure 6.25 takes this analysis a step further, displaying the cross-tabulation of political philosophy in each of the five regions along with the vote for president. Since it was clear from Figure 6.24 that moderates were on the rise in Philadelphia, the Philadelphia suburbs, and the Allegheny region, this final cross-tabulation was run in an effort to determine if those who were identifying as moderates had shifted their allegiance between the two major parties. Figure 6.25 indicates that the moderates have been increasingly voting more Democratic and in fact track more closely to the Democrats in all regions except for the central/ northern tier region. In Figure 6.25b, one striking trend is found in the Philadelphia suburbs: moderates there gave only 21 percent of their vote to the Democrat in 1968 but gave 58 percent to Kerry in 2004! Democratic voting of moderates has also increased proportionately since 1968 in Philadelphia and in the Northeast

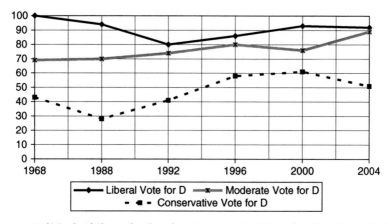

Fig. 6.25a. Political Philosophy by the Democratic Vote for President in Philadelphia, 1968–2004

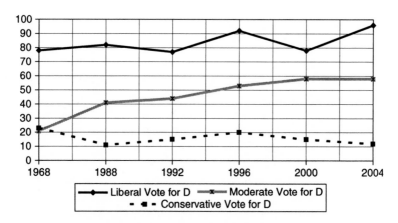

Fig. 6.25b. Political Philosophy by the Democratic Vote for President in the
Philadelphia Suburban Counties, 1968–2004

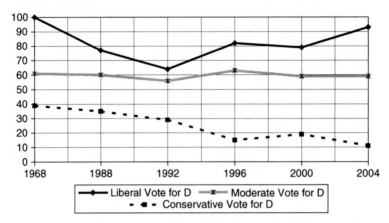

Fig. 6.25c. Political Philosophy by the Democratic Vote for President in the Allegheny Area, 1968–2004

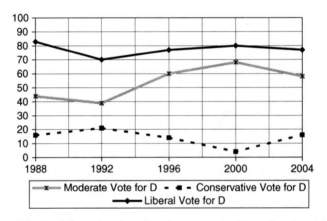

Fig. 6.25d. Political Philosophy by the Democratic Vote for President in the Northeast Region, 1988–2004

counties, as shown in Figures 6.25a and 6.25d, respectively. In the Pittsburgh area, Figure 6.25c illustrates that the moderates have remained even, voting for the Democrats steadily in the 56 to 61 percent range. Only in the central/northern region, charted in Figure 6.25e, do moderates seem to be trending downward in terms of the Democratic vote for president.

Throughout this chapter, I have relied on survey research to better understand the behavior of the Pennsylvania electorate, and in other chapters of this book, I have examined national electoral change in order to put the Keystone State's partisan path in context. Thus, there is no more fitting way to conclude this survey-based chapter than by perusing Table 6.25, which draws together a vast amount of polling data on both Pennsylvania and the nation.

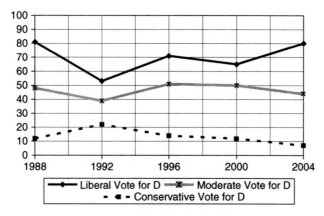

Fig. 6.25e. Political Philosophy by the Democratic Vote for President in the Central/ Northern Tier, 1988–2004

Note: Please refer to Table 6.5 for source.

The table presents findings from both the 2004 Pennsylvania exit poll and the national exit poll done that same Election Day. All the variables are cross-tabulated with the vote for president, and the nation is divided into its four standard regions.[20] Over half of these variables have been covered in this chapter in one form or another. They are party identification, political philosophy, race, education, income, religion, church attendance, and most important issue. Their presentation here in summary form allows for casual comparative inspection of the Pennsylvania presidential-vote cross-tabulations with results from across the nation's regions.

I want to comment briefly on a few of the variables I did not cover above. The gender and married/single variables are especially interesting. A gender gap has been noticeable in American electoral politics since at least the early 1980s, and it is present in Pennsylvania's 2004 presidential voting as well. As shown in Table 6.25, Keystone State men opted for Bush by 51 percent to 49 percent for Senator Kerry. Women chose Kerry by 54 percent to 46 percent for Bush. When one factors in

20. The exit-poll directors employ a sensible division of the country into the four regions. The Northeast (or East, as they call it) runs from New England to Delaware and Maryland and includes West Virginia, a border state that is sometimes included with the South or the Midwest. Ohio starts the Midwest in the east, and the region runs through the far western Great Plains states—North and South Dakota, Nebraska, and Kansas. The South, which is made up of the eleven states of the former Confederacy plus Kentucky and Oklahoma, stretches from Virginia to Texas. The West is made up of the disparate Rocky Mountain states and the Pacific coast states plus Hawaii and Alaska. Incidentally, this exit-poll division of the states into these regions is the same one Paul David used for his regional party-strength figures. I retained David's division of the states for my regional party-strength figures in chapters 1 and 2.

Table 6.25 Comparison of 2004 Election Results Between Pennsylvania
and the Four Regions of the Country

	PA		East		Midwest		South		West	
	Kerry	Bush	Kerry	Bush	Kerry	Bush	Kerry	Bush	Kerry	Bush
Vote for President	51	48	56	44	48	52	42	58	50	50
Party Identification										
Democrat	85	15	89	11	91	9	86	14	92	8
Republican	11	89	12	88	6	94	4	96	7	93
Independent	59	41	58	42	53	47	43	57	52	48
Political Philosophy										
Liberal	88	12	89	11	88	12	79	21	91	9
Moderate	57	43	60	40	55	45	52	48	52	48
Conservative	13	87	19	81	16	84	13	87	16	84
Vote by Gender										
Male	49	51	54	46	44	56	37	63	45	55
Female	54	46	58	42	52	48	46	54	55	45
Married/ Single										
Married	45	55	50	50	43	57	35	65	44	56
Single	60	40	65	35	59	41	53	47	60	40
Married male	41	59	49	51	39	61	33	67	41	59
Married female	50	50	52	48	46	54	37	63	47	53
Single male	59	41	65	35	56	44	45	55	51	49
Single female	60	40	66	34	61	39	59	41	65	35
Vote by Race										
White	46	54	50	50	43	57	30	70	46	54
Black	84	16	87	13	90	10	91	9	82	18
Hispanic/ Latino	72	28	71	29	67	33	36	64	60	40
Asian	44	56	57	43	46	54	46	54	63	37
Other	50	50	84	16	60	40	37	63	57	43
Vote by Age										
18–29	61	39	68	32	53	47	47	53	52	48
30–44	49	51	56	44	45	55	39	61	48	52
45–59	50	50	54	46	51	49	39	61	53	47
60 or over	48	52	49	51	45	55	42	58	49	51

Table 6.25 *(continued)*

	PA		East		Midwest		South		West	
	Kerry	Bush	Kerry	Bush	Kerry	Bush	Kerry	Bush	Kerry	Bush
Vote by Education										
Not a high school grad	57	43	74	26	52	48	40	60	46	54
High school graduate	49	51	54	46	51	49	43	57	42	58
Some college	54	46	52	48	49	51	40	60	45	55
College graduate	46	54	57	43	45	55	38	62	52	48
Postgraduate study	52	48	63	38	49	51	46	54	64	36
Vote by Income										
Under $30,000	60	40	69	31	60	40	56	44	59	41
$30,000–50,000	49	51	62	38	51	49	45	55	46	54
$50,000–75,000	48	52	51	49	43	57	35	65	47	53
$75,000–100,000	52	48	54	46	44	56	35	65	49	51
$100,000 or more	42	58	47	53	41	59	30	70	50	50
Financial Situation										
Better today	21	79	32	68	19	81	12	88	20	80
Worse today	84	16	86	14	79	21	78	22	79	21
About the same	47	53	57	43	45	55	43	57	60	40
Religion										
Protestant	40	60	54	46	42	58	36	64	38	62
Catholic	51	49	48	52	50	50	33	67	61	39
Jewish	70	30	76	24	73	27	74	26	75	25
Other	59	41	83	17	69	31	71	29	80	20
None	70	30	84	16	69	31	67	33	62	38
Church Attendance										
Regularly	43	57	48	52	39	61	35	65	37	63
Often	48	52	51	49	49	51	45	55	55	45
Seldom	56	44	61	39	55	45	45	55	57	43
Never	69	31	75	25	62	38	53	47	63	37

Table 6.25 (continued)

	PA		East		Midwest		South		West	
	Kerry	Bush	Kerry	Bush	Kerry	Bush	Kerry	Bush	Kerry	Bush
Gun Owner										
Yes	38	62	43	57	41	59	28	72	40	60
No	60	40	59	41	54	46	55	45	61	39
Most Important Issue										
Taxes	52	48	57	43	46	54	31	69	34	66
Education	74	26	86	14	67	33	64	36	78	22
Iraq	71	29	81	19	72	28	64	36	76	24
Terrorism	17	83	16	84	13	87	11	89	17	83
Economy/jobs	82	18	86	14	83	17	78	22	77	23
Moral values	19	81	32	68	15	85	10	90	27	73
Health care	82	18	82	18	73	27	76	24	77	23
Decision to go to war in Iraq										
Strongly approve	7	93	9	91	9	91	4	96	5	95
Somewhat approve	25	75	28	72	25	75	20	80	23	77
Somewhat disapprove	81	19	78	22	71	29	72	28	79	21
Strongly disapprove	93	7	95	5	94	6	93	7	96	4
How are things going in Iraq?										
Very well	12	88	19	81	8	92	5	95	7	93
Somewhat well	7	93	10	90	9	91	7	93	11	89
Somewhat badly	64	36	68	32	66	34	61	39	60	40
Very badly	93	7	94	6	95	5	94	6	94	6
Size of community										
Cities over 500,000	81	19	66	34	73	27	40	60	65	35
Cities 50,000–500,000	71	29	59	41	63	38	43	57	50	50
Suburbs	47	53	51	49	44	56	42	58	51	49
Cities 10,000–50,000	52	48	71	29	44	56	52	48	34	66
Rural	27	73	62	38	40	60	34	66	39	61

Source: 2004 Presidential Exit Poll in Pennsylvania and the Nation, conducted by Edison Media Research.

marriage, a different picture of the gender gap emerges. Both single men and single women preferred Kerry by about 59 percent to 40 percent for Bush. Married women, however, were evenly divided, but, married men overwhelmingly opted for the President over Kerry, 59 percent to 41 percent.

The breakdown of the Pennsylvania vote for president by age reveals that three of the four age groups were fairly evenly split between Bush and Kerry, but not the fourth. See Table 6.25. Those voters thirty to forty-four years of age favored Bush by 2 percentage points, while those forty-five to fifty-nine were evenly split. Voters over sixty gave Bush the edge by 4 percentage points. But, the big spread came among the youngest age group, those eighteen to twenty-nine. They opted for Kerry by 61 percent to 39 percent, which may offer a sign of hope for Democrats in Pennsylvania looking to the next generation.

In the next and final chapter, I examine the 2006 elections and offer my conclusions on Pennsylvania electoral change since 1960.

7

The Future of Pennsylvania Politics: The 2006 Election and Beyond

The Democratic party in Pennsylvania made sweeping advances in the 2006 election, winning a U.S. Senate seat, reelecting Governor Rendell, capturing four U.S. House seats from Republican incumbents, and gaining a one-seat majority in the state House of Representatives. In addition, analysis of the 2006 voting returns and exit polls indicates that in this election the partisan trends depicted throughout this book were strongly visible and continuing along the same lines.

In the first part of this final chapter, I analyze the historic 2006 election. Then, in the second and last part, my attention turns to the Keystone State's future partisan prospects in light of the state's past patterns, including the 2006 election outcomes.

The Historic 2006 Election

Governor Ed Rendell won reelection in a landslide over the Republican nominee, Lynn Swann, a businessman and former wide receiver for the Pittsburgh Steelers, with 60.4 percent to Swann's 39.6 percent. Senator Rick Santorum, the conservative, two-term Republican incumbent, was defeated decisively by state Treasurer Robert Casey Jr., a prolife Democrat, who received 58.7 percent of the vote to Santorum's 41.3 percent.

Governor Rendell ran a campaign that stressed his accomplishments in office, including expanding the state's program that helps the elderly receive prescription drugs at a lower cost, funneling state money into private–public economic-development efforts throughout Pennsylvania, and signing a slot-machine law that is expected to generate gambling revenue for school property tax relief.[1] He also raised over $30 million in campaign funds compared to Swann's $10 million.[2]

1. Anthony R. Wood, "Fizzle of Debate on Property Tax Benefits Rendell," *Philadelphia Inquirer*, October 26, 2006.

2. Angela Couloumbis and Amy Worden, "A Rendell Walkaway, Statewide," *Philadelphia Inquirer*, November 8, 2006.

Swann cast himself as a reformer and hoped to capitalize on widespread voter dissatisfaction with a 2005 legislative pay raise, which led to the ouster of seventeen state lawmakers in the May 2006 primaries and seven more in the general election. Rendell signed the pay increase, later acknowledged that it was a mistake, and then signed a law that repealed the increases.[3] The issue did not materialize as Swann had hoped, nor did his proposals to overhaul the state property-tax system and to shrink the size of the legislature through a constitutional amendment.

In the U.S. Senate seat battle, Casey, a seasoned statewide candidate who was recruited for the race by national Democrats, benefited from an anti-GOP mood in the country that translated into the Republican party's loss of control of both houses of Congress in the November balloting. Nationwide in 2006, Democrats gained thirty seats in the U.S. House and six in the Senate, making Pennsylvania's contribution to the party's 2006 victory quite substantial.[4] As two *Philadelphia Inquirer* reporters put it: "Casey . . . mined anger over the Iraq war, the economy, and Washington corruption to become the first Pennsylvania Democrat in more than 40 years to win a full Senate term."[5]

The airwaves during the fall campaign were full of sharp exchanges both in paid ads and in candidate debates. Casey hammered at Santorum for his support of President Bush's policies and sought to portray his Republican opponent as "too extreme" for Pennsylvania.[6]

Santorum fought back, asserting in one televised debate: "I'm a passionate guy. I'm tough, I'm a fighter. But you know what? I'm an Italian kid from a steel town. What do you expect from me? I'm a guy who had to grow up having to scratch and claw. I wasn't born into a family that had a great name [referring to his opponent's father, former Governor Robert Casey Sr.]. My dad's an immigrant to this country. I've worked hard, just like you do in western Pennsylvania to fight for the things you believe in."[7]

At another point in the debate after listening to Casey respond to a question, Santorum sneered: "I don't know how you can say so many words and say nothing." "Don't be a desperate campaigner," Casey shot back.[8]

Commenting on the campaign in late October, G. Terry Madonna, director of Franklin & Marshall College's Center for Politics and Public Affairs, noted: "Rick's

---

3. Sharon Smith, "Rendell Wins Despite Signing Pay Raise Bill," *Harrisburg Patriot-News*, November 8, 2006.

4. Since four of the thirty U.S. House seats won by Democrats in 2006 were from the Keystone State, Pennsylvania was responsible for 13.3 percent of the Democratic gain. Further, Casey's victory—one of six—amounted to 16.7 percent of the Democratic gain in the U.S. Senate.

5. Carrie Budoff and Emilie Lounsberry, "Pa. Landslide: State Overwhelmingly Rejects GOP's No. 3 Senate Leader," *Philadelphia Inquirer*, November 8, 2006.

6. Ibid.

7. Associated Press dispatch, "Santorum, Casey Hold Back Nothing During Stormy Debate," *Erie Times-News*, October 13, 2006.

8. Ibid.

unfavorables are the highest since we've been doing polls. That's remarkable. I think it's been the shrillness, the harshness of his campaign. The stridency, the negative commercials, the bad national environment for Republicans—I think there's a conflation of all those things going on."[9]

A *Los Angeles Times* reporter covering the campaign asserted that "Santorum is not just a victim of political circumstances. Even his admirers say he routinely suffers self-inflicted wounds from his sharp tongue." She added: "In 2002, he blamed Boston 'liberalism' for the Roman Catholic Church's sex abuse scandal. In a 2003 interview, he linked gay consensual sex with bigamy, polygamy, incest and adultery. In a 2005 book, he found fault with two-income families and working women. The ensuing controversies have so engulfed Santorum's image that his campaign website has a long feature, 'Myth vs. Fact,' to counter what people 'hear around the water cooler' about Santorum."[10]

Our effort to understand the voters' choices in these two major statewide elections is aided by exit-poll data, which add a measure of precision to the interpretation of the results as well as provide an opportunity to sample the Pennsylvania electorate at the time of the latest balloting.

Table 7.1, which cross-tabulates party identification with the vote for Rendell and Swann in the governor's race and Casey and Santorum in the U.S. Senate race, reveals that Democratic voters were quite faithful to their party's nominees but that Republicans were less so. Rendell garnered the most partisans of the other party, receiving 21 percent of the votes of Republicans, the famed "Rendellicans" from his first election as governor in 2002. Independents broke decisively for Rendell and Casey by over two to one.

Note that overall party identification percentages gave the Democrats a 5-percentage point edge in 2006—43 percent to the GOP's 38 percent. Republicans were down 3 percentage points from their 2004 showing of 41 percent; Democrats remained the same. The independent/other category came in at 19 percent, 3 percentage points higher than found in the 2004 exit poll. This latter finding is in keeping with the most recent trends found in Pennsylvania's party registration data. For example, the "other" party-registration category continued to inch upward, reaching 12.0 percent in May 2007.[11]

Table 7.2, which presents the 2006 vote by race, shows percentages familiar from earlier elections: most African Americans voting Democratic, Hispanics favoring Democrats three to one, and whites split but with the edge to Rendell and Casey in 2006. Interestingly, Swann, who is African American, scored only 3 percentage points ahead of Santorum among black voters, 13 percent to the white senator's 10 percent.

9. Tom Murse, "Are Rendell, Casey Sure Things? Analysts Say Swann, Santorum Face Very Tough Odds in Six Days," *Lancaster New Era*, November 1, 2006.

10. Janet Hook, "GOP on a Mission to Save Santorum," *Los Angeles Times*, October 16, 2006.

11. All statewide party-registration numbers and percentages from 1926 to 2007 are found in Table 5.5 in chapter 5.

Table 7.1 Cross-Tabulation of the 2006 Pennsylvania Vote for Governor and
U.S. Senator by Party Identification

| | | | Vote for Governor in 2006 | | |
			Rendell (D)	Swann (R)	Total
Party Identification	Democrat (43%)	N	853	91	944
			90%	10%	100%
	Republican (38%)	N	175	650	825
			21%	79%	100%
	Independent/Other (20%)	N	291	138	429
			68%	32%	100%
Total		N	1319	879	2198
			60%	40%	100%

| | | | Vote for Senator in 2006 | | |
			Casey (D)	Santorum (R)	Total
Party Identification	Democrat (43%)	N	872	63	935
			93%	7%	100%
	Republican (38%)	N	116	716	832
			14%	86%	100%
	Independent/Other (19%)	N	305	119	424
			72%	28%	100%
Total		N	1293	898	2191
			59%	41%	100%

Source: 2006 Exit Poll in Pennsylvania, conducted by Edison Media Research.

Education and income, depicted in Tables 7.3 and 7.4, do not strongly differentiate the candidates' supporters, revealing patterns familiar from the data in chapter 6. Likewise, cross-tabulation of the respondents' vote with his or her religion is consistent with the figures found in chapter 6; see Table 7.5. Incidentally, when comparing the 2006 breakdowns on these three variables with the 2004 presidential results in Table 6.25, keep in mind that the overall Kerry–Bush election was much closer than these two 2006 contests.

Two variables that do differentiate the Democratic and Republican candidates for governor and U.S. senator in 2006 are shown in Tables 7.6 and 7.7. The first set presents a cross-tabulation of the vote with whether respondents strongly approved, somewhat approved, somewhat disapproved, or strongly disapproved

Table 7.2 Cross-Tabulation of the 2006 Pennsylvania Vote for Governor and
U.S. Senator by Race

| | | | Vote for Governor in 2006 | | |
			Rendell (D)	Swann (R)	Total
Race	White (88%)	N	1206	907	2113
			57%	43%	100%
	Black (8%)	N	175	27	202
			87%	13%	100%
	Hispanic/ Latino (2%)	N	33	5	38
			87%	13%	100%
	Asian (1%)	N	21	0	21
			100%	0%	100%
	Other (1%)	N	21	6	27
			78%	22%	100%
Total		N	1456	945	2401
			61%	39%	100%

| | | | Vote for Senator in 2006 | | |
			Casey (D)	Santorum (R)	Total
Race	White (88%)	N	1170	947	2117
			55%	45%	100%
	Black (8%)	N	178	20	198
			90%	10%	100%
	Hispanic/ Latino (2%)	N	28	8	36
			78%	22%	100%
	Asian (1%)	N	20	3	23
			87%	13%	100%
	Other (1%)	N	18	8	26
			69%	31%	100%
Total		N	1414	986	2400
			59%	41%	100%

Source: 2006 Exit Poll in Pennsylvania, conducted by Edison Media Research.

Table 7.3 Cross-Tabulation of the 2006 Pennsylvania Vote for Governor and
U.S. Senator by Education

| | | | Vote for Governor in 2006 | | |
			Rendell (D)	Swann (R)	Total
What was the last grade in school you completed?	Did not complete high school (3%)	N	30	14	44
			68%	32%	100%
	High school graduate (22%)	N	215	174	389
			55%	45%	100%
	Some college or associate degree (26%)	N	277	187	464
			60%	40%	100%
	College graduate (27%)	N	263	215	478
			55%	45%	100%
	Postgraduate study (23%)	N	300	114	414
			72%	28%	100%
Total		N	1085	704	1789
			61%	39%	100%

| | | | Vote for Senator in 2006 | | |
			Casey (D)	Santorum (R)	Total
What was the last grade in school you completed?	Did not complete high school (3%)	N	32	12	44
			73%	27%	100%
	High school graduate (22%)	N	201	185	386
			52%	48%	100%
	Some college or associate degree (26%)	N	277	186	463
			60%	40%	100%
	College graduate (27%)	N	256	219	475
			54%	46%	100%
	Postgraduate study (23%)	N	290	122	412
			70%	30%	100%
Total		N	1056	724	1780
			59%	41%	100%

Source: 2006 Exit Poll in Pennsylvania, conducted by Edison Media Research.

Table 7.4 Cross-Tabulation of the 2006 Pennsylvania Vote for Governor and U.S. Senator by Income

| | | | Vote for Governor in 2006 | | |
			Rendell (D)	Swann (R)	Total
2005 Family Income	Under $30,000 (19%)	N	243	136	379
			64%	36%	100%
	$30,000–$50,000 (20%)	N	256	155	411
			62%	38%	100%
	$50,000–$75,000 (21%)	N	232	192	424
			55%	45%	100%
	$75,000–$100,000 (15%)	N	186	119	305
			61%	39%	100%
	$100,000 or more (26%)	N	321	206	527
			61%	39%	100%
Total		N	1238	808	2046
			61%	39%	100%

| | | | Vote for Senator in 2006 | | |
			Casey (D)	Santorum (R)	Total
2005 Family Income	Under $30,000 (18%)	N	232	140	372
			62%	38%	100%
	$30,000–$50,000 (20%)	N	254	157	411
			62%	38%	100%
	$50,000–$75,000 (21%)	N	228	198	426
			54%	46%	100%
	$75,000–$100,000 (15%)	N	190	114	304
			63%	38%	100%
	$100,000 or more (26%)	N	299	226	525
			57%	43%	100%
Total		N	1203	835	2038
			59%	41%	100%

Source: 2006 Exit Poll in Pennsylvania, conducted by Edison Media Research.

Table 7.5   Cross-Tabulation of the 2006 Pennsylvania Vote for Governor and
U.S. Senator by Religion

| | | | Vote for Governor in 2006 | | |
			Rendell (D)	Swann (R)	Total
Religion	Protestant/Other Christian (47%)	N	428	418	846
			51%	49%	100%
	Catholic (32%)	N	339	233	572
			59%	41%	100%
	Jewish (5%)	N	78	14	92
			85%	15%	100%
	Something else (5%)	N	72	14	86
			84%	16%	100%
	None (11%)	N	161	44	205
			79%	21%	100%
Total		N	1078	723	1801
			60%	40%	100%

| | | | Vote for Senator in 2006 | | |
			Casey (D)	Santorum (R)	Total
Religion	Protestant/Other Christian (47%)	N	431	418	849
			51%	49%	100%
	Catholic (32%)	N	337	234	571
			59%	41%	100%
	Jewish (5%)	N	72	20	92
			78%	22%	100%
	Something else (5%)	N	69	18	87
			79%	21%	100%
	None (11%)	N	169	34	203
			83%	17%	100%
Total		N	1078	724	1802
			60%	40%	100%

Source: 2006 Exit Poll in Pennsylvania, conducted by Edison Media Research.

Table 7.6 Cross-Tabulation of the 2006 Pennsylvania Vote for Governor and U.S. Senator by President Bush's Approval Rating

| | | | Vote for Governor in 2006 | | |
			Rendell (D)	Swann (R)	Total
Do you approve or disapprove of the way George W. Bush is handling his job as president?	Strongly approve (18%)	N	45	317	362
			12%	88%	100%
	Somewhat approve (20%)	N	110	278	388
			28%	72%	100%
	Somewhat disapprove (16%)	N	203	118	321
			63%	37%	100%
	Strongly disapprove (46%)	N	845	74	919
			92%	8%	100%
Total		N	1203	787	1990
			60%	40%	100%

| | | | Vote for Senator in 2006 | | |
			Casey (D)	Santorum (R)	Total
Do you approve or disapprove of the way George W. Bush is handling his job as president?	Strongly approve (18%)	N	32	333	365
			9%	91%	100%
	Somewhat approve (20%)	N	78	315	393
			20%	80%	100%
	Somewhat disapprove (16%)	N	213	109	322
			66%	34%	100%
	Strongly disapprove (46%)	N	874	39	913
			96%	4%	100%
Total		N	1197	796	1993
			60%	40%	100%

Source: 2006 Exit Poll in Pennsylvania, conducted by Edison Media Research.

Table 7.7 Cross-Tabulation of the 2006 Pennsylvania Vote for Governor and
U.S. Senator by Feelings on the War in Iraq

| | | | Vote for Governor in 2006 | | |
			Rendell (D)	Swann (R)	Total
How do you feel about the U.S. war in Iraq?	Strongly approve (18%)	N	67	337	404
			17%	83%	100%
	Somewhat approve (20%)	N	134	307	441
			30%	70%	100%
	Somewhat disapprove (19%)	N	289	131	420
			69%	31%	100%
	Strongly disapprove (43%)	N	845	103	948
			89%	11%	100%
Total		N	1335	878	2213
			60%	40%	100%

| | | | Vote for Senator in 2006 | | |
			Casey (D)	Santorum (R)	Total
How do you feel about the U.S. war in Iraq?	Strongly approve (18%)	N	44	364	408
			11%	89%	100%
	Somewhat approve (20%)	N	102	341	443
			23%	77%	100%
	Somewhat disapprove (19%)	N	284	134	418
			68%	32%	100%
	Strongly disapprove (43%)	N	877	64	941
			93%	7%	100%
Total		N	1307	903	2210
			59%	41%	100%

Source: 2006 Exit Poll in Pennsylvania, conducted by Edison Media Research.

of the way President Bush is handling his job. The President's overall rating in the 2006 Pennsylvania exit poll had plummeted since his reelection in 2004, standing at 62 percent disapproval compared to 49 percent disapproval just two years earlier. As Table 7.6 indicates, how voters felt about the President was closely related to their 2006 vote. For example, of the astonishingly high 46 percent who strongly disapproved of the President's job performance, 92 percent voted for Rendell and 96 percent for Casey!

Equally astounding is the sharp differentiation among the voters on the question "How do you feel about the war in Iraq?" Pennsylvanians' overall disapproval of the Iraq war was 62 percent in 2006, as shown in Table 7.7. Although the Iraq question asked in 2004 was worded a little differently from the one in 2006, it is clear that the President's Iraq policy had the overall approval of a bare majority of Pennsylvanians two years earlier, in sharp contrast to the reality in 2006.[12] Of the 43 percent who strongly disapproved of the war in 2006, 89 percent voted for Rendell and 93 percent for Casey; of the 19 percent who somewhat disapproved, over two-thirds favored the two statewide Democrats. Among the 38 percent who strongly or somewhat approved of the Iraq war, Swann and Santorum received the vast majority of their votes. Of course, the President's job approval rating and the voters' evaluation of the Iraq war were closely linked.

As displayed in Table 7.8, positions on abortion continued to divide the electorate. Prochoice voters overwhelmingly favored the two Democrats. Prolife voters favored the Republicans, although the support percentages for the GOP candidates were not as high. Interestingly, Casey received the support of 28 percent of those who said abortion should be illegal in all cases, but Rendell, at 30 percent, did slightly better in that category. These results are particularly noteworthy because Casey is prolife and Rendell is prochoice. These abortion findings are an indication that for many voters the abortion issue had lost its intensity by 2006. Overall, the exit poll found that slightly over 60 percent of Pennsylvanians adhered to a prochoice position in 2006.

Voters in 2006 were also differentiated to some extent by their view of the condition of the Pennsylvania economy, as shown in Table 7.9. Those who said the economy's condition is "poor" voted 73 percent for Casey; those choosing "excellent" opted for Santorum by 60 percent to Casey's 40 percent. These tendencies were less pronounced in the results for the governor's race. Overall, 64 percent of the exit-poll respondents viewed the condition of the state's economy as "good" or "excellent."

When the responses on the economy are examined in each of the state's five regions, prominent regional disparities appear; see Table 7.10. Respondents from the

---

12. In the 2004 exit poll, the comparable Iraq war question was worded as follows: "How do you feel about the U.S. decision to go to war with Iraq?" Of the 52 percent who approved of the decision to go to war, 89 percent voted for President Bush. Likewise, of the 48 percent of Pennsylvanians who disapproved of the war decision, an overwhelming 84 percent voted for Senator Kerry.

Table 7.8 Cross-Tabulation of the 2006 Pennsylvania Vote for Governor and U.S. Senator by Stance on Abortion

| | | | Vote for Governor in 2006 | | |
			Rendell (D)	Swann (R)	Total
Which comes closest to your position? Abortion should be:	Legal in all cases (25%)	N	307	62	369
			83%	17%	100%
	Legal in most cases (37%)	N	390	161	551
			71%	29%	100%
	Illegal in most cases (24%)	N	157	204	361
			43%	57%	100%
	Illegal in all cases (15%)	N	66	153	219
			30%	70%	100%
Total		N	920	580	1500
			61%	39%	100%

| | | | Vote for Senator in 2006 | | |
			Casey (D)	Santorum (R)	Total
Which comes closest to your position? Abortion should be:	Legal in all cases (24%)	N	308	58	366
			84%	16%	100%
	Legal in most cases (37%)	N	396	153	549
			72%	28%	100%
	Illegal in most cases (24%)	N	151	214	365
			41%	59%	100%
	Illegal in all cases (15%)	N	62	160	222
			28%	72%	100%
Total		N	917	585	1502
			61%	39%	100%

Source: 2006 Exit Poll in Pennsylvania, conducted by Edison Media Research.

Table 7.9 Cross-Tabulation of the 2006 Pennsylvania Vote for Governor and U.S. Senator by Condition of Economy

| | | | Vote for Governor in 2006 | | |
			Rendell (D)	Swann (R)	Total
Do you think the condition of Pennsylvania's economy is:	Excellent (6%)	N	41	45	86
			48%	52%	100%
	Good (58%)	N	572	322	894
			64%	36%	100%
	Not so good (29%)	N	256	186	442
			58%	42%	100%
	Poor (7%)	N	67	41	108
			62%	38%	100%
Total		N	936	594	1530
			61%	39%	100%

| | | | Vote for Senator in 2006 | | |
			Casey (D)	Santorum (R)	Total
Do you think the condition of Pennsylvania's economy is:	Excellent (6%)	N	34	51	85
			40%	60%	100%
	Good (58%)	N	536	354	890
			60%	40%	100%
	Not so good (29%)	N	285	159	444
			64%	36%	100%
	Poor (7%)	N	81	30	111
			73%	27%	100%
Total		N	936	594	1530
			61%	39%	100%

Source: 2006 Exit Poll in Pennsylvania, conducted by Edison Media Research.

Table 7.10 Cross-Tabulation of the Condition of the Pennsylvania Economy
by Region

| | | | Do you think the condition of Pennsylvania's economy is: | | | | |
			Excellent	Good	Not so good	Poor	Total
Region	Philadelphia	N	5	104	58	15	182
			3%	57%	32%	8%	100%
	Philadelphia suburbs	N	27	247	67	4	345
			8%	72%	19%	1%	100%
	Northeast	N	10	100	53	9	172
			6%	58%	31%	5%	100%
	Pittsburgh area/West	N	11	140	139	57	347
			3%	40%	40%	16%	100%
	Central/Northern tier	N	33	308	132	28	501
			7%	61%	26%	6%	100%
Total		N	86	899	449	113	1547
			6%	58%	29%	7%	100%

Source: 2006 Exit Poll in Pennsylvania, conducted by Edison Media Research.

prosperous Philadelphia suburbs stood out in their highly positive assessment of the state of the Pennsylvania economy; for example, 72 percent assessed the economy as "good" and 8 percent said "excellent" compared to 19 percent who picked "not so good" and only 1 percent who chose "poor." By contrast, 40 percent of the voters in the Pittsburgh/West region picked "not so good" and 16 percent "poor"; 40 percent of the respondents in these western counties selected "good" and 3 percent "excellent."

The county-by-county, two-party patterns in 2006 exhibited broad partisan continuity with those earlier in the decade. For example, Senator Kerry's successful Pennsylvania pattern correlates at 0.92 and 0.96 respectively with Governor Rendell and Treasurer Casey. Figure 7.1, a scattergram of the Kerry–Casey correlation, illustrates this stable configuration.

Since Rendell and Casey have their own particular bases of support in the state, it is not surprising that their 2006 patterns do not correlate quite as closely as was the case with Kerry. The Rendell–Casey correlation is 0.89. A scattergram of that relationship, pictured in Figure 7.2, isolates the differences,[13] which are also shown in another form in Table 7.11, a cross-tabulation of the 2006 vote by the state's five regions. Rendell, a former mayor of Philadelphia, ran about 10 percentage points

13. Of course, a similar scattergram depicting the Swann–Santorum correlation could be presented, which would show the county-by-county pattern from the GOP perspective.

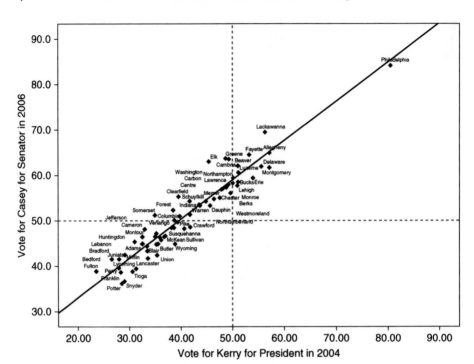

Fig. 7.1. Scattergram of the Democratic Vote for President in 2004 and Senator in 2006

ahead of Casey in the Philadelphia suburban counties. Casey, who made a concerted effort to campaign in rural, small-town counties, scored about 5 percentage points better in western Pennsylvania counties than did the Governor.[14]

The 2006 partisan support patterns are displayed in the book's final two maps, Figures 7.3 and 7.4, which place the state's sixty-seven counties into five categories (ranging from dark gray to light gray and white to dots) based on the partisan level of voter support for the 2006 statewide nominees of both major parties. When compared with similar maps presented earlier in this book, these two figures illustrate the extent of electoral change that has occurred in the Keystone State since the 1960 and 1962 elections.

Another confirmation of the extent of the changes that have occurred is found by comparing Casey's winning pattern in 2006 with his father's gubernatorial victory pattern in 1986. This is done through a scattergram of the father–son

14. "We can't have . . . a blue-state strategy in presidential campaigns, and I can't have a blue-county-only strategy," Casey was quoted as saying in a newspaper article. "You have to be willing to go into places where you may not get any votes, because part of it is to give people a sense of who you are, to listen to them. . . . If you ignore them and let your opponent tell them who you are, you're going to be in big trouble." Thomas Fitzgerald and Carrie Budoff, "Looking to Chip Off the Old Blocs–Out of Their Element, Seeking an Edge," *Philadelphia Inquirer*, October 18, 2006.

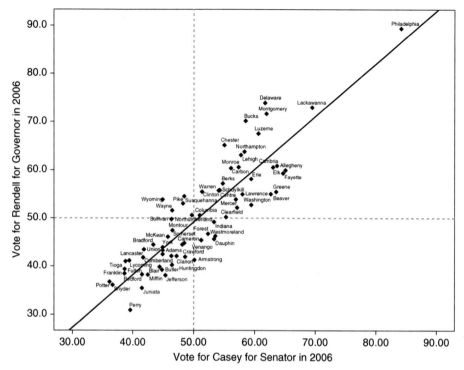

Fig. 7.2. Scattergram of the Democratic Vote for Senator and Governor in 2006

correlation coefficient of 0.62. See Figure 7.5, which captures once again the considerable change that occurred in the state's partisan patterns in recent decades. That members of the same political family would exhibit these by-now well-established tendencies is not surprising, only noteworthy because of the name.

The cross-tabulation in Table 7.12 reveals the extent of ticket-splitting in the 2006 gubernatorial and senatorial elections. Of those respondents who voted for Casey, 17 percent (or 165 people) also voted for Swann, and of the respondents who voted for Rendell, 13 percent (or 195 people) voted for Santorum.

Although the small percentages and numbers involved make it difficult via an exit poll to analyze further these ticket-splitters with any reliability, cross-tabulating the ticket-splitters with the five regional divisions provides a revealing hint as to who they are. As shown in Table 7.13, 39 percent of the Casey–Swann ticket-splitters resided in the Pittsburgh/West region, and 35 percent of the Rendell–Santorum voters resided in the Philadelphia suburbs, attesting to the continued relevance of the "friends-and-neighbors" phenomenon in voting behavior. Incidentally, the central/northern tier had sizable percentages among both categories of ticket-splitters, perhaps an indicator of an especially strong independent spirit in these counties.

Democratic challengers defeated four Republican members of Congress in 2006 to claim an 11-to-8 majority of the state's U.S. House delegation for their

Table 7.11   Cross-Tabulation of the 2006 Pennsylvania Vote for Governor and
U.S. Senator by Region

| | | | Vote for Governor in 2006 | | |
			Rendell (D)	Swann (R)	Total
Region	Philadelphia	N	235	29	264
			89%	11%	100%
	Philadelphia suburbs	N	385	161	546
			71%	29%	100%
	Northeast	N	219	125	344
			64%	36%	100%
	Pittsburgh Area/West	N	315	246	561
			56%	44%	100%
	Central/Northern Tier	N	326	397	723
			45%	55%	100%
Total		N	1480	958	2438
			61%	39%	100%

| | | | Vote for Senator in 2006 | | |
			Casey (D)	Santorum (R)	Total
Region	Philadelphia	N	224	40	264
			85%	15%	100%
	Philadelphia suburbs	N	325	219	544
			60%	40%	100%
	Northeast	N	199	136	335
			59%	41%	100%
	Pittsburgh Area/West	N	348	219	567
			61%	39%	100%
	Central/Northern Tier	N	343	384	727
			47%	53%	100%
Total		N	1439	998	2437
			59%	41%	100%

Source: 2006 Exit Poll in Pennsylvania, conducted by Edison Media Research.

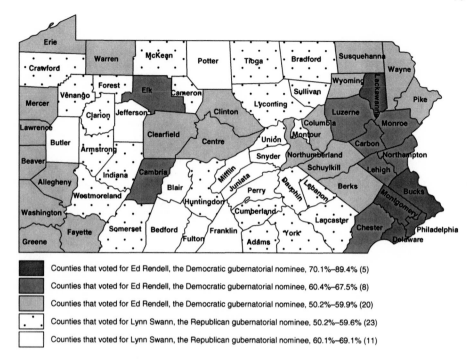

Counties that voted for Ed Rendell, the Democratic gubernatorial nominee, 70.1%–89.4% (5)

Counties that voted for Ed Rendell, the Democratic gubernatorial nominee, 60.4%–67.5% (8)

Counties that voted for Ed Rendell, the Democratic gubernatorial nominee, 50.2%–59.9% (20)

Counties that voted for Lynn Swann, the Republican gubernatorial nominee, 50.2%–59.6% (23)

Counties that voted for Lynn Swann, the Republican gubernatorial nominee, 60.1%–69.1% (11)

Fig. 7.3. Map of the Vote for Governor in 2006 with Five Levels of County Support

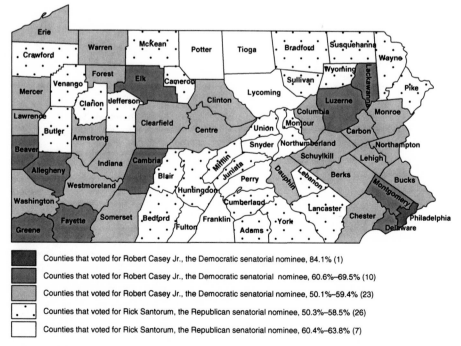

Counties that voted for Robert Casey Jr., the Democratic senatorial nominee, 84.1% (1)

Counties that voted for Robert Casey Jr., the Democratic senatorial nominee, 60.6%–69.5% (10)

Counties that voted for Robert Casey Jr., the Democratic senatorial nominee, 50.1%–59.4% (23)

Counties that voted for Rick Santorum, the Republican senatorial nominee, 50.3%–58.5% (26)

Counties that voted for Rick Santorum, the Republican senatorial nominee, 60.4%–63.8% (7)

Fig. 7.4. Map of the Vote for Senator in 2006 with Five Levels of County Support

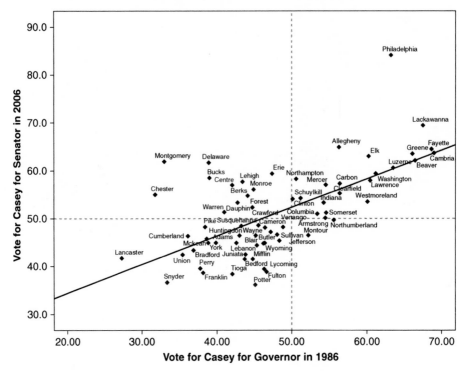

Fig. 7.5. Scattergram of the Democratic Vote for Governor in 1986 and Senator in 2006

Table 7.12 Cross-Tabulation of the 2006 Pennsylvania Vote for Governor and U.S. Senator

			Vote for Senator in 2006		
			Casey (D)	Santorum (R)	Total
Vote for Governor in 2006	Rendell (D)	N	1260	195	1455
			87%	13%	100%
	Swann (R)	N	165	785	950
			17%	83%	100%
Total		N	1425	980	2405
			59%	41%	100%

Source: 2006 Exit Poll in Pennsylvania, conducted by Edison Media Research.

Table 7.13 Cross-Tabulation of the 2006 Ticket-Splitters in Pennsylvania by Region

			2006 Ticket-splitters	
			Rendell & Santorum Voters	Swann & Casey Voters
Region	Philadelphia	N	18	8
			9%	5%
	Philadelphia suburbs	N	68	13
			35%	8%
	Northeast	N	27	15
			14%	9%
	Pittsburgh Area/West	N	34	65
			17%	39%
	Central/Northern Tier	N	48	65
			25%	39%
Total		N	195	166

Source: 2006 Exit Poll in Pennsylvania, conducted by Edison Media Research.

party. Two of the four districts were part of the Philadelphia suburbs: the 7th district (Delaware county), where retired Navy Admiral Joseph A. Sestak handily defeated veteran Congressman Curt Weldon, and the 8th district (Bucks county), where Patrick Murphy won a narrow victory over Congressman Mike Fitzpatrick. In the 6th district, encompassing much of Chester County, Congressman Jim Gerlach won reelection narrowly over Democrat Lois Murphy.

The other two Democratic gains were at opposite ends of the state. Republican Congressman Don Sherwood lost his one-time safe 10th district seat after he admitted to a five-year extramarital affair. Democrat Chris Carney won the election by 6 percentage points in this sprawling, rural, small-town district in the northeastern section of the state. In the 4th district west of Pittsburgh, Jason Altmire, a former congressional aide, defeated Congresswoman Melissa Hart by 3 percentage points in a stunning upset that demonstrated how powerful the anti-Bush, anti-GOP tide was in 2006.

Democrats also gained seats in the state House of Representatives, ending up with a one-vote majority after many weeks of dispute over several very close races. Then, in a surprise move, Democrats along with six Republicans elected state Representative Dennis M. O'Brien, a Republican from Philadelphia, House speaker. The Philadelphia Inquirer's lead paragraph of the article reporting the vote captured the drama: "In a twist that shocked even seasoned politicians, [O'Brien] was elected speaker of the House yesterday through a stealth maneuver pulled off by top Democrats, whose party narrowly controls the chamber."[15] Republicans retained their 29-to-21 majority in the state Senate.

Overall, the Democratic surge in 2006 propelled the David index of Democratic party strength in Pennsylvania to its highest recorded level—58.7 percent, up from 49.0 percent just two years earlier. See chapter 1, Figure 1.1.

From the Past to the Future

At the end of this long journey through decades of Pennsylvania electoral politics, a glance toward the future is in order. The effort to peer forward cautiously at the end of this final section follows a quick look back at the path just covered.

At the outset of the book, I thoroughly explored the question of national electoral change, mining the insights found in the literature on electoral realignments and party system change for assistance in placing the Pennsylvania experience in a broader context.

I started with an analysis of several major past realignments of the party system at the national and state levels, the last one being the powerful New Deal realignment of the 1930s and its aftershocks, which were still being felt in the 1960s. Then, I began to untangle yet another realignment that started in the middle to late 1960s, which I termed the culture-wars realignment. The crosscutting issues involved in this realignment were propelled by a series of divisive cultural issues that were quite different from the old New Deal economic-class cleavages that had defined the party system. They were the hot-button social issues of the era—race, abortion, prayer in the public schools, gay rights, and so on.

Drawing on the work of many analysts, I explained how these new crosscutting issues disrupted American political life and the party system over the next three decades. A pivotal figure at the national level was Ronald Reagan, who got his start in Republican politics in California in the mid-1960s as a champion of the conservative, "backlash" side of the new culture-wars divide.

To fully grasp the new realignment, which I rank below the New Deal realignment in magnitude, I analyzed in detail how the national party system was transformed by this latest realignment. In my view, the main work of the culture-wars realignment had been accomplished by the early 1990s, and the years since have witnessed a series of aftershocks of this realignment as it worked its way through the states and solidified the new party system along the basic cultural divide that was at the heart of this recent partisan reshuffling.

I illustrated this change at the national level by displaying a scattergram of the state-by-state vote for John Kennedy in 1960 and John Kerry in 2004 (chapter 2, Figure 2.11). The paths of the various states shown in this fascinating scattergram capture the transformation. In general, the more culturally liberal areas of the

---

15. Mario F. Cattabiani, Angela Couloumbis, and Amy Worden, "In a Stunning Move, Democrats Elected GOP Rep. Dennis M. O'Brien Speaker," *Philadelphia Inquirer*, January 3, 2007.

country have become the core support base for the Democratic party, and the more culturally conservative states make up the GOP base.

Shifting to Pennsylvania, I presented a similar scattergram of the Keystone State's county-by-county vote for Kennedy and Kerry (chapter 2, Figure 2.24), which offered a snapshot of the state's major changes over the period. This illustration showed that the populous, previously Republican suburban Philadelphia counties were voting Democratic by 2004. For example, Montgomery County, which had a population of 750,000 in the 2000 census, had given Kennedy only 39.2 percent of its votes in 1960, but the county's voters went for Kerry in 2004 by 55.6 percent. This scattergram also picked up another important trend— the weakening of Democratic voting strength in the counties surrounding Pittsburgh.

I linked these divergent Philadelphia and Pittsburgh metropolitan-area changes to aftershocks of the culture-wars realignment as the more culturally liberal Philadelphia suburban counties moved toward the national Democrats and the more culturally conservative Pittsburgh-area counties became more Republican, not unlike the path of various states depicted in the national scattergram.

This latest reshuffling gave the edge in Pennsylvania to the national Democrats. In fact, since 1960, Democratic presidential nominees have carried Pennsylvania eight times, three more times than the Democrats have been able to win the White House. The latest examples of this phenomenon occurred in 2000 and 2004, when Al Gore and John Kerry carried the Keystone State only to lose close presidential elections to the Republicans. This national Democratic success in Pennsylvania sets up a central problem that I then thoroughly investigated: Why did Pennsylvania Republicans do so well through 2004 in a period of impressive national Democratic strength in the state?

As I became acquainted with the victorious Republican U.S. Senate candidates—Hugh Scott, Richard Schweiker, John Heinz, Arlen Specter, and Rick Santorum—I came to appreciate how important it was for the first four of them that they were positioned as moderate-to-liberal Republicans. The lone exception, Senator Santorum, a solid conservative, was the last to be elected, in 1994, and in fact, he epitomized a dilemma faced by Republicans in so-called blue states, that is, those states arranged on the Democratic side of the culture-wars realignment as measured by presidential voting inclinations. Scott, Schweiker, Heinz, and Specter did well partly because they had appeal far beyond their party's registered voters.

The governor's races also featured an array of moderate-to-liberal Republican winners—William Scranton, Raymond Shafer, Richard Thornburgh, and Tom Ridge—and there is little doubt that their careful distancing from their party's conservative wing was an important reason for their success.

On the Democratic side, Governor Casey, a social conservative but an economic liberal, occupies a spot by himself in the typology, as does the current governor, Ed Rendell, a moderate on the divisive social issues of the day. Both were excellent campaigners attuned closely to current trends. Perhaps Rendell has tracked to the center for strategic reasons; Casey's social conservatism seemed completely sincere, even if the tactics he followed in his 1986 gubernatorial victory were less so.

Senator Santorum's overwhelming defeat in 2006 suggests the difficulty a social and economic conservative faces running in Pennsylvania in the transformed partisan environment at the end of the first decade of the twenty-first century. However, Santorum and his allies can argue that in 2006 he was caught up in a powerful national trend running against supporters of an unpopular president fighting an unpopular war. Certainly there are forces in the Pennsylvania GOP who want their major nominees to come from the conservative wing of the party, a faction that very nearly defeated Senator Specter's renomination in the Republican primary in 2004.

What can be said about future partisan prospects in Pennsylvania? More than a little depends on how the GOP resolves its ideological dilemmas. Weighing in quickly after the 2006 elections, Senator Specter delivered a speech in Philadelphia arguing that the Republican party had to become "a lot more progressive and a lot less ideological" in light of the "seismic earthquake," as he termed the 2006 election results.[16] Those conservatives who sought unsuccessfully to end Specter's career in the GOP primary in 2004 see the need to remain faithful to conservative principles, hope for a more favorable political climate than what they experienced in 2006, and plan to search for candidates with strong personal appeal to go along with their conservatism.

Robert A. Gleason Jr., who became the state GOP chairman in June 2006, has, in the words of a Harrisburg Patriot-News reporter, "focused on rallying Republicans around economic principles that unite them while encouraging room for disagreement on social issues."[17] If he and other moderates like him are unsuccessful, these intraparty disputes are likely to be fought out in highly divisive GOP primaries. My best guess is that moderate-to-liberal Republicans like Senator Specter are likely to have a tougher time winning GOP nominations in the future. The irony is that it is exactly this type of moderate-to-liberal candidate who has the best chance of getting elected statewide.

Of course, Pennsylvania Democrats could have their share of internal party squabbles as well. One factor that gives future hope to Democrats, however, is the increasing appeal their party is having among younger voters. For example, Table 7.14, which cross-tabulates party identification with age, shows that 47 percent of voters between eighteen and twenty-nine years of age identified with the Democratic party compared to only 25 percent in that age category opting for the Republican party. For other, older age groups in the 2006 Pennsylvania exit poll, the gap between the two parties was considerably smaller.

As for presidential elections, it is likely that the state will continue to be hotly contested for the same reason that Ohio is likely to be vigorously fought

16. Steve Goldstein, "For Casey, Party's Gains Could Give Him Added Clout," Philadelphia Inquirer, November 9, 2006.

17. Brett Lieberman, "GOP Fears Its Days at Top Might Be Ending," Harrisburg Patriot-News, October 15, 2006.

Table 7.14 Cross-Tabulation of 2006 Party Identification in Pennsylvania by Age

			Party Identification			
			Democrat	Republican	Independent/Other	Total
Age	18–29 (11%)	N	117	62	70	249
			47%	25%	28%	100%
	30–44 (24%)	N	224	215	96	535
			42%	40%	18%	100%
	45–59 (37%)	N	345	313	163	821
			42%	38%	20%	100%
	60 or over (28%)	N	262	247	103	612
			43%	40%	17%	100%
Total		N	948	837	432	2217
			43%	38%	19%	100%

Source: 2006 Exit Poll in Pennsylvania, conducted by Edison Media Research.

over by the major parties. Although national Democrats currently have the edge in the Keystone State, if the Republican party's presidential nominee can win here, it would be a major coup and could determine the outcome in a close election.

Likewise, as became apparent during the 2004 election, if the Democratic presidential standard-bearer could carry Ohio, that result could also make the difference in a close national election. In the last presidential election, Republicans in the Buckeye State had the edge, but the pro-Democratic swing in Ohio during the 2006 midterm elections could change those calculations. Such are the current realities of our closely balanced national party system.

Of course, the outcome of a closely contested presidential campaign in the Keystone State is going to depend on the quality and positioning of the candidates, among other things. Given the current partisan trends, the GOP stands a much better chance of carrying Pennsylvania's electoral votes with a nominee politically closer to Tom Ridge than to Rick Santorum, just as they do to win future statewide elections.

In thinking of the future, it is instructive to keep in mind the findings of the extensive factor analysis that I conducted because it captured the recent direction of partisan movement for all sixty-seven Pennsylvania counties. In the process, the factor analysis highlighted the striking, new pro-Democratic developments in the four populous suburban counties of Philadelphia—Montgomery, Bucks, Chester, and Delaware—as well as the growth of Republican voting strength in the western counties surrounding Pittsburgh. The recent, intriguing partisan paths of many other Pennsylvania counties are revealed as well.

All are depicted in chapter 5, Figure 5.1 and Table 5.2, two important illustrations that allowed me to show in a reasonably precise manner the diverse county-level partisan trends I observed from various data sources. To communicate that comprehensive county-by-county summary picture, I constructed a Pennsylvania map using the directional findings from the factor analysis. Figure 5.2 quickly conveys the 2000 to 2004 county movements relative to those in the 1960 to 2004 period.

After the 2006 election, I ran the same factor analysis including the latest election and found that the trends previously isolated were alive and well. For example, in the new factor analysis, comparing 2000 to 2006 county movements to those in the 1960 to 2006 period, Montgomery and Delaware counties advanced their Democratic consistency factor from 1.41 to 1.47 and 1.45 to 1.52 respectively. On the other hand, Beaver, Lawrence, and Washington, all western counties near Pittsburgh, moved in the opposite direction—Beaver going from 1.29 to 1.17, Lawrence from 1.18 to 1.02, and Washington from 1.11 to 0.96.

Although one can come right up to the present moment to capture direction and magnitude of change, those indicators are no guarantee of the course that the future will take. We cannot know what new crosscutting issues will rise to sunder the present alignment.

Also, it is important to keep in mind that any new realignment cannot carry enough force to fully displace what went before. Thus, the culture-wars realignment did not completely supplant the alignment left by the New Deal realignment. As Sundquist phrased it and as I quoted him at the outset of this book, "Successive realignments can best be understood as new patterns drawn on transparent overlays." It is not surprising, then, that a portion of the current political debate harkens back to the familiar issue conflicts that had their origins in the 1930s. Thus, by pointing to new cultural cleavages in the party system, I do not imply that the older cleavages were supplanted completely. Instead, the two sets of issues—cultural and economic—now share the political arena, existing side by side. It is likely that future transformations will follow this pattern.

Furthermore, it is equally important to keep in mind that when new issues arise at the national level, they are not necessarily absorbed into each state's party system in the same way. The impact will be determined by the type of people living in a state, the state's partisan history, the issues and interests of special concern to that particular state, the skill and ambitions of the particular individuals who arose in each state, among other things. These factors are the state-specific ones that make each state unique.

When the culture-wars realignment restructured the American party system over the course of several decades, it was restructuring the complex alignment most recently altered by the New Deal realignment and its aftershocks.

The exact outcome of a national alignment in each state at any particular date—let's say 1965, for example—has never been spelled out in any one study or even in any series of studies. For someone interested in what the partisan alignments were in all fifty states in 1965 or 1985 or 2005, there is only a sparse, state-specific literature that offers some information along these lines for some of the states. The reality of state party systems is that they differ from each other and yet are all subject to common influences that flow from national political developments—and, of course, they are invariably understudied. This mix in the fifty states can be comprehended, but not easily, because true understanding would require the existence of fifty detailed and up-to-date state studies.

My Pennsylvania study cannot explain what has occurred in the other forty-nine states or predict what will happen there. However, it does offer a case study of how national—and state and local—forces played out in a key battleground state. Drawing on the Pennsylvania experience, a researcher in another state might want to probe to see if the Keystone State's patterns apply to his or her state. For example, did the nomination of moderate-to-liberal Republican statewide candidates in another state work to forestall Democratic gains that might otherwise have resulted from having more conservative GOP nominees? Or, does the notion of aftershocks of the culture-wars realignment help explain voting-pattern shifts in the metropolitan regions of another state? In other words, was a "federalized accommodation," to draw on Speel's book, at work? Or, do the ideopolis ideas of Judis and Teixeira as well as my complementary notion of aftershocks of the culture-wars realignment help explain voting-pattern shifts in metropolitan regions of that state? Incidentally, the work of Richard Florida in *The Rise of the Creative Class*[18] goes beyond Judis and Teixeira in classifying urban areas throughout the country—large as well as reasonably small ones—in regard to how influential a new "creative class" is in those places. Perhaps Florida's extensive classifications, which are strikingly similar to Judis and Teixeira's notions, but more detailed, can be linked to county-level voter behavior in other states.

At the outset of this project, my main goal was to illuminate Pennsylvania's post-1960 electoral patterns. A secondary goal, if possible, was to advance understanding of national electoral change. My chief contribution to the latter comes in the case I make for the culture-wars realignment, grounding my interpretation squarely within Sundquist's theoretical explanation of how national electoral change occurs but applying it to a later period that overlapped the last era Sundquist analyzed. In this regard, other state-centered researchers may find value in my interpretation because it provides an overarching explanation of the national context in which their states operated.

Further, my explication of the Pennsylvania experience sheds light on possible paths that states similar to Pennsylvania may have followed. For example, consider the partisan paths of Ohio, Illinois, Michigan, and Wisconsin. Figures 7.6, 7.7, 7.8, and 7.9 portray the Democratic party-strength trends for these four Great Lakes states, constructed like the Pennsylvania figure and three Northeastern states located near Pennsylvania, which were introduced earlier in this book.

What are the dominant elements at play in these four Midwestern states in the post-1960 period? Three of them—all but Ohio—are reasonably solid members of

---

18. Richard Florida, *The Rise of the Creative Class: And How It's Transforming Work, Leisure, Community, and Everyday Life* (New York: Basic Books, 2002).

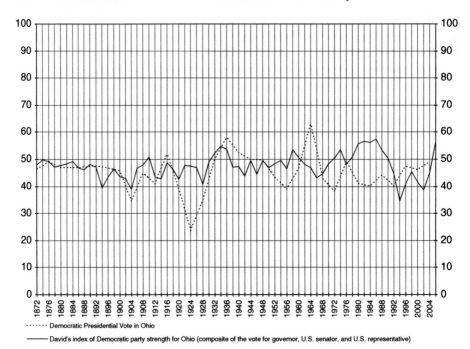

········ Democratic Presidential Vote in Ohio

———— David's index of Democratic party strength for Ohio (composite of the vote for governor, U.S. senator, and U.S. representative)

Fig. 7.6. Democratic Party Strength in Ohio, 1872–2006

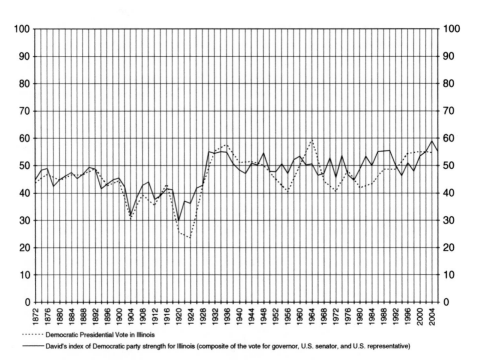

········ Democratic Presidential Vote in Illinois

———— David's index of Democratic party strength for Illinois (composite of the vote for governor, U.S. senator, and U.S. representative)

Fig. 7.7. Democratic Party Strength in Illinois, 1872–2006

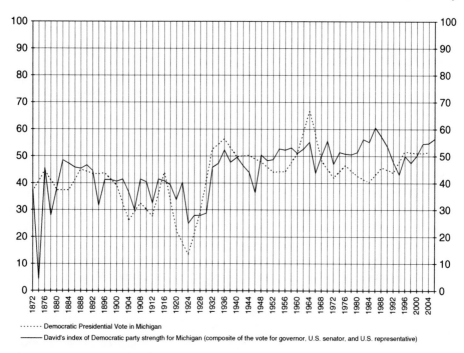

······· Democratic Presidential Vote in Michigan

——— David's index of Democratic party strength for Michigan (composite of the vote for governor, U.S. senator, and U.S. representative)

Fig. 7.8. Democratic Party Strength in Michigan, 1872–2006

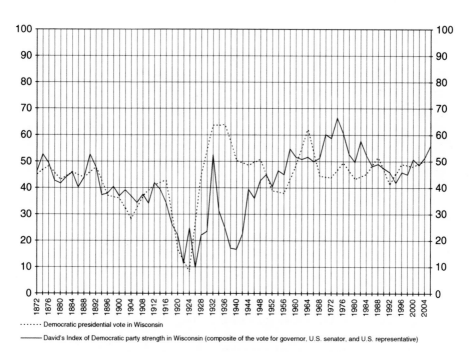

······· Democratic presidential vote in Wisconsin

——— David's Index of Democratic party strength in Wisconsin (composite of the vote for governor, U.S. senator, and U.S. representative)

Fig. 7.9. Democratic Party Strength in Wisconsin, 1872–2006

the new Democratic presidential coalition, which the map in Figure 7.10 depicts. How these four states reached their respective positions in red-and-blue America is suggested in rough fashion by my national analysis.

But, how does one explain fully the ups and down in both the party-strength index (solid line) and the presidential vote (dotted line) in these four state figures? There are explanations, and they may have parallels in the Pennsylvania experience.

My hope is that the approach in this book could be of use to researchers interested in understanding the patterns in other states. Certainly one has to start such a study with an investigation of national party system change and its links to a state's patterns. Further, the straightforward research method I use could be employed with profit, including analyzing newspaper accounts, county-level voting patterns, census data, and state surveys and exit polls.

A comparable factor analysis like mine could be helpful for charting voting trends in, for example, Illinois, to name one state where I am sure that movements similar to what occurred in the Philadelphia suburbs can be discerned in Chicago's diverse and populous suburban counties. I haven't studied them systematically, but my casual acquaintance with the Chicago metropolitan area leads me to think that this would be a fruitful avenue of research for a project on post-1960 Illinois two-party politics. Such state-specific studies could flesh out important, current aspects of the American party system.

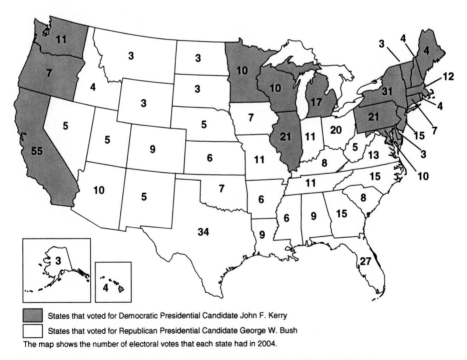

States that voted for Democratic Presidential Candidate John F. Kerry

States that voted for Republican Presidential Candidate George W. Bush

The map shows the number of electoral votes that each state had in 2004.

Fig. 7.10. U.S. Electoral College Map of the 2004 Presidential Election

Furthermore, the fact that the national partisan balance was tipped in the way it has been because of the grafting-on of these cultural issues does not mean that state politics in all the states must be dominated by cultural issues—or, for that matter, by the older economic issues. The reality is that the two coexist, and together with other issues—like foreign policy concerns—they define partisan politics in the national and the state arenas. What the mix is in any particular state—or even in individual voters—is something that must be determined by state-specific investigation.

As for regional differences in electoral change, I am not in a position to speculate with any confidence about various regional similarities or differences. In presenting Pennsylvania survey data, I reported Northern survey results for rough comparison with Pennsylvania, but in doing so, I had no intention of trying to explain the reasons for the diverse Northern patterns. Why survey percentages that are a collection of responses from respondents in thirty-seven Northern states should differ from or be similar to Pennsylvania's patterns would require considerable inquiry into these Northern patterns. Obviously, I have done that sort of investigation only for Pennsylvania.

However, the extensive survey information from the 2004 national exit poll in chapter 6, Table 6.25, allows anyone so inclined to engage in comparative speculation. The data are broken down by the country's four regions and cross-tabulated by the vote for president in 2004; the results from the comparable 2004 exit poll for Pennsylvania are also displayed in the table.

One learns, for example, that persons with family incomes under $30,000 in the Northeast voted overwhelmingly for Kerry, 69 percent compared to 31 percent for President Bush, the top region with such a spread. The Pennsylvania figure in this category was identical to the Midwest figure, not the Northeast's. In the South, among those with the highest incomes, over $100,000, 70 percent voted for Bush. In the West, it was 50–50. In Pennsylvania, 58 percent in that top income category voted for Bush, 42 percent for Kerry. As chapter 6, Table 6.25, shows, the Pennsylvania pattern was again closer to the Midwest than the Northeast. On other variables, Pennsylvania is closer to the Northeast; yet on some, the Keystone State is closer to the South. I would not attempt to draw any supportable generalizations from such crude comparisons as these. But, with good studies and data from many other states, the possibility for deeper understanding widens considerably.

In looking to the future, students of electoral change have to keep in mind that we don't know what major new developments will enter our politics. No doubt, in the mid-1920s, Pennsylvania Republicans had no idea a Great Depression was on the way that would sweep into office a charismatic national Democratic leader who would lead a New Deal revolution that would end the GOP's seven decades of dominance in the Keystone State.

Where the next cluster of crosscutting issues will take the party system in Pennsylvania and the nation is anyone's guess. But, as a firm believer in the value of realignment theory for understanding U.S. electoral change, I am confident that the concepts that have proven so useful in this book for comprehending the realignment of Pennsylvania politics since 1960 will be of value again.

Postscript
The 2008 Election

In the historic 2008 presidential election, Pennsylvania voters helped elect Senator Barack Obama of Illinois the nation's first African American president while continuing to exhibit in striking fashion the new electoral patterns that emerged in the state during the last decade.

The Democratic nominee carried the Keystone State with 54.7 percent of the vote to 44.3 percent for Senator John McCain of Arizona, the Republican standard-bearer, marking the fifth straight Democratic presidential victory in Pennsylvania. However, unlike 2000 and 2004, this election resulted in the Democratic party's recapture of the White House in an impressive victory that shattered the national partisan balance in existence since President George W. Bush's narrow win eight years earlier. Senator Obama and his vice-presidential running mate, Senator Joseph Biden of Delaware, a Scranton native, captured nine states that the party lost in 2004—three in the Midwest (Ohio, Indiana, and Iowa); three in the South (Virginia, North Carolina, and Florida); and three in the West (Colorado, New Mexico, and Nevada). The Democratic ticket won 52.8 percent of the popular vote nationwide and amassed 365 electoral votes compared to 45.7 percent and 173 electoral votes for Senator McCain and his running mate, Governor Sarah Palin of Alaska. Figure 8.1 displays the 2008 national electoral configuration.

Before examining the 2008 Pennsylvania voting patterns in detail, an overview of this exciting presidential election is in order, especially because the Keystone State figured so prominently both in the Democratic nomination battle and in the fall campaign. While Senator McCain's path to his party's nomination was far from easy, he was able to defeat a strong field of challengers by early March to insure that he would be the GOP standard-bearer after getting the official designation at the party's national convention in St. Paul, Minnesota, in early September.

Senator Obama, virtually unknown in national political circles before his electrifying keynote speech at the 2004 Democratic National Convention in Boston, was not the odds-on favorite to win the Democratic nomination when the campaign started in early 2007. Senator Hillary Rodham Clinton of New York, the nation's First Lady in the 1990s when her husband, President Bill Clinton, served two terms in the White House, had many advantages in her bid to become the country's first female president.

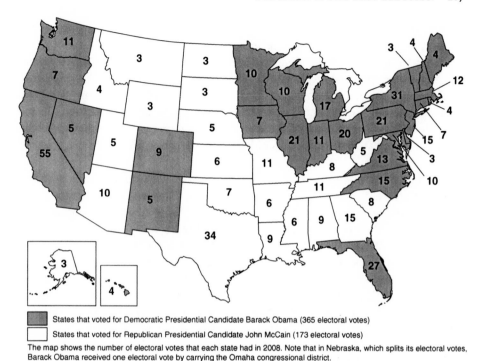

States that voted for Democratic Presidential Candidate Barack Obama (365 electoral votes)

States that voted for Republican Presidential Candidate John McCain (173 electoral votes)

The map shows the number of electoral votes that each state had in 2008. Note that in Nebraska, which splits its electoral votes, Barack Obama received one electoral vote by carrying the Omaha congressional district.

Fig. 8.1. U.S. Electoral College Map of the 2008 Presidential Election

They included wide name recognition among the voters, a vast network of supporters within the Democratic party's establishment, and the backing of many large donors. Further, the Democratic field consisted of a handful of prominent, experienced members or former members of Congress, including Senator Biden, as well as former Senator John Edwards of North Carolina, the party's 2004 vice-presidential running mate with Senator John Kerry, the party's losing nominee that year.

In the first major contest, the January 3 Iowa caucuses, Obama, in an upset, triumphed by winning the support of 38 percent of those attending the caucuses. Since only a small percentage of Iowans are African Americans (2.5 percent versus the national average of 12.8 percent, according to a 2006 U.S. census estimate[1]), the Illinois Democrat's victory boosted his prospects considerably by initially laying to rest doubt as to whether an African American could win the presidency in a pre-dominantly white country. This doubt was to return later and figure prominently in speculation about the vote in Pennsylvania both in the state's April 22 primary and in the general election. Edwards came in second in Iowa at 30 percent, followed closely by Clinton at 29 percent. Five days later Clinton rallied in New Hampshire to win a narrow victory over Obama despite trailing in the final pre-primary polls; Edwards finished a distant third there. The Nevada caucuses, held on January 19,

1. U.S. Census Bureau, State and County Quick Facts at http://quickfacts.census.gov.

were a virtual stand-off with Clinton claiming more caucus-goers but Obama winning slightly more convention delegates.

Then came the South Carolina primary on January 26, the fourth early delegate-selection event approved by the national Democratic party prior to Super Tuesday on February 5, when a score of states lined up at the "official" starting post to express their nomination preferences in delegate-selection primaries and caucuses. Obama won 55 percent of the vote in the Palmetto State to Clinton's 27 percent. Edwards, who could garner only 18 percent in this southern state bordering his home state, dropped out a few days later.

In the twenty-two contests on Super Tuesday, Clinton did well, winning primaries in California, New York, Massachusetts, New Jersey, and several other states. Obama also did well, winning primaries in Illinois, Georgia, Connecticut, Alabama, and Missouri, among others, and dominating all the caucus states holding events that day, which included Colorado, Minnesota, Kansas, and others. Since the Democratic delegate-selection process required proportional representation, Obama amassed sizable numbers of delegates even in the primary states he lost. Because Clinton's campaign gave only scant attention to the caucus states, Obama's superior grassroots organizations, fueled by an outpouring of support for Obama among young voters,[2] secured the vast majority of these delegates.[3]

Obama then won all of the next ten contests in the month after Super Tuesday, including decisive victories in the Virginia and Maryland primaries and a solid win in Wisconsin. But, on March 4, Clinton staved off impending defeat with victories in Ohio, Rhode Island, and Texas, although the Lone Star State's result was close. Obama won only liberal Vermont that day. Because Clinton's Ohio victory with 54 percent of the vote to Obama's 44 percent was built on overwhelming support for her among white Democrats (68 percent to Obama's 31 percent, according to the Ohio exit poll[4]), the question of the role of race in the election returned. Also, doubt was raised about Obama's appeal to Hispanic voters, who had voted heavily for Clinton in several key contests, including the California and Texas primaries.

Because the Pennsylvania primary on April 22 was the next major contest after the March 4 primaries,[5] this debate loomed large during the intervening seven weeks. Two *Washington Post* reporters, Jonathan Weisman and Shailagh Murray, explored the topic in a lengthy article published four days after the Ohio and Texas primaries, headlined, "Downside of Obama Strategy: Losses in Big States Spur General-Election Fears." They wrote: "If Obama becomes the Democratic nominee but cannot win support from working-class whites and Hispanics, [Clinton supporters] argue, then

2. David Von Drehle, "The Year of the Youth Vote," *Time Magazine*, January 31, 2008.

3. Peter Slevin, "Obama Mines Small, Traditionally Red States," *Washington Post*, January 29, 2008.

4. http://edition.cnn.com/election/2008/primaries.

5. There were only two contests before the Pennsylvania primary: the Wyoming caucuses on March 8 and the Mississippi primary on March 11. Obama won both with slightly over 60 percent.

Democrats will not retake the White House in November. 'If you can't win in the Southwest, if you don't win Ohio, if you don't win Pennsylvania, you've got problems in November,' said Sen. Robert Menendez (D-N.J.), a Clinton supporter." The reporters asked Obama's campaign manager, David Plouffe, to comment on the issue and relayed his response in their own words: "[Plouffe said] he is not going to be goaded into shifting from the current strategy, which is to get as many delegates from wherever he can. And he rejects what he says is the Clinton campaign's attempt to give greater legitimacy to certain states—especially Pennsylvania, where Clinton is expected to have an advantage because of her support from the Democratic establishment there and because its demographics are similar to Ohio's."[6]

Next, the *Post* reporters paraphrased Obama's response: "Obama rejects the charge that he has failed to reach important segments of the party, noting that he has shown he can crack Clinton's coalition of working-class voters, women and Latinos with his wins in the bellwether state of Missouri, the swing state of Virginia and the Rust Belt redoubt of Wisconsin. He also showed that he can expand the battleground into the coveted Mountain West, with his convincing win in Colorado." Then the reporters quoted the candidate directly: "I don't buy into this demographic argument. Missouri, Wisconsin, Virginia—in many of these states we've won the white vote and the blue-collar vote and so forth. I think it is very important not to somehow focus on a handful of states because the Clintons say those states are important and that the other states are unimportant."[7]

In mid-March, Obama was put on the defensive when portions of inflammatory sermons preached by his Chicago pastor of twenty years, the Rev. Jeremiah A. Wright, Jr., surfaced and began to flood the airwaves and the twenty-four-hour cable news networks. For example, in a 2003 sermon, Wright, an African American, preached in his fiery style: "The government gives them the drugs, builds bigger prisons, passes a three-strike law and then wants us to sing 'God Bless America.' No, no, no. God damn America, that's in the Bible for killing innocent people. God damn America for treating our citizens as less than human. God damn America for as long as she acts like she is God and she is supreme." In a sermon on the Sunday after the 9/11 terrorist attacks on New York and Washington in 2001, he said: "We bombed Hiroshima, we bombed Nagasaki, and we nuked far more than the thousands in New York and the Pentagon, and we never batted an eye. We have supported state terrorism against the Palestinians and black South Africans, and now we are indignant because the stuff we have done overseas is now brought right back to our own front yards. America's chickens are coming home to roost."[8]

---

6. Jonathan Weisman and Shailagh Murray, "Downside of Obama Strategy: Losses in Big States Spur General-Election Fears," *Washington Post*, March 8, 2008.

7. Ibid.

8. Brian Ross and Rehab El-Buri, "Obama's Pastor: God Damn America, U.S. to Blame for 9/11," March 13, 2008, article on the ABC News web site, found at http://abcnews.go.com, with a link to the television story on the topic.

Immediately Obama issued a statement condemning Wright's remarks: "All of the statements that have been the subject of controversy are ones that I vehemently condemn. They in no way reflect my attitudes and directly contradict my profound love for this country." The senator said he would not leave the church, the Trinity United Church of Christ on Chicago's south side, where Wright was in the process of retiring, adding that the controversial statements were not ones he "personally heard [Wright] preach while I sat in the pews of Trinity or heard him utter in private conversation."[9]

As the furor over the Wright remarks grew, Obama announced he would give a major speech on race in America at the National Constitution Center in Philadelphia. In the talk, which was well received around the county,[10] he sought to confront the role of race in American society in a straight-forward manner as a means toward future reconciliation. He asserted that the controversy over the Wright remarks "reflect the complexities of race in this country that we've never really worked through—a part of our union that we have yet to perfect."[11] As a child of two cultures—his father was a black man from Kenya who met his mother, a white woman born in Kansas, when they were college students in Hawaii—Obama sought to view the racial divide from both sides, saying:

> For the men and women of Reverend Wright's generation, the memories of humiliation and doubt and fear have not gone away, nor has the anger and bitterness of those years [of racial discrimination against African Americans]. That anger may not get expressed in public, in front of white co-workers or white friends, but it does find voice in the barbershop or the beauty shop or around the kitchen table.
>
> In fact, a similar anger exists within segments of the white community. . . . So when they are told to bus their children to a school across town, when they hear that an African American is getting an advantage in landing a good job or a spot in a good college because of an injustice that they themselves never committed, when they're told that their fears about crime in urban neighborhoods are somehow prejudiced, resentment builds over time.[12]

9. Peter Slevin, "Obama Condemns Pastor's Remarks," *Washington Post*, March 14, 2008.

10. The assessment of Dan Balz of the *Washington Post* is representative of the praise Obama received after the speech: "In so many ways, Obama's speech was remarkable: ambitious, lofty, gritty, honest and unnerving. In tone and substance, and in the challenge he laid down to the country about the need to somehow move beyond the racial stalemate, it was the kind of speech Americans should expect of a presidential candidate or a president." Dan Balz, "Will the Answer Outlive Questions? Obama's Speech Driven by Necessity," *Washington Post*, March 20, 2008.

11. Jeff Zeleny, "Obama Urges U.S. to Grapple With Racial Issue," *New York Times*, March 19, 2008.

12. Ibid.

Obama argued: "The profound mistake of Reverend Wright's sermons is not that he spoke about racism in our society. It's that he spoke as if our society was static." Further, he cautioned that, if Americans "walk away [from the path of racial reconciliation], if we simply retreat into our respective corners, we will never be able to come together and solve challenges like health care, or education, or the need to find good jobs for every American."[13]

By the time April 22 arrived, Pennsylvanians had been subjected to an expensive, vigorous campaign by both Clinton and Obama. One estimate put the amount spent at $20 million with Obama outspending his New York opponent by two to one.[14] Governor Edward Rendell, who had close ties with the Clintons over the years, spearheaded her effort in the state, which featured endorsements from many members of Congress and a hundred mayors, including the mayors of Philadelphia and Pittsburgh. Obama won an important endorsement himself in late March when Senator Robert P. Casey, Jr., backed him, joining Obama for a six-day bus tour across Pennsylvania. Casey told reporters in Pittsburgh, "I believe in this guy like I've never believed in a candidate in my life," adding at another tour stop, "He's been tested. He's appealed to the better angels of our nature under very difficult circumstances."[15]

On Primary Day, Clinton defeated Obama with 55 percent of the vote to the Illinois senator's 45 percent. Exit polls showed that 61 percent of white Pennsylvania Democrats voted for Clinton compared to 38 percent for Obama, a crushing defeat in that category. However, compared to the Ohio result among white Democrats, Obama had advanced seven percentage points. Right after the Pennsylvania primary, a New York Times reporter, Patrick Healy, published an insightful article assessing the relative strengths of the Democratic rivals in swing states in the general election. He quoted Peter Hart, a veteran Democratic pollster not affiliated with either candidate, as follows on the issue: "I think it differs state to state, and I think either Democrat will have a good chance of appealing to many Democrats who didn't vote for them the first time." In the words of the reporter, "Mr. Hart, as well as Obama advisers, also say that Mr. Obama appears better poised than Mrs. Clinton to pick up states that Democrats struggle to carry, or rarely do, in a general election, like Colorado, Iowa, Missouri and Virginia, all of which he carried in the primaries." He then quotes Hart's prescient conclusion: "Hillary goes deeper and stronger in the Democratic base than Obama, but her challenge is that she doesn't go as wide. Obama goes much further reaching into the independent and Republican vote, and has a greater chance of creating a new electoral map for the Democrats."[16]

13. Ibid.

14. Jeff Zeleny and Katharine Q. Seelye, "Obama, Trailing, Sharpens Attack in Pennsylvania," New York Times, April 21, 2008.

15. Katharine Q. Seelye and Michael Powell, "A Surprise Endorsement That Reflected Frustration and a Desire for Healing," New York Times, March 29, 2008.

16. Patrick Healy, "For Democrats, Questions Over Race and Electability: Assessing Strength of Contenders in Swing States," New York Times, April 24, 2008.

In a companion article, another *New York Times* reporter, Adam Nagourney, wrote:

> But just when it seemed that the Democratic Party was close to anointing Mr. Obama as its nominee, he lost yet again in a big general election state, dragged down by his weakness among blue-collar voters, older voters and white voters. The composition of Mrs. Clinton's support—or, looked at another way, the makeup of voters who have proved reluctant to embrace Mr. Obama—has Democrats wondering, if not worrying, about what role race may be playing.
>
> "I'm sure there is some of that," said David Axelrod, Mr. Obama's senior political adviser, as he considered how race was playing among voters in late primary states. Mr. Axelrod said Mrs. Clinton's biggest advantage had been among older voters, "and I think there is a general inclination on the part of the older voters to vote for what is more familiar." He added: "Here's a guy named Barack Obama, an African-American guy, relatively new. That's a lot of change."[17]

Despite her Pennsylvania victory, the remaining primary calendar offered little opportunity for the New York senator to catch Obama's lead in pledged delegates, that is, among those delegates won by the candidates in the primaries and caucuses. Two weeks later, on May 6, Obama won the North Carolina primary handily and only narrowly lost the Indiana primary. As the final contests played out over the next four weeks, more and more uncommitted "super-delegates," that is, party notables who received delegate status by virtue of their positions, shifted to Obama. On June 7, as the primary season came to an end, Clinton endorsed Obama, saying: "The way to continue our fight now, to accomplish the goals for which we stand, is to take our energy, our passion and our strength and do all we can to help elect Barack Obama the next president of the United States."[18]

In accepting the Democratic presidential nomination at the party's national convention in Denver in late August, Obama portrayed his Republican opponent as

17. Adam Nagourney, "For Democrats, Questions Over Race and Electability: Obama Struggling to Add Support of Key Blocs," *New York Times*, April 24, 2008. Incidentally, the Reverend Wright controversy burst back into the headlines less than a week after the Pennsylvania primary following a string of new inflammatory comments by Wright in a series of public appearances, including one at the National Press Club in Washington. At a news conference in North Carolina, Obama denounced these new statements by his former pastor and cut off ties with him. "His comments were not only divisive and destructive," Obama said, "but I believe that they end up giving comfort to those who prey on hate, and I believe that they do not portray accurately the perspective of the black church. They certainly don't portray accurately my values and beliefs." Jeff Zeleny and Adam Nagourney, "An Angry Obama Renounces Ties to His Ex-Pastor," *New York Times*, April 30, 2008.

18. Adam Nagourney and Jeff Zeleny, "Clinton Pledges an All-Out Push To Elect Obama," *New York Times*, June 8, 2008.

offering the country a third term of President Bush. "Senator McCain likes to talk about judgment, but really, what does it say about your judgment when you think George Bush was right more than 90 percent of the time? I don't know about you, but I'm not ready to take a 10 percent chance on change."[19] Later in his speech, the Democratic standard-bearer asserted:

> I don't believe that Senator McCain doesn't care what's going on in the lives of Americans; I just think he doesn't know. Why else would he define middle class as someone making under $5 million a year? How else could he propose hundreds of billions in tax breaks for big corporations and oil companies but not one penny of tax relief to more than 100 million Americans? How else could he offer a health-care plan that would actually tax people's benefits, or an education plan that would do nothing to help families pay for college, or a plan that would privatize Social Security and gamble your retirement? It's not because John McCain doesn't care. It's because John McCain doesn't get it.[20]

The next week, in accepting the Republican presidential nomination at the GOP's national convention in St. Paul, McCain, proudly describing himself as a maverick, vowed to end the "constant partisan rancor" in Washington. "It's what happens when people go to Washington to work for themselves and not you. Again and again, I've worked with members of both parties to fix problems that need to be fixed. That's how I will govern as president." He added: "Let me just offer an advance warning to the old, big-spending, do-nothing, me-first, country-second crowd: Change is coming."[21] Then, McCain contrasted his policies with Obama's:

> I will keep taxes low and cut them where I can. My opponent will raise them. I will open new markets to our goods and services. My opponent will close them. I will cut government spending. He will increase it. My tax cuts will create jobs; his tax increases will eliminate them. My health care plan will make it easier for more Americans to find and keep good health care insurance. His plan will force small businesses to cut jobs, reduce wages, and force families into a government-run health care system where a bureaucrat stands between you and your doctor.[22]

19. Jonathan Weisman and Shailagh Murray, "Obama, Accepting Nomination, Draws Sharp Contrast With McCain," *Washington Post*, August 29, 2008.

20. Ibid.

21. Adam Nagourney and Michael Cooper, "McCain Vows to End 'Partisan Rancor,'" *New York Times*, September 5, 2008.

22. "Transcript of John McCain's Acceptance Speech," *New York Times*, September 4, 2008.

The fall campaign was fought out against the backdrop of a major national financial crisis, symbolized by the collapse of a prominent securities company, Lehman Brothers, on September 14, and the near demise of the insurance giant American International Group (A.I.G.).[23] The financial turmoil, which started in the housing sector as a result of the collapse of the risky, sub-prime mortgage market, prompted an unprecedented $700 billion federal bailout passed by Congress and signed by President Bush on October 3.[24] Further, the severe economic downturn the country experienced during the fall along with the record-breaking, low-approval ratings registered by the incumbent Republican president—below 30 percent—worked to the disadvantage of the GOP nominee.[25] For example, a late September *Washington Post*/ABC News poll reported that slightly over 50 percent of the voters picked the economy as the most important issue facing the country, a very high number for a single issue.[26]

Obama, who had led McCain through most of the summer by between 2 to 6 percentage points in an average of fifteen major national polls, lost the lead to the Arizona Republican shortly after the GOP convention by up to 2 percentage points until September 17, when the two men registered a tie at 45.3 percent each. After that date, as the financial and economic crisis deepened, Obama's lead grew in fits and starts from 2 to 8 percentage points, registering 52.1 percent for Obama on Election Day to 44.5 percent for McCain in this average of major national polls.[27] In addition, Obama helped his candidacy by his performance in the three presidential debates, held on September 26, October 7, and October 15, because, despite his relatively brief experience in national politics, he was able to demonstrate an impressive command of the issues and to appear "presidential."[28]

Pennsylvanians had no reason to complain about lack of attention by the candidates in the general election. According to calculations by the *Philadelphia Inquirer*, Obama visited the state 9 times after he secured the nomination in June, holding 20 events. McCain visited 30 times after he wrapped up his nomination in early March, holding 43 events. Further, Biden made 7 visits with 14 events, and Palin

---

23. Andrew Ross Sorkin, "Lehman Files for Bankruptcy; Merrill Is Sold," *New York Times*, September 15, 2008.

24. David M. Herszenhorn, "Bailout Plan Wins Approval; Democrats Vow Tighter Rules," *New York Times*, October 4, 2008.

25. For example, Bush's approval rating registered at 26 percent in the September 27–29, 2008, Washington Post/ABC News Poll, reported under the "polls" category at http://www.washingtonpost.com.

26. Dan Balz and Jon Cohen, "Most Voters Worry About Economy," *Washington Post*, October 1, 2008.

27. These national averages of fifteen polls included those conducted by CBS News/*New York Times*, Gallup, ABC News/*Washington Post*, Reuters/C-Span/Zogby, Fox News, and NBC News/*Wall Street Journal* and were calculated by Real Clear Politics. The percentages are found on its web site at http://www.realclearpolitics.com/polls.

28. On this point, see Robert G. Kaiser, "The Debates: No Drama but a Dramatic Effect," *Washington Post*, October 31, 2008.

visited 14 times, appearing at 23 events.[29] For the Republicans, Pennsylvania was one of two large, Democratic-leaning ("blue") states—Michigan was the other—initially targeted as part of their national victory strategy. Then, in early October, the McCain campaign abandoned the Michigan effort, making the Keystone State even more important for the McCain-Palin ticket. "We need to carry Pennsylvania to win this thing," said former Governor Tom Ridge in late October, adding: "You don't want to write John McCain off, ever."[30] Howard Dean, the Democratic party's national chairman, ratified Ridge's view this way: "Pennsylvania is the Ohio of 2008. If we win Pennsylvania, we win the whole shooting match. McCain has chosen to make his last stand here."[31]

The GOP strategy was analyzed in a lengthy *New York Times* article, headlined "A Blue State, to McCain, Very Much Still in Play."[32] After noting that five major Pennsylvania polls gave Obama a double-digit lead in the state in mid-October, the article went on to explain that the GOP's strategy for winning the state rested on a dual appeal: "to the pro-gun working-class voters in the western coal country, many of whom supported Senator Hillary Rodham Clinton of New York in the Democratic primary, and to independents and moderates in the swing counties around Philadelphia," basing the latter pitch on McCain's maverick label.[33] The campaign also hoped that the choice of Palin, the first woman nominated by the Republican party to run for vice president, would win votes for the ticket in the more socially conservative parts of the state. Earlier in the campaign, a *Washington Post* reporter explained Palin's "energizing" appeal this way:

> The reaction has been remarkably instantaneous, with socially conservative voters who had barely heard of Palin electrified by the few facts they quickly learned: her longtime membership in the Assemblies of God, the largest Pentecostal denomination; her large family; her opposition to abortion even in cases of rape and incest; her decision to carry to term her fifth child after learning he has Down syndrome; and her belief in teaching creationism alongside evolution in public schools.[34]

Republican strategists also hoped she would attract disappointed Hillary Clinton supporters.

29. Thomas Fitzgerald, "McCain's Musts for Pa.; Turnout Is Key: Lots of His Base; Less of Obama's," *Philadelphia Inquirer*, November 2, 2008.

30. Larry Eichel, "Both Sides Targeting Red States," *Philadelphia Inquirer*, October 26, 2008.

31. Fitzgerald, "McCain's Musts for Pa."

32. Elisabeth Bumiller and Jeff Zeleny, "A Blue State, to McCain, Very Much Still in Play," *New York Times*, October 22, 2008.

33. Ibid.

34. Alec MacGillis, "For the Republican Base, Palin Pick Is Energizing," *Washington Post*, September 8, 2008.

In mid-October U.S. Representative John Murtha, a Democrat from Johnstown, ignited a minor firestorm with comments he made to *Pittsburgh Post-Gazette* editorial writers concerning the role of race in the presidential campaign. Murtha, an Obama supporter who backed Clinton in the primary, said that he expected the Democratic nominee to carry Pennsylvania despite "racist" sentiments in his region of the state. "There's no question Western Pennsylvania is a racist area," the veteran Democrat asserted. "The older population is more hesitant [to vote for an African American for president]."[35] Murtha later apologized for the remark, and a spokesman for him quickly issued the following clarification: "It's naïve to think that race or gender doesn't play a role in a voter's perception of a candidate. Mr. Murtha makes the point that while race may be an issue for some, it's evident that voters today are concerned about the issues that truly matter—issues like the economy, health care and energy independence."[36]

The role of race continued to be discussed around the state. For example, this exchange of views between two politicians in Northeast Pennsylvania—one a Democrat and the other a Republican—was reported in the *Scranton Times-Tribune* at the end of the campaign:

> "There is no other reason for John McCain and Sarah Palin to be in the state based on what the polls say, except that they're counting on us to be bigots," said former Scranton Mayor James McNulty, a Democrat. "Why else are they here? They're counting on Pennsylvania not voting for a black man."
>
> Ridiculous, says Republican Lackawanna County Commissioner A. J. Munchak.
>
> "He forgets that we were labeled bitter and hanging on to our guns and our Bibles," Mr. Munchak said. "I don't believe the polls. I honestly don't believe the polls. I think a lot of people, when asked, are afraid to say they're voting against Obama because people will put that [racist] label on them.... I think it's a lot closer than Mr. McNulty thinks."[37]

Munchak was making reference to controversial remarks Obama made at a San Francisco fund-raiser in early April when asked why he was behind in the polls in the then-upcoming Pennsylvania primary. Noting that many voters were "bitter" about their economic difficulties, Obama said: "So it's not surprising then that they get bitter, they cling to guns or religion or antipathy to people who aren't like them or anti-immigration sentiment or antitrade sentiment as a way to explain

35. Ed Blazina, "Murtha Says Obama Will Win Pennsylvania Despite Racism," *Pittsburgh Post-Gazette*, October 16, 2008.

36. Ibid.

37. Borys Krawczeniuk, "Is Pennsylvania McCain's Last Stand?" *Scranton Times-Tribune*, November 2, 2008.

their frustrations."[38] Obama later said he ought to have phrased his comments better. "I didn't say it as well as I should have," he noted during an Indiana campaign visit at the time of the controversy, but the Illinois Democrat stuck to his basic argument: "Lately, there's been a little typical sort of political flare-up because I said something that everybody knows is true, which is that there are a whole bunch of folks in small towns in Pennsylvania, in towns right here in Indiana, in my hometown in Illinois, who are bitter. They are angry, they feel like they've been left behind. They feel like nobody's paying attention to what they're going through."[39]

An aspect of the race issue returned at the end of the campaign when the Pennsylvania Republican party began airing, in the words of the *Philadelphia Daily News*, "hard-hitting TV ads attacking Obama and featuring his controversial former pastor, the Rev. Jeremiah Wright. 'If you think you could ever vote for Barack Obama, consider this: Obama chose as his spiritual leader this man,' an announcer says, as the ad cuts to Wright shouting, 'Not God bless America, God damn America!' "[40]

On Election Night, as the results became known, Governor Rendell offered his view of how Obama's race had played out in the election, as reported by Dave Davies of the *Philadelphia Daily News*: " 'The economy clearly trumped race,' Gov. Rendell said last night as he reviewed the intensely fought battle for Pennsylvania's 21 electoral votes. . . . Rendell said Obama 'blew the race open' when the financial crisis hit this fall, showing a steadier hand and more appealing ideas than Republican John McCain. 'When times got tough, people listened and gave Sen. Obama a fair chance to win them over,' Rendell said, 'and in many cases, I believe he did.' "[41] Rendell's interpretation was echoed in a lengthy post-election article in the *New York Times*, subtitled "How Did Obama Win Over White, Blue-Collar Levittown." The article's findings were summed up in the observations of Tina Davis, council president of Bristol Township, which contains many residents of the predominantly white Levittown community in lower Bucks county near Philadelphia:

> She said she had endless conversations with constituents who said they would not vote for Obama. "Most of them couldn't give me a real answer why," she said. "I had some of them reciting those stupid

38. Jeff Zeleny, "Obama Works to Limit Fallout Over Remark on 'Bitter' Working Class," *New York Times*, April 13, 2008.

39. Ibid.

40. William Bender and Dave Davies, "Both Campaigns To Spend Their Final Day in Pennsylvania," *Philadelphia Daily News*, November 3, 2008. The *Daily News* reporters added: "McCain had promised not to raise the issue of Wright in the campaign. McCain campaign spokesman Peter Feldman said yesterday that McCain 'is not the referee of every political ad in this election.' "

41. Dave Davies, "Obama Cruises in 'Racist' Pennsylvania," *Philadelphia Daily News*, November 5, 2008.

e-mails saying he was a Muslim. I'm pretty blunt. I would just say to them, "You're against him because he's black."

She thinks some of those who argued with her and insisted till the bitter end that they would vote for Mr. McCain just stubbornly did not want to acknowledge they had changed their minds. In the end, she believes they ended up voting out of a different kind of fear—fear for their own economic survival. Self-interest trumped racism. "They had to ask themselves if they wanted a really smart young black guy, or a stodgy old white guy from the same crowd who put us in this hole," she said.[42]

While a narrative, analytical account of the 2008 election sheds light on what happened and why, a detailed examination of the voting returns, party registration data, and exit polls offers the opportunity to illuminate further the behavior of the Pennsylvania electorate in this fascinating election.

Strikingly visible in Figure 8.2 is the continuation in the 2008 presidential election of two important Pennsylvania trends analyzed throughout this book. The map in Figure 8.2 depicts the 18 counties won by Obama and the 49 carried by McCain with the state's counties divided into four categories by strength of support for each candidate. Comparing Obama's 18 counties with the 13 counties won by Kerry in 2004 (see Figure 2.23 in Chapter 2) reveals that three southwestern Pennsylvania counties—Beaver, Washington, and Fayette—abandoned the Democratic standard-bearer in 2008. As a result of this latest balloting, the national Democratic presidential nominee, who amassed a Keystone State victory margin of 10.4 percentage points in a minor landslide over the GOP, was reduced in 2008 to carrying only one county (Allegheny) in the nine-county Pittsburgh metropolitan area, a region that had been a mainstay of Democratic support since the New Deal realignment. Obviously, the recent, important, on-going transformation in southwestern Pennsylvania, which I have linked to the culture wars realignment and its aftershocks, continued in 2008. Other illustrations introduced below confirm this trend.

While Obama was doing relatively poorly in the southwest, the Democratic standard-bearer added eight counties to Kerry's 2004 victory pattern—five in the eastern part of the state (Chester, Berks, Dauphin, Carbon and Monroe), Centre in the middle of the state, and Cambria and Elk in the west-central region. Thus, the 2008 outcome in the east reaffirms another key development visible in Pennsylvania's recent electoral development, namely, the growing Democratic

42. Michael Sokolove, "The Transformation," *New York Times*, November 9, 2008. Sokolove explained that Levittown is not an incorporated entity itself, but rather is defined by the Levitt-built homes that "extend into towns with large white working-class populations—Bristol, Middletown and Falls Townships, as well as Tullytown Borough—but it does not make up the entirety of any of those places. In those four jurisdictions, Obama defeated McCain, 44,110 to 25,034." Thus, according to Sokolove's calculations, Obama won there by a 3,200-vote margin higher than John Kerry's in 2004.

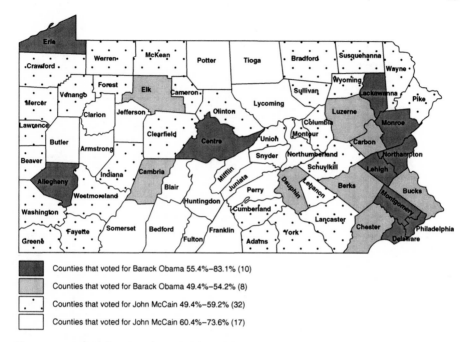

Counties that voted for Barack Obama 55.4%–83.1% (10)

Counties that voted for Barack Obama 49.4%–54.2% (8)

Counties that voted for John McCain 49.4%–59.2% (32)

Counties that voted for John McCain 60.4%–73.6% (17)

Fig. 8.2. Map of the Vote for President in 2008 with Four Levels of County Support

strength in the vicinity of Philadelphia. Other illustrations discussed below amplify this pattern as well.

Although Figure 8.2 starts the analysis by offering an overview of the 2008 results and by pointing to the 2008 continuation of key trends, Table 8.1 and Figure 8.3 present a more comprehensive way to look at the recent voting by directly comparing the 2008 presidential result by county with the 2004 vote. In Table 8.1, this is done by measuring the margin of victory for the winning candidate in each of Pennsylvania's sixty-seven counties for 2004 and 2008. Then, in the table's far-right column, the difference between the 2008 and 2004 margin of victory in each county is calculated, allowing for an ordering of all the counties by this margin difference.

For example, in 2008, McCain won 55.5 percent of the vote in Lancaster county to Obama's 43.7 percent, for a margin of minus 11.8 when viewed from the Democratic perspective. But, in 2004, Bush won 65.8 percent in Lancaster compared to Kerry's 33.6 percent, for a margin of minus 32.2 percent. The 2008–2004 difference between the margins is an astounding 20.4 percent, indicating a major advance for the national Democratic nominee in 2008 in this large, southeastern county compared to four years earlier and placing Lancaster at the top of the counties in Table 8.1.

Let's look at a second example on the other side of the state. In Westmoreland county near Pittsburgh, McCain won by 57.8 percent to 41.1 percent for Obama, for a 2008 margin of minus 16.7. In 2004, Bush won Westmoreland by 56.0 percent to Kerry's 43.5 percent, for a margin of minus 12.5 percent. The 2008–2004 difference between the margins is minus 4.2 percent, indicating an advance, albeit a small one, by

Table 8.1 Change in Presidential Voting Margin by County Between 2004 and 2008

| County | 2008 | | | 2004 | | | 2008–2004 |
	% for Obama	% for McCain	Margin	% for Kerry	% for Bush	Margin	Difference
Lancaster	43.7	55.5	−11.8	33.6	65.8	−32.2	20.4
Dauphin	54.0	45.0	9.1	45.6	53.9	−8.3	17.3
Monroe	57.6	41.3	16.3	49.6	49.7	0.0	16.3
Berks	53.9	44.7	9.2	46.4	53.0	−6.6	15.8
Centre	55.4	43.5	11.8	47.8	51.6	−3.7	15.6
Columbia	47.1	51.6	−4.4	39.7	59.7	−20.0	15.6
Lebanon	40.0	58.9	−18.9	32.5	66.6	−34.1	15.2
Adams	39.6	59.2	−19.6	32.6	66.9	−34.3	14.7
York	42.7	56.3	−13.6	35.5	63.7	−28.2	14.6
Cumberland	42.6	56.3	−13.6	35.8	63.9	−28.1	14.5
Union	42.1	56.7	−14.5	35.3	64.1	−28.8	14.3
Montour	41.9	57.0	−15.1	35.0	64.3	−29.3	14.3
Wyoming	45.6	53.2	−7.6	38.8	60.7	−21.8	14.2
Bradford	40.0	58.4	−18.4	33.5	66.1	−32.6	14.1
Cameron	39.2	58.9	−19.8	33.0	66.5	−33.5	13.7
Chester	54.2	45.0	9.2	47.5	52.0	−4.5	13.7
Pike	47.3	51.5	−4.2	40.6	58.4	−17.8	13.6
Wayne	43.3	55.6	−12.3	36.7	62.4	−25.7	13.4
Clinton	48.0	50.7	−2.8	41.7	57.5	−15.8	13.1
Elk	51.1	46.8	4.3	45.4	54.1	−8.7	13.0
Lehigh	57.1	41.6	15.5	51.0	48.4	2.6	12.9
Lycoming	37.3	61.5	−24.2	31.3	67.9	−36.5	12.4
Snyder	34.8	64.0	−29.2	29.0	70.5	−41.5	12.3
Lackawanna	62.6	36.6	26.0	56.3	42.3	14.0	12.0
Erie	59.3	39.4	19.9	54.0	45.6	8.4	11.5
Northampton	55.5	43.2	12.3	50.1	49.0	1.1	11.3
Tioga	35.5	63.0	−27.4	30.6	68.8	−38.2	10.7
Franklin	33.3	65.8	−32.6	28.3	71.4	−43.1	10.5
Susquehanna	43.5	55.1	−11.7	38.6	60.8	−22.2	10.5
Perry	32.4	66.1	−33.7	27.9	71.7	−43.7	10.0
McKean	40.5	57.8	−17.3	36.1	62.8	−26.7	9.4
Montgomery	60.0	39.2	20.8	55.6	44.0	11.6	9.2
Forest	42.5	55.9	−13.4	38.4	61.1	−22.6	9.2

Table 8.1 *(continued)*

County	2008			2004			2008–2004
	% for Obama	% for McCain	Margin	% for Kerry	% for Bush	Margin	Difference
Warren	46.1	52.3	−6.2	41.7	57.1	−15.3	9.1
Clearfield	43.0	55.2	−12.1	39.5	60.0	−20.5	8.3
Blair	37.3	61.6	−24.3	33.4	66.0	−32.6	8.3
Juniata	31.6	66.8	−35.2	28.0	71.4	−43.5	8.3
Jefferson	34.3	64.1	−29.8	31.1	68.4	−37.3	7.5
Huntingdon	35.5	63.0	−27.5	32.6	67.2	−34.6	7.1
Mifflin	32.6	66.2	−33.7	29.1	69.8	−40.7	7.0
Northumberland	42.2	56.0	−13.8	39.3	60.0	−20.6	6.8
Clarion	38.0	60.4	−22.4	35.2	64.4	−29.2	6.8
Delaware	60.2	38.8	21.4	57.2	42.3	14.8	6.6
Sullivan	39.5	59.0	−19.5	36.9	62.6	−25.7	6.2
Bucks	53.8	45.1	8.6	51.1	48.3	2.8	5.8
Philadelphia	83.1	16.3	66.7	80.4	19.3	61.1	5.6
Crawford	44.0	54.4	−10.4	41.8	57.3	−15.5	5.1
Indiana	45.7	52.9	−7.1	43.7	55.9	−12.2	5.1
Luzerne	53.6	45.2	8.4	51.2	47.8	3.4	5.0
Potter	30.6	68.1	−37.4	28.5	70.8	−42.4	4.9
Somerset	36.6	61.7	−25.0	34.9	64.7	−29.8	4.8
Fulton	25.0	73.6	−48.6	23.5	76.1	−52.6	4.0
Venango	39.6	58.9	−19.2	38.1	61.2	−23.0	3.8
Carbon	50.0	48.1	1.9	48.8	50.0	−1.2	3.1
Cambria	49.4	48.7	0.7	48.7	50.8	−2.2	2.9
Mercer	49.1	49.4	−0.3	48.2	51.0	−2.9	2.6
Bedford	27.0	71.8	−44.8	26.5	73.2	−46.7	1.8
Butler	35.7	63.1	−27.4	35.2	64.3	−29.1	1.7
Schuylkill	44.9	53.6	−8.7	44.8	54.6	−9.8	1.1
Allegheny	57.3	41.8	15.5	57.2	42.1	15.0	0.5
Greene	49.0	49.4	−0.4	49.3	50.0	−0.7	0.3
Armstrong	37.0	61.6	−24.6	38.7	60.9	−22.2	−2.4
Lawrence	46.8	51.9	−5.1	49.2	50.5	−1.3	−3.8
Westmoreland	41.1	57.8	−16.7	43.5	56.0	−12.5	−4.2
Washington	47.0	51.8	−4.7	50.1	49.6	0.6	−5.3
Beaver	47.9	50.8	−2.8	51.1	48.4	2.7	−5.5
Fayette	49.2	49.6	−0.4	53.2	45.8	7.5	−7.9

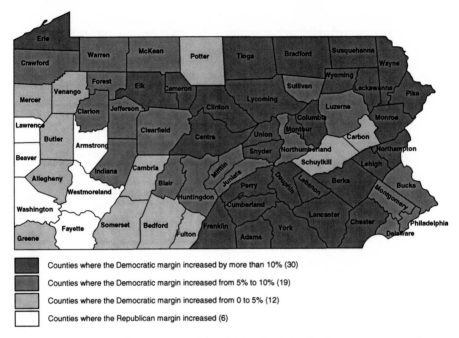

Counties where the Democratic margin increased by more than 10% (30)

Counties where the Democratic margin increased from 5% to 10% (19)

Counties where the Democratic margin increased from 0 to 5% (12)

Counties where the Republican margin increased (6)

Fig. 8.3. Map of the Change in Presidential Voting Margin Between 2004 and 2008

the losing Republican standard-bearer in 2008 compared to four years earlier, putting Westmoreland in league with only five other counties that showed a margin-difference gain for the GOP in 2008. All six of these counties—Fayette, Beaver, Washington, Lawrence, and Armstrong, plus Westmoreland—are in western Pennsylvania, located in the vicinity of Pittsburgh. Note that the map in Figure 8.3 depicts these margin differences in four categories with three of them for Obama, who "advanced" in 61 counties in this category compared to Kerry. The fourth category is made up of the six western counties just discussed above where McCain "advanced."

The scattergram in Figure 8.4 shows the relationship of the Kerry and Obama county patterns (correlation coefficient of 0.95). The eight counties that Obama added to the Democratic column are located in the upper left-hand quadrant.[43] A close examination of this scattergram reveals many other interesting patterns, some just now taking shape in this pair of 21st century presidential elections while others have been in the works for decades. For example, in addition to showing the continued decline of the national Democratic nominee in the western counties surrounding Pittsburgh, the scattergram also indicates that Allegheny county itself, despite giving Obama 57.3 percent of its votes, has slipped from its previous high place of prominence among Democratic counties statewide. Allegheny's diamond marker

43. Of the eight counties, only seven—Berks, Cambria, Carbon, Centre, Chester, Dauphin, and Monroe—are labeled on the scattergram. For Elk, the diamond marking is visible, but the county name could not be labeled on the scattergram due to lack of space.

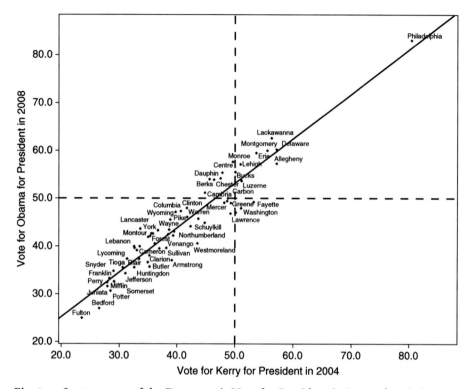

Fig. 8.4. Scattergram of the Democratic Vote for President in Pennsylvania in 2004 and 2008

is now located to the right of the "best-fit" line while several other counties are registering higher, more consistent Democratic support, including Erie, the other western urban center. For comparison, see Allegheny's position on the Gore–Kerry scattergram in Figure 2.27 and on the Dukakis–Kerry scattergram in Figure 2.26.

In fact, Allegheny county is worth examining more closely. To understand better what is going on inside of Allegheny county, one must separate the vote in Pittsburgh itself from the other 129 municipal entities within the county. Keep in mind that, in the 2000 census, Pittsburgh's population of 334,563 was only 26.1 percent of the total Allegheny county population of 1,281,666. In 2008, Obama won 75.2 percent of the vote in Pittsburgh, but he received only 51.2 percent in the rest of the county.[44] These

44. These percentages were calculated by William (Bill) Egar, a Case Western Reserve University undergraduate majoring in political science, from the Allegheny County Elections Division's web site at http://www.alleghenycounty.us/elect. This was no easy task because for 2008 the Elections Division did not present total figures for each municipality. Instead, it reported the returns for each election subdivision within all 130 municipalities, a total of 1,321 units! I much appreciate Bill's assistance, which also included gathering scores of Pennsylvania newspaper articles on the 2008 election from various sources.

percentages are similar to what Kerry received in winning Allegheny county with 57.1 percent: 74.4 percent in Pittsburgh and 51.8 percent in the rest of the county.

However, when compared to Michael Dukakis's showing within Allegheny county in 1988, one finds an erosion of Democratic support in the suburban municipalities of Allegheny county outside of Pittsburgh. Dukakis, who carried the county with 59.5 percent in his losing effort to capture Pennsylvania's electoral votes that year, received 73.7 percent in Pittsburgh and 54.3 percent in the rest of Allegheny county. A fall-off of 3.1 percentage points over two decades may not seem like a significant decline until you compare the result in these close-in Pittsburgh suburbs with what happened over the same twenty-year period in the Philadelphia area. In the four suburban counties closest to Philadelphia, Dukakis received only 37.8 percent of the vote in 1988; in those same four suburban counties in 2008, Obama received 57.9 percent of the vote! (Incidentally, Philadelphia itself gave Dukakis 66.6 percent and Obama 83.1 percent.) Thus, although Allegheny county remains a Democratic stronghold in the western part of Pennsylvania, its position in comparative terms has diminished, affected outside of Pittsburgh itself by the general trends already noted in the region. One further comparison between the 1988 and 2008 elections is worth making. In 1988, Dukakis received 58.8 percent of the vote in the eight counties surrounding Allegheny to George H. W. Bush's 41.2 percent. In 2008, Obama received 43.9 percent in these eight western counties compared to 56.1 percent for McCain.

A remarkable surge in Democratic party registration preceded the 2008 Democratic presidential victory in Pennsylvania. Between May 2007 and November 2008, Democrats nearly doubled their registration advantage over Republicans, advancing to a record 1.2 million more Democrats than Republicans. The Democratic party added 608,673 registered voters after May 2007. During the same 18-month period, the Republican party lost 15,852 registered voters. Voters choosing the "other" category increased modestly—by 57,777. Thus, on Election Day 2008, registered Democrats consisted of 51.2 percent of Pennsylvania voters, registered Republicans 37.0 percent, and others 11.8 percent.[45]

Democratic registration gains occurred across the state—in 61 of the 67 counties! Only Beaver, Washington, Greene, Fayette, and Westmoreland counties in the Pittsburgh area and the southern-border county of Fulton bucked the trend to post small Republican gains. In the process, Democrats increased significantly the number of counties where their party has a registration edge, going from 20 in 2004 to 27 in 2008. Included in the seven were the populous Philadelphia suburban counties of Montgomery and Bucks along with Dauphin, Centre, Clearfield,

45. The May 2007 party-registration figures used to make these calculations are found in the last entry in Table 5.5, which traces state party registration from November 1926 to May 2007. For comparison, the May 2007 percentages were: Democrats, 47.8 percent; Republicans, 40.2 percent, and others, 12.0 percent. Also, the November 2008 numbers are: Democrats, 4,480,691; Republicans, 3,243,391; others, 1,033,949. Total registration came to 8,758,031 voters. The November 2008 figures are from the Pennsylvania Department of State's Bureau of Commissions, Elections, and Legislation.

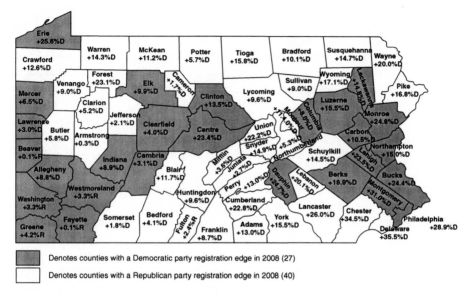

Denotes counties with a Democratic party registration edge in 2008 (27)

Denotes counties with a Republican party registration edge in 2008 (40)

Fig. 8.5. Map of Percent Net Gain in Democratic and Republican Party Registration from 2004 to 2008

Clinton, and Columbia. See Figure 8.5, which displays in gray the 27 counties with a 2008 Democratic registration edge and, in white, the 40 counties with a Republican registration advantage. The percentage under each county's name in Figure 8.5 indicates the net partisan-percentage gain in that county between 2004 and 2008.

The 61 counties that experienced a Democratic gain are indicated by the letter D while the 6 counties that had a gain in Republican registration are indicated by the letter R. The map in Figure 8.5 is similar to the one I used in Chapter 5—Figure 5.23—to illustrate the change in party registration between 2000 and 2004. In sharp contrast to 2008, Figure 5.23 shows that in 2004 only 26 counties experienced a net gain in Democratic registration while 41 counties had a net gain in Republican registration then.

The 2008 Democratic registration breakthrough in two of the Philadelphia suburban counties—Montgomery and Bucks—demonstrates that party registration is finally catching up with pro-Democratic voting trends there. When the registration books closed for the November 2008 election, Montgomery county had 264,043 registered Democrats to 239,629 registered Republicans, or 45.1 percent to 41.0. In 2004 there were 214,233 Democrats and 268,755 Republicans; thus, in four years, there was an increase of 49,810 Democrats and a loss of 29,126 Republicans. For Bucks county, the 2008 figures were 195,794 Democrats to 184,378 Republicans, or 44.0 percent to 41.4 percent. In 2004, there were 173,803 Democrats and 208,639 Republicans in Bucks.

As Figure 8.5 further indicates, Democrats were closing the gap in Chester and Delaware counties as well, gaining 34.5 percent and 35.5 percent, respectively.

Commenting on the trend, Tom Curtin, a Democratic councilman in Parkesburg in Chester county, said, "I think, overall, people in the region are becoming less conservative than they were in the past." Curtin, who moved to the county from western New York to take advantage of a better economic opportunity, added: "I know it's been said that Republicans in Chester County are more liberal than the Democrats outside of Pittsburgh."[46] "Democrats are coming out of the closet [in Chester]," asserted Lorraine Stanish, a retired nurse who moved to the county from South Philadelphia thirty years ago. "[M]any people had Democratic views but weren't out in the open because there had been such a heavy Republican presence."[47]

Also, in 2008, voter turnout in Pennsylvania increased to 61.5 percent of the voting age population (VAP) from 60.3 percent in 2004. The turnout in both of these presidential elections far exceeded the 2000 turnout rate of 52.5 percent.

Because I had such good fortune using factor analysis in Chapter 5, I decided to rerun the analysis adding in the most recent statewide elections—the 2006 gubernatorial and U.S. Senate elections and the 2008 presidential election. The well-understood changes in the Philadelphia suburbs and in the southwestern counties around Pittsburgh are still present in the findings of the factor analysis, of course. But, including the 2006 and 2008 elections revealed fascinating new patterns taking shape. These involved shifts in the south-central region of the state, which is comprised of eight counties—Adams, Cumberland, Dauphin, Franklin, Lancaster, Lebanon, Perry, and York—and in the northeast portion of the state, spanning the following thirteen counties: Berks, Carbon, Columbia, Lackawanna, Lehigh, Luzerne, Monroe, Northampton, Pike, Schuylkill, Susquehanna, Wayne, and Wyoming. Many of these counties broke out into a new factor that carried important explanatory value.

It is too early to know how these new forces will play out, but it appears that demographic changes may offer the key to understanding them. A *Philadelphia Inquirer* reporter, Paul Nussbaum, explored these changes in an April 2008 article, headlined "Shift in Pa. Population Has a Liberal, Urban Edge." He wrote: "The separation between new and old Pennsylvania runs roughly from Franklin County in the central south to Wayne County in the northeast, tracing a cultural and demographic divide as pronounced as the geographical boundary provided by the Appalachian Mountains."[48] Then, focusing on several rapidly growing border counties, Nussbaum captured the situation this way:

> The thousands of new residents streaming into Pennsylvania's border counties often continue to commute to work in another state.

46. Paul Nussbaum, "Shift in Pa. Population Has a Liberal, Urban Edge," *Philadelphia Inquirer*, April 10, 2008.

47. Ibid.

48. Ibid.

From Monroe County, "We have 22,000 people a day who commute to New Jersey and New York," said Robert Phillips, chief executive officer of the Greater Pocono County Chamber of Commerce in Monroe County. That is 20 percent of the county's working-age population.

About 60 New York-bound buses a day roll out of the depots in Mount Pocono and Delaware Water Gap, starting at 4 a.m. The trip takes nearly two hours, each way, and a monthly ticket costs about $450.

"It's a tough life, but people are willing to make the sacrifice," Phillips said. "For so many people, they find an oasis here. . . . It's a great place to raise a family."

Likewise, Pennsylvania's southern border has been discovered by workers in the Baltimore and Washington regions.

Adams County's population swelled by 10,000—11 percent—between 2000 and 2006. Neighboring Franklin County grew 8 percent, and York County added about 35,000 people, or 9 percent.[49]

Leif Jensen, a professor of rural sociology and demography at Pennsylvania State University, told Nussbaum: "Demographically, the two parts of the state are very different. In the west, the youth are moving out and leaving behind an aging population. . . . In the east, you have the stresses of the population increase." Jensen added that new arrivals from urban areas "are going to bring with them more cosmopolitan attitudes."[50]

Analysis of presidential election returns in the northeast and south-central regions uncovered the emergence of these new voting patterns, which were isolated by the factor analysis. In 1988, for example, Michael Dukakis lost the northeast region's thirteen counties to George H. W. Bush by 81,556 votes, or 43.9 percent to Bush's 56.1 percent. In 2008, Obama won the northeast by 94,210 votes, or 54.9 percent to McCain's 45.1 percent. In the south-central region, Democrats have not yet turned the region "blue," but there is definitely a trend in that direction. In 1988, Dukakis lost the region's eight counties to Bush by 168,438 votes, or 33.6 percent to Bush's 66.4 percent. In 2008, Obama lost the region by only 104,226 votes, or 43.8 percent to McCain's 56.2 percent.

Tom Infield, a *Philadelphia Inquirer* reporter, reached a similar conclusion in a post-election article seeking to explain Obama's strong, if losing, vote in Lancaster county. "Obama's 10-point improvement over Kerry's performance," he wrote, "may be yet another signal that a bigger, wealthier and better-educated Lancaster County slowly is being drawn into the long arms of metropolitan areas to the east and south—not just Philadelphia, but also Baltimore and Washington." He then quoted Bruce Beardsley, the chairman of the Lancaster county Democratic

49. Ibid.
50. Ibid.

party: "Lancaster County is one of the fastest-growing counties in the state. People are moving in from the Philadelphia region—even from New Jersey. They're younger and more professional, and that's the Democratic demographic." Infield added: "Much the same kind of change is happening in other areas of south-central Pennsylvania beyond the wide arc of the Philadelphia region. Berks,[51] Lebanon, Dauphin and York were among the top eight counties in the state where Obama outperformed Kerry. . . ."[52] Senator Casey weighed in along the same lines in a pre-election interview with the *Morning Call*. "Part of south-central Pennsylvania . . . demographically and income-wise is starting to resemble an extension of the Philly suburbs," Casey said.[53]

Turning to other 2008 elections in Pennsylvania, Democrats picked up a U.S. House seat in the 2008 election when Kathy Dahlkemper, an Erie businesswoman making her first bid for public office, defeated a seven-term Republican incumbent, Phil English, with 51.2 percent of the vote to English's 48.8 percent in the 3rd district, which stretches from Erie through several western Pennsylvania counties to slightly north of Pittsburgh. The victory meant that, when the new Congress convened in January 2009, Democrats held twelve U.S. House seats from Pennsylvania to seven for the Republicans, an exact reversal of the result in the 2002 election following the controversial redistricting after the 2000 census.

All other U.S. House incumbents were re-elected, including the four freshmen Democrats—Jason Altmire, Joseph Sestak, Patrick Murphy, and Chris Carney—

---

51. One indication of the demographic change occurring in Berks and other northeast counties is the influx of Hispanic Americans. The Hispanic population in Berks was 2.8 percent in 1990, 9.7 percent in 2000, and 13.3 percent in 2007. In Reading, the county seat of Berks, the Hispanic population went from 18.5 percent in 1990 (or 14,486) to 52.6 percent in 2007, while Reading's overall population has remained stagnant. Reading's 1990 total population was 78,380 while the 2007 estimate is 78,446, and of those, 41,252 are Hispanic or Latino—an increase of 185 percent over 1990. Reporter Carrie Budoff, in a May 19, 2003, *Philadelphia Inquirer* article headlined, "Battle Over Bilingual Ballot," had this to say about the impact of the changing demographics in Reading: "The culture shift could be felt on the streets, in restaurants, churches and bodegas, and in travel agencies promoting fares to Puerto Rico and beyond. Census numbers also told the story: Between 1990 and 2000, the Hispanic population doubled to 30,302, or 37.3 percent of the city. Puerto Ricans make up the majority of the city's Hispanics. For decades, Reading has been a magnet for Hispanics in search of better pay, much like Allentown, Lancaster and southern Chester County." In addition, Lehigh's Hispanic population was 15.1 percent in 2007, Monroe's was 11.6 percent, and Northampton's was 8.8 percent. For comparison purposes, Philadelphia's Hispanic population stands at 10.7 percent. The 1990 census data can be found at http://pasdc.hbg.psu.edu/pasdc/PA_Stats/census_data/historical_census/july2005/PAtab.htm. The U.S. Census Bureau, 2007 American Community Survey, can be found at http://factfinder.census.gov. And, for 2007 estimates, go to the U.S. Census Bureau, USA Counties, General Profile at http://censtats.census.gov/cgi-bin/usac/usacomp.pl.

52. Tom Infield, "A Surprising Bump for Obama in Conservative Lancaster County," *Philadelphia Inquirer*, November 8, 2008.

53. Josh Drobnyk and Scott Kraus, "Heartland Is McCain's Hope," *Allentown Morning Call*, October 26, 2008.

elected in the impressive 2006 Democratic advance. Three-term Republican Jim Gerlach won re-election with 52.1 percent to 47.9 percent for his Democratic challenger, Bob Roggio. Paul Kanjorski, a veteran Democratic congressman, held back a stiff challenge from Lou Barletta, the Republican mayor of Hazleton, a vociferous advocate of restrictive laws against illegal immigrants whose stance had gained considerable national attention. Kanjorski won with 51.6 percent of the vote to Barletta's 48.4 percent.

Two Democrats won "row" offices in 2008. Auditor General Jack Wagner was re-elected, and Rob McCord, a venture capitalist, was elected state treasurer. Tom Corbett, the Republican attorney general, defeated a challenge from Democrat John Morganelli, Northampton county's district attorney.

Democrats in the state House, who had won a narrow 102-to-101 majority two years earlier, added two seats in the 2008 election, giving them a 104-to-99 advantage. They did especially well in contests in several counties in the Philadelphia suburbs.[54] Republicans increased their majority in the state Senate by one seat, giving them a 29-to-20 margin, with one vacancy.

Incidentally, David's index of Democratic party strength in Pennsylvania, a measure I used in Figure 1.1 and referred to throughout the book, declined to 55.4 percent in 2008 from its record high of 58.7 percent two years earlier. However, the 2008 figure is only preliminary because there was not a U.S. Senate or governor's race in 2008. After the 2010 election, which will feature both of these major statewide contests, the permanent 2008 index can then be calculated by adding to the formula an average of the Democratic statewide vote in 2006 and 2010.[55] The Democratic presidential vote line used with the David index in Figure 1.1 rose to 55.4 percent in 2008 from 51.0 in 2004 as a result of Barack Obama's strong presidential victory in the Keystone State.

The 2008 exit polls provide further insight into the behavior of Pennsylvania's voters. Table 8.2 displays the results for the state next to the national figures, which allows for easy comparison. Among the first three panels, the most startling finding comes in the age breakdown. Pennsylvanians 18 to 29 years old gave Obama 65 percent of their votes, an amazing edge, although it was widely anticipated because of the highly visible support the Illinois Democrat received among young people throughout the campaign.[56] Neither the gender gap nor the racial division of the votes, visible in the second and third panels of Table 8.2, is particularly striking given past exit-poll patterns.

---

54. Derrick Nunnally, "Democrats Gain in Pa. Suburbs," *Philadelphia Inquirer*, November 6, 2008.

55. See Notes 18 and 19 on Page 6 for more on the construction of the David index. For 2008, the index consisted solely of the average percentage Democrats attained in the state's 19 U.S. House elections.

56. Kerry also did well among young Pennsylvanians, receiving 61 percent of their vote in this same age category, according to the 2004 exit polls. See Table 6.25.

Table 8.2 Exit Polls for President in 2008

		Pennsylvania (2,752 Respondents)				National (17,836 Respondents)	
		Obama	McCain			Obama	McCain
Gender				Gender			
Male	(46%)	51%	48%	Male	(47%)	49%	48%
Female	(54%)	59%	41%	Female	(53%)	56%	43%
		Obama	McCain			Obama	McCain
Age				Age			
18–29	(18%)	65%	35%	18–29	(18%)	66%	32%
30–44	(28%)	51%	47%	30–44	(29%)	52%	46%
45–64	(39%)	55%	43%	45–64	(37%)	50%	49%
65+	(15%)	49%	50%	65+	(16%)	45%	53%
		Obama	McCain			Obama	McCain
Race				Race			
White	(81%)	48%	51%	White	(74%)	43%	55%
Black	(13%)	95%	5%	Black	(13%)	95%	4%
Hispanic/ Latino	(4%)	72%	28%	Hispanic/ Latino	(9%)	67%	31%
Asian	(1%)	—	—	Asian	(2%)	62%	35%
Other	(1%)	—	—	Other	(3%)	66%	31%
		Obama	McCain			Obama	McCain
What was the last grade of school you completed?				What was the last grade of school you completed?			
Did not complete high school	(3%)	—	—	Did not complete high school	(4%)	63%	35%
High school graduate	(21%)	52%	47%	High school graduate	(20%)	52%	46%
Some college or associate degree	(25%)	53%	46%	Some college or associate degree	(31%)	51%	47%
College graduate	(27%)	52%	47%	College graduate	(28%)	50%	48%
Postgraduate study	(23%)	60%	39%	Postgraduate study	(17%)	58%	40%

Table 8.2 *(continued)*

		Pennsylvania (2,752 Respondents)				National (17,836 Respondents)	
		Obama	McCain			Obama	McCain
Religion				**Religion**			
Protestant/ Other Christian	(48%)	50%	49%	Protestant/ Other Christian	(54%)	45%	54%
Catholic	(32%)	48%	52%	Catholic	(27%)	54%	45%
Jewish	(4%)	—	—	Jewish	(2%)	78%	21%
Something else	(5%)	81%	16%	Something else	(6%)	73%	22%
None	(11%)	84%	15%	None	(12%)	75%	23%
		Obama	McCain			Obama	McCain
Which one of these five issues is the most important facing the country?				**Which one of these five issues is the most important facing the country?**			
Energy policy	(11%)	53%	45%	Energy policy	(7%)	50%	46%
The war in Iraq	(11%)	66%	34%	The war in Iraq	(10%)	59%	39%
The economy	(57%)	58%	41%	The economy	(63%)	53%	44%
Terrorism	(9%)	9%	90%	Terrorism	(9%)	13%	86%
Health care	(9%)	71%	27%	Health care	(9%)	73%	26%
		Obama	McCain			Obama	McCain
How do you feel about the U.S. war in Iraq?				**How do you feel about the U.S. war in Iraq?**			
Strongly approve	(14%)	7%	93%	Strongly approve	(14%)	4%	96%
Somewhat approve	(23%)	17%	83%	Somewhat approve	(22%)	18%	80%
Somewhat disapprove	(22%)	58%	39%	Somewhat disapprove	(21%)	55%	44%
Strongly disapprove	(41%)	91%	8%	Strongly disapprove	(41%)	87%	11%
		Obama	McCain			Obama	McCain
No matter how you voted today, do you usually think of yourself as a:				**No matter how you voted today, do you usually think of yourself as a:**			
Democrat	(44%)	90%	10%	Democrat	(39%)	89%	10%
Republican	(37%)	13%	87%	Republican	(32%)	9%	90%
Independent or something else	(18%)	58%	39%	Independent or something else	(29%)	52%	44%

Table 8.2 *(continued)*

	Pennsylvania (2,752 Respondents)			National (17,836 Respondents)	
	Obama	McCain		Obama	McCain
On most political matters, do you consider yourself:			On most political matters, do you consider yourself:		
Liberal (23%)	91%	9%	Liberal (22%)	89%	10%
Moderate (50%)	58%	41%	Moderate (44%)	60%	39%
Conservative (27%)	19%	79%	Conservative (34%)	20%	78%
	Obama	McCain		Obama	McCain
Pennsylvania Regions			National Regions		
Philadelphia (12%)	83%	16%	East (21%)	59%	40%
Philly Suburbs (21%)	58%	41%	Midwest (24%)	54%	44%
Northeast (14%)	57%	42%	South (32%)	45%	54%
Pitt Area/West (23%)	53%	46%	West (23%)	57%	40%
Central/ Northern Tier (30%)	42%	57%			

Note: The percentage in parenthesis is the percent of respondents in that category.

Source: The 2008 Presidential Exit Polls for Pennsylvania and the Nation, conducted by Edison Media Research.

But, of course, how Obama, the first African-American presidential nominee, would do among white voters drew considerable attention. The 48 percent of the vote among white Pennsylvanians that Obama received was, in fact, two percentages points higher than Kerry's percentage among whites four years earlier; see Table 6.6. Nationwide, Obama's white percentage was lower, partly reflecting the abysmal percentage of white support he received in several states in the American South. For example, the exit polls showed that Obama received only 11 percent of the white vote in Mississippi and 10 percent in Alabama![57] That result alone debunks James Carville's trite, but much-quoted remark that "Pennsylvania is made up of Philadelphia and Pittsburgh with Alabama in between."[58]

The figures on education level reveal the continuation of strong Democratic support among the most highly educated Pennsylvanians. Of the 23 percent who have studied beyond a college degree, Obama won 60 percent of their votes compared to 39 percent for McCain. The national results are similar. Another panel shows that Obama did less well among Pennsylvania Catholics than he did among Catholics nationwide. However, Obama did better among Protestants than Kerry (see Table 6.25) and even slightly edged out McCain in this category.

57. http://www.cnn.com/election/results/polls.

58. Quoted by Scott LaMar, WITF-TV (PBS) Harrisburg, in "Voter Turnout May Be the Key to Winning Pennsylvania," September 22, 2004, found at http://www.pbs.org/elections/archives/essays_shell.html?essay_scottlamar.

The overriding concern with the economy that permeated the fall campaign is reflected in the exit poll question asking respondents which of five specified issues was "the most important [issue] facing the country." Fifty-seven percent of Pennsylvanians chose the economy, and, of those, 58 percent voted for Obama. Nine percent of the sample picked terrorism, and, of them, 90 percent voted for McCain. Of the 11 percent who chose the war in Iraq, 66 percent cast a ballot for Obama. When asked, "How do you feel about the U.S. war in Iraq?" 63 percent of the sample disapproved. Of those who "strongly disapproved," (41 percent of the Pennsylvania sample), 91 percent voted for Obama.

Another exit-poll panel reveals that 90 percent of self-identified Democrats in Pennsylvania voted for Obama. In 2004, the figure for Kerry was 85 percent; see Table 6.25. For McCain, 87 percent of self-identified Republicans supported him, slightly below the percentage backing President Bush four years earlier. Independents preferred the Illinois Democrat by 58 percent to 39 percent for McCain. Of the overall 2008 exit-poll sample, 44 percent identified with the Democratic party, 37 percent with the Republican party, and 18 percent said they were Independents or something else. In another panel, self-identified liberals gave Obama 91 percent of their votes; self-identified conservatives gave McCain 79 percent of their votes. Moderates, who occupied 50 percent of the Pennsylvania sample, broke for Obama, 58 percent to 41 percent for McCain.

Finally, the last panel reports the presidential vote of Pennsylvania respondents by the state's five geographical divisions introduced in Chapter 6 and used for the last several decades by exit-poll takers. The boundaries of the five divisions are displayed in the map in Figure 6.23. Compared to the 2004 presidential-vote results, which are found in Table 6.7, the 2008 results are quite revealing and fully supportive of the aggregate data analysis of the 2008 outcome already done in this postscript. Obama did 6 percentage points better than Kerry among respondents living in the Northeast counties; 5 percentage points better among residents of the Central and Northern Tier; 4 percentage points better among those in the Philadelphia suburbs, and 2 percentage points better among Philadelphia residents. Kerry had a one-percentage-point edge over Obama in the Pittsburgh area/West.[59]

Soon after the votes were counted and the exit-poll results released, speculation began concerning whether the 2008 results indicated that a new realignment of the American political party system was under way.[60] Certainly the Obama victory broke new ground, apart from what it said about the electorate's racial tolerance. The 2008 electoral configuration amassed by Obama, which is displayed in Figure 8.1 at the beginning of this postscript, shattered the closely balanced party

---

59. One would like to do further analysis of the 2008 exit-poll data using these five geographical divisions, as I did in Chapter 6, but the exit polls won't be made available to scholars for their own independent analysis until later in 2009.

60. For a sampling of the conjecture, see Robert G. Kaiser, "Pollsters Debate America's Political Realignment," *Washington Post*, November 23, 2008.

system in existence during the 2000 and 2004 elections and is truly national in scope, leaving no region of the country behind.

Is there evidence in Obama's path-breaking victory of a major upheaval in the party system? Before addressing that question, further investigation of what propelled Obama's election is in order. After hearing the analysis of the campaign managers, reading the insider accounts of the campaign, studying the polls, and considering everything the nominees did, including their vice-presidential selections, ultimately one must conclude that the 2008 election turned on the state of the economy. Following months of dire warning signs, the financial and economic crisis that descended during the fall 2008 campaign had no counterpart in an American presidential election since the 1932 election, which was fought out three years after the famous stock market crash of October 1929 and the onset of the Great Depression. The 2008 pre-election surveys point to the importance of the economy as do the exit polls just covered above.

Further, impressionistic data from the voters and politicians show it, too. Interviewing voters shopping in Butler in early October, an Associated Press reporter quoted a lifelong Republican, Ruth Ann Michel, a 64-year-old retiree, as follows: "I don't know that there's anything I particularly like about him [Obama], but I dislike McCain, and I dislike the way the country is, and Republicans need to change." "She said her vote for Mr. Obama would be her first for a Democratic presidential candidate," the AP reporter, Kimberly Hefling, noted.[61] In a late October article, headlined "Looking for Election Cues in Scranton," a *Philadelphia Inquirer* reporter, Thomas Fitzgerald, wrote:

> Melissa Yanchak, who was bowling with her grandmother . . . and a few other women Tuesday, said that she planned to back Obama because "his policies are for everyone as a whole." She thinks McCain favors business.
>
> "I don't feel he'll lead the country in the direction I want it to go," said Yanchak, 29, who works in a bank's call center. "I didn't care for him in the debates, the way he was interrupting Obama, the facial expressions he was making. He seems very shady."
>
> Her grandmother, Reggie, 78, said McCain offered nothing for the economic struggles of working people. "People are losing their jobs, they're going overseas," said Reggie, who declined to give her last name. "Bush is worse than Herbert Hoover."
>
> Mayor Chris Doherty [of Scranton], a Democrat who backed Clinton in the primary, said that he had lately found it easier to persuade skeptics to support Obama. "The downturn in the economy has

---

61. Kimberly Hefling, "Region Belatedly Moving to Obama," *Pittsburgh Post-Gazette* (Associated Press dispatch), October 12, 2008.

changed this election," he said. "People are upset at Republican policies, and they vote their pocketbooks."[62]

Governor Rendell summed it up as follows: "This election is going to be decided
when a husband and wife sit at a kitchen table, or a single parent sits at the kitchen
table, looks at their bills and figures out who is most likely to help them with their
financial condition. If the answer's Barack Obama, nobody's going to care whether
he's black, green, orange, purple, fuschia, or whatever."[63] On Election Night, as the
results became clear, Bob Asher, co-chairman of McCain's Pennsylvania campaign
and a resident of Montgomery county, said that he was optimistic McCain could
carry the Keystone State "up until about six weeks ago." "We really felt," Asher continued, "we were very much in the game. But then the economy went south. That
was very difficult for us. It refocused the whole campaign more on the economy
and President Bush."[64]

Of course, other factors aside from the economy were at play. They included
widespread dissatisfaction with the Iraq war, as captured in the exit polls; disap-
pointment in the overall performance of the Republican incumbent, President
Bush; the impressive "ground game" of the Obama team, which put field offices in
counties around the country that hadn't seen such retail politics from Democrats
in decades, and McCain's selection of Palin as his running-mate, which energized
the socially conservative GOP base while, at the same time, alienating moderates.

Recognizing that Obama won the 2008 election in large part because of the
poor condition of the economy suggests that what happened in 1932 is likely to
be our guide for the future. Thus, the answer to the realignment question must
be that it depends on how President Obama and his administration cope with the
many challenges they face. Keep in mind that the New Deal realignment, as related
in Chapter 1, came about because of the substantive actions and achievements of
President Roosevelt and his Democratic allies in Congress during the dramatic
events of FDR's first term. Winning the 1932 election only gave them the chance to
succeed—or to fail.

We don't know, of course, what the future holds, but the current political situation does suggest a core issue or cluster of issues that could serve as the linchpin
for a new realignment: the challenges of the new global economy and how to
restructure American society to become a winner in this competition in a way that
economically benefits a large segment of the country and protects the environment
while at the same time finding new, environmentally safe sources of energy. Related
to this could be a new strategy for leading effective international cooperation to
deal with the global aspects of these domestic initiatives. If substantive, successful

---

62. Thomas Fitzgerald, "Looking for Election Clues in Scranton," *Philadelphia Inquirer*,
October 24, 2008.

63. Hefling, "Region Belatedly Moving to Obama."

64. Tom Infield, "Philadelphia Region a Key to Obama's Win in Penna.," *Philadelphia Inquirer*,
November 5, 2008.

change along these lines is accomplished by President Obama and his Democratic party, the impact on our politics would likely be measured at the high level reached by the New Deal realignment, and Pennsylvania certainly would be at the epicenter of any such transformation. But, all of that is—or is not—in the future.

What do the 2008 results tells us more immediately about the direction of the Keystone State's politics? The recent successes of the Democratic party in Pennsylvania are impressive—from the surge in overall party registration as reported above to the party's emerging strength in rapidly growing and changing parts of the state where it had not been competitive previously. The Democrats' statewide victories in 2006 and 2008 illustrate a breadth of appeal that ought not to be overlooked.

Consider, for example, a scattergram of Senator Casey's 58.6 percent victory pattern in 2006 with President Obama's 54.7 percent winning pattern in 2008. See Figure 8.6. The two Democrats—one prolife, the other prochoice—yield a correlation coefficient of 0.88, indicating more than a little divergence among the counties in support for these two Democrats as displayed in the scattergram. All of the counties to the right of the vertical 50-percent line and below the horizontal 50-percent line—the bulk of them in western Pennsylvania—were carried

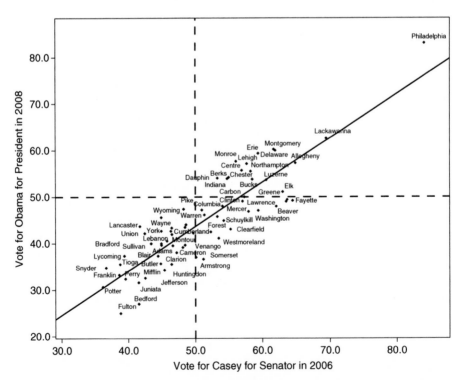

Fig. 8.6. Scattergram of the Democratic Vote for Senator in 2006 and President in 2008

by Casey, but not Obama. Of course, the pair shared all the counties above the horizontal line.

Obama and Casey, who has a more socially conservative image than the Illinois Democrat, are political allies and friends. If the issues that dominate national politics in the immediate years ahead are not the divisive social issues of the past, it seems plausible that Obama, with Casey's help and guidance, could improve his support in areas where Casey is the stronger of the two. Governor Rendell's victory pattern in 2006 is closer to Obama's—correlation coefficient of 0.92. As I illustrated in Chapter 7 with a scattergram of Casey and Rendell in 2006 (correlation coefficient of 0.89), these two leading Pennsylvania Democratic politicians draw from broad, overlapping areas of support; see Figure 7.2. Whether that broad coalition continues to win statewide elections for the Democratic party is yet to be determined, but its potential for continued success should not be minimized.

As for Pennsylvania's Republicans, they have their work cut out for them. They are in their weakest position in years for all the reasons cited above as to why the state's Democrats are on the ascendancy. Most telling of all, apart from the weak McCain performance in the state and the recent success of Democrats in U.S. House races, are the stark party-registration figures. To watch your opposition party gain 600,000 registered voters in the eighteen months before the November 2008 election while your party's total of registered voters decline by 15,000 has to be disquieting.

Detailed examination of registration figures from April 21, the day before the 2008 Pennsylvania primary, until November 2, two days before the general election, contain even more bad news. Of the 492,838 Pennsylvanians who registered to vote during that period, 55.6 percent chose to register as Democrats, 21.0 percent as Republicans, and 23.4 percent opted for the "other" category. Over the same period, 106,971 registered voters chose to change their registration to one of the two major parties from the other major party or from the "other" category. Of these switchers, 70.5 percent picked the Democratic party and 29.5 percent the GOP. If those numbers aren't bad enough for the Republican party, newly released official information on the age of all Pennsylvania registered voters by party ought to jolt them. Of the 754,447 voters in the 18 to 24 year old range who were registered with either the Democratic or Republican parties as of November 2, 2008, 67.3 percent were Democrats and 32.7 percent were Republicans. Needless to say, a political party that is not attracting young people has a shaky future.[65]

Right after the election, Michael Smerconish, the Philadelphia radio talk show host, gave this blistering assessment of the GOP's plight in his *Philadelphia Inquirer* column. Arguing that McCain played "to the party's base to the exclusion of more independent-thinking suburbanites," he wrote: "There was no pitch

65. The web site of the Pennsylvania Department of State's Bureau of Commissions, Elections, and Legislation, Voter Registration Statistics at http://www.dos.state.pa.us/bcel/site/default.asp.

made to moderates. Instead, there were direct and indirect efforts by the McCain campaign to whip up the base." Smerconish concluded: "The GOP will continue to lose Pennsylvania, and hence the nation, until it comes to grips with the fact that it is ideologically out of touch with concerns of residents here and in similar communities across the country. The campaign needed a platform that spoke to the constituency that votes for Sen. Arlen Specter and [Governor] Rendell regardless of their party affiliation."[66]

At the end of the first decade of the 21st century, the national political environment, as noted above, is drastically different from what it was when Ronald Reagan was riding high. The first Democratic president from the North since John F. Kennedy in 1961 has taken office. President Obama enters the White House with solid Democratic majorities in both houses of Congress, and his Democratic allies are in broad sympathy with his policy outlook. This has not happened for the party of the New Deal since its modern formation during the twenty-year era of Franklin Roosevelt and Harry Truman. The new president has assembled an experienced team of advisers and executive branch officials widely representative of his reasonably unified Democratic party. Daunting challenges await the new Democratic administration in Washington. Upon the outcome of these upcoming political struggles and challenges rests, among other things, the likely shape of the electoral landscape of the nation and Pennsylvania for years to come.

---

66. Michael Smerconish, "Head Strong: Ignoring Suburbs Doomed the GOP," *Philadelphia Inquirer*, November 9, 2008.

Appendix A
Correlations of Pennsylvania County-Level Election Returns

Table A.1 Correlations of the Democratic Vote for President, 1896–2004

	P1896D	P1900D	P1904D	P1908D	P1912D	P1916D	P1920D	P1924D	P1928D	P1932D	P1936D	P1940D	P1944D	P1948D
P1896D	1	0.943	0.852	0.905	0.850	0.898	0.796	0.718	0.317	0.677	0.370	0.340	0.293	0.385
P1900D	0.943	1	0.943	0.981	0.937	0.930	0.874	0.799	0.308	0.659	0.370	0.365	0.286	0.330
P1904D	0.852	0.943	1	0.956	0.961	0.892	0.861	0.851	0.239	0.628	0.338	0.345	0.248	0.281
P1908D	0.905	0.981	0.956	1	0.963	0.937	0.897	0.830	0.342	0.688	0.428	0.424	0.345	0.376
P1912D	0.850	0.937	0.961	0.963	1	0.920	0.886	0.881	0.201	0.608	0.311	0.316	0.224	0.255
P1916D	0.898	0.930	0.892	0.937	0.920	1	0.904	0.850	0.228	0.677	0.419	0.411	0.323	0.372
P1920D	0.796	0.874	0.861	0.897	0.886	0.904	1	0.894	0.239	0.687	0.488	0.521	0.403	0.425
P1924D	0.718	0.799	0.851	0.830	0.881	0.850	0.894	1	0.064	0.555	0.253	0.280	0.150	0.207
P1928D	0.317	0.308	0.239	0.342	0.201	0.228	0.239	0.064	1	0.682	0.566	0.558	0.654	0.638
P1932D	0.677	0.659	0.628	0.688	0.608	0.677	0.687	0.555	0.682	1	0.742	0.722	0.692	0.743
P1936D	0.370	0.370	0.338	0.428	0.311	0.419	0.488	0.253	0.566	0.742	1	0.967	0.944	0.916
P1940D	0.340	0.365	0.345	0.424	0.316	0.411	0.521	0.280	0.558	0.722	0.967	1	0.956	0.907
P1944D	0.293	0.286	0.248	0.345	0.224	0.323	0.403	0.150	0.654	0.692	0.944	0.956	1	0.953
P1948D	0.385	0.330	0.281	0.376	0.255	0.372	0.425	0.207	0.638	0.743	0.916	0.907	0.953	1
P1952D	0.225	0.170	0.143	0.231	0.123	0.216	0.297	0.064	0.620	0.664	0.894	0.900	0.956	0.954
P1956D	0.216	0.166	0.144	0.232	0.133	0.219	0.319	0.107	0.587	0.663	0.847	0.865	0.913	0.918
P1960D	0.089	0.048	-0.009	0.106	-0.031	0.026	0.078	-0.141	0.798	0.544	0.722	0.731	0.849	0.809
P1964D	0.331	0.244	0.140	0.263	0.121	0.201	0.246	-0.006	0.682	0.600	0.763	0.742	0.844	0.851
P1968D	0.172	0.092	0.004	0.126	-0.013	0.063	0.104	-0.156	0.704	0.520	0.734	0.718	0.843	0.825
P1972D	0.098	0.030	-0.031	0.077	-0.030	0.024	0.079	-0.143	0.638	0.473	0.659	0.662	0.776	0.754
P1976D	0.247	0.153	0.056	0.182	0.046	0.134	0.175	-0.059	0.662	0.563	0.712	0.715	0.808	0.824
P1980D	0.127	-0.011	-0.103	0.018	-0.108	0.009	0.055	-0.154	0.600	0.512	0.665	0.643	0.759	0.796
P1984D	0.024	-0.089	-0.155	-0.049	-0.162	-0.048	-0.020	-0.239	0.567	0.458	0.674	0.641	0.761	0.763
P1988D	0.030	-0.099	-0.169	-0.067	-0.178	-0.065	-0.042	-0.250	0.581	0.452	0.652	0.615	0.742	0.761
P1992D	-0.024	-0.114	-0.148	-0.061	-0.143	-0.071	-0.037	-0.234	0.541	0.382	0.616	0.592	0.724	0.706
P1996D	-0.021	-0.060	-0.101	-0.005	-0.090	-0.041	-0.007	-0.215	0.578	0.325	0.560	0.562	0.693	0.631
P2000D	-0.035	-0.025	-0.049	0.040	-0.033	-0.019	0.000	-0.203	0.576	0.296	0.545	0.546	0.667	0.574
P2004D	-0.062	-0.043	-0.052	0.022	-0.033	-0.047	-0.040	-0.222	0.537	0.223	0.464	0.464	0.588	0.481

Table A.1 (continued)

	P1952D	P1956D	P1960D	P1964D	P1968D	P1972D	P1976D	P1980D	P1984D	P1988D	P1992D	P1996D	P2000D	P2004D
P1896D	0.225	0.216	0.089	0.331	0.172	0.098	0.247	0.127	0.024	0.030	-0.024	-0.021	-0.035	-0.062
P1900D	0.170	0.166	0.048	0.244	0.092	0.030	0.153	-0.011	-0.089	-0.099	-0.114	-0.060	-0.025	-0.043
P1904D	0.143	0.144	-0.009	0.140	0.004	-0.031	0.056	-0.103	-0.155	-0.169	-0.148	-0.101	-0.049	-0.052
P1908D	0.231	0.232	0.106	0.263	0.126	0.077	0.182	0.018	-0.049	-0.067	-0.061	-0.005	0.040	0.022
P1912D	0.123	0.133	-0.031	0.121	-0.013	-0.030	0.046	-0.108	-0.162	-0.178	-0.143	-0.090	-0.033	-0.033
P1916D	0.216	0.219	0.026	0.201	0.063	0.024	0.134	0.009	-0.048	-0.065	-0.071	-0.041	-0.019	-0.047
P1920D	0.297	0.319	0.078	0.246	0.104	0.079	0.175	0.055	-0.020	-0.042	-0.037	-0.007	0.000	-0.040
P1924D	0.064	0.107	-0.141	-0.006	-0.156	-0.143	-0.059	-0.154	-0.239	-0.250	-0.234	-0.215	-0.203	-0.222
P1928D	0.620	0.587	0.798	0.682	0.704	0.638	0.662	0.600	0.567	0.581	0.541	0.578	0.576	0.537
P1932D	0.664	0.663	0.544	0.600	0.520	0.473	0.563	0.512	0.458	0.452	0.382	0.325	0.296	0.223
P1936D	0.894	0.847	0.722	0.763	0.734	0.659	0.712	0.665	0.674	0.652	0.616	0.560	0.545	0.464
P1940D	0.900	0.865	0.731	0.742	0.718	0.662	0.715	0.643	0.641	0.615	0.592	0.562	0.546	0.464
P1944D	0.956	0.913	0.849	0.844	0.843	0.776	0.808	0.759	0.761	0.742	0.724	0.693	0.667	0.588
P1948D	0.954	0.918	0.809	0.851	0.825	0.754	0.824	0.796	0.763	0.761	0.706	0.631	0.574	0.481
P1952D	1	0.973	0.879	0.845	0.867	0.827	0.861	0.846	0.848	0.832	0.798	0.718	0.662	0.568
P1956D	0.973	1	0.861	0.814	0.827	0.822	0.858	0.841	0.823	0.810	0.786	0.711	0.641	0.545
P1960D	0.879	0.861	1	0.870	0.931	0.896	0.899	0.858	0.864	0.853	0.851	0.843	0.817	0.750
P1964D	0.845	0.814	0.870	1	0.957	0.901	0.930	0.865	0.839	0.843	0.811	0.785	0.734	0.664
P1968D	0.867	0.827	0.931	0.957	1	0.932	0.940	0.902	0.914	0.906	0.889	0.865	0.830	0.760
P1972D	0.827	0.822	0.896	0.901	0.932	1	0.925	0.878	0.893	0.887	0.904	0.886	0.848	0.797
P1976D	0.861	0.858	0.899	0.930	0.940	0.925	1	0.935	0.905	0.905	0.877	0.844	0.776	0.691
P1980D	0.846	0.841	0.858	0.865	0.902	0.878	0.935	1	0.950	0.954	0.899	0.811	0.705	0.614
P1984D	0.848	0.823	0.864	0.839	0.914	0.893	0.905	0.950	1	0.987	0.956	0.865	0.797	0.713
P1988D	0.832	0.810	0.853	0.843	0.906	0.887	0.905	0.954	0.987	1	0.957	0.863	0.777	0.696
P1992D	0.798	0.786	0.851	0.811	0.889	0.904	0.877	0.899	0.956	0.957	1	0.949	0.891	0.831
P1996D	0.718	0.711	0.843	0.785	0.865	0.886	0.844	0.811	0.865	0.863	0.949	1	0.966	0.924
P2000D	0.662	0.641	0.817	0.734	0.830	0.848	0.776	0.705	0.797	0.777	0.891	0.966	1	0.978
P2004D	0.568	0.545	0.750	0.664	0.760	0.797	0.691	0.614	0.713	0.696	0.831	0.924	0.978	1

Table A.2   Correlations of the Republican Vote for President, 1896–2004

	P1896R	P1900R	P1904R	P1908R	P1912R	P1916R	P1920R	P1924R	P1928R	P1932R	P1936R	P1940R	P1944R	P1948R
P1896R	1	0.963	0.928	0.936	0.536	0.903	0.829	0.764	0.302	0.640	0.328	0.295	0.257	0.317
P1900R	0.963	1	0.956	0.952	0.548	0.874	0.807	0.769	0.310	0.623	0.318	0.309	0.252	0.283
P1904R	0.928	0.956	1	0.937	0.492	0.856	0.767	0.754	0.256	0.606	0.290	0.264	0.221	0.265
P1908R	0.936	0.952	0.937	1	0.534	0.917	0.842	0.801	0.393	0.714	0.452	0.409	0.390	0.440
P1912R	0.536	0.548	0.492	0.534	1	0.519	0.434	0.435	0.187	0.380	0.130	0.093	0.050	0.145
P1916R	0.903	0.874	0.856	0.917	0.519	1	0.883	0.786	0.210	0.652	0.413	0.353	0.321	0.402
P1920R	0.829	0.807	0.767	0.842	0.434	0.883	1	0.832	0.290	0.708	0.553	0.549	0.483	0.529
P1924R	0.764	0.769	0.754	0.801	0.435	0.786	0.832	1	0.436	0.839	0.575	0.582	0.500	0.562
P1928R	0.302	0.310	0.256	0.393	0.187	0.210	0.290	0.436	1	0.682	0.640	0.586	0.673	0.652
P1932R	0.640	0.623	0.606	0.714	0.380	0.652	0.708	0.839	0.682	1	0.797	0.764	0.733	0.776
P1936R	0.328	0.318	0.290	0.452	0.130	0.413	0.553	0.575	0.640	0.797	1	0.949	0.948	0.918
P1940R	0.295	0.309	0.264	0.409	0.093	0.353	0.549	0.582	0.586	0.764	0.949	1	0.955	0.903
P1944R	0.257	0.252	0.221	0.390	0.050	0.321	0.483	0.500	0.673	0.733	0.948	0.955	1	0.961
P1948R	0.317	0.283	0.265	0.440	0.145	0.402	0.529	0.562	0.652	0.776	0.918	0.903	0.961	1
P1952R	0.177	0.143	0.136	0.312	0.026	0.248	0.391	0.435	0.638	0.701	0.889	0.898	0.956	0.963
P1956R	0.169	0.142	0.135	0.302	-0.010	0.229	0.397	0.459	0.609	0.695	0.836	0.867	0.914	0.927
P1960R	0.051	0.039	0.007	0.192	-0.079	0.057	0.164	0.260	0.805	0.566	0.752	0.734	0.849	0.827
P1964R	0.300	0.240	0.194	0.379	0.071	0.292	0.374	0.404	0.695	0.633	0.794	0.744	0.847	0.858
P1968R	0.120	0.080	0.061	0.260	-0.047	0.161	0.252	0.309	0.700	0.595	0.803	0.767	0.879	0.874
P1972R	0.091	0.056	0.032	0.223	-0.107	0.103	0.181	0.250	0.651	0.513	0.701	0.677	0.789	0.778
P1976R	0.216	0.162	0.118	0.310	0.028	0.210	0.310	0.352	0.669	0.587	0.733	0.722	0.815	0.833
P1980R	0.104	0.035	0.008	0.210	-0.078	0.139	0.217	0.254	0.570	0.489	0.703	0.667	0.785	0.798
P1984R	-0.013	-0.073	-0.077	0.128	-0.083	0.064	0.130	0.199	0.574	0.472	0.685	0.645	0.766	0.784
P1988R	-0.001	-0.075	-0.078	0.124	-0.077	0.069	0.138	0.208	0.587	0.467	0.668	0.617	0.746	0.777
P1992R	0.087	0.009	0.016	0.202	-0.067	0.118	0.148	0.170	0.569	0.422	0.613	0.550	0.701	0.729
P1996R	0.069	0.037	0.022	0.177	-0.105	0.049	0.113	0.126	0.641	0.355	0.542	0.509	0.656	0.636
P2000R	-0.034	-0.008	-0.012	0.119	-0.225	-0.023	0.033	0.076	0.590	0.312	0.561	0.538	0.658	0.587
P2004R	-0.076	-0.049	-0.045	0.072	-0.275	-0.074	-0.021	0.007	0.545	0.247	0.502	0.469	0.591	0.506

Table A.2 *(continued)*

	P1952R	P1956R	P1960R	P1964R	P1968R	P1972R	P1976R	P1980R	P1984R	P1988R	P1992R	P1996R	P2000R	P2004R
P1896R	0.177	0.169	0.051	0.300	0.120	0.091	0.216	0.104	−0.013	−0.001	0.087	0.069	−0.034	−0.076
P1900R	0.143	0.142	0.039	0.240	0.080	0.056	0.162	0.035	−0.073	−0.075	0.009	0.037	−0.008	−0.049
P1904R	0.136	0.135	0.007	0.194	0.061	0.032	0.118	0.008	−0.077	−0.078	0.016	0.022	−0.012	−0.045
P1908R	0.312	0.302	0.192	0.379	0.260	0.223	0.310	0.210	0.128	0.124	0.202	0.177	0.119	0.072
P1912R	0.026	−0.010	−0.079	0.071	−0.047	−0.107	0.028	−0.078	−0.083	−0.077	−0.067	−0.105	−0.225	−0.275
P1916R	0.248	0.229	0.057	0.292	0.161	0.103	0.210	0.139	0.064	0.069	0.118	0.049	−0.023	−0.074
P1920R	0.391	0.397	0.164	0.374	0.252	0.181	0.310	0.217	0.130	0.138	0.148	0.113	0.033	−0.021
P1924R	0.435	0.459	0.260	0.404	0.309	0.250	0.352	0.254	0.199	0.208	0.170	0.126	0.076	0.007
P1928R	0.638	0.609	0.805	0.695	0.700	0.651	0.669	0.570	0.574	0.587	0.569	0.641	0.590	0.545
P1932R	0.701	0.695	0.566	0.633	0.595	0.513	0.587	0.489	0.472	0.467	0.422	0.355	0.312	0.247
P1936R	0.889	0.836	0.752	0.794	0.803	0.701	0.733	0.703	0.685	0.668	0.613	0.542	0.561	0.502
P1940R	0.898	0.867	0.734	0.744	0.767	0.677	0.722	0.667	0.645	0.617	0.550	0.509	0.538	0.469
P1944R	0.956	0.914	0.849	0.847	0.879	0.789	0.815	0.785	0.766	0.746	0.701	0.656	0.658	0.591
P1948R	0.963	0.927	0.827	0.858	0.874	0.778	0.833	0.798	0.784	0.777	0.729	0.636	0.587	0.506
P1952R	1	0.973	0.881	0.846	0.917	0.836	0.866	0.839	0.851	0.835	0.771	0.684	0.646	0.569
P1956R	0.973	1	0.864	0.814	0.891	0.828	0.860	0.822	0.823	0.808	0.742	0.676	0.626	0.548
P1960R	0.881	0.864	1	0.870	0.943	0.897	0.898	0.856	0.868	0.856	0.826	0.834	0.813	0.752
P1964R	0.846	0.814	0.870	1	0.935	0.901	0.933	0.893	0.841	0.845	0.855	0.804	0.741	0.672
P1968R	0.917	0.891	0.943	0.935	1	0.938	0.937	0.933	0.930	0.914	0.891	0.823	0.804	0.739
P1972R	0.836	0.828	0.897	0.901	0.938	1	0.937	0.929	0.897	0.886	0.889	0.859	0.843	0.796
P1976R	0.866	0.860	0.898	0.933	0.937	0.937	1	0.938	0.911	0.909	0.904	0.872	0.783	0.704
P1980R	0.839	0.822	0.856	0.893	0.933	0.929	0.938	1	0.956	0.955	0.935	0.861	0.803	0.746
P1984R	0.851	0.823	0.868	0.841	0.930	0.897	0.911	0.956	1	0.987	0.933	0.846	0.791	0.718
P1988R	0.835	0.808	0.856	0.845	0.914	0.886	0.909	0.955	0.987	1	0.947	0.858	0.774	0.702
P1992R	0.771	0.742	0.826	0.855	0.891	0.889	0.904	0.935	0.933	0.947	1	0.914	0.826	0.769
P1996R	0.684	0.676	0.834	0.804	0.823	0.859	0.872	0.861	0.846	0.858	0.914	1	0.920	0.870
P2000R	0.646	0.626	0.813	0.741	0.804	0.843	0.783	0.803	0.791	0.774	0.826	0.920	1	0.980
P2004R	0.569	0.548	0.752	0.672	0.739	0.796	0.704	0.746	0.718	0.702	0.769	0.870	0.980	1

Table A.3   Correlations of the Democratic Vote for President, Governor, and Senator, 1960–2004

	P1960D	G1962D	S1962D	P1964D	S1964D	G1966D	P1968D	S1968D	G1970D	S1970D	P1972D	S1974D	G1974D	P1976D
P1960D	1	0.922	0.926	0.870	0.795	0.893	0.931	0.892	0.819	0.627	0.896	0.686	0.761	0.899
G1962D	0.922	1	0.964	0.896	0.865	0.942	0.895	0.943	0.835	0.641	0.871	0.668	0.818	0.920
S1962D	0.926	0.964	1	0.922	0.857	0.963	0.929	0.940	0.885	0.671	0.886	0.784	0.784	0.929
P1964D	0.870	0.896	0.922	1	0.846	0.926	0.957	0.933	0.916	0.693	0.901	0.673	0.770	0.930
S1964D	0.795	0.865	0.857	0.846	1	0.839	0.816	0.858	0.806	0.634	0.757	0.593	0.751	0.862
G1966D	0.893	0.942	0.963	0.926	0.839	1	0.927	0.921	0.927	0.684	0.881	0.772	0.769	0.913
P1968D	0.931	0.895	0.929	0.957	0.816	0.927	1	0.945	0.915	0.657	0.932	0.707	0.774	0.940
S1968D	0.892	0.943	0.940	0.933	0.858	0.921	0.945	1	0.855	0.610	0.899	0.639	0.803	0.924
G1970D	0.819	0.835	0.885	0.916	0.806	0.927	0.915	0.855	1	0.713	0.854	0.757	0.783	0.869
S1970D	0.627	0.641	0.671	0.693	0.634	0.684	0.657	0.610	0.713	1	0.608	0.529	0.508	0.658
P1972D	0.896	0.871	0.886	0.901	0.757	0.881	0.932	0.899	0.854	0.608	1	0.648	0.790	0.925
S1974D	0.686	0.668	0.784	0.673	0.593	0.772	0.707	0.639	0.757	0.529	0.648	1	0.481	0.699
G1974D	0.761	0.818	0.784	0.770	0.751	0.769	0.774	0.803	0.783	0.508	0.790	0.481	1	0.767
P1976D	0.899	0.920	0.929	0.930	0.862	0.913	0.940	0.924	0.869	0.658	0.925	0.699	0.767	1
S1976D	0.658	0.714	0.599	0.668	0.679	0.589	0.646	0.714	0.523	0.451	0.691	0.200	0.668	0.741
G1978D	0.730	0.725	0.812	0.730	0.670	0.832	0.771	0.683	0.820	0.560	0.691	0.936	0.552	0.782
P1980D	0.858	0.862	0.904	0.865	0.745	0.893	0.902	0.864	0.821	0.628	0.878	0.772	0.678	0.935
S1980D	0.718	0.707	0.811	0.754	0.646	0.837	0.787	0.701	0.796	0.566	0.708	0.908	0.483	0.786
G1982D	0.699	0.754	0.738	0.696	0.751	0.748	0.711	0.724	0.679	0.521	0.676	0.603	0.624	0.811

Table A.3 *(continued)*

	P1960D	G1962D	S1962D	P1964D	S1964D	G1966D	P1968D	S1968D	G1970D	S1970D	P1972D	S1974D	G1974D	P1976D
S1982D	0.869	0.895	0.884	0.834	0.824	0.862	0.856	0.862	0.783	0.661	0.850	0.703	0.689	0.942
P1984D	0.864	0.828	0.887	0.839	0.715	0.875	0.914	0.859	0.850	0.582	0.893	0.793	0.710	0.905
G1986D	0.814	0.789	0.814	0.755	0.737	0.821	0.806	0.755	0.714	0.534	0.741	0.730	0.570	0.860
S1986D	0.884	0.881	0.909	0.857	0.792	0.904	0.902	0.874	0.848	0.591	0.880	0.783	0.774	0.913
P1988D	0.853	0.817	0.873	0.843	0.699	0.871	0.906	0.840	0.846	0.572	0.887	0.787	0.680	0.905
S1988D	0.851	0.838	0.813	0.773	0.705	0.793	0.832	0.836	0.741	0.598	0.879	0.581	0.757	0.876
G1990D	0.574	0.584	0.590	0.575	0.627	0.619	0.582	0.573	0.521	0.368	0.470	0.522	0.423	0.576
S1991D	0.880	0.827	0.863	0.856	0.732	0.838	0.925	0.869	0.812	0.536	0.897	0.694	0.690	0.919
P1992D	0.851	0.798	0.835	0.811	0.655	0.815	0.889	0.835	0.793	0.527	0.904	0.683	0.713	0.877
S1992D	0.802	0.783	0.815	0.855	0.715	0.798	0.885	0.861	0.763	0.575	0.869	0.591	0.643	0.892
G1994D	0.780	0.752	0.728	0.670	0.644	0.693	0.754	0.754	0.617	0.373	0.771	0.517	0.748	0.783
S1994D	0.865	0.818	0.809	0.800	0.724	0.787	0.878	0.852	0.734	0.485	0.883	0.539	0.762	0.878
P1996D	0.843	0.768	0.773	0.785	0.646	0.738	0.865	0.822	0.715	0.483	0.886	0.516	0.720	0.844
G1998D	0.810	0.794	0.793	0.749	0.666	0.755	0.819	0.819	0.693	0.454	0.868	0.588	0.712	0.863
S1998D	0.740	0.706	0.705	0.631	0.604	0.695	0.708	0.685	0.623	0.326	0.722	0.633	0.572	0.758
P2000D	0.817	0.703	0.717	0.734	0.601	0.668	0.830	0.778	0.669	0.443	0.848	0.448	0.694	0.776
S2000D	0.857	0.769	0.804	0.759	0.649	0.755	0.861	0.814	0.733	0.464	0.870	0.649	0.710	0.828
G2002D	0.717	0.611	0.602	0.633	0.534	0.548	0.720	0.678	0.614	0.390	0.764	0.319	0.706	0.661
P2004D	0.750	0.611	0.628	0.664	0.509	0.578	0.760	0.696	0.604	0.378	0.797	0.371	0.629	0.691
S2004D	0.787	0.678	0.705	0.696	0.578	0.661	0.799	0.745	0.678	0.440	0.836	0.502	0.693	0.755

Table A.3 *(continued)*

	S1976D	G1978D	P1980D	S1980D	G1982D	S1982D	P1984D	G1986D	S1986D	P1988D	S1988D	G1990D	S1991D	P1992D
P1960D	0.658	0.730	0.858	0.718	0.699	0.869	0.864	0.814	0.884	0.853	0.851	0.574	0.880	0.851
G1962D	0.714	0.725	0.862	0.707	0.754	0.895	0.828	0.789	0.881	0.817	0.838	0.584	0.827	0.798
S1962D	0.599	0.812	0.904	0.811	0.738	0.884	0.887	0.814	0.909	0.873	0.813	0.590	0.863	0.835
P1964D	0.668	0.730	0.865	0.754	0.696	0.834	0.839	0.755	0.857	0.843	0.773	0.575	0.856	0.811
S1964D	0.679	0.670	0.745	0.646	0.751	0.824	0.715	0.737	0.792	0.699	0.705	0.627	0.732	0.655
G1966D	0.589	0.832	0.893	0.837	0.748	0.862	0.875	0.821	0.904	0.871	0.793	0.619	0.838	0.815
P1968D	0.646	0.771	0.902	0.787	0.711	0.856	0.914	0.806	0.902	0.906	0.832	0.582	0.925	0.889
S1968D	0.714	0.683	0.864	0.701	0.724	0.862	0.859	0.755	0.874	0.840	0.836	0.573	0.869	0.835
G1970D	0.523	0.820	0.821	0.796	0.679	0.783	0.850	0.714	0.848	0.846	0.741	0.521	0.812	0.793
S1970D	0.451	0.560	0.628	0.566	0.521	0.661	0.582	0.534	0.591	0.572	0.598	0.368	0.536	0.527
P1972D	0.691	0.691	0.878	0.708	0.676	0.850	0.893	0.741	0.880	0.887	0.879	0.470	0.897	0.904
S1974D	0.200	0.936	0.772	0.908	0.603	0.703	0.793	0.730	0.783	0.787	0.581	0.522	0.694	0.683
G1974D	0.668	0.552	0.678	0.483	0.624	0.689	0.710	0.570	0.774	0.680	0.757	0.423	0.690	0.713
P1976D	0.741	0.782	0.935	0.786	0.811	0.942	0.905	0.860	0.913	0.905	0.876	0.576	0.919	0.877
S1976D	1	0.307	0.552	0.264	0.570	0.724	0.478	0.526	0.598	0.476	0.756	0.249	0.604	0.550
G1978D	0.307	1	0.843	0.952	0.688	0.766	0.844	0.813	0.850	0.845	0.632	0.590	0.765	0.740
P1980D	0.552	0.843	1	0.880	0.787	0.885	0.950	0.885	0.913	0.954	0.813	0.643	0.905	0.899
S1980D	0.264	0.952	0.880	1	0.708	0.759	0.862	0.846	0.837	0.871	0.587	0.624	0.777	0.751
G1982D	0.570	0.688	0.787	0.708	1	0.879	0.749	0.863	0.793	0.743	0.671	0.715	0.731	0.639

Table A.3 (continued)

	S1976D	G1978D	P1980D	S1980D	G1982D	S1982D	P1984D	G1986D	S1986D	P1988D	S1988D	G1990D	S1991D	P1992D
S1982D	0.724	0.766	0.885	0.759	0.879	1	0.855	0.880	0.888	0.841	0.862	0.603	0.865	0.800
P1984D	0.478	0.844	0.950	0.862	0.749	0.855	1	0.830	0.915	0.987	0.828	0.607	0.947	0.956
G1986D	0.526	0.813	0.885	0.846	0.863	0.880	0.830	1	0.867	0.840	0.716	0.738	0.825	0.739
S1986D	0.598	0.850	0.913	0.837	0.793	0.888	0.915	0.867	1	0.913	0.849	0.619	0.890	0.866
P1988D	0.476	0.845	0.954	0.871	0.743	0.841	0.987	0.840	0.913	1	0.824	0.613	0.942	0.957
S1988D	0.756	0.632	0.813	0.587	0.671	0.862	0.828	0.716	0.849	0.824	1	0.410	0.844	0.865
G1990D	0.249	0.590	0.643	0.624	0.715	0.603	0.607	0.738	0.619	0.613	0.410	1	0.561	0.485
S1991D	0.604	0.765	0.905	0.777	0.731	0.865	0.947	0.825	0.890	0.942	0.844	0.561	1	0.950
P1992D	0.550	0.740	0.899	0.751	0.639	0.800	0.956	0.739	0.866	0.957	0.865	0.485	0.950	1
S1992D	0.708	0.657	0.827	0.680	0.640	0.823	0.835	0.731	0.832	0.837	0.851	0.423	0.904	0.866
G1994D	0.623	0.589	0.771	0.571	0.700	0.756	0.787	0.771	0.787	0.774	0.825	0.516	0.819	0.818
S1994D	0.685	0.639	0.859	0.645	0.725	0.826	0.889	0.786	0.848	0.877	0.862	0.572	0.929	0.930
P1996D	0.682	0.581	0.811	0.582	0.588	0.774	0.865	0.675	0.793	0.863	0.878	0.423	0.916	0.949
G1998D	0.706	0.608	0.808	0.603	0.692	0.836	0.832	0.741	0.810	0.817	0.907	0.409	0.888	0.876
S1998D	0.526	0.700	0.752	0.675	0.672	0.783	0.771	0.749	0.775	0.766	0.787	0.512	0.748	0.754
P2000D	0.656	0.482	0.705	0.478	0.492	0.694	0.797	0.580	0.717	0.777	0.831	0.331	0.871	0.891
S2000D	0.570	0.662	0.811	0.646	0.612	0.785	0.904	0.706	0.821	0.885	0.872	0.474	0.925	0.948
G2002D	0.669	0.345	0.529	0.285	0.356	0.565	0.634	0.398	0.598	0.601	0.760	0.118	0.733	0.750
P2004D	0.611	0.394	0.614	0.388	0.374	0.594	0.713	0.473	0.630	0.696	0.763	0.228	0.794	0.831
S2004D	0.624	0.529	0.696	0.501	0.474	0.673	0.789	0.560	0.733	0.765	0.852	0.276	0.842	0.884

Table A.3 (continued)

	S1992D	G1994D	S1994D	P1996D	G1998D	S1998D	P2000D	S2000D	G2002D	P2004D	S2004D
P1960D	0.802	0.780	0.865	0.843	0.810	0.740	0.817	0.857	0.717	0.750	0.787
G1962D	0.783	0.752	0.818	0.768	0.794	0.706	0.703	0.769	0.611	0.611	0.678
S1962D	0.815	0.728	0.809	0.773	0.793	0.705	0.717	0.804	0.602	0.628	0.705
P1964D	0.855	0.670	0.800	0.785	0.749	0.631	0.734	0.759	0.633	0.664	0.696
S1964D	0.715	0.644	0.724	0.646	0.666	0.604	0.601	0.649	0.534	0.509	0.578
G1966D	0.798	0.693	0.787	0.738	0.755	0.695	0.668	0.755	0.548	0.578	0.661
P1968D	0.885	0.754	0.878	0.865	0.819	0.708	0.830	0.861	0.720	0.760	0.799
S1968D	0.861	0.754	0.852	0.822	0.819	0.685	0.778	0.814	0.678	0.696	0.745
G1970D	0.763	0.617	0.734	0.715	0.693	0.623	0.669	0.733	0.614	0.604	0.678
S1970D	0.575	0.373	0.485	0.483	0.454	0.326	0.443	0.464	0.390	0.378	0.440
P1972D	0.869	0.771	0.883	0.886	0.868	0.722	0.848	0.870	0.764	0.797	0.836
S1974D	0.591	0.517	0.539	0.516	0.588	0.633	0.448	0.649	0.319	0.371	0.502
G1974D	0.643	0.748	0.762	0.720	0.712	0.572	0.694	0.710	0.706	0.629	0.693
P1976D	0.892	0.783	0.878	0.844	0.863	0.758	0.776	0.828	0.661	0.691	0.755
S1976D	0.708	0.623	0.685	0.682	0.706	0.526	0.656	0.570	0.669	0.611	0.624
G1978D	0.657	0.589	0.639	0.581	0.608	0.700	0.482	0.662	0.345	0.394	0.529
P1980D	0.827	0.771	0.859	0.811	0.808	0.752	0.705	0.811	0.529	0.614	0.696
S1980D	0.680	0.571	0.645	0.582	0.603	0.675	0.478	0.646	0.285	0.388	0.501
G1982D	0.640	0.700	0.725	0.588	0.692	0.672	0.492	0.612	0.356	0.374	0.474

Table A.3 *(continued)*

	S1992D	G1994D	S1994D	P1996D	G1998D	S1998D	P2000D	S2000D	G2002D	P2004D	S2004D
S1982D	0.823	0.756	0.826	0.774	0.836	0.783	0.694	0.785	0.565	0.594	0.673
P1984D	0.835	0.787	0.889	0.865	0.832	0.771	0.797	0.904	0.634	0.713	0.789
G1986D	0.731	0.771	0.786	0.675	0.741	0.749	0.580	0.706	0.398	0.473	0.560
S1986D	0.832	0.787	0.848	0.793	0.810	0.775	0.717	0.821	0.598	0.630	0.733
P1988D	0.837	0.774	0.877	0.863	0.817	0.766	0.777	0.885	0.601	0.696	0.765
S1988D	0.851	0.825	0.862	0.878	0.907	0.787	0.831	0.872	0.760	0.763	0.852
G1990D	0.423	0.516	0.572	0.423	0.409	0.512	0.331	0.474	0.118	0.228	0.276
S1991D	0.904	0.819	0.929	0.916	0.888	0.748	0.871	0.925	0.733	0.794	0.842
P1992D	0.866	0.818	0.930	0.949	0.876	0.754	0.891	0.948	0.750	0.831	0.884
S1992D	1	0.728	0.855	0.876	0.853	0.712	0.842	0.843	0.735	0.788	0.833
G1994D	0.728	1	0.903	0.810	0.864	0.770	0.771	0.832	0.690	0.683	0.782
S1994D	0.855	0.903	1	0.946	0.892	0.770	0.899	0.918	0.783	0.832	0.872
P1996D	0.876	0.810	0.946	1	0.880	0.723	0.966	0.956	0.847	0.924	0.925
G1998D	0.853	0.864	0.892	0.880	1	0.741	0.857	0.901	0.787	0.791	0.870
S1998D	0.712	0.770	0.770	0.723	0.741	1	0.652	0.767	0.511	0.580	0.689
P2000D	0.842	0.771	0.899	0.966	0.857	0.652	1	0.948	0.922	0.978	0.959
S2000D	0.843	0.832	0.918	0.956	0.901	0.767	0.948	1	0.826	0.898	0.935
G2002D	0.735	0.690	0.783	0.847	0.787	0.511	0.922	0.826	1	0.927	0.915
P2004D	0.788	0.683	0.832	0.924	0.791	0.580	0.978	0.898	0.927	1	0.958
S2004D	0.833	0.782	0.872	0.925	0.870	0.689	0.959	0.935	0.915	0.958	1

330   THE REALIGNMENT OF PENNSYLVANIA POLITICS SINCE 1960

Table A.4 Correlations of the Republican Vote for President, Governor, and Senator, 1960–2004

	P1960R	G1962R	S1962R	P1964R	S1964R	G1966R	P1968R	S1968R	G1970R	S1970R	P1972R	S1974R	G1974R	P1976R
P1960R	1	0.924	0.927	0.870	0.799	0.892	0.943	0.882	0.805	0.612	0.897	0.687	0.767	0.898
G1962R	0.924	1	0.966	0.899	0.868	0.944	0.922	0.928	0.829	0.622	0.873	0.673	0.822	0.921
S1962R	0.927	0.966	1	0.921	0.859	0.960	0.959	0.921	0.874	0.651	0.895	0.786	0.792	0.931
P1964R	0.870	0.899	0.921	1	0.847	0.915	0.935	0.901	0.889	0.662	0.901	0.670	0.778	0.933
S1964R	0.799	0.868	0.859	0.847	1	0.847	0.823	0.852	0.815	0.631	0.769	0.599	0.757	0.865
G1966R	0.892	0.944	0.960	0.915	0.847	1	0.952	0.903	0.922	0.664	0.884	0.755	0.807	0.907
P1968R	0.943	0.922	0.959	0.935	0.823	0.952	1	0.922	0.905	0.643	0.938	0.765	0.821	0.937
S1968R	0.882	0.928	0.921	0.901	0.852	0.903	0.922	1	0.808	0.578	0.882	0.606	0.813	0.905
G1970R	0.805	0.829	0.874	0.889	0.815	0.922	0.905	0.808	1	0.678	0.836	0.741	0.803	0.847
S1970R	0.612	0.622	0.651	0.662	0.631	0.664	0.643	0.578	0.678	1	0.599	0.501	0.501	0.638
P1972R	0.897	0.873	0.895	0.901	0.769	0.884	0.938	0.882	0.836	0.599	1	0.671	0.796	0.937
S1974R	0.687	0.673	0.786	0.670	0.599	0.755	0.765	0.606	0.741	0.501	0.671	1	0.495	0.702
G1974R	0.767	0.822	0.792	0.778	0.757	0.807	0.821	0.813	0.803	0.501	0.796	0.495	1	0.784
P1976R	0.898	0.921	0.931	0.933	0.865	0.907	0.937	0.905	0.847	0.638	0.937	0.702	0.784	1
S1976R	0.653	0.708	0.594	0.667	0.676	0.591	0.608	0.726	0.502	0.449	0.683	0.191	0.662	0.732
G1978R	0.737	0.739	0.819	0.736	0.679	0.818	0.811	0.641	0.805	0.525	0.715	0.928	0.571	0.788
P1980R	0.856	0.851	0.897	0.893	0.743	0.873	0.933	0.865	0.827	0.591	0.929	0.717	0.751	0.938
S1980R	0.724	0.719	0.818	0.760	0.655	0.814	0.812	0.662	0.767	0.534	0.729	0.900	0.500	0.796
G1982R	0.707	0.762	0.747	0.703	0.759	0.752	0.724	0.715	0.656	0.504	0.695	0.605	0.636	0.817

Table A.4 (continued)

	P1960R	G1962R	S1962R	P1964R	S1964R	G1966R	P1968R	S1968R	G1970R	S1970R	P1972R	S1974R	G1974R	P1976R
S1982R	0.871	0.896	0.885	0.839	0.826	0.853	0.864	0.845	0.746	0.635	0.864	0.700	0.701	0.942
P1984R	0.868	0.835	0.890	0.841	0.722	0.869	0.930	0.830	0.822	0.552	0.897	0.787	0.721	0.911
G1986R	0.815	0.793	0.818	0.753	0.741	0.795	0.798	0.742	0.680	0.513	0.745	0.729	0.572	0.854
S1986R	0.883	0.885	0.910	0.857	0.795	0.896	0.918	0.837	0.828	0.550	0.880	0.778	0.773	0.913
P1988R	0.856	0.823	0.876	0.845	0.705	0.857	0.914	0.800	0.813	0.538	0.886	0.783	0.688	0.909
S1988R	0.854	0.840	0.820	0.788	0.716	0.797	0.848	0.812	0.716	0.575	0.880	0.592	0.760	0.885
G1990R	0.574	0.586	0.590	0.572	0.628	0.612	0.569	0.577	0.535	0.359	0.464	0.518	0.423	0.576
S1991R	0.880	0.830	0.864	0.855	0.735	0.828	0.915	0.846	0.784	0.509	0.896	0.693	0.697	0.920
P1992R	0.826	0.791	0.855	0.855	0.677	0.813	0.891	0.792	0.787	0.552	0.889	0.736	0.650	0.904
S1992R	0.737	0.735	0.779	0.838	0.695	0.761	0.807	0.766	0.735	0.564	0.829	0.645	0.568	0.871
G1994R	0.712	0.632	0.652	0.590	0.537	0.650	0.699	0.596	0.630	0.494	0.640	0.587	0.683	0.636
S1994R	0.850	0.811	0.802	0.785	0.725	0.788	0.856	0.828	0.728	0.452	0.861	0.543	0.775	0.868
P1996R	0.834	0.765	0.776	0.804	0.651	0.722	0.823	0.794	0.655	0.461	0.859	0.539	0.645	0.872
G1998R	0.754	0.687	0.763	0.716	0.622	0.746	0.802	0.646	0.719	0.666	0.797	0.794	0.573	0.801
S1998R	0.751	0.715	0.723	0.656	0.629	0.696	0.723	0.668	0.618	0.325	0.737	0.662	0.581	0.768
P2000R	0.813	0.697	0.710	0.741	0.602	0.670	0.804	0.785	0.641	0.442	0.843	0.436	0.688	0.783
S2000R	0.856	0.772	0.804	0.764	0.655	0.766	0.871	0.806	0.718	0.446	0.872	0.654	0.721	0.841
G2002R	0.719	0.614	0.607	0.648	0.541	0.579	0.721	0.704	0.605	0.390	0.770	0.322	0.714	0.675
P2004R	0.752	0.614	0.629	0.672	0.514	0.593	0.739	0.709	0.582	0.378	0.796	0.373	0.638	0.704
S2004R	0.771	0.666	0.721	0.709	0.582	0.707	0.817	0.707	0.717	0.494	0.838	0.633	0.682	0.768

Table A.4 (continued)

	S1976R	G1978R	P1980R	S1980R	G1982R	S1982R	P1984R	G1986R	S1986R	P1988R	S1988R	G1990R	S1991R	P1992R
P1960R	0.653	0.737	0.856	0.724	0.707	0.871	0.868	0.815	0.883	0.856	0.854	0.574	0.880	0.826
G1962R	0.708	0.739	0.851	0.719	0.762	0.896	0.835	0.793	0.885	0.823	0.840	0.586	0.830	0.791
S1962R	0.594	0.819	0.897	0.818	0.747	0.885	0.890	0.818	0.910	0.876	0.820	0.590	0.864	0.855
P1964R	0.667	0.736	0.893	0.760	0.703	0.839	0.841	0.753	0.857	0.845	0.788	0.572	0.855	0.855
S1964R	0.676	0.679	0.743	0.655	0.759	0.826	0.722	0.741	0.795	0.705	0.716	0.628	0.735	0.677
G1966R	0.591	0.818	0.873	0.814	0.752	0.853	0.869	0.795	0.896	0.857	0.797	0.612	0.828	0.813
P1968R	0.608	0.811	0.933	0.812	0.724	0.864	0.930	0.798	0.918	0.914	0.848	0.569	0.915	0.891
S1968R	0.726	0.641	0.865	0.662	0.715	0.845	0.830	0.742	0.837	0.800	0.812	0.577	0.846	0.792
G1970R	0.502	0.805	0.827	0.767	0.656	0.746	0.822	0.680	0.828	0.813	0.716	0.535	0.784	0.787
S1970R	0.449	0.525	0.591	0.534	0.504	0.635	0.552	0.513	0.550	0.538	0.575	0.359	0.509	0.552
P1972R	0.683	0.715	0.929	0.729	0.695	0.864	0.897	0.745	0.880	0.886	0.880	0.464	0.896	0.889
S1974R	0.191	0.928	0.717	0.900	0.605	0.700	0.787	0.729	0.778	0.783	0.592	0.518	0.693	0.736
G1974R	0.662	0.571	0.751	0.500	0.636	0.701	0.721	0.572	0.773	0.688	0.760	0.423	0.697	0.650
P1976R	0.732	0.788	0.938	0.796	0.817	0.942	0.911	0.854	0.913	0.909	0.885	0.576	0.920	0.904
S1976R	1	0.302	0.579	0.263	0.571	0.722	0.474	0.513	0.586	0.471	0.748	0.248	0.598	0.517
G1978R	0.302	1	0.789	0.947	0.698	0.766	0.847	0.815	0.856	0.851	0.653	0.590	0.772	0.803
P1980R	0.579	0.789	1	0.824	0.718	0.842	0.956	0.799	0.898	0.955	0.842	0.547	0.925	0.935
S1980R	0.263	0.947	0.824	1	0.712	0.761	0.865	0.851	0.843	0.876	0.612	0.622	0.786	0.815
G1982R	0.571	0.698	0.718	0.712	1	0.883	0.761	0.863	0.803	0.753	0.692	0.713	0.744	0.652
S1982R	0.722	0.766	0.842	0.761	0.883	1	0.861	0.876	0.890	0.848	0.878	0.595	0.870	0.817

Table A.4 (continued)

	S1976R	G1978R	P1980R	S1980R	G1982R	S1982R	P1984R	G1986R	S1986R	P1988R	S1988R	G1990R	S1991R	P1992R
P1984R	0.474	0.847	0.956	0.865	0.761	0.861	1	0.835	0.917	0.987	0.840	0.608	0.948	0.933
G1986R	0.513	0.815	0.799	0.851	0.863	0.876	0.835	1	0.870	0.843	0.724	0.738	0.828	0.774
S1986R	0.586	0.856	0.898	0.843	0.803	0.890	0.917	0.870	1	0.913	0.854	0.620	0.890	0.863
P1988R	0.471	0.851	0.955	0.876	0.753	0.848	0.987	0.843	0.913	1	0.837	0.609	0.945	0.947
S1988R	0.748	0.653	0.842	0.612	0.692	0.878	0.840	0.724	0.854	0.837	1	0.411	0.855	0.838
G1990R	0.248	0.590	0.547	0.622	0.713	0.595	0.608	0.738	0.620	0.609	0.411	1	0.561	0.462
S1991R	0.598	0.772	0.925	0.786	0.744	0.870	0.948	0.828	0.890	0.945	0.855	0.561	1	0.941
P1992R	0.517	0.803	0.935	0.815	0.652	0.817	0.933	0.774	0.863	0.947	0.838	0.462	0.941	1
S1992R	0.628	0.719	0.865	0.760	0.664	0.804	0.817	0.753	0.824	0.841	0.794	0.473	0.858	0.896
G1994R	0.345	0.648	0.677	0.595	0.636	0.623	0.726	0.677	0.707	0.703	0.659	0.575	0.659	0.624
S1994R	0.656	0.669	0.874	0.654	0.743	0.810	0.883	0.783	0.849	0.870	0.836	0.581	0.912	0.848
P1996R	0.695	0.626	0.861	0.635	0.646	0.820	0.846	0.748	0.799	0.858	0.860	0.432	0.920	0.914
G1998R	0.378	0.817	0.815	0.817	0.707	0.797	0.854	0.780	0.796	0.845	0.755	0.515	0.792	0.830
S1998R	0.513	0.724	0.731	0.695	0.680	0.792	0.784	0.747	0.787	0.780	0.794	0.515	0.760	0.748
P2000R	0.662	0.479	0.803	0.485	0.509	0.707	0.791	0.583	0.708	0.774	0.828	0.327	0.868	0.826
S2000R	0.563	0.679	0.875	0.666	0.642	0.797	0.911	0.719	0.825	0.895	0.872	0.488	0.927	0.890
G2002R	0.670	0.356	0.673	0.305	0.380	0.580	0.644	0.409	0.598	0.614	0.756	0.132	0.743	0.696
P2004R	0.615	0.404	0.746	0.403	0.397	0.612	0.718	0.479	0.628	0.702	0.767	0.232	0.796	0.769
S2004R	0.482	0.657	0.837	0.628	0.530	0.682	0.847	0.610	0.760	0.832	0.832	0.373	0.841	0.852

Table A.4 (continued)

	S1992R	G1994R	S1994R	P1996R	G1998R	S1998R	P2000R	S2000R	G2002R	P2004R	S2004R
P1960R	0.737	0.712	0.850	0.834	0.754	0.751	0.813	0.856	0.719	0.752	0.771
G1962R	0.735	0.632	0.811	0.765	0.687	0.715	0.697	0.772	0.614	0.614	0.666
S1962R	0.779	0.652	0.802	0.776	0.763	0.723	0.710	0.804	0.607	0.629	0.721
P1964R	0.838	0.590	0.785	0.804	0.716	0.656	0.741	0.764	0.648	0.672	0.709
S1964R	0.695	0.537	0.725	0.651	0.622	0.629	0.602	0.655	0.541	0.514	0.582
G1966R	0.761	0.650	0.788	0.722	0.746	0.696	0.670	0.766	0.579	0.593	0.707
P1968R	0.807	0.699	0.856	0.823	0.802	0.723	0.804	0.871	0.721	0.739	0.817
S1968R	0.766	0.596	0.828	0.794	0.646	0.668	0.785	0.806	0.704	0.709	0.707
G1970R	0.735	0.630	0.728	0.655	0.719	0.618	0.641	0.718	0.605	0.582	0.717
S1970R	0.564	0.494	0.452	0.461	0.666	0.325	0.442	0.446	0.390	0.378	0.494
P1972R	0.829	0.640	0.861	0.859	0.797	0.737	0.843	0.872	0.770	0.796	0.838
S1974R	0.645	0.587	0.543	0.539	0.794	0.662	0.436	0.654	0.322	0.373	0.633
G1974R	0.568	0.683	0.775	0.645	0.573	0.581	0.688	0.721	0.714	0.638	0.682
P1976R	0.871	0.636	0.868	0.872	0.801	0.768	0.783	0.841	0.675	0.704	0.768
S1976R	0.628	0.345	0.656	0.695	0.378	0.513	0.662	0.563	0.670	0.615	0.482
G1978R	0.719	0.648	0.669	0.626	0.817	0.724	0.479	0.679	0.356	0.404	0.657
P1980R	0.865	0.677	0.874	0.861	0.815	0.731	0.803	0.875	0.673	0.746	0.837
S1980R	0.760	0.595	0.654	0.635	0.817	0.695	0.485	0.666	0.305	0.403	0.628
G1982R	0.664	0.636	0.743	0.646	0.707	0.680	0.509	0.642	0.380	0.397	0.530

Table A.4 (continued)

	S1992R	G1994R	S1994R	P1996R	G1998R	S1998R	P2000R	S2000R	G2002R	P2004R	S2004R
S1982R	0.804	0.623	0.810	0.820	0.797	0.792	0.707	0.797	0.580	0.612	0.682
P1984R	0.817	0.726	0.883	0.846	0.854	0.784	0.791	0.911	0.644	0.718	0.847
G1986R	0.753	0.677	0.783	0.748	0.780	0.747	0.583	0.719	0.409	0.479	0.610
S1986R	0.824	0.707	0.849	0.799	0.796	0.787	0.708	0.825	0.598	0.628	0.760
P1988R	0.841	0.703	0.870	0.858	0.845	0.780	0.774	0.895	0.614	0.702	0.832
S1988R	0.794	0.659	0.836	0.860	0.755	0.794	0.828	0.872	0.756	0.767	0.832
G1990R	0.473	0.575	0.581	0.432	0.515	0.515	0.327	0.488	0.132	0.232	0.373
S1991R	0.858	0.659	0.912	0.920	0.792	0.760	0.868	0.927	0.743	0.796	0.841
P1992R	0.896	0.624	0.848	0.914	0.830	0.748	0.826	0.890	0.696	0.769	0.852
S1992R	1	0.511	0.770	0.845	0.732	0.723	0.726	0.757	0.604	0.664	0.740
G1994R	0.511	1	0.773	0.589	0.774	0.665	0.576	0.709	0.528	0.519	0.735
S1994R	0.770	0.773	1	0.903	0.752	0.755	0.862	0.908	0.781	0.805	0.846
P1996R	0.845	0.589	0.903	1	0.728	0.744	0.920	0.911	0.798	0.870	0.822
G1998R	0.732	0.774	0.752	0.728	1	0.749	0.641	0.776	0.534	0.583	0.806
S1998R	0.723	0.665	0.755	0.744	0.749	1	0.658	0.780	0.528	0.596	0.719
P2000R	0.726	0.576	0.862	0.920	0.641	0.658	1	0.936	0.927	0.980	0.883
S2000R	0.757	0.709	0.908	0.911	0.776	0.780	0.936	1	0.825	0.895	0.929
G2002R	0.604	0.528	0.781	0.798	0.534	0.528	0.927	0.825	1	0.934	0.828
P2004R	0.664	0.519	0.805	0.870	0.583	0.596	0.980	0.895	0.934	1	0.882
S2004R	0.740	0.735	0.846	0.822	0.806	0.719	0.883	0.929	0.828	0.882	1

Appendix B
Interest-Group Ratings of Major Pennsylvania Politicians

Key

ADA	=	Americans for Democratic Action
ACLU	=	American Civil Liberties Union
CFA	=	Consumer Federation of America
COPE	=	Committee on Political Education (AFL-CIO)
LCV	=	League of Conservation Voters
NEA	=	National Education Association
CCUS	=	Chamber of Commerce of the U.S.
ACU	=	American Conservative Union

Clark, Joseph

Year	ADA	ACLU	CFA	COPE	LCV	NEA	CCUS	ACU
1957	100			100				
1958	92			100				
1959	100			100				
1960	100			100				
1961	100			100				
1962	92			100				
1963	100			90				
1964	89			90				
1965	88			100			0	
1966	90			100			0	
1967	92			92			50	
1968	93			92			50	
Average Ratings	**95**			**97**			**25**	
Liberal Rating	**96**							
Conservative Rating	**25**							

Scott, Hugh

Year	ADA	ACLU	CFA	COPE	LCV	NEA	CCUS	ACU
1959	31			40				
1960	67			40				
1961	40			36				
1962	25			36				
1963	59			78				
1964	68			78				
1965	47			64			44	
1966	30			64			44	
1967	38			75			60	
1968	57			75			60	
1969	56			77		17	20	
1970	25			77		17	20	
1971	26		25	50	26	67	40	50
1972	35		63	60	26	67	40	41
1973	25		23	55	52	38	56	58
1974	43		44	70	52	38	44	38
1975	39		65	73	40	100	56	26
1976	40		64	53	40	100	33	29
Average Ratings	**42**		**47**	**61**	**39**	**56**	**43**	**40**
Liberal Rating	**49**							
Conservative Rating	**42**							

Schweiker, Richard

Year	ADA	ACLU	CFA	COPE	LCV	NEA	CCUS	ACU
HOUSE 1961	40			27				
1962	38			27				
1963	33			64				
1964	23			64				
1965	47			62			30	
1966	47			62			30	
1967	40			58			70	
1968	50			58			70	
SENATE 1969	78			100		67	20	
1970	70			100		67	20	
1971	70		86	50	79	100	20	25
1972	60		100	100	79	100	20	19
1973	75		77	100	76	89	22	20

Schweiker, Richard (continued)

Year	ADA	ACLU	CFA	COPE	LCV	NEA	CCUS	ACU
1974	81		88	91	76	89	11	25
1975	89		100	100	74	100	13	9
1976	80		93	94	74	100	25	16
1977	15		52	47	35	45	53	47
1978	20		35	63	35	45	59	79
1979	16	30	33	47	44	22	50	88
1980	17	30	13	37	44	22	87	85
Average Ratings	49	30	68	68	62	71	37.5	41
Liberal Rating	58							
Conservative Rating	39							

Scranton, William

Year	ADA	ACLU	CFA	COPE	LCV	NEA	CCUS	ACU
1961	40			55				
1962	63			55				
Average Ratings	52			55				
Liberal Rating	53							
Conservative Rating								

Ridge, Tom

Year	ADA	ACLU	CFA	COPE	LCV	NEA	CCUS	ACU
1983	35	55	50	47	71	80	80	39
1984	50	55	58	38	66	80	60	36
1985	30	35	67	47	53	38	73	48
1986	35	35	58	64	53	38	61	41
1987	44	61	50	60	75	50	64	19
1988	50	61	73	86	75	50	71	36
1989	45	35	50	67	30	43	80	57
1990	22	35	72	33	75	43	57	58
1991	15	35	33	58	8	42	90	70
1992	30	35	40	50	19	42	63	68
1993	10	29	10	25	20	0	80	78
1994	30	29	40	29	19	0	90	61
Average Ratings	33	42	50	50	47	42	72	51
Liberal Rating	44							
Conservative Rating	62							

Heinz, John

Year	ADA	ACLU	CFA	COPE	LCV	NEA	CCUS	ACU
HOUSE 1971	67			100	83	100	20	43
1972	63		100	55	81	100	20	8
1973	60		88	56	68	73	40	36
1974	57		69	82	61	73	30	26
1975	68		77	74	74	78	40	44
1976	30		45	67	53	78	20	21
SENATE 1977	50		64	65	66	82	39	33
1978	60		40	78	66	82	50	23
1979	42	90	29	59	67	50	56	56
1980	50	90	33	67	67	50	63	55
1981	35	61	36	61	50	75	71	36
1982	70	61	64	75	49	75	29	17
1983	35	38	42	44	44	64	37	25
1984	50	38	50	45	44	64	56	41
1985	35	38	57	71	90	50	59	55
1986	55	38	47	60	90	50	59	43
1987	70	60	67	89	50	43	50	35
1988	55	60	75	79	50	43	46	41
1989	35	50	46	80	70	64	75	54
1990	33	50	58	78	58	64	42	48
1991						100		100
Average Ratings	**51**	**56**	**57**	**69**	**64**	**69**	**45**	**40**
Liberal Rating	**61**							
Conservative Rating	**43**							

Santorum, Rick

Year	ADA	ACLU	CFA	COPE	LCV	NEA	CCUS	ACU
HOUSE 1991	15	17	28	42	0	23	80	80
1992	20	17	33	58	19	23	88	83
1993	20	23	20	50	25	41	73	70
1994	15	23	10	22	15	41	100	81
SENATE 1995	5	17	13	8	0	6	100	83
1996	15	17	29	43	15	6	77	95
1997	15	14	29	14	14	26	90	84
1998	0	14	10	0	7	26	98	84
1999	5			25			81	88
2000	0			0			93	100

Santorum, Rick (continued)

Year	ADA	ACLU	CFA	COPE	LCV	NEA	CCUS	ACU
2001	10			13			86	100
2002	5			15			95	95
2003	10			0			100	90
2004	15			10			94	96
Average Ratings	11	18	22	21	12	24	90	88
Liberal Rating	18							
Conservative Rating	89							

Wofford, Harris

Year	ADA	ACLU	CFA	COPE	LCV	NEA	CCUS	ACU
1991	9	82	87	89	86	100	0	22
1992	100	82	83	92	67	100	20	0
1993	85	42	70	91	94	95	18	24
1994	85	42	83	75	92	95	30	16
Average Ratings	70	62	81	87	85	98	17	16
Liberal Rating	80							
Conservative Rating	16							

Specter, Arlen

Year	ADA	ACLU	CFA	COPE	LCV	NEA	CCUS	ACU
1981	50	86	36	58	39	33	72	40
1982	70	86	64	60	49	33	35	26
1983	80	60	67	76	44	83	37	16
1984	50	60	50	45	44	83	68	36
1985	55	64	33	71	75	57	55	36
1986	75	64	80	87	75	57	44	33
1987	80	67	83	90	30	57	47	15
1988	60	67	58	83	30	57	62	33
1989	40	59	54	50	80	73	75	57
1990	39	59	67	89	50	73	50	48
1991	40	59	61	58	40	79	50	71
1992	65	59	75	83	50	79	60	30
1993	45	56	33	45	38	68	100	57
1994	55	56	58	38	54	68	60	46
1995	55	33	44	33	50	39	79	36
1996	50	33	57	57	52	39	77	50
1997	70	50	57	57	43	74	50	32

Specter, Arlen *(continued)*

Year	ADA	ACLU	CFA	COPE	LCV	NEA	CCUS	ACU
1998	45	50	50	83	47	74	60	33
1999	40			44			47	48
2000	40			50			53	62
2001	40			63			79	56
2002	35			46			85	50
2003	25			16			87	65
2004	45			64			87	75
Average Ratings	**52**	**59**	**57**	**60**	**49**	**63**	**63**	**44**
Liberal Rating	**57**							
Conservative Rating	**54**							

The manner in which each interest group computed its scores is explained in the introduction of the *Directory of Congressional Voting Scores and Interest Group Ratings*. For instance, the "ADA assigns each member a 'liberal quotient,' which is defined as 'the percentage of votes cast or paired live, in support of liberal policy, measured against the number of votes counted' " (ix).

Source: J. Michael Sharp, *Directory of Congressional Voting Scores and Interest Group Ratings*, (Washington, DC: CQ Press), 2000; and Jackie Koszczuk and H. Amy Stern, *CQ's Politics in America 2006: The 109th Congress* (Washington, DC: CQ Press), 2006.

Appendix C
Tables Supporting the Pennsylvania Factor Analyses

Table C.1 Factor Analysis of the Democratic Vote for President, Governor, and U.S. Senator in Pennsylvania, 1896–2004

	Total Variance Explained					
	Initial Eigenvalues			Extraction Sums of Squared Loadings		
Component	Total	% of Variance	Cumulative %	Total	% of Variance	Cumulative %
1	48.939	54.988	54.988	48.939	54.988	54.988
2	20.785	23.354	78.342	20.785	23.354	78.342
3	4.476	5.029	83.371	4.476	5.029	83.371
4	2.587	2.907	86.279	2.587	2.907	86.279
5	1.966	2.209	88.488	1.966	2.209	88.488
6	1.556	1.749	90.236	1.556	1.749	90.236
7	1.165	1.309	91.545	1.165	1.309	91.545

Extraction Method: Principal Component Analysis.

	Component Matrix(a)						
	Component						
	1	2	3	4	5	6	7
P2004D	0.642	−0.388	0.584	−0.116	0.040	−0.078	0.189
S2004D	0.727	−0.380	0.465	−0.120	0.120	−0.090	0.187
G2002D	0.635	−0.284	0.596	−0.253	0.080	−0.171	0.052
P2000D	0.729	−0.390	0.502	−0.111	0.068	−0.023	0.140
S2000D	0.795	−0.433	0.290	−0.044	0.153	0.046	0.194
G1998D	0.809	−0.304	0.302	−0.054	0.192	0.167	0.000
S1998D	0.721	−0.356	0.033	0.044	0.046	0.218	0.103
P1996D	0.775	−0.435	0.384	−0.063	0.118	0.041	0.058

Component Matrix(a) *(continued)*

	Component						
	1	2	3	4	5	6	7
G1994D	0.803	−0.236	0.142	−0.232	0.162	0.288	0.077
S1994D	0.849	−0.345	0.231	−0.100	0.114	0.176	0.045
S1992D	0.821	−0.245	0.328	0.185	0.144	−0.017	−0.043
P1992D	0.811	−0.469	0.164	0.020	0.228	−0.011	0.119
S1991D	0.851	−0.374	0.180	0.136	0.177	0.093	0.064
G1990D	0.628	−0.148	−0.417	0.052	−0.126	0.361	0.035
P1988D	0.834	−0.460	−0.040	0.153	0.180	0.023	0.080
S1988D	0.823	−0.342	0.251	−0.071	0.066	0.039	−0.106
S1986D	0.901	−0.303	−0.071	0.086	0.061	0.030	−0.014
G1986D	0.815	−0.273	−0.154	0.236	−0.019	0.327	−0.068
P1984D	0.845	−0.450	−0.030	0.118	0.203	0.010	0.085
S1982D	0.883	−0.206	0.040	0.175	0.055	0.211	−0.201
G1982D	0.793	−0.115	−0.194	0.095	0.054	0.357	−0.201
P1980D	0.858	−0.375	−0.091	0.174	0.156	0.085	−0.069
S1980D	0.745	−0.320	−0.316	0.429	0.122	−0.012	0.092
G1978D	0.761	−0.295	−0.309	0.348	0.138	−0.086	0.082
P1976D	0.921	−0.246	0.086	0.134	0.081	0.043	−0.174
S1976D	0.698	0.047	0.452	−0.125	−0.066	0.125	−0.403
S1974D	0.699	−0.283	−0.305	0.358	0.139	−0.120	0.180
G1974D	0.840	−0.084	0.051	−0.361	0.026	−0.164	−0.119
P1972D	0.865	−0.346	0.191	0.026	0.072	−0.046	−0.080
S1970D	0.634	−0.113	−0.029	0.240	−0.100	−0.260	−0.348
G1970D	0.865	−0.221	−0.055	0.159	0.028	−0.309	−0.092
P1968D	0.904	−0.310	0.121	0.126	−0.016	−0.090	−0.053
S1968D	0.929	−0.147	0.111	0.017	0.043	−0.038	−0.129
G1966D	0.933	−0.185	−0.105	0.136	−0.035	−0.109	−0.089
P1964D	0.910	−0.145	0.084	0.168	−0.031	−0.137	−0.133
S1964D	0.889	0.021	−0.031	0.046	−0.077	−0.017	−0.216
S1962D	0.945	−0.171	−0.038	0.111	−0.001	−0.077	−0.056
G1962D	0.949	−0.103	0.003	−0.014	−0.042	0.016	−0.153
P1960D	0.896	−0.321	0.109	0.015	−0.175	0.024	−0.014
G1958D	0.950	−0.048	−0.087	−0.120	−0.081	−0.032	−0.056
S1958D	0.930	0.083	−0.145	−0.160	−0.058	−0.017	−0.130
S1956D	0.933	−0.038	−0.242	−0.117	0.080	−0.059	−0.034
P1956D	0.932	−0.104	−0.164	−0.161	0.078	−0.021	−0.042

Component Matrix(a) *(continued)*

	Component						
	1	2	3	4	5	6	7
G1954D	0.903	0.143	−0.298	−0.048	0.013	−0.120	−0.077
S1952D	0.938	−0.082	−0.185	−0.173	−0.010	−0.131	0.050
P1952D	0.952	−0.117	−0.177	−0.117	0.015	−0.101	0.016
G1950D	0.927	0.189	−0.151	−0.115	−0.036	−0.095	−0.033
S1950D	0.921	0.177	−0.216	−0.093	−0.050	−0.022	−0.037
P1948D	0.944	0.053	−0.209	−0.043	−0.031	−0.120	−0.003
G1946D	0.869	0.322	−0.235	−0.159	−0.066	0.022	0.015
S1946D	0.886	0.268	−0.219	−0.188	−0.104	0.023	0.012
S1944D	0.951	0.038	−0.081	−0.189	−0.085	−0.136	0.050
P1944D	0.944	0.004	−0.094	−0.180	−0.104	−0.150	0.027
G1942D	0.877	0.265	−0.170	−0.113	−0.167	0.051	0.023
S1940D	0.897	0.182	−0.157	−0.307	−0.086	−0.100	0.013
P1940D	0.890	0.148	−0.169	−0.311	−0.089	−0.117	0.004
G1938D	0.850	0.207	−0.282	−0.202	−0.119	0.066	0.083
S1938D	0.839	0.182	−0.214	−0.247	−0.159	0.148	0.076
P1936D	0.892	0.139	−0.192	−0.202	−0.063	−0.159	0.114
S1934D	0.809	0.238	−0.262	0.139	−0.052	−0.131	0.255
G1934D	0.783	0.268	−0.279	0.142	−0.027	−0.149	0.242
P1932D	0.765	0.468	−0.172	0.110	−0.094	0.208	0.190
S1932D	0.745	0.466	−0.098	−0.002	0.000	0.141	0.196
S1930D	0.494	0.694	0.188	0.141	−0.243	−0.097	−0.017
G1930D	0.517	0.530	0.305	0.200	−0.267	−0.209	0.016
P1928D	0.731	−0.014	0.168	0.236	−0.464	0.263	0.118
S1928D	0.776	0.206	0.111	0.183	−0.383	0.258	0.092
S1926D	−0.229	0.625	−0.331	0.130	0.552	−0.057	−0.103
G1926D	0.332	0.816	0.185	−0.067	−0.052	0.064	0.019
P1924D	0.174	0.897	0.009	−0.139	0.156	0.144	0.000
G1922D	0.036	0.848	−0.237	−0.168	0.255	0.085	−0.134
S1922DR	0.147	0.908	−0.041	−0.170	0.206	−0.019	0.038
S1922DP	0.216	0.905	−0.093	−0.175	0.175	0.049	0.014
P1920D	0.414	0.847	0.029	−0.126	0.133	0.070	−0.055
S1920D	0.440	0.822	0.012	−0.158	0.142	0.077	0.012
G1918D	0.563	0.706	0.200	0.116	−0.234	0.055	−0.032
P1916D	0.365	0.878	0.077	0.080	0.123	0.024	0.010
S1916D	0.336	0.902	0.105	0.052	0.103	0.032	0.045

Component Matrix(a) *(continued)*

	Component						
	1	2	3	4	5	6	7
S1914D	0.189	0.855	0.141	−0.011	0.280	0.002	−0.004
G1914D	0.140	0.896	0.043	0.039	0.266	0.065	−0.046
P1912D	0.274	0.909	0.224	0.032	0.085	0.008	0.090
G1910D	0.228	0.733	0.377	0.154	−0.177	−0.139	0.033
P1908D	0.399	0.873	0.200	0.106	0.002	0.019	0.013
G1906D	0.156	0.761	0.313	−0.062	−0.184	0.089	−0.106
P1904D	0.290	0.900	0.185	0.063	−0.005	−0.016	0.089
G1902D	0.162	0.831	0.175	0.248	−0.009	−0.099	0.020
P1900D	0.348	0.881	0.174	0.181	−0.014	0.024	−0.039
G1898D	0.425	0.760	0.101	0.342	0.026	−0.181	0.083
P1896D	0.393	0.792	0.064	0.383	0.080	−0.012	−0.082

Extraction Method: Principal Component Analysis.
a. Seven components extracted.

Case Summaries(a)					
	County	REGR factor score 1 for analysis 1	REGR factor score 2 for analysis 1	REGR factor score 3 for analysis 1	REGR factor score 4 for analysis 1
1	Adams	−0.11503	1.59910	−0.02115	0.04926
2	Allegheny	1.10085	−1.53602	−0.74346	−0.71927
3	Armstrong	0.19869	−0.87342	−1.00613	1.04354
4	Beaver	1.48388	−1.27914	−0.83720	0.60824
5	Bedford	−0.57017	0.44724	−1.20860	−0.36176
6	Berks	0.66847	1.20263	0.63079	−0.78621
7	Blair	−0.64878	−0.37571	−1.10704	0.10456
8	Bradford	−1.53234	−0.61947	0.55777	0.11432
9	Bucks	−0.00537	0.12946	1.78941	−0.54603
10	Butler	−0.29187	−0.30711	−0.76247	1.87883
11	Cambria	1.46639	−0.49161	−0.82273	0.29397
12	Cameron	−0.69410	−0.70461	−0.17492	1.09976
13	Carbon	1.00649	0.26194	0.61987	−0.43186
14	Centre	−0.05199	0.57868	0.70937	−0.42577
15	Chester	−0.89882	−0.34950	0.97351	−1.57024
16	Clarion	−0.02073	1.14556	−0.41548	1.67438
17	Clearfield	0.55116	0.03445	−0.95940	−0.09272
18	Clinton	0.54143	0.09506	0.53897	−0.19966

Case Summaries(a) *(continued)*

	County	REGR factor score 1 for analysis 1	REGR factor score 2 for analysis 1	REGR factor score 3 for analysis 1	REGR factor score 4 for analysis 1
19	Columbia	0.69848	1.84095	0.02403	−0.29218
20	Crawford	−0.30913	−0.00213	0.21959	1.66270
21	Cumberland	−0.48436	1.18239	−0.73533	−1.31556
22	Dauphin	−0.56380	−0.46631	−0.19388	−1.89572
23	Delaware	−0.45431	−1.42353	1.66303	−1.40124
24	Elk	0.92573	−0.18465	0.01915	2.42654
25	Erie	0.60207	−0.67811	0.41206	1.56727
26	Fayette	2.15881	−0.56779	−0.53465	0.15175
27	Forest	−0.70761	−0.86419	−0.15856	0.81433
28	Franklin	−0.38577	0.73994	−0.95701	−0.96657
29	Fulton	0.38178	2.06932	−0.98465	−0.27912
30	Greene	2.28008	1.38477	0.06966	1.13690
31	Huntingdon	−1.05491	−0.59469	−0.65809	−0.61552
32	Indiana	−0.12381	−1.58704	−0.80474	−0.11999
33	Jefferson	−0.50923	−0.38567	−1.10550	0.84855
34	Juniata	−0.01768	0.95895	−1.43853	−1.18070
35	Lackawanna	1.51473	−0.34139	0.89228	−1.01038
36	Lancaster	−1.36953	−0.30807	−0.81943	−1.64716
37	Lawrence	0.76924	−1.66442	−0.34364	0.38995
38	Lebanon	−0.87517	−0.24019	−1.24967	−1.98202
39	Lehigh	0.54824	0.76026	1.48783	−0.09242
40	Luzerne	1.08600	−0.39851	0.70369	−0.09862
41	Lycoming	−0.27228	0.55995	−0.58353	0.15457
42	McKean	−1.15592	−0.49018	0.80803	0.94168
43	Mercer	0.51156	−0.67296	0.34085	0.89178
44	Mifflin	−0.19430	0.29112	−1.28047	−1.33769
45	Monroe	0.67669	2.51937	1.48389	0.49392
46	Montgomery	−0.59466	−0.41027	2.62524	−0.60296
47	Montour	0.30376	1.55706	−0.14536	0.20497
48	Northampton	1.30214	0.75717	0.93992	−0.19224
49	Northumberland	0.44349	0.36788	−0.24444	−0.21238
50	Perry	−0.81726	0.95453	−0.98469	−0.93385
51	Philadelphia	2.13552	−2.60811	2.86119	−2.28846
52	Pike	−0.46506	1.94806	1.78867	0.86263

Case Summaries(a) *(continued)*

	County	REGR factor score 1 for analysis 1	REGR factor score 2 for analysis 1	REGR factor score 3 for analysis 1	REGR factor score 4 for analysis 1
53	Potter	−1.05273	−0.12879	−0.48032	0.39311
54	Schuylkill	0.47741	0.16145	0.62903	0.09282
55	Snyder	−1.89021	0.13665	−0.22588	−0.33224
56	Somerset	−0.19762	−1.27076	−1.33904	−0.23052
57	Sullivan	−0.01975	0.82790	0.34944	0.36781
58	Susquehanna	−0.90723	0.03993	0.69198	0.35296
59	Tioga	−1.76590	−1.16490	0.30772	0.32267
60	Union	−1.74010	−0.08807	0.27488	−0.02641
61	Venango	−0.98238	−0.88490	0.46122	2.38732
62	Warren	−0.74601	−0.84383	0.46659	0.97176
63	Washington	1.70586	−0.89402	−1.48911	−0.32234
64	Wayne	−1.52829	0.02821	1.35361	0.62531
65	Westmoreland	1.37143	−0.62873	−1.59422	0.41925
66	Wyoming	−1.26194	0.34448	0.62289	0.35224
67	York	0.36580	1.40434	−0.90680	−1.18985
Total N	67	67	67	67	67

Limited to first sixty-seven cases.

Table C.2 Factor Analysis of the Democratic Vote for President, Governor, and U.S. Senator in Pennsylvania, 1960–2004

Total Variance Explained						
	Initial Eigenvalues			Extraction Sums of Squared Loadings		
Component	Total	% of Variance	Cumulative %	Total	% of Variance	Cumulative %
1	29.633	75.982	75.982	29.633	75.982	75.982
2	3.066	7.861	83.844	3.066	7.861	83.844
3	1.440	3.693	87.537	1.440	3.693	87.537
4	1.125	2.885	90.422	1.125	2.885	90.422
5	0.611	1.567	91.989			
6	0.544	1.394	93.383			
7	0.395	1.014	94.397			

Extraction Method: Principal Component Analysis.

Component Matrix(a)			
	Component		
	1	2	3	4
P2004D	0.775	−0.566	−0.129	−0.115
S2004D	0.844	−0.460	−0.159	−0.081
G2002D	0.734	−0.611	0.038	−0.136
P2000D	0.854	−0.475	−0.105	−0.049
S2000D	0.917	−0.259	−0.234	0.003
G1998D	0.899	−0.238	−0.062	0.145
S1998D	0.798	0.031	−0.217	0.290
P1996D	0.908	−0.346	−0.117	0.015
G1994D	0.844	−0.164	−0.089	0.338
S1994D	0.934	−0.201	−0.072	0.180
S1992D	0.904	−0.151	0.000	−0.048
P1992D	0.939	−0.138	−0.239	−0.060
S1991D	0.957	−0.060	−0.155	0.015
G1990D	0.597	0.467	−0.014	0.353
P1988D	0.943	0.113	−0.237	−0.043
S1988D	0.909	−0.197	0.057	0.072
S1986D	0.944	0.160	−0.029	0.027
G1986D	0.855	0.328	−0.069	0.266
P1984D	0.952	0.092	−0.224	−0.049
S1982D	0.922	0.149	0.127	0.158
G1982D	0.784	0.323	0.126	0.369
P1980D	0.938	0.202	−0.098	0.019
S1980D	0.798	0.493	−0.263	−0.127
G1978D	0.801	0.457	−0.231	−0.137
P1976D	0.970	0.070	0.119	0.024
S1976D	0.686	−0.315	0.508	0.223
S1974D	0.739	0.449	−0.289	−0.228
G1974D	0.803	−0.123	0.290	−0.014
P1972D	0.948	−0.108	0.047	−0.095
S1970D	0.639	0.215	0.337	−0.377
G1970D	0.884	0.177	0.111	−0.301
P1968D	0.966	0.019	0.055	−0.132
S1968D	0.937	0.009	0.202	−0.035
G1966D	0.926	0.236	0.131	−0.128

Component Matrix(a) *(continued)*

	Component			
	1	2	3	4
P1964D	0.919	0.095	0.210	−0.173
S1964D	0.829	0.178	0.372	0.037
S1962D	0.942	0.171	0.115	−0.114
G1962D	0.922	0.105	0.251	0.012
P1960D	0.940	−0.009	0.070	−0.027

Extraction Method: Principal Component Analysis.
a. Four components extracted.

Case Summaries(a)			
	County	REGR factor score 1 for analysis 2	REGR factor score 2 for analysis 2
1	Adams	−0.61007	0.28757
2	Allegheny	1.24397	−0.17750
3	Armstrong	0.54673	1.34146
4	Beaver	1.80973	0.99187
5	Bedford	−0.88844	0.74552
6	Berks	0.23162	−0.43495
7	Blair	−0.74761	0.71834
8	Bradford	−1.20572	−0.59493
9	Bucks	0.10296	−1.77032
10	Butler	−0.08180	1.50495
11	Cambria	1.35856	0.81340
12	Cameron	−0.37672	0.94068
13	Carbon	0.95306	−0.48049
14	Centre	−0.16589	−1.13598
15	Chester	−0.75538	−1.88923
16	Clarion	−0.24185	1.20825
17	Clearfield	0.37165	0.80657
18	Clinton	0.57859	−0.41129
19	Columbia	0.07981	0.06276
20	Crawford	−0.17141	0.37231
21	Cumberland	−0.98806	−0.24386
22	Dauphin	−0.41786	−0.74012
23	Delaware	0.02912	−2.43691
24	Elk	0.71521	1.30715

Case Summaries(a) *(continued)*

	County	REGR factor score 1 for analysis 2	REGR factor score 2 for analysis 2
25	Erie	0.75266	0.14666
26	Fayette	2.19224	0.61604
27	Forest	−0.29216	0.37215
28	Franklin	−0.70525	0.57464
29	Fulton	−0.41801	1.18578
30	Greene	1.97499	0.78162
31	Huntingdon	−0.84649	0.21548
32	Indiana	0.34854	0.25940
33	Jefferson	−0.39247	1.25359
34	Juniata	−0.45438	0.89494
35	Lackawanna	1.50684	−0.56684
36	Lancaster	−1.51149	−0.23951
37	Lawrence	1.34672	0.25909
38	Lebanon	−1.09697	0.06100
39	Lehigh	0.39595	−1.15677
40	Luzerne	1.24248	−0.05072
41	Lycoming	−0.50891	0.66641
42	McKean	−0.86463	−0.31713
43	Mercer	0.86674	−0.12781
44	Mifflin	−0.41826	0.50407
45	Monroe	0.07830	−0.84106
46	Montgomery	−0.22671	−3.02210
47	Montour	−0.22560	0.44702
48	Northampton	1.09524	−0.60275
49	Northumberland	0.27944	0.35565
50	Perry	−1.20096	0.57768
51	Philadelphia	3.05875	−3.49631
52	Pike	−0.85316	−1.15899
53	Potter	−0.96239	0.49371
54	Schuylkill	0.42405	−0.13150
55	Snyder	−1.84368	−0.23092
56	Somerset	0.06858	1.00479
57	Sullivan	−0.28306	0.06240
58	Susquehanna	−0.79082	−0.41573

Case Summaries(a) *(continued)*

	County	REGR factor score 1 for analysis 2	REGR factor score 2 for analysis 2
59	Tioga	−1.21683	−0.19901
60	Union	−1.46857	−0.62847
61	Venango	−0.30391	0.54137
62	Warren	−0.25779	−0.21944
63	Washington	1.70085	0.91367
64	Wayne	−1.27236	−0.83552
65	Westmoreland	1.24619	1.47233
66	Wyoming	−1.16037	−0.53085
67	York	−0.37351	0.32671
Total N	67	67	67

a. Limited to first sixty-seven cases.

Table C.3   Factor Analysis of the Democratic Vote for President, Governor, and U.S. Senator in Pennsylvania, 2000–2004

Total Variance Explained						
	Initial Eigenvalues			Extraction Sums of Squared Loadings		
Component	Total	% of Variance	Cumulative %	Total	% of Variance	Cumulative %
1	4.708	94.156	94.156	4.708	94.156	94.156
2	0.180	3.594	97.750			
3	0.059	1.182	98.932			
4	0.045	0.897	99.829			
5	0.009	0.171	100.000			

Extraction Method: Principal Component Analysis.

Component Matrix(a)	
	Component
	1
P2004D	0.982
S2004D	0.983
G2002D	0.946
P2000D	0.991
S2000D	0.950

Extraction Method: Principal Component Analysis.
a. One component extracted.

Case Summaries(a)		
	County	REGR factor score 1 for analysis 3
1	Adams	−0.79398
2	Allegheny	1.56068
3	Armstrong	−0.06914
4	Beaver	1.28911
5	Bedford	−1.25099
6	Berks	0.50399
7	Blair	−0.81974
8	Bradford	−0.92894
9	Bucks	1.02107
10	Butler	−0.49034
11	Cambria	0.80750
12	Cameron	−0.70941
13	Carbon	0.87166
14	Centre	0.25010
15	Chester	0.46667
16	Clarion	−0.54355
17	Clearfield	−0.13880
18	Clinton	0.26044
19	Columbia	−0.14624
20	Crawford	−0.24441
21	Cumberland	−0.60693
22	Dauphin	0.24915
23	Delaware	1.44860
24	Elk	0.21825
25	Erie	0.71260
26	Fayette	1.61206
27	Forest	−0.40691
28	Franklin	−1.12052
29	Fulton	−1.42396
30	Greene	1.20264
31	Huntingdon	−0.96655
32	Indiana	0.19983
33	Jefferson	−0.89448
34	Juniata	−1.15313

Case Summaries(a) *(continued)*

	County	REGR factor score 1 for analysis 3
35	Lackawanna	1.51182
36	Lancaster	−0.88864
37	Lawrence	1.18238
38	Lebanon	−0.72024
39	Lehigh	0.90730
40	Luzerne	0.97743
41	Lycoming	−0.87441
42	McKean	−0.71447
43	Mercer	0.78164
44	Mifflin	−1.00508
45	Monroe	0.62596
46	Montgomery	1.40618
47	Montour	−0.56031
48	Northampton	1.01216
49	Northumberland	−0.12207
50	Perry	−1.35384
51	Philadelphia	4.04467
52	Pike	−0.03547
53	Potter	−1.30854
54	Schuylkill	0.31678
55	Snyder	−1.32890
56	Somerset	−0.36982
57	Sullivan	−0.58401
58	Susquehanna	−0.51892
59	Tioga	−1.12921
60	Union	−0.76437
61	Venango	−0.26073
62	Warren	−0.12627
63	Washington	1.10578
64	Wayne	−0.56047
65	Westmoreland	0.51430
66	Wyoming	−0.58503
67	York	−0.54195
Total N	67	67

a. Limited to first sixty-seven cases.

Appendix D
Census Demographic Data on Pennsylvania's Sixty-Seven Counties

Table D.1 Population in 1960, 1980, and 2000

County	1960 Population	1980 Population	2000 Population	Change 1960–2000	% Change 1960–2000	Change 1980–2000	% Change 1980–2000
Adams	51,906	68,292	91,292	39,386	75.9%	23,000	33.7%
Allegheny	1,628,587	1,450,085	1,281,666	−346,921	−21.3%	−168,419	−11.6%
Armstrong	79,524	77,768	72,392	−7,132	−9.0%	−5,376	−6.9%
Beaver	206,948	204,441	181,412	−25,536	−12.3%	−23,029	−11.3%
Bedford	42,451	46,784	49,984	7,533	17.7%	3,200	6.8%
Berks	275,414	312,509	373,638	98,224	35.7%	61,129	19.6%
Blair	137,270	136,621	129,144	−8,126	−5.9%	−7,477	−5.5%
Bradford	54,925	62,919	62,761	7,836	14.3%	−158	−0.3%
Bucks	308,567	479,211	597,635	289,068	93.7%	118,424	24.7%
Butler	114,639	147,912	174,083	59,444	51.9%	26,171	17.7%
Cambria	203,283	183,263	152,598	−50,685	−24.9%	−30,665	−16.7%
Cameron	7,586	6,674	5,974	−1,612	−21.2%	−700	−10.5%
Carbon	52,889	53,285	58,802	5,913	11.2%	5,517	10.4%
Centre	78,580	112,760	135,758	57,178	72.8%	22,998	20.4%
Chester	210,608	316,660	433,501	222,893	105.8%	116,841	36.9%
Clarion	37,408	43,362	41,765	4,357	11.6%	−1,597	−3.7%
Clearfield	81,534	83,578	83,382	1,848	2.3%	−196	−0.2%
Clinton	37,619	38,971	37,914	295	0.8%	−1,057	−2.7%
Columbia	53,489	61,967	64,151	10,662	19.9%	2,184	3.5%
Crawford	77,956	88,869	90,366	12,410	15.9%	1,497	1.7%
Cumberland	124,816	178,541	213,674	88,858	71.2%	35,133	19.7%

Table D.1 *(continued)*

County	1960 Population	1980 Population	2000 Population	Change 1960–2000	% Change 1960–2000	Change 1980–2000	% Change 1980–2000
Dauphin	220,255	232,317	251,798	31,543	14.3%	19,481	8.4%
Delaware	553,154	555,007	550,864	−2,290	−0.4%	−4,143	−0.7%
Elk	37,328	38,338	35,112	−2,216	−5.9%	−3,226	−8.4%
Erie	250,682	279,780	280,843	30,161	12.0%	1,063	0.4%
Fayette	169,340	159,417	148,644	−20,696	−12.2%	−10,773	−6.8%
Forest	4,485	5,072	4,946	461	10.3%	−126	−2.5%
Franklin	88,172	113,629	129,313	41,141	46.7%	15,684	13.8%
Fulton	10,597	12,842	14,261	3,664	34.6%	1,419	11.0%
Greene	39,424	40,476	40,672	1,248	3.2%	196	0.5%
Huntingdon	39,457	42,253	45,586	6,129	15.5%	3,333	7.9%
Indiana	75,366	92,281	89,605	14,239	18.9%	−2,676	−2.9%
Jefferson	46,792	48,303	45,932	−860	−1.8%	−2,371	−4.9%
Juniata	15,874	19,188	22,821	6,947	43.8%	3,633	18.9%
Lackawanna	234,531	227,908	213,295	−21,236	−9.1%	−14,613	−6.4%
Lancaster	278,359	362,346	470,658	192,299	69.1%	108,312	29.9%
Lawrence	112,965	107,150	94,643	−18,322	−16.2%	−12,507	−11.7%
Lebanon	90,853	108,582	120,327	29,474	32.4%	11,745	10.8%
Lehigh	227,536	272,349	312,090	84,554	37.2%	39,741	14.6%
Luzerne	346,972	343,079	319,250	−27,722	−8.0%	−23,829	−6.9%
Lycoming	109,367	118,416	120,044	10,677	9.8%	1,628	1.4%
McKean	54,517	50,635	45,936	−8,581	−15.7%	−4,699	−9.3%
Mercer	127,519	128,299	120,293	−7,226	−5.7%	−8,006	−6.2%
Mifflin	44,348	46,908	46,486	2,138	4.8%	−422	−0.9%
Monroe	39,567	69,409	138,687	99,120	250.5%	69,278	99.8%
Montgomery	516,682	643,621	750,097	233,415	45.2%	106,476	16.5%
Montour	16,730	16,675	18,236	1,506	9.0%	1,561	9.4%
Northampton	201,412	225,418	267,066	65,654	32.6%	41,648	18.5%
Northumberland	104,138	100,381	94,556	−9,582	−9.2%	−5,825	−5.8%
Perry	26,582	35,718	43,602	17,020	64.0%	7,884	22.1%
Philadelphia	2,002,512	1,688,210	1,517,550	−484,962	−24.2%	−170,660	−10.1%
Pike	9,158	18,271	46,302	37,144	405.6%	28,031	153.4%
Potter	16,483	17,726	18,080	1,597	9.7%	354	2.0%

Table D.1 (continued)

County	1960 Population	1980 Population	2000 Population	Change 1960–2000	% Change 1960–2000	Change 1980–2000	% Change 1980–2000
Schuylkill	173,027	160,630	150,336	−22,691	−13.1%	−10,294	−6.4%
Snyder	25,922	33,584	37,546	11,624	44.8%	3,962	11.8%
Somerset	77,450	81,243	80,023	2,573	3.3%	−1,220	−1.5%
Sullivan	6,251	6,349	6,556	305	4.9%	207	3.3%
Susquehanna	33,137	37,876	42,238	9,101	27.5%	4,362	11.5%
Tioga	36,614	40,973	41,373	4,759	13.0%	400	1.0%
Union	25,646	32,870	41,624	15,978	62.3%	8,754	26.6%
Venango	65,295	64,444	57,565	−7,730	−11.8%	−6,879	−10.7%
Warren	45,582	47,449	43,863	−1,719	−3.8%	−3,586	−7.6%
Washington	217,271	217,074	202,897	−14,374	−6.6%	−14,177	−6.5%
Wayne	28,237	35,237	47,722	19,485	69.0%	12,485	35.4%
Westmoreland	352,629	392,294	369,993	17,364	4.9%	−22,301	−5.7%
Wyoming	16,813	26,433	28,080	11,267	67.0%	1,647	6.2%
York	238,336	312,963	381,751	143,415	60.2%	68,788	22.0%
Pennsylvania	11,319,366	11,863,895	12,281,054	961,688	8.5%	417,159	3.5%

Table D.2 Minority Population of Blacks/African Americans, Asians, and Latinos/Hispanics, 1980 and 2000

County	Black Population 1980	Percent Black 1980	Black Population 2000	Percent Black 2000	Percent Asian 1980	Percent Asian 2000	Percent Latino 1980	Percent Latino 2000
Adams	705	1.0	1,126	1.2	0.3	0.5	0.9	3.6
Allegheny	150,246	10.4	158,002	12.4	0.5	1.7	0.6	0.9
Armstrong	713	0.9	658	0.8	0.1	0.1	0.3	0.4
Beaver	11,393	5.6	10,544	6.0	0.2	0.3	0.5	0.7
Bedford	154	0.3	130	0.4	0.1	0.3	0.3	0.5
Berks	7,722	2.5	13,057	3.7	0.4	1.0	2.9	9.7
Blair	956	0.7	1,281	1.2	0.2	0.4	0.3	0.5
Bradford	83	0.1	151	0.4	0.2	0.5	0.4	0.6
Bucks	11,950	2.5	18,454	3.3	0.8	2.3	1.2	2.3
Butler	731	0.5	1,125	0.8	0.3	0.6	0.3	0.6
Cambria	3,398	1.9	4,407	2.8	0.2	0.4	0.5	0.9
Cameron	6	0.1	16	0.4	0.0	0.1	0.3	0.6

Table D.2 *(continued)*

County	Black Population 1980	Percent Black 1980	Black Population 2000	Percent Black 2000	Percent Asian 1980	Percent Asian 2000	Percent Latino 1980	Percent Latino 2000
Carbon	30	0.1	354	0.6	0.2	0.3	0.6	1.5
Centre	1,468	1.3	3,330	2.6	1.1	4.0	0.7	1.7
Chester	23,085	7.3	26,421	6.2	0.6	2.0	1.8	3.7
Clarion	246	0.6	236	0.8	0.2	0.3	0.4	0.4
Clearfield	165	0.2	1,225	1.5	0.2	0.3	0.3	0.6
Clinton	129	0.3	241	0.5	0.2	0.4	0.4	0.5
Columbia	198	0.3	574	0.8	0.3	0.5	0.3	0.9
Crawford	1,091	1.2	1,313	1.6	0.2	0.3	0.4	0.6
Cumberland	2,457	1.4	5,111	2.4	0.7	1.7	0.5	1.3
Dauphin	31,275	13.5	41,439	16.9	0.6	2.0	1.5	4.1
Delaware	49,989	9.0	79,260	14.5	0.8	3.3	0.8	1.5
Elk	13	0.0	33	0.1	0.2	0.3	0.2	0.4
Erie	12,414	4.4	16,991	6.1	0.4	0.7	0.7	2.2
Fayette	6,041	3.8	5,109	3.5	0.2	0.2	0.4	0.4
Forest	11	0.2	108	2.2	0.1	0.1	0.3	1.2
Franklin	2,086	1.8	3,087	2.3	0.3	0.6	0.6	1.8
Fulton	96	0.8	86	0.7	0.1	0.1	0.5	0.4
Greene	316	0.8	1,603	3.9	0.1	0.2	0.6	0.9
Huntingdon	969	2.3	2,322	5.1	0.1	0.2	0.3	1.1
Indiana	952	1.0	1,499	1.6	0.2	0.7	0.4	0.5
Jefferson	37	0.1	46	0.1	0.1	0.2	0.3	0.4
Juniata	17	0.1	51	0.4	0.1	0.2	0.4	1.6
Lackawanna	1,109	0.5	2,432	1.3	0.3	0.8	0.4	1.4
Lancaster	6,972	1.9	12,722	2.8	0.6	1.4	2.5	5.7
Lawrence	3,042	2.8	3,568	3.6	0.2	0.3	0.4	0.6
Lebanon	462	0.4	1,187	1.3	0.5	0.9	1.5	5.0
Lehigh	4,134	1.5	10,449	3.6	0.5	2.1	2.6	10.2
Luzerne	2,311	0.7	5,479	1.7	0.3	0.6	0.4	1.2
Lycoming	1,749	1.5	4,988	4.3	0.3	0.4	0.3	0.7
McKean	96	0.2	907	1.9	0.2	0.3	0.3	1.1
Mercer	5,447	4.3	6,056	5.3	0.2	0.4	0.3	0.7
Mifflin	96	0.2	221	0.5	0.1	0.3	0.3	0.6
Monroe	982	1.4	8,291	6.0	0.4	1.1	0.8	6.6

Table D.2 *(continued)*

County	Black Population 1980	Percent Black 1980	Black Population 2000	Percent Black 2000	Percent Asian 1980	Percent Asian 2000	Percent Latino 1980	Percent Latino 2000
Montgomery	30,864	4.8	55,190	7.5	1.2	4.0	0.8	2.0
Montour	21	0.1	135	1.0	0.5	1.3	0.3	0.9
Northampton	3,974	1.8	7,258	2.8	0.5	1.4	3.1	6.7
Northumber-land	162	0.2	1,450	1.5	0.1	0.2	0.3	1.1
Perry	28	0.1	126	0.4	0.1	0.1	0.4	0.7
Philadelphia	638,878	37.8	653,364	43.2	1.1	4.5	3.8	8.5
Pike	55	0.3	1,396	3.3	0.2	0.6	1.3	5.0
Potter	30	0.2	64	0.3	0.2	0.5	0.4	0.6
Schuylkill	310	0.2	3,227	2.1	0.2	0.4	0.3	1.1
Snyder	145	0.4	288	0.8	0.2	0.4	0.3	1.0
Somerset	57	0.1	1,382	1.6	0.1	0.2	0.3	0.7
Sullivan	40	0.6	137	2.2	0.1	0.2	0.6	1.1
Susquehanna	46	0.1	125	0.3	0.1	0.2	0.4	0.7
Tioga	177	0.4	253	0.6	0.1	0.3	0.4	0.5
Union	919	2.8	2,826	6.9	0.3	1.1	0.7	3.9
Venango	316	0.5	623	1.1	0.2	0.2	0.3	0.5
Warren	47	0.1	51	0.2	0.2	0.3	0.2	0.3
Washington	7,525	3.5	6,522	3.3	0.2	0.4	0.6	0.6
Wayne	82	0.2	740	1.6	0.1	0.4	0.5	1.7
Westmore-land	6,439	1.6	7,169	2.0	0.3	0.5	0.3	0.5
Wyoming	74	0.3	138	0.5	0.1	0.3	0.4	0.7
York	9,079	2.9	13,515	3.7	0.4	0.9	0.9	3.0
Pennsylvania	**1,046,810**	**8.8**	**1,211,669**	**9.9**	**0.5**	**1.8**	**1.3**	**3.2**

Table D.3   Percent Employed in Agriculture, Forestry, Fishing, and Hunting Industries; Percent Employed in Manufacturing Industry; and Percent Urban

County	Agriculture, Forestry, Fishing, Hunting Industries		Manufacturing Industry		Percent Urban	
	1980	2000	1980	2000	1980	2000
Adams	6.0	3.2	36.9	22.6	18.8	40.2
Allegheny	0.3	0.1	21.4	9.0	95.6	97.3
Armstrong	3.8	2.7	30.5	21.7	15.5	36.9
Beaver	0.7	0.4	36.3	15.2	75.9	73.2
Bedford	6.8	4.2	23.9	22.4	7.1	15.6
Berks	2.4	1.7	38.2	24.1	60.5	72.8
Blair	1.6	1.4	23.8	15.9	64.5	74.0
Bradford	7.8	5.8	38.4	26.0	22.4	27.8
Bucks	1.3	0.4	32.8	15.5	80.6	90.1
Butler	2.9	1.0	32.2	18.3	28.1	53.3
Cambria	0.9	0.8	20.8	11.5	53.2	67.6
Cameron	1.6	0.9	58.8	41.5	42.5	56.4
Carbon	0.9	0.6	39.1	22.1	57.6	49.5
Centre	3.2	1.5	18.4	10.6	54.2	64.3
Chester	4.0	1.9	31.9	14.8	54.6	81.0
Clarion	2.8	2.5	22.3	17.4	15.4	21.4
Clearfield	1.0	1.5	22.7	18.6	23.9	46.0
Clinton	2.6	2.4	41.9	24.5	24.7	49.2
Columbia	2.8	1.7	35.5	24.1	38.1	55.7
Crawford	4.0	3.1	35.6	26.3	25.2	34.6
Cumberland	1.9	1.2	19.0	10.1	62.3	74.9
Dauphin	1.0	0.7	18.4	11.1	74.8	85.3
Delaware	0.6	0.2	23.5	9.9	97.1	98.9
Elk	0.8	1.2	57.0	44.0	41.6	52.2
Erie	1.6	0.9	36.9	23.8	72.4	80.4
Fayette	1.3	1.0	26.1	14.8	32.2	53.2
Forest	3.8	3.9	26.8	19.8	0.0	0.0
Franklin	5.2	2.7	35.0	21.0	30.7	52.8
Fulton	7.6	4.0	29.2	26.9	0.0	0.0
Greene	2.5	1.4	11.4	8.9	11.1	31.3
Huntingdon	4.3	3.5	30.0	21.6	24.0	30.7
Indiana	2.8	2.3	14.9	10.5	21.9	37.9
Juniata	9.8	5.3	36.3	23.6	0.0	14.6

Table D.3 (continued)

County	Agriculture, Forestry, Fishing, Hunting Industries		Manufacturing Industry		Percent Urban	
	1980	2000	1980	2000	1980	2000
Lackawanna	0.7	0.4	30.0	15.7	83.2	82.5
Lancaster	5.1	2.7	34.7	22.5	54.6	75.3
Lawrence	1.9	1.1	35.1	16.9	48.0	58.9
Lebanon	3.3	2.4	40.3	21.9	41.0	68.9
Lehigh	1.1	0.4	39.9	20.2	81.6	90.3
Luzerne	0.7	0.5	30.6	16.6	73.8	79.6
Lycoming	1.9	1.6	35.7	22.5	55.7	64.0
McKean	1.3	1.4	37.5	28.4	37.0	36.6
Mercer	2.1	1.5	33.9	20.1	50.0	51.9
Mifflin	5.2	4.1	41.5	30.2	21.0	44.2
Monroe	1.3	0.4	25.3	13.0	19.0	50.4
Montgomery	1.0	0.2	31.1	15.0	88.4	96.5
Montour	3.7	3.0	26.8	17.0	47.1	45.7
Northampton	1.0	0.5	42.4	20.7	69.7	84.7
Northumberland	2.0	1.7	33.8	21.8	51.0	63.0
Perry	3.8	2.7	21.3	12.1	6.9	13.7
Philadelphia	0.2	0.1	17.9	8.8	100.0	100.0
Pike	1.7	0.4	14.6	10.0	0.0	10.6
Potter	7.2	6.0	32.3	21.9	15.8	0.0
Schuylkill	1.6	1.1	41.8	26.0	47.9	63.5
Snyder	6.3	4.0	32.1	27.0	15.6	28.7
Somerset	4.7	3.3	23.1	16.9	19.9	25.5
Sullivan	8.0	4.6	40.4	21.6	0.0	0.0
Susquehanna	7.5	4.7	33.4	20.2	0.0	18.5
Tioga	7.4	4.5	27.3	24.0	17.4	15.7
Union	4.7	2.8	30.0	22.0	26.0	55.0
Venango	1.1	1.2	33.1	19.8	43.4	46.0
Warren	3.0	2.3	35.9	26.6	25.6	45.4
Washington	1.2	0.7	25.8	14.9	57.8	63.1
Wayne	7.2	3.1	25.9	10.6	14.6	16.1
Westmoreland	0.9	0.4	31.8	17.1	64.6	74.3
Wyoming	6.6	2.8	39.1	18.8	0.0	15.0
York	2.1	0.9	43.1	23.9	51.1	71.5
Pennsylvania	**1.6**	**1.0**	**28.4**	**16.0**	**69.3**	**77.0**

Appendix E
Pennsylvania Party Registration and Turnout Data

Table E.1a Party Registration in Pennsylvania in 1960

County	1960 Dem Reg	1960 Rep Reg	1960 Others	Total 1960 Reg	Dem/ Rep Plurality		Percent Dem Reg	Percent Rep Reg	Percent Others
Adams	11,391	12,289	388	24,068	898	R	47.3%	51.1%	1.6%
Allegheny	536,601	323,048	6,067	865,716	213,553	D	62.0%	37.3%	0.7%
Armstrong	17,693	22,084	155	39,932	4,391	R	44.3%	55.3%	0.4%
Beaver	51,380	43,340	905	95,625	8,040	D	53.7%	45.3%	0.9%
Bedford	10,259	11,658	83	22,000	1,399	R	46.6%	53.0%	0.4%
Berks	79,765	45,753	3,026	128,544	34,012	D	62.1%	35.6%	2.4%
Blair	24,002	38,138	341	62,481	14,136	R	38.4%	61.0%	0.5%
Bradford	7,962	17,589	227	25,778	9,627	R	30.9%	68.2%	0.9%
Bucks	59,559	76,354	4,725	140,638	16,795	R	42.3%	54.3%	3.4%
Butler	20,532	31,808	408	52,748	11,276	R	38.9%	60.3%	0.8%
Cambria	61,216	40,808	348	102,372	20,408	D	59.8%	39.9%	0.3%
Cameron	1,253	2,677	46	3,976	1,424	R	31.5%	67.3%	1.2%
Carbon	14,846	13,346	234	28,426	1,500	D	52.2%	46.9%	0.8%
Centre	12,086	17,947	842	30,875	5,861	R	39.1%	58.1%	2.7%
Chester	24,900	66,170	2,095	93,165	41,270	R	26.7%	71.0%	2.2%
Clarion	8,760	9,415	138	18,313	655	R	47.8%	51.4%	0.8%
Clearfield	19,943	17,724	374	38,041	2,219	D	52.4%	46.6%	1.0%
Clinton	7,535	9,368	136	17,039	1,833	R	44.2%	55.0%	0.8%
Columbia	15,666	11,905	285	27,856	3,761	D	56.2%	42.7%	1.0%
Crawford	13,492	21,671	245	35,408	8,179	R	38.1%	61.2%	0.7%
Cumberland	23,793	35,650	1,224	60,667	11,857	R	39.2%	58.8%	2.0%
Dauphin	35,541	77,228	2,103	114,872	41,687	R	30.9%	67.2%	1.8%

Table E.1a (continued)

County	1960 Dem Reg	1960 Rep Reg	1960 Others	Total 1960 Reg	Dem/ Rep Plurality		Percent Dem Reg	Percent Rep Reg	Percent Others
Delaware	59,500	229,012	6,610	295,122	169,512	R	20.2%	77.6%	2.2%
Elk	10,243	7,115	195	17,553	3,128	D	58.4%	40.5%	1.1%
Erie	59,559	58,391	1,308	119,258	1,168	D	49.9%	49.0%	1.1%
Fayette	59,147	23,642	344	83,133	35,505	D	71.1%	28.4%	0.4%
Forest	1,154	1,546	62	2,762	392	R	41.8%	56.0%	2.2%
Franklin	18,690	20,380	708	39,778	1,690	R	47.0%	51.2%	1.8%
Fulton	2,885	2,231	34	5,150	654	D	56.0%	43.3%	0.7%
Greene	15,422	4,626	35	20,083	10,796	D	76.8%	23.0%	0.2%
Huntingdon	6,162	12,322	106	18,590	6,160	R	33.1%	66.3%	0.6%
Indiana	16,720	20,329	337	37,386	3,609	R	44.7%	54.4%	0.9%
Jefferson	11,380	14,581	232	26,193	3,201	R	43.4%	55.7%	0.9%
Juniata	4,073	4,259	64	8,396	186	R	48.5%	50.7%	0.8%
Lackawanna	97,825	50,601	699	149,125	47,224	D	65.6%	33.9%	0.5%
Lancaster	34,144	87,010	4,877	126,031	52,866	R	27.1%	69.0%	3.9%
Lawrence	23,379	29,991	439	53,809	6,612	R	43.4%	55.7%	0.8%
Lebanon	13,738	26,687	447	40,872	12,949	R	33.6%	65.3%	1.1%
Lehigh	52,079	51,760	1,311	105,150	319	D	49.5%	49.2%	1.2%
Luzerne	81,763	115,050	594	197,407	33,287	R	41.4%	58.3%	0.3%
Lycoming	23,413	30,475	581	54,469	7,062	R	43.0%	55.9%	1.1%
McKean	7,177	17,133	222	24,532	9,956	R	29.3%	69.8%	0.9%
Mercer	29,207	30,499	428	60,134	1,292	R	48.6%	50.7%	0.7%
Mifflin	8,155	9,264	97	17,516	1,109	R	46.6%	52.9%	0.6%
Monroe	11,720	8,054	270	20,044	3,666	D	58.5%	40.2%	1.3%
Montgomery	61,654	189,550	6,370	257,574	127,896	R	23.9%	73.6%	2.5%
Montour	3,353	3,991	212	7,556	638	R	44.4%	52.8%	2.8%
Northampton	58,172	34,067	1,089	93,328	24,105	D	62.3%	36.5%	1.2%
Northumber- land	23,427	32,958	310	56,695	9,531	R	41.3%	58.1%	0.5%
Perry	5,279	8,002	116	13,397	2,723	R	39.4%	59.7%	0.9%
Philadelphia	587,157	408,694	22,046	1,017,897	178,463	D	57.7%	40.2%	2.2%
Pike	2,307	4,003	132	6,442	1,696	R	35.8%	62.1%	2.0%
Potter	3,509	5,316	98	8,923	1,807	R	39.3%	59.6%	1.1%
Schuylkill	37,582	65,420	1,178	104,180	27,838	R	36.1%	62.8%	1.1%

Table E.1a *(continued)*

County	1960 Dem Reg	1960 Rep Reg	1960 Others	Total 1960 Reg	Dem/ Rep Plurality		Percent Dem Reg	Percent Rep Reg	Percent Others
Snyder	3,207	8,402	72	11,681	5,195	R	27.5%	71.9%	0.6%
Somerset	19,871	21,186	189	41,246	1,315	R	48.2%	51.4%	0.5%
Sullivan	1,632	1,957	37	3,626	325	R	45.0%	54.0%	1.0%
Susquehanna	6,446	11,471	80	17,997	5,025	R	35.8%	63.7%	0.4%
Tioga	4,337	12,642	147	17,126	8,305	R	25.3%	73.8%	0.9%
Union	2,770	7,843	103	10,716	5,073	R	25.8%	73.2%	1.0%
Venango	9,684	19,110	538	29,332	9,426	R	33.0%	65.2%	1.8%
Warren	7,240	12,977	488	20,705	5,737	R	35.0%	62.7%	2.4%
Washington	71,831	33,424	451	105,706	38,407	D	68.0%	31.6%	0.4%
Wayne	5,477	10,235	133	15,845	4,758	R	34.6%	64.6%	0.8%
Westmore-land	118,024	58,078	831	176,933	59,946	D	66.7%	32.8%	0.5%
Wyoming	3,753	6,403	44	10,200	2,650	R	36.8%	62.8%	0.4%
York	62,780	45,580	1,339	109,699	17,200	D	57.2%	41.6%	1.2%
Pennsylvania	**2,805,202**	**2,802,237**	**80,398**	**5,687,837**	**2,965**	**D**	**49.3%**	**49.3%**	**1.4%**

Table E.1b Party Registration in Pennsylvania in 2004

County	2004 Dem Reg	2004 Rep Reg	2004 Others	Total 2004 Reg	Dem/ Rep Plurality		Percent Dem Reg	Percent Rep Reg	Percent Others
Adams	18,100	32,137	7,788	58,025	14,037	R	31.2%	55.4%	13.4%
Allegheny	557,900	262,692	98,285	918,877	295,208	D	60.7%	28.6%	10.7%
Armstrong	20,442	20,739	4,080	45,261	297	R	45.2%	45.8%	9.0%
Beaver	73,401	37,538	11,411	122,350	35,863	D	60.0%	30.7%	9.3%
Bedford	11,033	19,395	2,450	32,878	8,362	R	33.6%	59.0%	7.5%
Berks	103,541	98,170	33,455	235,166	5,371	D	44.0%	41.7%	14.2%
Blair	26,213	46,047	8,338	80,598	19,834	R	32.5%	57.1%	10.3%
Bradford	10,624	22,509	4,019	37,152	11,885	R	28.6%	60.6%	10.8%
Bucks	173,803	208,639	69,457	451,899	34,836	R	38.5%	46.2%	15.4%
Butler	42,466	57,737	12,740	112,943	15,271	R	37.6%	51.1%	11.3%
Cambria	56,390	28,849	6,530	91,769	27,541	D	61.4%	31.4%	7.1%
Cameron	1,562	1,862	294	3,718	300	R	42.0%	50.1%	7.9%
Carbon	17,807	14,626	4,187	36,620	3,181	D	48.6%	39.9%	11.4%
Centre	32,867	38,367	15,598	86,832	5,500	R	37.9%	44.2%	18.0%

Table E.1b *(continued)*

County	2004 Dem Reg	2004 Rep Reg	2004 Others	Total 2004 Reg	Dem/ Rep Plurality		Percent Dem Reg	Percent Rep Reg	Percent Others
Chester	98,765	170,419	55,563	324,747	71,654	R	30.4%	52.5%	17.1%
Clarion	9,638	12,148	2,046	23,832	2,510	R	40.4%	51.0%	8.6%
Clearfield	22,226	22,768	4,505	49,499	542	R	44.9%	46.0%	9.1%
Clinton	9,018	9,328	2,093	20,439	310	R	44.1%	45.6%	10.2%
Columbia	18,422	18,640	5,872	42,934	218	R	42.9%	43.4%	13.7%
Crawford	23,212	30,037	5,320	58,569	6,825	R	39.6%	51.3%	9.1%
Cumberland	42,970	81,752	20,005	144,727	38,782	R	29.7%	56.5%	13.8%
Dauphin	67,345	83,699	22,183	173,227	16,354	R	38.9%	48.3%	12.8%
Delaware	131,317	213,030	42,256	386,603	81,713	R	34.0%	55.1%	10.9%
Elk	11,026	7,930	2,061	21,017	3,096	D	52.5%	37.7%	9.8%
Erie	92,922	73,308	18,388	184,618	19,614	D	50.3%	39.7%	10.0%
Fayette	61,475	21,421	6,038	88,934	40,054	D	69.1%	24.1%	6.8%
Forest	1,248	1,715	189	3,152	467	R	39.6%	54.4%	6.0%
Franklin	24,235	48,084	9,762	82,081	23,849	R	29.5%	58.6%	11.9%
Fulton	3,269	5,025	636	8,930	1,756	R	36.6%	56.3%	7.1%
Greene	17,151	6,514	1,579	25,244	10,637	D	67.9%	25.8%	6.3%
Huntingdon	9,782	16,987	2,912	29,681	7,205	R	33.0%	57.2%	9.8%
Indiana	23,770	23,699	6,201	53,670	71	D	44.3%	44.2%	11.6%
Jefferson	11,289	15,213	2,345	28,847	3,924	R	39.1%	52.7%	8.1%
Juniata	4,757	7,875	1,131	13,763	3,118	R	34.6%	57.2%	8.2%
Lackawanna	96,804	46,882	10,778	154,464	49,922	D	62.7%	30.4%	7.0%
Lancaster	82,172	184,852	45,854	312,878	102,680	R	26.3%	59.1%	14.7%
Lawrence	32,881	21,995	4,774	59,650	10,886	D	55.1%	36.9%	8.0%
Lebanon	21,307	42,980	9,331	73,618	21,673	R	28.9%	58.4%	12.7%
Lehigh	88,149	79,364	30,284	197,797	8,785	D	44.6%	40.1%	15.3%
Luzerne	120,420	75,529	17,171	213,120	44,891	D	56.5%	35.4%	8.1%
Lycoming	24,756	37,261	7,416	69,433	12,505	R	35.7%	53.7%	10.7%
McKean	8,634	16,368	2,957	27,959	7,734	R	30.9%	58.5%	10.6%
Mercer	36,745	31,626	7,702	76,073	5,119	D	48.3%	41.6%	10.1%
Mifflin	9,293	14,883	2,347	26,523	5,590	R	35.0%	56.1%	8.8%
Monroe	40,959	39,271	18,554	98,784	1,688	D	41.5%	39.8%	18.8%
Montgomery	214,233	268,755	81,970	564,958	54,522	R	37.9%	47.6%	14.5%
Montour	4,428	5,871	1,488	11,787	1,443	R	37.6%	49.8%	12.6%

Table E.1b *(continued)*

County	2004 Dem Reg	2004 Rep Reg	2004 Others	Total 2004 Reg	Dem/ Rep Plurality		Percent Dem Reg	Percent Rep Reg	Percent Others
Northampton	83,694	67,193	27,812	178,699	16,501	D	46.8%	37.6%	15.6%
Northumber-land	22,958	24,901	4,074	51,933	1,943	R	44.2%	47.9%	7.8%
Perry	7,004	17,196	3,082	27,282	10,192	R	25.7%	63.0%	11.3%
Philadelphia	796,033	175,434	90,972	1,062,439	620,599	D	74.9%	16.5%	8.6%
Pike	12,762	18,488	6,975	38,225	5,726	R	33.4%	48.4%	18.2%
Potter	3,736	7,341	969	12,046	3,605	R	31.0%	60.9%	8.0%
Schuylkill	36,200	47,213	8,158	91,571	11,013	R	39.5%	51.6%	8.9%
Snyder	5,034	13,689	2,121	20,844	8,655	R	24.2%	65.7%	10.2%
Somerset	22,487	25,987	3,698	52,172	3,500	R	43.1%	49.8%	7.1%
Sullivan	1,699	2,528	351	4,578	829	R	37.1%	55.2%	7.7%
Susquehanna	8,561	15,467	2,746	26,774	6,906	R	32.0%	57.8%	10.3%
Tioga	7,594	17,071	2,574	27,239	9,477	R	27.9%	62.7%	9.4%
Union	6,260	12,741	3,074	22,075	6,481	R	28.4%	57.7%	13.9%
Venango	13,756	19,774	3,826	37,356	6,018	R	36.8%	52.9%	10.2%
Warren	10,604	14,577	3,327	28,508	3,973	R	37.2%	51.1%	11.7%
Washington	88,941	47,351	13,424	149,716	41,590	D	59.4%	31.6%	9.0%
Wayne	8,669	17,488	3,907	30,064	8,819	R	28.8%	58.2%	13.0%
Westmore-land	142,979	88,727	24,659	256,365	54,252	D	55.8%	34.6%	9.6%
Wyoming	6,102	10,909	1,986	18,997	4,807	R	32.1%	57.4%	10.5%
York	89,646	136,667	37,821	264,134	47,021	R	33.9%	51.7%	14.3%
Pennsylvania	**3,985,486**	**3,405,278**	**975,899**	**8,366,663**	**580,208**	**D**	**47.6%**	**40.7%**	**11.7%**

Table E.2 Percent Net Gain of Democratic and Republican Registration from 1960 and 2004

County	1960 Democratic Registration	2004 Democratic Registration	Difference	% Dem Change	County	1960 Republican Registration	2004 Republican Registration	Difference	% Rep Change	% Gain for Dems & Reps	
Adams	11,391	18,100	6,709	58.9%	Adams	12,289	32,137	19,848	161.5%	102.6%	R
Allegheny	536,601	557,900	21,299	4.0%	Allegheny	323,048	262,692	−60,356	−18.7%	22.7%	D
Armstrong	17,693	20,442	2,749	15.5%	Armstrong	22,084	20,739	−1,345	−6.1%	21.6%	D
Beaver	51,380	73,401	22,021	42.9%	Beaver	43,340	37,538	−5,802	−13.4%	56.2%	D
Bedford	10,259	11,033	774	7.5%	Bedford	11,658	19,395	7,737	66.4%	58.8%	R
Berks	79,765	103,541	23,776	29.8%	Berks	45,753	98,170	52,417	114.6%	84.8%	R
Blair	24,002	26,213	2,211	9.2%	Blair	38,138	46,047	7,909	20.7%	11.5%	R
Bradford	7,962	10,624	2,662	33.4%	Bradford	17,589	22,509	4,920	28.0%	5.5%	D
Bucks	59,559	173,803	114,244	191.8%	Bucks	76,354	208,639	132,285	173.3%	18.6%	D
Butler	20,532	42,466	21,934	106.8%	Butler	31,808	57,737	25,929	81.5%	25.3%	D
Cambria	61,216	56,390	−4,826	−7.9%	Cambria	40,808	28,849	−11,959	−29.3%	21.4%	D
Cameron	1,253	1,562	309	24.7%	Cameron	2,677	1,862	−815	−30.4%	55.1%	D
Carbon	14,846	17,807	2,961	19.9%	Carbon	13,346	14,626	1,280	9.6%	10.4%	D
Centre	12,086	32,867	20,781	171.9%	Centre	17,947	38,367	20,420	113.8%	58.2%	D
Chester	24,900	98,765	73,865	296.6%	Chester	66,170	170,419	104,249	157.5%	139.1%	R
Clarion	8,760	9,638	878	10.0%	Clarion	9,415	12,148	2,733	29.0%	19.0%	R
Clearfield	19,943	22,226	2,283	11.4%	Clearfield	17,724	22,768	5,044	28.5%	17.0%	R
Clinton	7,535	9,018	1,483	19.7%	Clinton	9,368	9,328	−40	−0.4%	20.1%	D
Columbia	15,666	18,422	2,756	17.6%	Columbia	11,905	18,640	6,735	56.6%	39.0%	R
Crawford	13,492	23,212	9,720	72.0%	Crawford	21,671	30,037	8,366	38.6%	33.4%	D

Table E.2 *(continued)*

County	1960 Democratic Registration	2004 Democratic Registration	Difference	% Dem Change	County	1960 Republican Registration	2004 Republican Registration	Difference	% Rep Change	% Gain for Dems & Reps	
Cumberland	23,793	42,970	19,177	80.6%	Cumberland	35,650	81,752	46,102	129.3%	48.7%	R
Dauphin	35,541	67,345	31,804	89.5%	Dauphin	77,228	83,699	6,471	8.4%	81.1%	D
Delaware	59,500	131,317	71,817	120.7%	Delaware	229,012	213,030	-15,982	-7.0%	127.7%	D
Elk	10,243	11,026	783	7.6%	Elk	7,115	7,930	815	11.5%	3.8%	R
Erie	59,559	92,922	33,363	56.0%	Erie	58,391	73,308	14,917	25.5%	30.5%	D
Fayette	59,147	61,475	2,328	3.9%	Fayette	23,642	21,421	-2,221	-9.4%	13.3%	D
Forest	1,154	1,248	94	8.1%	Forest	1,546	1,715	169	10.9%	2.8%	R
Franklin	18,690	24,235	5,545	29.7%	Franklin	20,380	48,084	27,704	135.9%	106.3%	R
Fulton	2,885	3,269	384	13.3%	Fulton	2,231	5,025	2,794	125.2%	111.9%	R
Greene	15,422	17,151	1,729	11.2%	Greene	4,626	6,514	1,888	40.8%	29.6%	R
Huntingdon	6,162	9,782	3,620	58.7%	Huntingdon	12,322	16,987	4,665	37.9%	20.9%	D
Indiana	16,720	23,770	7,050	42.2%	Indiana	20,329	23,699	3,370	16.6%	25.6%	D
Jefferson	11,380	11,289	-91	-0.8%	Jefferson	14,581	15,213	632	4.3%	5.1%	R
Juniata	4,073	4,757	684	16.8%	Juniata	4,259	7,875	3,616	84.9%	68.1%	R
Lackawanna	97,825	96,804	-1,021	-1.0%	Lackawanna	50,601	46,882	-3,719	-7.3%	6.3%	D
Lancaster	34,144	82,172	48,028	140.7%	Lancaster	87,010	184,852	97,842	112.4%	28.2%	D
Lawrence	23,379	32,881	9,502	40.6%	Lawrence	29,991	21,995	-7,996	-26.7%	67.3%	D
Lebanon	13,738	21,307	7,569	55.1%	Lebanon	26,687	42,980	16,293	61.1%	6.0%	R
Lehigh	52,079	88,149	36,070	69.3%	Lehigh	51,760	79,364	27,604	53.3%	15.9%	D
Luzerne	81,763	120,420	38,657	47.3%	Luzerne	115,050	75,529	-39,521	-34.4%	81.6%	D
Lycoming	23,413	24,756	1,343	5.7%	Lycoming	30,475	37,261	6,786	22.3%	16.5%	R

Table E.2 (*continued*)

County	1960 Democratic Registration	2004 Democratic Registration	Difference	% Dem Change	County	1960 Republican Registration	2004 Republican Registration	Difference	% Rep Change	% Gain for Dems & Reps	
McKean	7,177	8,634	1,457	20.3%	McKean	17,133	16,368	−765	−4.5%	24.8%	D
Mercer	29,207	36,745	7,538	25.8%	Mercer	30,499	31,626	1,127	3.7%	22.1%	D
Mifflin	8,155	9,293	1,138	14.0%	Mifflin	9,264	14,883	5,619	60.7%	46.7%	R
Monroe	11,720	40,959	29,239	249.5%	Monroe	8,054	39,271	31,217	387.6%	138.1%	R
Montgomery	61,654	214,233	152,579	247.5%	Montgomery	189,550	268,755	79,205	41.8%	205.7%	D
Montour	3,353	4,428	1,075	32.1%	Montour	3,991	5,871	1,880	47.1%	15.0%	R
Northampton	58,172	83,694	25,522	43.9%	Northampton	34,067	67,193	33,126	97.2%	53.4%	R
Northumberland	23,427	22,958	−469	−2.0%	Northumberland	32,958	24,901	−8,057	−24.4%	22.4%	D
Perry	5,279	7,004	1,725	32.7%	Perry	8,002	17,196	9,194	114.9%	82.2%	R
Philadelphia	587,157	796,033	208,876	35.6%	Philadelphia	408,694	175,434	−233,260	−57.1%	92.6%	D
Pike	2,307	12,762	10,455	453.2%	Pike	4,003	18,488	14,485	361.9%	91.3%	D
Potter	3,509	3,736	227	6.5%	Potter	5,316	7,341	2,025	38.1%	31.6%	R
Schuylkill	37,582	36,200	−1,382	−3.7%	Schuylkill	65,420	47,213	−18,207	−27.8%	24.2%	D
Snyder	3,207	5,034	1,827	57.0%	Snyder	8,402	13,689	5,287	62.9%	6.0%	R
Somerset	19,871	22,487	2,616	13.2%	Somerset	21,186	25,987	4,801	22.7%	9.5%	R
Sullivan	1,632	1,699	67	4.1%	Sullivan	1,957	2,528	571	29.2%	25.1%	R
Susquehanna	6,446	8,561	2,115	32.8%	Susquehanna	11,471	15,467	3,996	34.8%	2.0%	R
Tioga	4,337	7,594	3,257	75.1%	Tioga	12,642	17,071	4,429	35.0%	40.1%	D

Table E.2 *(continued)*

County	1960 Democratic Registration	2004 Democratic Registration	Difference	% Dem Change	County	1960 Republican Registration	2004 Republican Registration	Difference	% Rep Change	% Gain for Dems & Reps	
Union	2,770	6,260	3,490	126.0%	Union	7,843	12,741	4,898	62.5%	63.5%	D
Venango	9,684	13,756	4,072	42.0%	Venango	19,110	19,774	664	3.5%	38.6%	D
Warren	7,240	10,604	3,364	46.5%	Warren	12,977	14,577	1,600	12.3%	34.1%	D
Washington	71,831	88,941	17,110	23.8%	Washington	33,424	47,351	13,927	41.7%	17.8%	R
Wayne	5,477	8,669	3,192	58.3%	Wayne	10,235	17,488	7,253	70.9%	12.6%	R
Westmoreland	118,024	142,979	24,955	21.1%	Westmoreland	58,078	88,727	30,649	52.8%	31.6%	R
Wyoming	3,753	6,102	2,349	62.6%	Wyoming	6,403	10,909	4,506	70.4%	7.8%	R
York	62,780	89,646	26,866	42.8%	York	45,580	136,667	91,087	199.8%	157.0%	R
Pennsylvania	**2,805,202**	**3,985,486**	**1,180,284**	**42.1%**	**Pennsylvania**	**2,802,237**	**3,405,278**	**603,041**	**21.5%**	**20.6%**	**D**

Table E.3 Percent Net Gain of Democratic and Republican Registration, 2000–2004

County	2000 Democratic Registration	2004 Democratic Registration	Difference	% Dem Change	County	2000 Republican Registration	2004 Republican Registration	Difference	% Rep Change	% Gain for Dems & Reps	
Adams	15,925	18,100	2,175	13.7	Adams	26,774	32,137	5,363	20.03	6.4	R
Allegheny	568,560	557,900	−10,660	−1.9	Allegheny	260,791	262,692	1,901	0.73	2.6	R
Armstrong	20,600	20,442	−158	−0.8	Armstrong	18,927	20,739	1,812	9.57	10.3	R
Beaver	73,045	73,401	356	0.5	Beaver	33,451	37,538	4,087	12.22	11.7	R
Bedford	10,500	11,033	533	5.1	Bedford	16,955	19,395	2,440	14.39	9.3	R
Berks	94,861	103,541	8,680	9.2	Berks	89,731	98,170	8,439	9.4	0.3	R
Blair	25,224	26,213	989	3.9	Blair	40,852	46,047	5,195	12.72	8.8	R
Bradford	10,375	10,624	249	2.4	Bradford	22,345	22,509	164	0.73	1.7	D
Bucks	145,625	173,803	28,178	19.4	Bucks	192,498	208,639	16,141	8.39	11.0	D
Butler	42,516	42,466	−50	−0.1	Butler	51,557	57,737	6,180	11.99	12.1	R
Cambria	57,060	56,390	−670	−1.2	Cambria	28,818	28,849	31	0.11	1.3	R
Cameron	1,547	1,562	15	1.0	Cameron	1,771	1,862	91	5.14	4.2	R
Carbon	16,826	17,807	981	5.8	Carbon	13,755	14,626	871	6.33	0.5	R
Centre	33,215	32,867	−348	−1.1	Centre	40,000	38,367	−1,633	−4.08	3.0	D
Chester	82,428	98,765	16,337	19.8	Chester	163,833	170,419	6,586	4.02	15.8	D
Clarion	9,412	9,638	226	2.4	Clarion	11,431	12,148	717	6.27	3.9	R
Clearfield	20,778	22,226	1,448	7.0	Clearfield	20,572	22,768	2,196	10.67	3.7	R
Clinton	8,911	9,018	107	1.2	Clinton	9,508	9,328	−180	−1.89	3.1	D
Columbia	16,717	18,422	1,705	10.2	Columbia	15,851	18,640	2,789	17.6	7.4	R

Table E.3 (continued)

County	2000 Democratic Registration	2004 Democratic Registration	Difference	% Dem Change	County	2000 Republican Registration	2004 Republican Registration	Difference	% Rep Change	% Gain for Dems & Reps	
Crawford	20,680	23,212	2,532	12.2	Crawford	27,955	30,037	2,082	7.45	4.8	D
Cumberland	39,060	42,970	3,910	10.0	Cumberland	76,801	81,752	4,951	6.45	3.6	D
Dauphin	59,138	67,345	8,207	13.9	Dauphin	83,185	83,699	514	0.62	13.3	D
Delaware	110,104	131,317	21,213	19.3	Delaware	230,741	213,030	-17,711	-7.68	26.9	D
Elk	10,409	11,026	617	5.9	Elk	7,292	7,930	638	8.75	2.8	R
Erie	89,994	92,922	2,928	3.3	Erie	67,154	73,308	6,154	9.16	5.9	R
Fayette	60,069	61,475	1,406	2.3	Fayette	18,375	21,421	3,046	16.58	14.2	R
Forest	1,170	1,248	78	6.7	Forest	1,660	1,715	55	3.31	3.4	D
Franklin	22,387	24,235	1,848	8.3	Franklin	41,274	48,084	6,810	16.5	8.3	R
Fulton	3,286	3,269	-17	-0.5	Fulton	4,279	5,025	746	17.43	18.0	R
Greene	16,774	17,151	377	2.3	Greene	5,659	6,514	855	15.11	12.9	R
Huntingdon	8,941	9,782	841	9.4	Huntingdon	15,149	16,987	1,838	12.13	2.7	R
Indiana	21,670	23,770	2,100	9.7	Indiana	20,647	23,699	3,052	14.78	5.1	R
Jefferson	10,628	11,289	661	6.2	Jefferson	13,444	15,213	1,769	13.16	6.9	R
Juniata	4,610	4,757	147	3.2	Juniata	6,897	7,875	978	14.18	11.0	R
Lackawanna	92,065	96,804	4,739	5.2	Lackawanna	45,246	46,882	1,636	3.6	1.5	D
Lancaster	67,932	82,172	14,240	21.0	Lancaster	166,272	184,852	18,580	11.2	9.8	D
Lawrence	31,709	32,881	1,172	3.7	Lawrence	19,967	21,995	2,028	10.2	6.5	R
Lebanon	20,073	21,307	1,234	6.2	Lebanon	40,764	42,980	2,216	5.4	0.7	D
Lehigh	84,391	88,149	3,758	4.5	Lehigh	80,324	79,364	-960	-1.2	5.7	D
Luzerne	111,902	120,420	8,518	7.6	Luzerne	69,603	75,529	5,926	8.5	0.9	R

Table E.3 (continued)

County	2000 Democratic Registration	2004 Democratic Registration	Difference	% Dem Change	County	2000 Republican Registration	2004 Republican Registration	Difference	% Rep Change	% Gain for Dems & Reps	
Lycoming	23,405	24,756	1,351	5.8	Lycoming	34,440	37,261	2,821	8.2	2.4	R
McKean	8,089	8,634	545	6.7	McKean	15,704	16,368	664	4.2	2.5	D
Mercer	36,130	36,745	615	1.7	Mercer	30,029	31,626	1,597	5.3	3.6	R
Mifflin	8,982	9,293	311	3.5	Mifflin	13,222	14,883	1,661	12.6	9.1	R
Monroe	31,716	40,959	9,243	29.1	Monroe	33,546	39,271	5,725	17.1	12.1	D
Montgomery	173,503	214,233	40,730	23.5	Montgomery	272,615	268,755	-3,860	-1.4	24.9	D
Montour	3,959	4,428	469	11.9	Montour	5,069	5,871	802	15.8	4.0	R
Northampton	78,941	83,694	4,753	6.0	Northampton	62,906	67,193	4,287	6.8	0.8	R
Northumberland	23,829	22,958	-871	-3.7	Northumberland	23,393	24,901	1,508	6.5	10.1	R
Perry	6,709	7,004	295	4.4	Perry	15,480	17,196	1,716	11.1	6.7	R
Philadelphia	760,315	796,033	35,718	4.7	Philadelphia	198,007	175,434	-22,573	-11.4	16.1	D
Pike	9,943	12,762	2,819	28.4	Pike	15,184	18,488	3,304	21.8	6.6	D
Potter	3,644	3,736	92	2.5	Potter	7,036	7,341	305	4.3	1.8	R
Schuylkill	34,655	36,200	1,545	4.5	Schuylkill	46,093	47,213	1,120	2.4	2.0	D
Snyder	4,458	5,034	576	12.9	Snyder	12,674	13,689	1,015	8.0	4.9	D
Somerset	21,770	22,487	717	3.3	Somerset	23,998	25,987	1,989	8.3	5.0	R
Sullivan	1,712	1,699	-13	-0.8	Sullivan	2,570	2,528	-42	-1.6	0.9	D
Susquehanna	8,273	8,561	288	3.5	Susquehanna	15,061	15,467	406	2.7	0.8	D
Tioga	7,179	7,594	415	5.8	Tioga	16,294	17,071	777	4.8	1.0	D
Union	5,123	6,260	1,137	22.2	Union	11,380	12,741	1,361	12.0	10.2	D

Table E.3 *(continued)*

County	2000 Democratic Registration	2004 Democratic Registration	Difference	% Dem Change	County	2000 Republican Registration	2004 Republican Registration	Difference	% Rep Change	% Gain for Dems & Reps	
Venango	12,728	13,756	1,028	8.1	Venango	17,786	19,774	1,988	11.2	3.1	R
Warren	10,464	10,604	140	1.3	Warren	14,222	14,577	355	2.5	1.2	R
Washington	85,898	88,941	3,043	3.5	Washington	40,948	47,351	6,403	15.6	12.1	R
Wayne	7,750	8,669	919	11.9	Wayne	16,700	17,488	788	4.7	7.1	D
Westmore-land	141,652	142,979	1,327	0.9	Westmore-land	77,227	88,727	11,500	14.9	14.0	R
Wyoming	5,696	6,102	406	7.1	Wyoming	10,963	10,909	−54	−0.5	7.6	D
York	78,664	89,646	10,982	14.0	York	116,109	136,667	20,558	17.7	3.8	R
Pennsylvania	3,736,304	3,985,486	249,182	6.7	**Pennsylvania**	3,250,764	3,405,278	154,514	4.8	1.9	**D**

Table E.4 Turnout in 2004 Based on Registered Voters and Voting Age Population (VAP)

County	2004 Total Vote	2004 Total Registration	2004 Turnout of Reg Voters	2004 VAP	Percent VAP Registered	2004 Turnout of VAP
Adams	42,228	58,025	72.78	75,672	76.7%	55.8%
Allegheny	645,469	918,877	70.25	983,336	93.4%	65.6%
Armstrong	31,097	45,261	68.71	56,334	80.3%	55.2%
Beaver	82,543	122,350	67.46	140,224	87.3%	58.9%
Bedford	22,679	32,878	68.98	39,009	84.3%	58.1%
Berks	164,487	235,166	69.95	298,437	78.8%	55.1%
Blair	54,178	80,598	67.22	99,850	80.7%	54.3%
Bradford	25,652	37,152	69.05	47,693	77.9%	53.8%
Bucks	319,816	451,899	70.77	469,452	96.3%	68.1%
Butler	85,425	112,943	75.64	138,701	81.4%	61.6%
Cambria	66,983	91,769	72.99	118,972	77.1%	56.3%
Cameron	2,406	3,718	64.71	4,403	84.4%	54.6%
Carbon	25,043	36,620	68.39	48,509	75.5%	51.6%
Centre	64,253	86,832	74	117,095	74.2%	54.9%
Chester	230,823	324,747	71.08	349,673	92.9%	66.0%
Clarion	17,184	23,832	72.1	32,931	72.4%	52.2%
Clearfield	34,233	49,499	69.16	65,554	75.5%	52.2%
Clinton	13,967	20,439	68.34	29,716	68.8%	47.0%
Columbia	26,869	42,934	62.58	52,542	81.7%	51.1%
Crawford	38,322	58,569	65.43	69,070	84.8%	55.5%
Cumberland	105,842	144,727	73.13	175,348	82.5%	60.4%
Dauphin	121,208	173,227	69.97	192,819	89.8%	62.9%
Delaware	284,538	386,603	73.6	421,265	91.8%	67.5%
Elk	14,550	21,017	69.23	26,599	79.0%	54.7%
Erie	125,898	184,618	68.19	215,068	85.8%	58.5%
Fayette	54,707	88,934	61.51	114,192	77.9%	47.9%
Forest	2,573	3,152	81.63	3,903	80.8%	65.9%
Franklin	58,569	82,081	71.36	103,603	79.2%	56.5%
Fulton	6,271	8,930	70.22	11,262	79.3%	55.7%
Greene	15,565	25,244	61.66	31,910	79.1%	48.8%
Huntingdon	18,058	29,681	60.84	36,563	81.2%	49.4%
Indiana	36,248	53,670	67.54	72,199	74.3%	50.2%
Jefferson	19,560	28,847	67.81	35,942	80.3%	54.4%
Juniata	10,006	13,763	72.7	17,787	77.4%	56.3%

Table E.4 *(continued)*

County	2004 Total Vote	2004 Total Registration	2004 Turnout of Reg Voters	2004 VAP	Percent VAP Registered	2004 Turnout of VAP
Lackawanna	105,819	154,464	68.51	166,176	93.0%	63.7%
Lancaster	221,278	312,878	70.72	361,414	86.6%	61.2%
Lawrence	43,442	59,650	72.83	72,785	82.0%	59.7%
Lebanon	55,665	73,618	75.61	96,193	76.5%	57.9%
Lehigh	145,091	197,797	73.35	249,385	79.3%	58.2%
Luzerne	136,028	213,120	63.83	250,479	85.1%	54.3%
Lycoming	50,049	69,433	72.08	92,766	74.8%	54.0%
McKean	17,426	27,959	62.33	34,802	80.3%	50.1%
Mercer	51,564	76,073	67.78	93,159	81.7%	55.4%
Mifflin	16,802	26,523	63.35	35,192	75.4%	47.7%
Monroe	56,342	98,784	57.04	119,466	82.7%	47.2%
Montgomery	399,591	564,958	70.73	592,022	95.4%	67.5%
Montour	7,624	11,787	64.68	13,850	85.1%	55.0%
Northampton	126,740	178,699	70.92	220,079	81.2%	57.6%
Northumber-land	37,134	51,933	71.5	73,752	70.4%	50.3%
Perry	19,427	27,282	71.21	34,054	80.1%	57.0%
Philadelphia	674,069	1,062,439	63.45	1,097,609	96.8%	61.4%
Pike	21,298	38,225	55.72	41,177	92.8%	51.7%
Potter	7,962	12,046	66.1	13,555	88.9%	58.7%
Schuylkill	65,269	91,571	71.28	118,643	77.2%	55.0%
Snyder	14,983	20,844	71.88	29,486	70.7%	50.8%
Somerset	36,778	52,172	70.49	63,257	82.5%	58.1%
Sullivan	3,285	4,578	71.76	5,124	89.3%	64.1%
Susquehanna	19,040	26,774	71.11	32,268	83.0%	59.0%
Tioga	17,475	27,239	64.15	32,736	83.2%	53.4%
Union	16,133	22,075	73.08	34,727	63.6%	46.5%
Venango	23,659	37,356	63.33	43,600	85.7%	54.3%
Warren	19,273	28,508	67.61	33,059	86.2%	58.3%
Washington	96,177	149,716	64.24	162,312	92.2%	59.3%
Wayne	21,967	30,064	73.07	38,615	77.9%	56.9%
Westmoreland	178,696	256,365	69.7	292,636	87.6%	61.1%
Wyoming	12,832	18,997	67.55	21,644	87.8%	59.3%
York	179,269	264,134	67.87	307,628	85.9%	58.3%
Pennsylvania	5,765,764	8,366,663	68.91	9,569,283	87.4%	60.3%

Table E.5 2004 Turnout by County Sorted by Democratic Registration

Counties with Highest Percent Registered Democrats in 2004

County	2004 Total Vote	2004 Total Registration	2004 Turnout	2004 Registered Democrats
Philadelphia	674,069	1,062,439	63.5	74.9
Fayette	54,707	88,934	61.5	69.1
Greene	15,565	25,244	61.7	67.9
Lackawanna	105,819	154,464	68.5	62.7
Cambria	66,983	91,769	73.0	61.5
Allegheny	645,469	918,877	70.3	60.7
Beaver	82,543	122,350	67.5	60.0
Washington	96,177	149,716	64.2	59.4
Luzerne	136,028	213,120	63.8	56.5
Westmoreland	178,696	256,365	69.7	55.8
Lawrence	43,442	59,650	72.8	55.1
Elk	14,550	21,017	69.2	52.5
Erie	125,898	184,618	68.2	50.3
Carbon	25,043	36,620	68.4	48.6
Mercer	51,564	76,073	67.8	48.3
Northampton	126,740	178,699	70.9	46.8
Armstrong	31,097	45,261	68.7	45.2
Total RVT04	2,474,390	3,685,216	67.1	

Counties with Second-Highest Percent Registered Democrats in 2004

County	2004 Total Vote	2004 Total Registration	2004 Turnout	2004 Registered Democrats
Clearfield	34,233	49,499	69.2	44.9
Lehigh	145,091	197,797	73.4	44.6
Indiana	36,248	53,670	67.5	44.3
Northumberland	37,134	51,933	71.5	44.2
Clinton	13,967	20,439	68.3	44.1
Berks	164,487	235,166	70.0	44.0
Somerset	36,778	52,172	70.5	43.1
Columbia	26,869	42,934	62.6	42.9
Cameron	2,406	3,718	64.7	42.0
Monroe	56,342	98,784	57.0	41.5
Clarion	17,184	23,832	72.1	40.4
Crawford	38,322	58,569	65.4	39.6
Forest	2,573	3,152	81.6	39.6
Schuylkill	65,269	91,571	71.3	39.5
Jefferson	19,560	28,847	67.8	39.1
Dauphin	121,208	173,227	70.0	38.9
Bucks	319,816	451,899	70.8	38.5
Total RVT04	1,137,487	1,637,209	69.5	

Counties with Third-Highest Percent Registered Democrats in 2004

County	2004 Total Vote	2004 Total Registration	2004 Turnout	2004 Registered Democrats
Montgomery	399,591	564,958	70.7	37.9
Centre	64,253	86,832	74.0	37.9
Butler	85,425	112,943	75.6	37.6
Montour	7,624	11,787	64.7	37.6
Warren	19,273	28,508	67.6	37.2
Sullivan	3,285	4,578	71.8	37.1
Venango	23,659	37,356	63.3	36.8
Fulton	6,271	8,930	70.2	36.6
Lycoming	50,049	69,433	72.1	35.7
Mifflin	16,802	26,523	63.4	35.0
Juniata	10,006	13,763	72.7	34.6
Delaware	284,538	386,603	73.6	34.0
York	179,269	264,134	67.9	33.9
Bedford	22,679	32,878	69.0	33.6
Pike	21,298	38,225	55.7	33.4
Huntingdon	18,058	29,681	60.8	33.0
Blair	54,178	80,598	67.2	32.5
Total RVT04	1,266,258	1,797,730	70.4	

Counties with Lowest Percent Registered Democrats in 2004

County	2004 Total Vote	2004 Total Registration	2004 Turnout	2004 Registered Democrats
Wyoming	12,832	18,997	67.6	32.1
Susquehanna	19,040	26,774	71.1	32.0
Adams	42,228	58,025	72.8	31.2
Potter	7,962	12,046	66.1	31.0
McKean	17,426	27,959	62.3	30.9
Chester	230,823	324,747	71.1	30.4
Cumberland	105,842	144,727	73.1	29.7
Franklin	58,569	82,081	71.4	29.5
Lebanon	55,665	73,618	75.6	28.9
Wayne	21,967	30,064	73.1	28.8
Bradford	25,652	37,152	69.1	28.6
Union	16,133	22,075	73.1	28.4
Tioga	17,475	27,239	64.2	27.9
Lancaster	221,278	312,878	70.7	26.3
Perry	19,427	27,282	71.2	25.7
Snyder	14,983	20,844	71.9	24.2
Total RVT04	887,302	1,246,508	71.2	

Table E.6 2004 Turnout by County Sorted by Republican Registration

Counties with Highest Percent Registered Republicans in 2004

County	2004 Total Vote	2004 Total Registration	2004 Turnout	2004 Registered Republicans
Snyder	14,983	20,844	71.9%	65.7%
Perry	19,427	27,282	71.2%	63.0%
Tioga	17,475	27,239	64.2%	62.7%
Potter	7,962	12,046	66.1%	60.9%
Bradford	25,652	37,152	69.0%	60.6%
Lancaster	221,278	312,878	70.7%	59.1%
Bedford	22,679	32,878	69.0%	59.0%
Franklin	58,569	82,081	71.4%	58.6%
McKean	17,426	27,959	62.3%	58.5%
Lebanon	55,665	73,618	75.6%	58.4%
Wayne	21,967	30,064	73.1%	58.2%
Susquehanna	19,040	26,774	71.1%	57.8%
Union	16,133	22,075	73.1%	57.7%
Wyoming	12,832	18,997	67.5%	57.4%
Huntingdon	18,058	29,681	60.8%	57.2%
Juniata	10,006	13,763	72.7%	57.2%
Blair	54,178	80,598	67.2%	57.1%
Total RVT04	613,330	875,929	70.0%	

Counties with Second-Highest Percent Registered Republicans in 2004

County	2004 Total Vote	2004 Total Registration	2004 Turnout	2004 Registered Republicans
Cumberland	105,842	144,727	73.1%	56.5%
Fulton	6,271	8,930	70.2%	56.3%
Mifflin	16,802	26,523	63.3%	56.1%
Adams	42,228	58,025	72.8%	55.4%
Sullivan	3,285	4,578	71.8%	55.2%
Delaware	284,538	386,603	73.6%	55.1%
Forest	2,573	3,152	81.6%	54.4%
Lycoming	50,049	69,433	72.1%	53.7%
Venango	23,659	37,356	63.3%	52.9%
Jefferson	19,560	28,847	67.8%	52.7%
Chester	230,823	324,747	71.1%	52.5%
York	179,269	264,134	67.9%	51.7%
Schuylkill	65,269	91,571	71.3%	51.6%
Crawford	38,322	58,569	65.4%	51.3%
Warren	19,273	28,508	67.6%	51.1%
Butler	85,425	112,943	75.6%	51.1%
Clarion	17,184	23,832	72.1%	51.0%
Total RVT04	1,190,372	1,672,478	71.2%	

Counties with Third-Highest Percent Registered Republicans in 2004

County	2004 Total Vote	2004 Total Registration	2004 Turnout	2004 Registered Republicans
Cameron	2,406	3,718	64.7%	50.1%
Somerset	36,778	52,172	70.5%	49.8%
Montour	7,624	11,787	64.7%	49.8%
Pike	21,298	38,225	55.7%	48.4%
Dauphin	121,208	173,227	70.0%	48.3%
Northumberland	37,134	51,933	71.5%	47.9%
Montgomery	399,591	564,958	70.7%	47.6%
Bucks	319,816	451,899	70.8%	46.2%
Clearfield	34,233	49,499	69.2%	46.0%
Armstrong	31,097	45,261	68.7%	45.8%
Clinton	13,967	20,439	68.3%	45.6%
Centre	64,253	86,832	74.0%	44.2%
Indiana	36,248	53,670	67.5%	44.2%
Columbia	26,869	42,934	62.6%	43.4%
Berks	164,487	235,166	69.9%	41.7%
Mercer	51,564	76,073	67.8%	41.6%
Lehigh	145,091	197,797	73.4%	40.1%
Total RVT04	1,513,664	2,155,590	70.2%	

Counties with Lowest Percent Registered Republicans in 2004

County	2004 Total Vote	2004 Total Registration	2004 Turnout	2004 Registered Republicans
Carbon	25,043	36,620	68.4%	39.9%
Monroe	56,342	98,784	57.0%	39.8%
Erie	125,898	184,618	68.2%	39.7%
Elk	14,550	21,017	69.2%	37.7%
Northampton	126,740	178,699	70.9%	37.6%
Lawrence	43,442	59,650	72.8%	36.9%
Luzerne	136,028	213,120	63.8%	35.4%
Westmoreland	178,696	256,365	69.7%	34.6%
Washington	96,177	149,716	64.2%	31.6%
Cambria	66,983	91,769	73.0%	31.4%
Beaver	82,543	122,350	67.5%	30.7%
Lackawanna	105,819	154,464	68.5%	30.4%
Allegheny	645,469	918,877	70.2%	28.6%
Greene	15,565	25,244	61.7%	25.8%
Fayette	54,707	88,934	61.5%	24.1%
Philadelphia	674,069	1,062,439	63.4%	16.5%
Total RVT04	2,448,071	3,662,666	66.8%	

Bibliographical Essay

In this bibliographical essay, I explore the main sources available on recent Pennsylvania politics and political history as well as those on national electoral and party system change. As the footnotes to this book's chapters attest, I have relied on many fine works on these subjects. Also included in this essay are the main digital data sources I used along with a survey of the state's major newspapers, the latter an invaluable source for keeping up with day-to-day developments in Pennsylvania politics.

Far and away the best detailed, single-volume general history is Philip S. Klein and Ari Hoogenboom, *A History of Pennsylvania*, 2nd ed. (University Park: Pennsylvania State University Press, 1980). While this well-written, 600-page work is a comprehensive historical survey, the political story is central to the book's narrative. In particular, chapter 27, "A Two-Party State," provided me with excellent historical perspective on the era from the early 1950s to the end of the 1970s. The senior author, the late Professor Klein of the Pennsylvania State University history department, died in 1993. He was informally known as "Mr. Pennsylvania History."

A delightful and highly readable short history of the state is Paul A. W. Wallace's *Pennsylvania: Seed of a Nation* (New York: Harper & Row, 1964). Wallace, a Canadian by birth with a Ph.D. in English from the University of Toronto, moved to Pennsylvania in 1925, taught at Lebanon Valley College for decades, then joined the Pennsylvania Historical and Museum Commission as editor of the magazine *Pennsylvania History* in 1949. Although Wallace's 300-page book covers few topics treated in my book, it remains the best general historical introduction to the state.

Two fairly recent edited books offer a wealth of information on a variety of Pennsylvania topics. One is Randall M. Miller and William Pencak, eds., *Pennsylvania: A History of the Commonwealth* (University Park: Pennsylvania State University Press, 2002). The first part of this book contains seven chapters tracing the state's history from "the first Pennsylvanians" to "the postindustrial age." The nine insightful chapters in the second part cover topics from architecture to folklore and genealogy to literature. The second book, E. Willard Miller, ed., *A Geography of Pennsylvania* (University Park: Pennsylvania State University Press, 1995), contains twenty-one chapters grouped into four general topics: natural landscapes, the people, the economy, and the cities. In a section about the people, for example, are chapters on ethnic, cultural, and political geography, plus an overview chapter on the characteristics of Pennsylvania's population as well as its growth patterns.

The best book on the Keystone State's politics up to the end of the 1970s is Paul B. Beers, *Pennsylvania Politics Today and Yesterday: The Tolerable Accommodation* (University Park: Pennsylvania State University Press, 1980). Beers, a veteran journalist with the *Harrisburg Patriot-News*, begins his invaluable book with a delightful introduction entitled "Vest-Pocket Edition of the World" and continues with 450 pages of insightful stories about all the important Pennsylvania politicians from the Civil War through the late 1970s.

Jack M. Treadway's *Elections in Pennsylvania: A Century of Partisan Conflict in the Keystone State* (University Park: Pennsylvania State University Press, 2005) is a first-rate overview of 100 years of party conflict in the state, including several chapters on state legislative elections and party primaries. John J. Kennedy's *Pennsylvania Elections: Statewide Contests from 1950–2004* (Lanham, MD: University Press of America, 2006) offers capsule accounts of all of Pennsylvania's statewide elections from 1950 to 2004 and a valuable introduction to the personalities and issues of those many campaigns, including especially hard-to-find information on down-ticket contests, known in the Keystone State as "row office" elections.

Neal R. Peirce and Michael Barone offer an excellent mid-1970s profile of the state, entitled "Pennsylvania: Twilight Time?" in their *The Mid-Atlantic States of America: People, Politics, and Power in the Five Mid-Atlantic States and the Nation's Capital* (New York: W. W. Norton, 1977), 113–205. Two other useful profiles are "Pennsylvania: Business as Usual," in A. James Reichley, *States in Crisis: Politics in Ten American States, 1950–1962* (Chapel Hill: University of North Carolina Press, 1964), 54–71; and G. Terry Madonna and Robert J. Bresler, "Pennsylvania," in Andrew M. Appleton and Daniel S. Ward, eds., *State Party Profiles: A 50-State Guide to Development, Organization, and Resources* (Washington, DC: Congressional Quarterly, 1997), 272–79.

S. A. Paolantonio's *Rizzo: The Last Big Man in Big City America* (Philadelphia: Camino Books, 2003) is a readable account of the political life of Philadelphia's controversial police commissioner and mayor. Governor Robert P. Casey provides insight into his political career in his autobiography, *Fighting for Life: The Story of a Courageous Pro-Life Democrat Whose Own Brush with Death Made Medical History* (Dallas, TX: Word Publishing, 1996). Vincent P. Carocci, a Pennsylvania journalist and an aide to Governor Casey and state Senate Democrats, published an engaging memoir, *A Capitol Journey: Reflections on the Press, Politics, and the Making of Public Policy in Pennsylvania* (University Park: Pennsylvania State University Press, 2005).

The best overall treatment of national politics from the end of World War II through the end of the twentieth century is found in two books by the historian James T. Patterson, the latest volumes in the Oxford History of the United States series: *Grand Expectations: The United States, 1945–1974* (New York: Oxford University Press, 1996), and *Restless Giant: The United States from Watergate to Bush v. Gore* (New York: Oxford University Press, 2005).

My favorite book on electoral change is James L. Sundquist's *Dynamics of the Party System: Alignment and Realignment of Political Parties in the United States*, rev. ed. (Washington, DC: Brookings Institution, 1983), which provided me with the theoretical framework I used at key places in this book to help me understand the Pennsylvania patterns. Robert W. Speel's *Changing Patterns of Voting in the Northern United States: Electoral Realignment, 1952–1996* (University Park: Pennsylvania State University Press, 1998) served as a model for my study in addition to offering a keen insight concerning the political positioning of Pennsylvania Republicans in recent decades.

Theodore Rosenof wrote a comprehensive historical survey of the field of American electoral change in his *Realignment: The Theory That Changed the Way We Think About American Politics* (Lanham, MD: Rowman & Littlefield, 2003), offering fascinating profiles of the scholars who have developed the field in the twentieth century. In contrast to Rosenof's meticulous scholarship, David R. Mayhew in *Electoral Realignments: A Critique of an American Genre* (New Haven: Yale University Press, 2002) offers an unpersuasive, long essay critical of the value of the realignment concept.

Two broad analyses of American electoral change are found in Walter Dean Burnham, *Critical Elections and the Mainsprings of American Politics* (New York: W. W. Norton, 1970), and Jerome M. Clubb, William H. Flanigan, and Nancy H. Zingale, *Partisan Realignment: Voters, Parties, and Government in American History* (Beverly Hills, CA: Sage, 1980). Six scholars offer their perspectives on recent electoral change in Byron E. Shafer, ed., *The End of Realignment? Interpreting American Electoral Eras* (Madison: University of Wisconsin Press, 1991). John B. Judis and Ruy Teixeira in *The Emerging Democratic Majority* present their valuable "ideopolis" concept along with a prophecy: the Democratic party will become the country's majority party toward the end of the first decade of the twenty-first century.

Leading efforts to understand the post-1960 realignment of the party system are Kevin P. Phillips, *The Emerging Republican Majority* (New Rochelle, NY: Arlington House, 1969); Samuel Lubell, *The Hidden Crisis in American Politics* (New York: W. W. Norton, 1970); Edward G. Carmines and James A. Stimson, *Issue Evolution: Race and the Transformation of American Politics* (Princeton, NJ: Princeton University Press, 1989); and Thomas Byrne Edsall and Mary D. Edsall, *Chain Reaction: The Impact of Race, Rights, and Taxes on American Politics* (New York: W. W. Norton, 1991).

Five helpful works emphasizing the cultural and religious aspects of the recent realignment are James Davison Hunter, *Culture Wars: The Struggle to Define America* (New York: Basic Books, 1991); John Kenneth White, *The Values Divide: American Politics and Culture in Transition* (New York: Chatham House Publishers, 2003); David C. Leege, Kenneth D. Wald, Brian S. Krueger, and Paul D. Mueller, *The Politics of Cultural Differences: Social Change and Voter Mobilization Strategies in the Post–New Deal Period* (Princeton, NJ: Princeton University Press, 2002); Geoffrey Layman, *The Great Divide: Religious and Cultural Conflict in American Party*

Politics (New York: Columbia University Press, 2001); and William B. Prendergast, *The Catholic Voter in American Politics: The Passing of the Democratic Monolith* (Washington, DC: Georgetown University Press, 1999).

My main digital source for the county-level election returns was Professor Harold Cox's excellent Wilkes University Election Statistics Project, a Web site found at http://staffweb.wilkes.edu/harold.cox/index.html. Professor Cox, a retired Wilkes University historian, founded the site in 1996 when he discovered there was no readily available digital source for county-level election returns for major offices in Pennsylvania. For an informative article on Cox and the Web site, see Mark E. Jones, "Free Election History Database Feast for Party Animals," *Wilkes-Barre Times Leader*, July 26, 2004.

In addition to making extensive use of the University of Michigan's National Election Studies, found at http://www.umich.edu/~nes/, I was fortunate to be able to analyze the following Pennsylvania surveys and exit polls:

Harris 1964 Presidential Election Survey in Pennsylvania, No. 1357 [Computer file]. Conducted by Louis Harris & Associates, Inc., 1964. Chapel Hill: University of North Carolina, The Odom Institute [distributor].

Kovenock, David M., and James W. Prothro. Comparative State Elections Project, 1968 [Computer file]. Chapel Hill: University of North Carolina, Institute for Research in Social Science, 1970 [producer]. Ann Arbor, MI: Inter-university Consortium for Political and Social Research [distributor], 1977.

Yankelovich Voter Study, 1972 [Computer file]. Conducted by Daniel Yankelovich, Inc. *Time Magazine* [producer]. ICPSR ed. Ann Arbor, MI: Inter-university Consortium for Political and Social Research [distributor], 1975.

CBS News. CBS News Election Day Surveys, 1984: State Surveys [Computer file]. Conducted by CBS News. ICPSR ed. Ann Arbor, MI: Inter-university Consortium for Political and Social Research [producer and distributor], 1985.

CBS News/*New York Times*. CBS News/*New York Times* Election Day Surveys, 1986 [Computer file]. ICPSR ed. Ann Arbor, MI: Inter-university Consortium for Political and Social Research [producer and distributor], 1988.

ABC News. ABC News "Good Morning America" Five State Poll, October–November 1988 [Computer file]. Radnor, PA: Chilton Research Services [producer], 1989. Ann Arbor, MI: Inter-university Consortium for Political and Social Research [distributor], 1990.

Voter Research and Surveys. Voter Research and Surveys General Election Exit Polls, 1992 [Computer file]. New York: Voter Research and Surveys [producer], 1992, 2nd ICPSR release.

Ann Arbor, MI: Inter-university Consortium for Political and Social Research [distributor], 1993.

Voter News Service. Voter News Service General Election Exit Polls, 1994 [Computer file]. New York: Voter News Service [producer], 1994. Ann Arbor, MI: Inter-university Consortium for Political and Social Research [distributor], 1995.

Voter News Service. Voter News Service General Election Exit Polls, 1996 [Computer file]. ICPSR version. New York: Voter News Service [producer], 1996. Ann Arbor, MI: Inter-university Consortium for Political and Social Research [distributor], 1997.

Voter News Service. Voter News Service General Election Exit Polls, 2000 [Computer file]. 2nd ICPSR version. New York: Voter News Service [producer], 2000. Ann Arbor, MI: Inter-university Consortium for Political and Social Research [distributor], 2004.

National Election Pool. Edison Media Research and Mitofsky International. National Election Pool General Election Exit Polls, 2004 [Computer file]. ICPSR version. Somerville, NJ: Edison Media Research/New York: Mitofsky International [producers], 2004. Ann Arbor, MI: Inter-university Consortium for Political and Social Research [distributor], 2005.

National Election Pool. Edison Media Research and Mitofsky International. National Election Pool General Election Exit Polls, 2006 [Computer file]. ICPSR04684-v1. Somerville, NJ: Edison Media Research/New York: Mitofsky International [producers], 2006. Ann Arbor, MI: Inter-university Consortium for Political and Social Research [distributor], 2007.

The state's major daily newspapers are an excellent source for understanding Pennsylvania elections as well as general state political developments. The largest and most influential newspaper is the *Philadelphia Inquirer*, with a circulation in 2000 of 400,000 daily and 800,000 on Sunday, according to *Editor and Publisher Yearbook*. Next in importance is the *Pittsburgh Post-Gazette*, which had a daily circulation of 240,000 and Sunday circulation of 411,000 in 2000. The *Philadelphia Daily News* is in third place with a daily-only circulation of 154,000 in 2000. Fourth place goes to the *Allentown Morning Call* with a daily circulation of 127,000 and 170,000 on Sunday. The fifth largest Keystone State paper is in the capital, the *Harrisburg Patriot-News*, which in 2000 had a daily circulation of 99,000 and 155,000 on Sunday.

Throughout the state, there are many substantial dailies of note, such as the *Erie Times-News*, the *Greensburg Tribune-Review* in Westmoreland County, the *Lancaster Intelligencer Journal*, the *Bucks County Courier Times*, the *Reading Times*, the *Scranton Times*, and the *Wilkes-Barre Times Leader*.

Finally, a useful Web site for keeping up with daily Pennsylvania political developments is PoliticsPA.com at www.politicspa.com.

Index

CPSIA information can be obtained at www.ICGtesting.com
Printed in the USA
BVOW01s2114160115

383688BV00001B/60/P